RASPUTIN

RASPUTIN
A LIFE

JOSEPH T. FUHRMANN

PRAEGER

New York
Westport, Connecticut
London

Library of Congress Cataloging-in-Publication Data

Fuhrmann, Joseph T., 1940–
    Rasputin : a life / Joseph T. Fuhrmann.
      p.   cm.
    Bibliography: p.
    Includes index.
    ISBN 0–275–93215–X (alk. paper)
    1. Rasputin, Grigori Efimovich, ca. 1870–1916. 2. Soviet Union—
Court and courtiers—Biography. 3. Soviet Union—History—Nicholas
II, 1894–1917.   I. Title.
DK254.R3F78   1990
947.08—dc19   89–3651

Library of Congress Catalog Card Number: 89–3651
ISBN: 0–275–93215–X

First published in 1990

Praeger Publishers, One Madison Avenue, New York, NY 10010
A division of Greenwood Press, Inc.

Printed in the United States of America

The paper used in this book complies with the
Permanent Paper Standard issued by the National
Information Standards Organization (Z39.48–1984).

10 9 8 7 6 5 4 3 2 1

To the memory of my father,

Paul T. Fuhrmann

My mind filled with vast and wonderful thoughts
as I immersed myself in the Russian past.
It was as if I were some terrible steppe nomad and Russia,
having been conquered, lay helpless at my feet.

Contents

Photographs follow page 112.

Acknowledgments

When I began this project nine years ago, I had no idea it would occupy me for so long. The little I knew about Rasputin made me think he would be an easy subject. As time passed complexity entered the picture in larger and larger measures. Even now there is so much more to be said about the Siberian holy man who befriended the royal family, healed the tsarevich—and helped destroy an empire.

Many people and organizations have helped me, and I am anxious to thank each. I spent the summer of 1984 at Yale University as an NEH Seminar participant, working under the direction of Firuz Kazemzadeh. I was a fellow of the Russian and East European Institute of Indiana University during the summer of 1985. Access to the fine libraries of these two institutions was important to my work, as were the services of Murray State University's interlibrary loan librarian, Betty Hornsby. Murray State University gave me generous financial support over the years. The Committee for Institutional Studies and Research (CISR) awarded me several research grants, culminating in a Presidential Fellowship for the summer of 1986. I am grateful to CISR and its director, Peter Whaley, and to Dean Kenneth E. Harrell, who administered the summer faculty development program that supported my writing during the summer of 1987. Department Chairmen Joseph H. Cartwright and Kenneth Wolf were friendly and helpful. My colleagues T. Wayne Beasley and Burton W. Folsom read an early draft of the manuscript and offered useful suggestions. Robert F. Byrnes and Mark Kulikowski gave generously of their knowledge. My special thanks are due Hughie Lawson and Melvin E. Page for helping me to learn to use a word processor. I am also grateful to my wife, Mary, and to my children, Maria and Christopher, for the love and understanding a family person needs in a large undertaking such as this.

These people and organizations improved my work, but the errors and short-comings that remain are entirely my responsibility.

PART I

RISE TO POWER

=== 1 ===
Siberian Childhood

Grigory Rasputin was born in western Siberia, in the town of Pokrovskoe. Peasants were casual in keeping track of such events, so we do not know the exact date. Estimates of the year are as early as 1860 and as late as 1873. Rasputin himself thought he was 52 in 1915, which would have him born in 1863 or 1864. The name "Grigory" may indicate that he was born on January 10, the church day dedicated to St. Grigory of Nicea.

Grigory's father, Efim Akovlevich Rasputin, farmed and worked as a state carter on the track from Tyumen to Tobolsk. He also drove sleighs and wagons for private customers. Efim had a large farm with a dozen cows and 18 horses. He seemed "well-to-do" to his young granddaughter Maria, who found the family's eight-room *izba* to be "spacious if not comfortable." Alexander Spiridovich, one of Grigory's reliable biographers, concluded the Rasputin family "lived as peasants with moderate means," comfortable "if not rich."[1]

Rasputin's origins shed light on his ability to impress the tsar and other important people. Siberian peasants owned property; they were never serfs or intimidated by nobles. But schooling was rare in Siberia: Although 20 percent of the tsar's subjects were literate in 1900, no more than 2 percent of the adults in an average Siberian village could read and write. Efim was in this elite group. He read the Bible to his family each night. The government commission that investigated Rasputin and his family in 1917 noted that Efim "drank strong vodka"; but it conceded the man and his wife Anna were "healthy people with no history of mental illness in their families." Efim was described in 1909 as an "old, thick-set, typical Siberian peasant."[2]

Pokrovskoe is 200 miles east of the Ural Mountains, halfway between Tyumen and Tobolsk. Tyumen was a stopping point for prisoners on their way to Siberian exile; by 1890, over 900,000 convicts had passed through here on their way farther east. The area declined after the Trans-Siberian Railroad bypassed it in the 1890s. Tobolsk claimed a mere 21,000 citizens in 1900.[3]

A white gilded-dome church stands on Pokrovskoe's circular plaza. The houses sparkled with bright paint, their elaborate wood carvings testified to Siberians' unique sense of beauty. Foreigners were not impressed with such displays; Siberian towns generally struck them as "colorless." Siberia's distances and travel conditions were even more disturbing. It took a steamship three days to travel from Tyumen to Tobolsk. An English visitor described her trip over the ice and snow from eastern Siberia to Tyumen as the "worst bit of sledging I ever experienced." The holes were so deep that the driver often had to stop and measure them; surface obstacles looked like the "remains of ancient buildings."[4] Travel during the early spring was equally difficult. The melting ice and snow turned roads into belts of mud, which at some points were barely passable.

At the age of eight Grigory suffered his greatest childhood tragedy, the death of his ten-year-old brother Dmitry. It happened on a warm summer day when the two boys went for a swim. Dmitry undressed first and jumped into the river, but when he tried to stand up he began sinking into a hole. Grigory ran to the stream and extended his arm to Dmitry, but the older boy simply pulled his brother into the water. The rapid current carried them along until a bystander got them to shore. Both boys came down with pneumonia. The nearest physician was at Tyumen, so Efim and Anna turned to the local midwife. Maria Rasputin reported that "the good woman did what she could, but Misha's illness was beyond her poor powers, and at the tender age of ten, he slipped away from his grieving family."[5]

Dmitry's death plunged Grigory into deep depression. His behavior suddenly became unpredictable. One day he avoided people, the next he was underfoot— driving his mother to tears. "His psychic powers vanished for a time," Maria claimed, "and when they did return . . . they were never restored to their former intensity." But the clairvoyance Grigory's admirers claimed for him was sufficient for his first miracle: the capture of a horse thief through second sight.

Grigory was 12 years old at the time. He lay in bed with a fever while his father and friends discussed the recent theft of a horse. Grigory got out of bed, approached the adults and, pointing to one man, cried out, "He's the one who stole the horse!" The lad had obviously not seen the crime; Efim apologized for his apparently delirious son. The accused man expressed no hard feelings. But two peasants followed him home, discovered the horse—and gave the thief a severe beating. "Thus Grigory obtained a place apart in his village."[6]

Adolescence threw Rasputin's life into a very different direction. He drank heavily and became a "sly, insolent young man with a violently rakish, expansive nature." When drunken and boastful—and that was often—he harnessed up his horses and bolted around town, shouting harsh words in every direction. Young women often found this attractive. Grigory offered them adventure as well as romance, the sense of a raw power they had never encountered. Grigory soon realized that the way to learn his limits was to test them, and when he encountered an attractive new girl, he frequently reached out and began undoing buttons. Grigory was a celebrated ladies' man by the time he staggered to his eighteenth birthday.[7]

At the age of 19, Rasputin fell in love. The young lady, Praskovaya Dubrovina, was from a neighboring village. Although her friends did not consider Praskovaya "actually pretty," they recalled her as a "charming" woman with black eyes and blond hair. Grigory was not bothered by the fact that Praskovaya was some four years his senior. Grigory escorted Praskovaya home from the festival at the local monastery where they met and left a "fervent kiss upon her willing lips." Unlike the other girls Praskovaya would not give in to Grigory's advances. Grigory courted her with boundless affection, and six months later they were married.[8]

Grigory's parents were pleased over his marriage. Efim and Anna realized their son was slovenly and untidy, that neighbors called him a "sniveller" and a "snotnose." As was the custom in Siberia, the bride joined her husband in his parents' home.

Grigory loved Praskovaya, but he was not ready to abandon his disorderly life. If anything his drunkenness grew more pronounced—and now he added petty thievery to his misdeeds. Neighbors told the Investigatory Commission of 1917 of the woes they suffered at the young man's hand. V. I. Kartavtsev recalled the time he "caught Grigory stealing pieces of my fence." Kartavtsev tried to drag Rasputin to the authorities, but he resisted and Kartavtsev "hit him with a stake so strongly that a stream of blood poured from his nose and mouth." After further blows "he actually came of his own accord."

A pair of Kartavtsev's horses disappeared soon after this. Suspicion fell upon Grigory and two friends, Constantine and Trofim. A town meeting dealt with the troublemakers. Rasputin's cohorts were convicted of horse stealing and expelled from Pokrovskoe. Grigory was cleared of this crime but formally arraigned on lesser charges in the district court at Tyumen. Rasputin was found guilty of stealing Kartavtsev's stakes; the sentence was temporary banishment from Pokrovskoe. Grigory suggested a different punishment: He offered to do penance at the Verkhoturie Monastery 260 miles northwest of Pokrovskoe. He noted that his father had promised to make a pilgrimage there on foot, but had not done so. Grigory would go in his place.[9]

Rasputin probably had his own reasons for making a pilgrimage. He and Praskovaya had just suffered a tragedy; their first child, a boy, died at six months. Grigory was certainly familiar with Verkhoturie; he and his father often brought passengers and cargo there. Grigory Rasputin journeyed to the monastery in about 1885 and remained there for three months.[10]

The trip to Verkhoturie was a turning point in Rasputin's life; it set him on the path to power and fame. Grigory was especially impressed by Makary, one of Russia's most celebrated religious figures. Makary was a *hermit*—his prayers and devotions were not part of the communal life. He lived in a hut some 70 miles from the monastery, and he wore chains to mortify his flesh. At the age of 50, Makary spoke in a faint, dry voice. People said his words were penetrating; what your ear did not grasp, your heart would comprehend.

Makary told Grigory that his son's death was a sign from God. Rasputin should return to Pokrovskoe and discover the vocation God intended for him. Grigory should develop his spiritual gifts, become a Man of God, and help others find the truth. Makary was inviting this semiliterate peasant lad to join him as a religious teacher. "These were awesome words spoken by [someone] known for holiness and wisdom."[11]

Pokrovskoe was amazed at Rasputin when he returned. Grigory was nervous and restless, alternating between religious ecstasy and severe depression. His movements were impetuous, his speech disconnected. One villager thought Rasputin was "abnormal." Grigory was "without a cap, his hair was rumpled," and he "sang away while waving his hands." Another noted that in church Rasputin "shot wild glances to the side and often began to sing in an improper voice." Rasputin's old nemesis Kartavtsev found him "strange," even "rather stupid." Kartavtsev attributed the changes to the beatings Grigory had received from him.[12]

Rasputin changed in other important respects. He gave up alcohol and tobacco, and he no longer ate meat. Grigory shunned people and prayed continually. He also attracted followers. Early members of this circle included his cousin Nicholas Rasputin, Nicholas Raspopov, Ilya Aropov, and the Pecherkin sisters, Katya and Dunya. Rumors held their "services" began with the Pecherkin girls washing Grigory at the bathhouse. Dunya and Katya then supposedly conducted Grigory to the basement of his father's house where the faithful sang religious songs and danced. Villagers tried to confirm these tales, but outsiders were unable to penetrate the meetings.[13]

Rasputin's neighbors concluded he had joined the *khlysty*, or "Flagellants," a radical religious sect. Russians believed the members of this secret group blended religious ecstasy and sex. The 120,000 khlysty scattered from Tobolsk to Kazan and Saratov were said to gather at night in houses or remote places. Forming a circle, they supposedly moved in a ring, holding hands as they chanted, sang, and prayed. The leader of the "ship"—as each congregation was called— whipped any member who flagged or broke formation. When the ritual reached a certain point, the khlysty cast off their white linen gowns and joined in sexual intercourse. Then they lay about, exhausted and dozing. The charge that Rasputin was a Flagellant dogged him to the end and was always a threat to his career.[14] The Russian Orthodox church was an established church, and the government supported it in many ways. The khlysty and other "sects" were banned before 1905, and their leaders were imprisoned in such monasteries as Verkhoturie. The khlysty were among the few groups that Nicholas refused to legalize under his edict of April 17, 1905, which generally established religious toleration in

Russia. The accusation of being a Flagellant was serious, then, and the charge concerned Rasputin whenever it appeared.

Rasputin was not a Flagellant—nor did members of the group mingle sex and worship. Splinter groups practiced "holy intercourse," but most khlysty were devout pentecostalists who condemned such behavior. But the Flagellants did influence Grigory in certain ways, even if he was not a member of the group. The members of Grigory's circle at Pokrovskoe sang khlyst hymns, and they addressed each other as "brother" and "sister" while praying and bathing together.[15] All this gave credence to the notion that Grigory was a Flagellant.

Other sectarians visited Rasputin after his conversion at the Verkhoturie Monastery. These men and women belonged to the "underground" of Russian Christianity. They were devoted to "mystical ecstasy"; official church observers lumped them into a single category as "khlysty." "There were Baptists at [nearby] Tyumen," Smitten notes, and "evangelists from Samara." Rasputin likewise might have talked with followers of the heretic priest Yakov Barbarin, who was imprisoned at the Abalaksky Monastery where Grigory met Praskovaya, his future bride.[16]

* * *

Rasputin had no sooner returned from Verkhoturie when an experience confirmed Makary's suggestion that a religious vocation lay ahead for young Grigory. As Grigory was plowing he was suddenly dazzled by an apparition. "Before him in the sky, veiling the sun from him, was the Virgin, looking at him and making gestures with her hand." Maria Rasputin tells us her father fell to his knees, ready to obey Our Lady. Mary did not speak to him, but she continued to beckon to the horizon. Rasputin concluded he should become a *strannik,* a "wandering pilgrim." These men and women roamed the lands of Holy Russia, exchanging teaching and counseling for the hospitality offered along the way.

If Praskovaya objected to Rasputin leaving home, she kept it to herself. Maria thought her mother was proud of Grigory, who was blessed with contemplative faculties she did not possess. Praskovaya was a capable woman, but also could rely upon her father-in-law for help in running their farm. Thrilled as she was to see Grigory when he returned home, she did well without him during his increasingly lengthy absences. Rasputin set out on his first pilgrimage beyond the familiar confines of Tobolsk and Verkhoturie. He was headed on foot for the Balak Monastery in Siberia.[17]

It is impossible to establish an exact chronology of Rasputin's life from the late 1880s to 1902. The period was important, however, for during that time Grigory extended his reputation and made some important decisions about his life. He also sharpened his wits against increasingly important people and, by 1902, was positioned for bolder strikes against Kazan and St. Petersburg.

Praskovaya gave birth to three children in these years: Dmitry (1897); Matriona, usually called "Maria" (1898); and Varvara, known as "Varya" (1900). As Grigory's family grew, so did his desire to establish his own home away from that of his parents. It was becoming increasingly difficult for Grigory and his father to live under the same roof. Efim was not impressed with his son's religious calling. The father thought his son was mainly interested in escaping work. This may be true. Aron Simanovich, Rasputin's business manager and the man who knew him best in later years, thought Rasputin avoided "regular work" because he was "lazy"—though Grigory could do "physical labor in cases of necessity." Grigory by nature did not worry about the future. "In general he was a carefree person [who] lived for the present day."[18] But Rasputin loved his family, and for their sake he built a new home, probably with the financial aid of his father.

Grigory's house was located on the main street of the village. Maria Rasputin remembered it as "huge" and "bright," the "largest dwelling in Pokrovskoe." Actually Rasputin did not have the full two-storied house characteristic of more prosperous Siberian peasants. His was a more typical single-floor-dwelling with double wood walls to fend off the cold. A little garden surrounded by an iron railing stretched along a facade whose high windows were decorated with wood mouldings. A wall with a wide gate surrounded the large yard, enclosing the out-buildings and forming what in Russia is known as a *dvor,* a courtyard. This wall also encircled a storage cellar five or six feet deep, a stable, and a small bathhouse.

The door of the house gave access to a vestibule beyond which were two rooms. The family lived and ate in the larger room to the right. It was equipped with a large, solid, red-brick stove whose chimney rose in direct lines to the ceiling except for a large niche where a lucky person could curl up and sleep. The "icon corner" to the left of the chimney was illuminated by a lamp whose blue flame perpetually burned. The smaller adjacent room was comparable to what Americans call the living room or the parlor. Guests here sat on benches flanking the walls; the stove was small since it was used for heating rather than cooking. The family slept in the attic, near the trunk of the stove. By one of those strange twists of fate, the fallen Tsar Nicholas and part of his family passed through Pokrovskoe in 1918 on their way to the bloody fate that claimed their lives several weeks later, and one of the girls made a quick drawing of the house. The sketch is not accurate, Maria Rasputin wrote. "For one thing, it gives our house more windows than it actually had." But Rasputin's daughter found she could never look at the drawing "without emotion."[19]

Rasputin's fortunes as a religious teacher were mixed in these early years. Grigory awed his growing circle of admirers with descriptions of the monasteries, churches, and shrines he visited on his pilgrimages. He also faced ridicule, being called "Grisha the prophet." One day when some neighbors were taunting him in this way, he suddenly thrust his spade into a heap of grain and set off on another pilgrimage to the "holy places." Rasputin was gone for a year on this occasion. When he returned, he dug a cave and spent two weeks in intense prayer.[20]

Rasputin's wanderings in these years took him throughout Siberia to the great churches and monasteries of Kiev. It was said that he also travelled to Jerusalem, throughout Mesopotamia, and to Mount Athos in Greece. The last trip was especially important, for it came early in Grigory's career and resolved the thought that God might intend for him to end his marriage and become a monk. (This was after the death of his first son and before the birth of his next child, Dmitry.) Makary advised Grigory to make this pilgrimage. Rasputin was accompanied by his best friend, Dmitry Pecherkin, who was also considering becoming a novice.

Athos is famous as the monastic center of the entire Eastern Orthodox Church. It is a rocky peninsula that cuts its way into a stormy corner of the Aegean Sea and soars to a height of 6,670 feet. Greeks established the first cloister here in 963. Other nations followed, and by Rasputin's time the entire peninsula bristled with monasteries and hermit cells. The 3,496 Russian brothers formed the largest nationality, accounting for 47 percent of the total number of monks in 1903.

Rasputin was not favorably impressed with the "holy mountain." He noticed that in the absence of women—female animals even were banned from Athos—some of the monks enjoyed each other. In later years Rasputin had close friends who were homosexuals. But homosexuality itself filled him with disgust. Rasputin bade Pecherkin farewell and immediately set out for home. Since Makary had urged him to make the pilgrimage to Athos, Grigory was anxious to share his experiences with his teacher.

Makary reminded the young man how often God's intentions are unfathomable. Evil exists everywhere, and temptation is sometimes strongest where it should not exist at all. Makary agreed that Grigory's feelings about Athos proved that the monastic calling was not for him. Makary advised Rasputin that he would develop his gifts not through meditation, the "inner way," but by the "outer way," through pilgrimages. "Remember your mission," Makary concluded. "Since you have not found salvation in the monastery, try to save your soul in the outside world."[21]

Rasputin made several pilgrimages throughout Siberia over the next several years. The life of a *strannik* suited Grigory's temperament better than a monk's existence. "He took clear stock of the fact that the monastic life would keep him from [sex]," a friend noted, "and for this reason he embraced the world which gave him the most personal satisfaction, the world of renowned sanctimonious people, 'wanderers' and 'fools in Christ.' He studied them to perfection from his earliest years."[22]

The life of a wandering pilgrim also brought the restless Rasputin before educated and upper-class-Russians. Free from the confines of Pokrovskoe, he could act boldly and sharpen his deadliest weapon: an intuitive grasp of the

problems, needs, and longings of every man or woman he met. Rasputin learned
to size up a person, to begin with the right expression, to use the right word; to
arouse curiosity; and to blend just the right mixture of courtesy and familiarity,
sternness and sympathy. He especially came to understand women, their secret
fantasies and needs for intimacy. Grigory learned to put on an act every minute,
ending with an understanding of his fellow humans that some took for clairvoyance.

Although he wandered far from Pokrovskoe, Rasputin usually returned within
a year. On one such occasion he encountered a neighbor who asked where he
had been so long.

"I've walked over all of Siberia, crossed the Urals," Rasputin answered.
"I've seen Russia. I've been looking for God."

"Where did you look for him?"

"In Russian monasteries, in small and out-of-the-way monasteries—and in
ships."[23]

Maria Rasputin's first memory of Grigory involved his Ulysses-like return to
Pokrovskoe after an unusually long absence of two years. Maria was so young
she could hardly remember her father. On this occasion she saw a man in a
dusty coat, a bag at his side, lumbering along with effort. "He was a tall man
with a long brown beard; [his eyes were] a little strange but gentle, set in a tired
face." The figure looked like any number of wandering pilgrims who came by
the house. Praskovaya took advantage of such people to trade food and a place
to stay for any news that might be had about her husband.

"What do you want, my good man?" Praskovaya asked as this particular
man approached with a searching glance. Suddenly she cried out, "Grigory!"
and rushed to his arms. Maria remembered Rasputin's joy at seeing his wife and
children. Then he "looked at me tenderly before coming with us into the house,
where my mother helped him take off his boots."[24]

The first major crisis of Rasputin's career broke a few days after this return.
With less luck it would have ended Grigory's ascent to fame before it really
began.

Disturbed over Rasputin's growing popularity, the village priest finally struck
out at his rival. Father Peter filed a report with government authorities at Tobolsk
in 1901 charging that Grigory was a khlyst. The denunciation was forwarded to
the governor who referred it to Anthony, archbishop of Tobolsk and Siberia.
Anthony sent V. M. Skvortsov, an expert on the sects, to investigate the charges.
Skvortsov was soon scurrying about Pokrovskoe, interrogating people.

The police finally appeared at Rasputin's door, hoping to find such telltale
signs of the Flagellants as white linen gowns or whips with lead weights. Praskovaya was so furious to hear her house was about to be searched that the police
retreated. But the authorities returned, and this time they had their way. They
were especially interested in the bathhouse and storage cellar where Grigory
supposedly celebrated his khlyst services. The cellar doubled as a shelter for

Rasputin's fellow pilgrims. Rasputin decorated it with icons, and indeed it was the site for his religious gatherings. To do a thorough search the police moved the sacks of potatoes and flour about the floor. They found nothing incriminating, but emerged covered with white flour from head to foot.

Rasputin was not amused when he returned. He carefully removed all the icons from the cellar and brought them to his house.[25]

Grigory might have fled—or he might have kept still while his enemies prepared their case. Rasputin did neither. Rather he settled upon a bold counterattack. Grigory sensed that the way to survive this crisis was to broaden his power base—to shift the battle to different terrain where he could win the support of new and important people.

So in 1902 Rasputin set out for Kazan, the gateway between Europe and Siberia. Self-confident as he was, he must have known this was a gamble. Grigory aspired to become the holy man of a large and important city. He was raising the stakes of his own game. But the gamble could bring great rewards. Rasputin would conquer Kazan—and Russia.

===== 2 =====
From Kazan to St. Petersburg

Rasputin's conquest of Kazan began with a Russian furrier by the name of Katkov. Grigory impressed Katkov, who invited Rasputin to stay at his house and presented him to church leaders. Rasputin made an excellent impression on these people, one of whom recalled his original views and simple language, brief and filled with images. His eyes "seemed to see straight through you" they "hypnotized" those who came under their spell.

Father Michael, a professor at the St. Petersburg Seminary, was one of Rasputin's first and most fervent admirers in the city. He was a thin, short man of slight build. Michael's bald pate contrasted with a thick black beard, and his excitable disposition was linked to a keen, scholarly mind. Michael was attracted to bold choices. Born a Jew, he converted to the Orthodox Church; he later joined the Old Believers, becoming a bishop and a harsh critic of the established Church. Another early admirer was Abbot Chrisanthos, diocesan curate and director of Russian Orthodox missions in Korea. Chrisanthos was convinced that Rasputin was a holy man, a voice of the common people. Grigory finally met and charmed the bishop, Andrew.[1]

Bishop Andrew insisted that Rasputin visit church leaders of the capital. He wrote a letter of introduction to Feofan, Inspector of the St. Petersburg Seminary. The bishop even sent Chrisanthos along with Rasputin. They arrived in St. Petersburg during Lent of 1903. Grigory was bewildered at how quickly his good fortune was unfolding; he admitted he felt "like a blind man on the road." But the Siberian peasant was adequate to his challenges. His first stop was the Alexander Nevsky Monastery. Rasputin did homage to the saints buried there; he paid three kopecks for a *Te Deum,* another two to light a candle. Within a dozen years, Grigory would be an honored guest at this cloister, one of the most important Russian monasteries. For the moment, he put away a cache of dirty underwear and got ready to meet Feofan.[2]

Feofan had been anxiously awaiting Rasputin's arrival. What he heard of Rasputin in Kazan prepared him to be favorably impressed—and Grigory did not disappoint him. Rasputin could have found no better patron than Feofan, one of those rare people nearly everyone admired. Ambition seemed foreign to Feofan, and he was universally esteemed for high integrity. His sterling character probably put Feofan at a disadvantage in judging Rasputin. Once Feofan decided Rasputin was a true *starets* (holy man), it did not occur to him that Grigory could be less than what men and women of this calling were known to be. Feofan told Rasputin about St. Petersburg and introduced him to important people.[3]

Rasputin met Bishop Serge, head of the Alexander Nevsky Monastery, and Hermogen, bishop of Saratov and one of Russia's most highly regarded church leaders. In time Hermogen would turn against Rasputin and try to drive him back to Siberia. For the moment he was an enthusiastic partisan. But Rasputin's grandest conquest was the most famous preacher in all of Russia, Father John of Kronstadt.

Kronstadt is a Russian naval base on the island of Kotlin in the Gulf of Finland, 15 miles from St. Petersburg. Ivan Ilych Sergeev, known as "John of Kronstadt," was born in 1829. His career at Kronstadt began in 1874, when he became the pastor of St. Andrew's Cathedral. John was soon famous for his work among the poor. He established a fraternal association and a center with an impressive array of social services and education programs. His devoted followers claimed he performed miracles. John was popular among the upper classes, and under his influence, many educated people turned from socialism and science to conservatism and religion. John's preaching was tinged with figures of speech taken from the sects and the Old Believers, who split from the official Church in protest against reforms of Patriarch Nikon during the seventeenth century. He had a gift of bringing people under his spell. John was a friend of the royal family; he tended Alexander III on his death bed and played a prominent role in Nicholas II's coronation. If there was one person whom Rasputin might have viewed as a model, it was John of Kronstadt.

John advocated frequent Communion, which was not the practice in Russia at this time. Throngs of people came to him for Confession. Since he could not hear them individually, John resorted to group Confession. Just before Communion people began reciting their sins for all to hear. "Papa thought this was one of the most curious sights he had ever witnessed," Maria Rasputin notes. Yet Grigory was impressed with John, for his basilica was an island of peace in a stormy sea. Even this confusing scene was the first display of true devotion he had seen in a long time. Overcome, Rasputin fell to his knees in prayer.[4]

According to the lore that surrounds Rasputin, at this moment Father John discerned a person with religious gifts in the congregation. John called Rasputin from the back to the front of the church just before Communion. He blessed

Grigory and then asked for his blessing. The two talked after the Liturgy. John finally dismissed Rasputin telling him to wander, to develop his gifts, and to help people renew their faith.[5]

Rasputin stayed in St. Petersburg for only five months on his first visit. He spent his first few days in the Alexander Nevsky Monastery and then moved in with the journalist G. P. Sazonov. Sazonov became a conservative after the Revolution of 1905, but in 1903 he was a liberal; he and his friends tried to win Rasputin to their side. These efforts failed, as did those of alarmed members of the opposite camp. Rasputin would never be very political—least of all in 1903. Grigory was far more interested in the ladies. The story was similar to Kazan, where a "few hysterical ladies [with] headaches suddenly found themselves better" after meeting Grigory, "and they spread his fame outside the small circle which had adopted him." Rasputin received many society ladies at Sazonov's home.[6]

*   *   *

One of the highest honors a Russian could attain in Rasputin's time was to be recognized as a starets. It was a popular title, not a church order. *Startsy* were ascetics whose lives brought them close to God, and they possessed obvious moral authority. Startsy were wise and eloquent; one felt the presence of God in their company.

Dostoevsky explains in *The Brothers Karamazov* that a starets is someone "who [takes] your soul, your will, into his soul and his will. When you select a starets, you renounce your own will and yield it to him in complete submission, complete self-abnegation." One does this "voluntarily in the hope of self-conquest, of self-mastery, to attain, after a life of obedience, perfect freedom." This freedom is freedom from self, "to escape the lot of those who have lived to the end without finding their true selves in themselves."[7]

Grigory's enemies charged that he was nothing but cynical, and that he used religion to mask his drive for sex, money, and power. But the evidence suggests that, at the outset, Rasputin sincerely sought a path of service to God. Yet his sex life was so outrageous as to make one wonder how anyone could have accepted "Father Grigory" as a starets. Startsy wore rags and chains and renounced the world for meditation and prayer. Although Rasputin was a man of simple tastes, he was certainly no ascetic. His most naive followers could see he was constantly in female company. Knowledgeable people were aware he enjoyed sex and was said to be a remarkable lover. Even if Rasputin was also a God-seeker, how could he have survived as a starets?

In part Rasputin benefitted from good luck. His timing, for example, could not have been better. Grigory appeared on the scene at the precise moment church leaders were seeking people of his type. The bishops were worried about the Church and feared it was losing contact with ordinary people. Rasputin seemed to be an ideal person to help bring the Church closer to the masses. He was an ordinary peasant: simple, forceful, direct. Rasputin expounded complex truths in a casual way. Experts were amazed at his knowledge of scripture and his ability to present settled doctrines in a fresh, original way. Rasputin even benefited from a willingness to dispute some church teachings. This showed he was "his own man"; he was bold, creative—exciting.

Rasputin also established a momentum that carried him to increasingly important groups of church leaders. News of his triumphs in Siberia ensured a hearing in Kazan. The elders there marvelled at Rasputin's spiritual gifts, and they eagerly shared the news with their counterparts in the capital. By the time Rasputin set out for St. Petersburg, its clergymen were certain that a starets was on the way and were ready to greet him in the proper fashion.

The norms of the Russian Orthodox Church were also changing at this time. Startsy were not necessarily what they had been in the past. "Along with those who might be called 'official *startsy*,' who are in monasteries and obedient to their codes, is another type one meets in Russia but is unknown to Europe," Prince Zhevakov, an astute observer of the contemporary scene, noted. "These are so-called 'God's people.' [They are often laymen and are rarely found in monasteries] . . . , but wander from place to place, preaching God's word to people and calling them to penitence."[8] One could say that Rasputin was a starets of this type—not entirely traditional and yet a part of the tradition.

The fact that Rasputin dealt with women in various ways also worked to his advantage. Not all his advances were sexual. Grigory taught the society women of Kazan that through him they could learn to *resist* temptation. A Kazanite hostile to Rasputin admitted that she did not know of a single case of a "lady actually giving herself to him." She recalled a "most respectable lady, a wife and mother" who yielded to his "suggestion that he share her bed." Several people observed this scene—all testified that Rasputin was entirely proper. He taught his disciples to transcend desire through concentration on the good.[9]

Rasputin showed such restraint during religious moods. At other times he was carnal. A distraught mother wrote Feofan from Kazan, complaining that Rasputin had captured the minds of her daughters, one 20, the other not quite 16. One afternoon she saw Rasputin coming out of a bathhouse with the two girls. The prophet turned and said: "Now you may feel at peace, the day of salvation has dawned for your daughters!"[10]

Similar reports came from Pokrovskoe after Rasputin returned there in the autumn of 1903. A woman reported seeing Grigory "surrounded by a large number of noble ladies who considered him a great prophet." Rasputin kissed them as they strolled about the village. "He said there was no reason to be ashamed, because all people were of the same kin." A lower-class woman had a different experience: Rasputin all but raped her in a cellar. He said there was no sin in what they did, only the Holy Trinity.[11]

Rasputin's various "lines" produced conflicting accounts of his behavior. When rumors that "Father Grigory has been with women" reached the Kazan Seminary, his admirers dismissed them in favor of more appealing accounts. If trapped, Rasputin admitted some of the charges were true. "All men sin, and

I, being a man, am also a sinner,'' he often said. One could make of that what
one wished. If a person was determined to think Rasputin was a ''holy man,''
evidence could be found to support that view. Opposite claims—even if they
were more common—could be discounted as misinformation or lies. Or one
might think that temptation got the upper hand—a lapse occurred—but it was
temporary.

Rasputin also profited from the campaign against Christianity at this time. His
first critics during 1902 and 1903 were ''people who were indifferent to religion,
who rejected even John of Kronstadt, bishop Feofan and the accepted zealots.''
Ridicule from these ''rationalists'' enhanced Grigory's reputation. To doubt
Rasputin was to side with those who were hostile to religion. Rasputin's partisans
sensed that the rumors against him were calculated to destroy a ''saint.'' One
did not demand proof of saintliness from a saint—nor was it wise to throw stones
at someone who might prove to be a prophet.[12]

Rasputin's warmest admirers eventually doubted him. Not even Rasputin could
conceal the truth forever. One of the most striking aspects of his rise to power
is the train of broken friendships left in its wake. The pattern was already visible
at Kazan. Within a year, Bishop Andrew decided his faith in Grigory was
misplaced, and he attacked him as a false starets. It made no difference. By this
time Rasputin was charming a still more important group: Feofan's circle. Feofan
not only ignored Andrew's sudden warnings, but also was anxiously awaiting
Rasputin's return to St. Petersburg. Two years would pass before Grigory made
this second trip in 1905. This time Rasputin was not escorted by church dignitaries. He did not need them. Rasputin was about to befriend Nicholas II, Tsar
and Autocrat of All the Russias.

* * *

Nicholas II was pursued by the conviction that he was unlucky, born to rule
and yet to fail.

''Do you know on what day my birthday falls?'' he asked Prime Minister
Peter Arkadievich Stolypin in 1909.

''How could I forget it?'' came the reply. ''It is May 6.''

''What Saint's Day is it?''

''Forgive me, Sire, I'm afraid I've forgotten.''

''The patriarch Job,'' Nicholas continued.

''Then God be praised!'' Stolypin tactfully observed. ''Your Majesty's reign
will end gloriously, for Job, after piously enduring the most cruel tests of his
faith, found blessings and rewards showered upon his head!''

''No, no, Peter Arkadievich, believe me! I have a presentiment—more than
a presentiment, a secret conviction—that I am destined for terrible trials. But I
shall not receive my reward on *this* earth. How often have I not applied to myself
the words of Job: *Hardly have I entertained a fear than it comes to pass, and
all the evils I foresee descend upon my head.*''[13]

, Nicholas Romanov, last of the tsars, was born on May 6, 1868, at Tsarskoe Selo, near St. Petersburg. His parents Alexander III and Maria Fedorovna had six children. Nicholas, the eldest child, was shy and withdrawn, known for dreamy moods and a sickly disposition. His father was huge and domineering, gifted with an ability to wield power that earned universal respect. The gap was widened by the tsar's determination that his children would not be spoiled by the luxury that came to all Romanovs in time. Nicholas and his brothers George and Michael slept on plain army cots with hard pillows, took cold showers, and had porridge for breakfast. The royal children were often hungry, for court etiquette specified that they were served after parents and guests and had to stop eating when the tsar finished.[14] Alexander prided himself on gobbling his food.

Nicholas met his future bride in 1890. She was Victoria Alix Helena Louise Beatrice of the German duchy of Hesse-Darmstadt. Alix was not quite 18 at the time. She came to Russia to visit her older sister, Elizabeth, who married Nicholas's uncle Serge. Nicholas visited his aunt by marriage and was captivated by her shy sister. Alix fell in love with the tsarevich, though she did not realize it at the time. "It was only on her return to Darmstadt that she felt she had left her heart in Russia."[15]

Alix was a beautiful woman in these early years. A Russian officer described her as "quite young, very pretty, slender and rather shy." Another person remembered her as "tall and slender." She carried herself superbly, but above all she impressed people with her eyes, "those sparkling, gray-blue eyes which mirrored the emotions of a sensitive soul." Alix was English in manner, for she had grown up at Kensington Palace under Queen Victoria's watchful eye. Nicky and Alix kept in touch by mail, and they managed to see each other on several occasions. Alexander was surprised when his son told him in 1893 that he would have no one for a wife but Alix. For diplomatic reasons Alexander preferred that his son not marry a German princess, much less a German reared at the English court. But Nicholas could be stubborn, and for the first time in his life, the callow youth stood up to his gruff father.

The impasse was broken in 1894 when Nicholas attended the marriage of Alix's brother at Coburg, Germany. Nicholas and Alexandra announced their engagement here on April 20, 1894. "This is a marvelous, unforgettable day," the tsarevich wrote in his diary, ". . . the day of my engagement to my darling, adorable Alix." Nicky felt as if a mountain had passed from his shoulders, and he spoke of "walking in a dream the entire day without fully realizing what was happening to me." If Nicholas's parents were displeased at the news, they kept it to themselves. The tsar and his wife fired off congratulatory telegrams within a few hours of hearing of their son's engagement. "Your dear Alix [is] already quite like a daughter to me," Maria Fedorovna wrote her son, and "I am waiting impatiently to see [her]." The tsarina admitted only one complaint: In a letter Alix addressed the empress as "Aunty-Mama"; the older lady asked to be called "Mother dear." Alix honored this request even at moments when it must have been difficult to pretend she really regarded her mother-in-law in such a friendly way. Maria addressed Alix as "Dushka," an affectionate term meaning "dear one."[16]

The young couple's marriage was moved forward by an unexpected event: Alexander III suddenly took ill and died on October 20, 1894. The next day Alix was received into the Russian Orthodox Church as the "truly believing Grand Duchess Alexandra Fedorovna."[17] Nicholas and Alexandra were married on November 26, 1894.

Life was difficult for Alix in her first months in Russia. The young German woman was on her own, plunged into a swirl of people whose relative standing at court was a mystery to her. Her slights and oversights were "irrelevant in themselves but tantamount to formidable crimes in the eyes of St. Petersburg society." This upset Alexandra and increased her natural reserve, which further soured the impression she was making on the people she needed to charm and captivate.

A kind and generous mother-in-law would have been helpful to Alexandra at this juncture, especially considering Maria Fedorovna's popularity. Outwardly they were friends. Nicholas' mother showered his fiancée with presents at her engagement; when her husband died Maria fainted into Alix's arms. When Nicky and his bride returned to the Anichkov Palace after their marriage, "Mother dear" greeted them with bread and salt. On the surface all was friendly. Yet Maria wore no jewels at her son's wedding, and during the service she fought back tears in vain.[18]

Maria and Alexandra were both strong-willed women who hoped to stand first in Nicholas's affections. Each was too jealous to extend true friendship to the other. Nicholas had always been close to his mother. Maria understood state affairs, and at the beginning of his reign Nicholas spent hours in conference with her. Alix did not reveal an interest in politics in these years, but worked on French, the court language, and on Russian. Her mastery of both was soon complete, but her fear of mistakes made her reluctant to start conversations, though she spoke Russian with but a slight accent.

Alexandra's second year of marriage saw a vast improvement. Maria left on a long summer visit to Denmark. Nicky and Alix moved to the Alexander palace at Tsarskoe Selo, the elegant residential town 15 miles south of the capital. Best of all Alexandra was pregnant. Olga was born on September 3, 1895. Tatyana and Maria arrived in the next three and one-half years. The family was warm and close, but the absence of a male heir presented a problem. Although women ruled Russia during the eighteenth century, the Emperor Paul's resentment against his mother Catherine the Great drove him to revise the succession law to exclude females. According to this time-sanctioned decree, if Nicholas died without a son the throne would pass to his brother Michael. The fourth child was another girl, Anastasia, born on June 14, 1901.

By this time Nicholas and Alexandra turned to the mystical realm for help in gaining a son. It is probably not true—though one often reads it as established fact—that Nicholas and Alexandra took part in table-tapping and spiritualism.

But they were superstitious. Alexandra would not seat 13 people at a table, and the sight of three candles together made her frantic. She knew a green dress brought bad luck, and she looked at a new moon from the right side. It was bad luck to begin any undertaking on Friday, but a bright day was good for a journey. Alexandra believed in miracles, and she venerated relics that had been kissed by hordes of unwashed peasants.[19] In fact Alexandra was seeking what appeared to be available only as a miracle—the birth of a son.

The first person with "mystical gifts" to aid the empress was Matrëna the "Barefooted." This retarded peasant woman was nearly 80 when she was fetched to the royal household from a St. Petersburg slum in 1900. The tsar and his wife were said to spend hours listening to her baffling speech, which supposedly predicted a male heir. Another occult expert, Mitya Kolyaba, was a noisier and more outlandish figure. Bow-legged and misshapen, his speech ranged from ordinary conversation to shrieks and groans, which his epileptic attacks changed into animal-like, high-pitched shrieking. Mitya was said to cast out devils; he could heal the sick and foretell the future. When he arrived at the capital in 1901, Kolyaba impressed Feofan and the same circle at the seminary which later received Rasputin so favorably. Mitya was finally presented to Nicholas and Alexandra. The empress hoped that Mitya could predict the birth of a son, but she soon found him a bother and dismissed him. Nevertheless Mitya returned home in great triumph.[20]

A third mystic was "Monsieur Philippe." He was born Philippe Nizier-Vachot in a peasant family in Savoy in 1849, and was apprenticed to an uncle in Lyons who was a butcher. Such work did not appeal to Philippe, who even as a boy possessed a love of solitude, "a hankering after the mysterious and a strong inclination for sorcerers, fortune-tellers, mesmerists and somnambulists." After a brief study at the medical college of Lyons, he opened an office on an elegant boulevard. Philippe practiced "occult medicine," treating his patients with "psychic fluids and astral forces." Philippe impressed his patients. His eyes were "limpid, fascinating and penetrating"— "blue eyes half-hidden by heavy eyelids," which shone with "a curious soft light." On three occasions Vachot was punished for practicing medicine without a license.[21]

These trials added to "Doctor Philippe's" reputation. Even patients who did not respond to his cures testified to his "kindness, pity and unselfishness, the soothing and strengthening power of his presence and the gentle balm that flowed from his slightest movement." Philippe continued to practice medicine through associates. His early patients were artisans, shopkeepers, and cooks, but after 1896 "they were joined by society people, well-dressed women, magistrates, actresses, officers and priests."[22]

Philippe met the tsar and his wife in France in 1901. Alexandra had just delivered her fourth daughter. The Frenchman charmed the royal couple, and at their first meeting they invited him to Russia. The empress was especially fascinated by Philippe's ability to select the sex of an embryo through "the most transcendental practices of hermetic medicine, astronomy and psychurgy."[23]

Dr. Philippe was busy during his three years in Russia. Much of the "medicine" he practiced involved praying with the people who sought him out. Philippe's admirers called him "Our Father" and "Lord." Above all Philippe cultivated Nicholas and Alexandra. Incredible things were said about their relationship. Philippe supposedly held seances in which Alexander III gave advice to his faltering son. Philippe was rumored to perform experiments in "hypnotism, prophecy, incarnation and necromancy" before the tsar and his wife. Best of all Philippe could become invisible! Gossips held that Alexandra went about in an open carriage with Philippe in this state.[24].

Even failure did not shake the confidence Nicholas and Alexandra showed in Philippe. The empress announced she was pregnant in the spring of 1902, and this time she was confident her child would be a boy. Unfortunately it was a false pregnancy or a miscarriage—and a blow to Philippe's reputation. His enemies at court sprang into action, spreading rumors that Philippe had the "evil eye" and the "mark of the Antichrist." The Frenchman's partisans disowned him; the tsarist secret police (the Okhrana) joined the attack. Philippe attracted the attention of General Rachkovsky, who from Paris directed the Okhrana's foreign information-gathering activities. Working with the French Sûreté, Rachkovsky prepared a detailed report that claimed that Philippe was a "shady and suspicious character of Jewish nationality" with connections to the Martinists (a branch of international Freemasonry) and a society called the "Grande Alliance Israelite."

Philippe's career in Russia soon came to an end. Perhaps Nicholas was finally convinced that Philippe was a fraud. It is also possible that Alexandra's confessor Feofan persuaded the empress and her husband that their faith in the occult arts exceeded permissible bounds of the Christian faith. Philippe departed graciously, showered with honors and gifts. This was typical of Nicholas; it was his way of showing that dismissal from a high position was for political reasons, not personal animosity. Philippe left his former hosts with a present and a prophecy. He gave Alexandra an icon with a little bell that would ring to warn her when evil people approached. Philippe also assured the empress she would not be alone. "You will someday have another friend like me who will speak to you of God."[25]

*   *   *

The birth of a tsar's daughter was announced with a 101-gun salute; 102 shots signaled a boy. Alexandra gave birth four times in less than seven years between 1894 and 1901. Each time the crowds listened intensely, wondering if an extra round would indicate the birth of a royal son. Alexandra's fifth delivery was marked by that additional shot. St. Petersburg cheered at the hundred and second round.

Alexandra was relieved at her marvelous fortune, though an event a few days before Alexis's birth seemed to be a bad omen. Alexandra was dressing, attended by Madame Mouchanow, a lady-in-waiting. Suddenly an enormous wall mirror fell with a crash, shattering into a thousand fragments. The empress cried out;

she grew deadly pale and predicted she would die in childbirth. On the day Alexis was christened, Mouchanow reminded Alexandra of her earlier fright, adding that it proved superstition was silly. The empress smiled sadly, and replied, "My good Martha, we do not know yet what is going to befall my baby, and whether his will be a happy life or not. Perhaps the bad omen was for him and not for me."[26]

Nicholas and Alexandra were thrilled with their new son. Yet within two months of Alexis's birth, his father was already confiding that

Alix and I have been very much worried. A hemorrhage began this morning without the slightest cause from the navel of our small Alexis. It lasted with but a few interruptions until evening. We had to call . . . the surgeon Fedorov who at seven o'clock applied a bandage. The child was remarkably quiet and even merry but it was a dreadful thing to have to live through such anxiety.

This was Alexis's first bout with the affliction that would change the history of his nation—and the world. Hemophilia came gently at the beginning: The bleeding stopped on the third day; at no point was the boy's pain great.

Alexis and his parents were spared further attacks for more than a year. The baby developed beautifully in these months; his parents were so proud of his yellow curls, his blue eyes, his fat body. He trotted about independently after his first birthday, taking the tumbles one expects from a child learning to walk. But the empress noticed a difference. She realized that Alexis suffered more from these bumps than the small blows warranted. "In deadly terror, but without speaking of it to anyone. Alexandra Fedorovna watched her darling with a fear in her heart she did not dare to put into words."[27]

Alexis suffered his first major blow from hemophilia in July 1905. He fell out of his baby carriage. It was not a bad tumble, and the skin was not even broken. But Alexandra was terror stricken as she heard, clearly and for the first time, a new cry of pain in Alexis's voice. Weeping bitterly Alexandra rushed to her husband to tell him the grim news before the doctors could speak. Such a bruise was more dangerous than a cut: It signified a massive internal hemorrhage, which lancing could not relieve lest the patient bleed to death. Alexis's agony increased with the swelling. The physicians admitted they could do nothing. They could only confirm Alexandra's worst fears: Her son had hemophilia.[28]

Alexandra's agony was compounded by the realization that Alexis took this terrible disease from her, his mother. Nicholas offered any price for the specialist who would cure his son. But the physicians had to concede they were powerless against hemophilia.

"Your majesty must realize that the heir apparent will never be completely cured of his disease," Dr. Fedorov said. "The attacks of hemophilia will recur now and then. Strenuous measures of protection will have to be taken to guard [your son] against falls, cuts and scratches, because the slightest bleeding may prove fatal to persons afflicted with hemophilia."

Nicholas aged ten years in as many days. Yet in one sense he was fortunate: As tsar he could bury himself in his work—and he did. Alexandra had no escape. She haunted the nursery, playing with Alexis when he was well, comforting him when he was sick. "Life lost all meaning for the imperial parents," one observer recalled. "We were afraid to smile in their presence. When visiting the palace, we acted as we would in a house of mourning." Alexandra refused to accept the opinions of the "experts." She rambled endlessly about the ignorance of physicians and declared an open preference for "true medicine men" such as "Doctor Philippe." Alexandra threw herself into prayer with all of the intensity of her passionate nature. Her prayers and devotions were "tinged with a certain hysteria."[29]

Alexandra believed faith could move mountains. If her own prayers were useless, this only proved she was a sinner not yet worthy of God's grace. But "God is just," she often observed. Perhaps more prayers and greater efforts would bring a better result. Alexandra's reading turned to the *Lives* of the saints. They were close to God and had pleased Him with their lives. Alexandra noticed that many saints were common people. Might there be saints of this type right now, living in the villages and distant corners of Russia? Would God finally hear the prayers of a suffering mother? Would he finally send a modern saint to her?

===== 3 =====
A Man of God from Tobolsk

Rasputin arrived in St. Petersburg during the Revolution of 1905. In October Nicholas finally agreed to create a legislature, the Duma. The tsar still called himself an autocrat, and monarchists supported the claim. Others hoped Russia was taking a step toward democracy. The "October Manifesto" announcing the Duma served as a constitution, for Nicholas conceded that his subjects would enjoy free speech and press, the right to form unions and political parties, etc. Conflicts continued throughout 1906 and 1907, but generally the feeling was Russia had surmounted a crisis and the system, as modified, would survive.

A conservative mood took hold of Russian society after the Revolution of 1905. Members of the working class turned increasingly to fiery evangelists such as John of Kronstadt, priests who combined work among the poor with anti-Semitism and monarchist politics. The upper classes displayed a heightened interest in the occult. Medlums summoned spirits; tables floated and tapped in dark rooms. Writers and socialites were fascinated by the cults, especially the Flagellants who had influenced Rasputin. Political upheaval led to ennui—and a search for teachings that were spiritually "fulfilling." Educated people mingled with members of the upper class in salons and discussion groups. There was a sense that a stage of Russian history was drawing to a close, that something new was emerging and defining itself. Conservatives deplored the flux that had descended upon Russia, "decadent" writers celebrated it; all agreed something important was about to occur. The poet Alexander Blok put the matter well when he observed "the gypsy caravan was moving on."[1]

Rasputin fitted well into the capital's social scene in these months. Feofan introduced him to the "Montenegrin sisters," and they in turn brought him before the royal family. The sisters, Militsa and Anastasia, were the beautiful daughters of the king of Montenegro, a small state in the Balkans. They were passionately devoted to the occult and to "religious truth" often found in exotic, nonwestern religions. Militsa was versed in eastern mysticism and philosophy, and she learned Farsi to read Persian texts in the original.

Militsa married Peter Nicholaevich Romanov, one of Nicholas II's first cousins once removed. Anastasia became attached to Peter's brother Nicholas Nicholaevich, the bluff soldier who would lead the Russian army on the western front at the beginning of the war. Alexandra's concerns harmonized with those of Militsa and Anastasia; they discussed books and ideas. The relationship deepened during 1905. Militsa dined with Alexandra at least seven times in the last three weeks of October; Anastasia failed to visit the palace only two days in the same period. The sisters were also constantly on the phone with Alexandra during the most critical days of 1905.[2]

Feofan introduced Rasputin to Militsa during the fall of 1905. The sisters were quite taken with Grigory. There was fire and conviction in his speech; his gray piercing eyes sparkled. Rasputin claimed he could heal all illness, foretell the future, and charm away unhappiness. As Simanovich put it, he seemed to be the "miracle worker their hearts were seeking." The sisters promptly brought their tales of Rasputin to Nicholas and Alexandra.[3]

Nicholas and Alexandra dined with the Montenegrins and their mates on October 31, 1905. The following day Nicholas inscribed in his diary a simple notation: "We became acquainted today with Grigory, a man of God from Tobolsk province."[4]

Sources say little about the early meetings between Rasputin and the royal family. The first was at the royal family's home at the Alexander Palace. Rasputin arrived in a taxi about nine o'clock at night. Nicholas and Alexandra received the starets in the cozy little parlor that adjoined the tsar's study. Rasputin knew the grand dukes and their women had recommended him, so he was relaxed and self-confident. Grigory addressed the tsar and his wife as *ty*.[5] He talked about his life and spiritual interests and in general made an excellent impression. Although Nicholas and Alexandra craved simplicity and honesty, their lives were filled with stuffy people. Rasputin was a welcome change. His discussion of the Gospels, and above all the apocalypse, made a strong impression on the royal couple.[6]

Rasputin probably met the tsar and his wife on other occasions later in 1905. The second *recorded* meeting occurred on July 18, 1906. This was the "first audience proper" and was an encounter "of long duration." At this point Grigory impressed the royal family as a starets, a voice of the common people—not as a healer. This revelation began with Rasputin's third visit to the palace on October 12, 1906.[7]

At that time Nicholas instructed Prince Putyatin, a court officer, to arrange a reception for Rasputin at 6:30 the following evening. The prince met the peasant at Tsarskoe Selo's railway station and brought him to the Alexander Palace. Rasputin showed the royal family the miracle-working icon of St. Simeon of Verkhoturie. Grigory gave a small icon to each of the children along with consecrated bread and a blessing. The company then had tea. When Grigory left, Nicholas asked Putyatin for his opinion of the visitor. The prince replied that he found Rasputin to be insincere and scatterbrained. The tsar did not care for this answer and looked askance while stroking his moustache and beard. Nicholas insisted he was glad Grigory made the visit, for it gave the family the opportunity to see a famous icon. Nicholas thanked the prince—and never spoke to him again about Rasputin.[8]

The tsar was so taken with Rasputin that he wrote Prime Minister Peter Stolypin about it three days later. Revolutionaries had recently bombed the minister's home. The explosions did not claim their intended victim, but they killed 33 people and smashed the feet of Stolypin's 14-year-old daughter Natalya. The physicians thought it necessary to amputate both her feet. Nicholas was moved by this misfortune. In a letter dated October 16, 1906, he told Stolypin that Rasputin "made a remarkably strong impression both on her Majesty and me, so that our conversation with him lasted for *more than an hour* instead of five minutes." The tsar hoped Stolypin could "find a minute to receive him next week."

The family humored Nicholas and received Grigory. No healing occurred, and when the distinguished visitor left, Natalya had her room sprinkled with eau de Cologne. Stolypin himself was not present. It was fortunate he asked the doctors to postpone amputation. Natalya was in agony and remained crippled, but the physicians saved her feet.

Nicholas and Alexandra were not bothered by the coolness of others toward Rasputin. The royal couple's admiration for the Siberian peasant continued despite the skepticism of others. "Militsa and Stana [her sister Anastasia] dined with us," Nicholas wrote in his diary under December 9, 1906. "All evening we spoke of Grigory."[9]

We would like to know when Rasputin first healed Alexis, but records of these events—if kept—are not available. Nicholas and Alexandra were secretive about their son's condition. They feared Alexis would be excluded from the throne if his hemophilia were known, so only a few intimates were aware of the disorder. Alexis's poor health could not be concealed, and rumors held he might die as a child. But the word "hemophilia" was never officially attached to the tsarevich.

Maria Rasputin thought her father healed Alexis for the first time in 1906. If so it must have been late in that year. The royal family's meeting with the starets on October 12, 1906, just described, obviously had nothing to do with hemophilia. Maria Rasputin tells us the attack that first brought Grigory to Alexis's bedside was serious. Dr. Botkin, the royal family's chief physician, did not expect the boy to recover. Nicholasha suggested they send for Rasputin. By the time Grigory arrived Alexis was too weak to even open his eyes. Alexandra was on her knees, weeping. Grigory ordered everyone to kneel and pray; he fixed Alexis in a steady gaze and placed his hand on his forehead. The tsarevich gave a small sigh and opened his eyes. Alexis smiled at Rasputin, then at his mother. The spark of life returned, the hemorrhage stopped, and the child recovered.

A very different account of Rasputin's first healing of Alexis comes from V. A. Telyakovsky, director of the imperial theaters. The painter Korovin was chatting with Telyakovsky when the conversation turned to the Siberian starets who was the rage of St. Petersburg. Telyakovsky understood that Rasputin healed Alexis who was afflicted with a bleeding leg due to "weak veins." Rasputin touched the tsarevich; the blood ceased to flow. "That's a good little boy," Rasputin said. "You'll be well. But God Alone knows what the future will be."

"Now, of course, they think he's a saint."[10]

*   *   *

Contemporary doctors viewed hemophilia as a "disease" whose symptoms were a "remarkable disposition to bleed with or without the provocation of an injury." They were fascinated by the fact that "neither structural change of the blood vessels nor peculiar composition of the blood has been made out, and there is nothing remarkable in the ordinary appearance of a bleeder." In cases of spontaneous bleeding, "it comes from the mucous membranes, especially from the nose, but also from the mouth, bowel, and bronchial tubes." Manifestations of the disorder are "incredibly painful" and provoked by injuries so minor as to go unnoticed by ordinary people. "Even slight bruises are very apt to be followed by extravasations of blood into the tissues." The swollen joints of a hemophiliac, especially the knee, "are probably due, in the first instance, to the escape of blood into the joint-cavity or into the synovial membrane." Blood flows from the smallest vessels, "and from these it may escape in such quantities as to cause death within a few hours."[11]

The physicians of the day could not relieve the sufferings of hemophilia—but Rasputin successfully treated Alexis. The "power" Rasputin possessed has been a source of endless fascination. What was his "secret?" How could Rasputin prevail where men of science and medicine were powerless?

Rasputin did not actually *cure* Alexis of hemophilia. The boy suffered from the disorder throughout his life, and he had it when he died. But Rasputin's ability to control Alexis's symptoms is indisputable, for it comes from people who resented Grigory's ability to bring relief where the experts stood helpless. General Lukhomsky recalls hearing "from people whose honesty I cannot doubt that there were several cases when the doctors were unable to stop the hemorrhage which ceased as soon as Rasputin appeared on the scene." An eyewitness at court adds that "Rasputin had incontestable success in the art of healing; I have no idea how he managed it." Professor S. P. Fedorov, M.D., the specialist in charge of the team of physicians who treated Alexis, admitted that for all his study of and experience with hemophilia, "when Alexis was bleeding, I was unable to stop it with any method." Rasputin, on the other hand, "would arrive, go up to the sick fellow, look at him without a single worry. After the very briefest time, the bleeding would stop." Fedorov did not know if this was a series of coincidences, but it was a "fact."

Similar testimony comes from Ostrogorsky, another of Alexis's doctors. Someone who heard of Rasputin's "cures" asked if it was true that Rasputin successfully treated Alexis. "Ostrogorsky categorically affirmed this, describing in detail how he had personally witnessed the relief [Rasputin brought] to the Heir [by halting] the flow of blood."

The impact of Rasputin's "healing" was heightened by the terrible condition in which he often found his patient. His aunt Olga recalled that on one occasion,

the poor child lay in pain, dark patches under his eyes and his little body all distorted, and the leg terribly swollen. The doctors were just useless, . . . more frightened than any of us, . . . whispering among themselves. . . . It was getting late and I was persuaded to go to my rooms. Alicky [the empress Alexandra] then sent a message to Rasputin in St. Petersburg. He reached the palace about midnight or even later. By that time, I had reached my apartments and early in the morning Alicky called me to go to Alexis's room. I just could not believe my eyes. The little boy was not just alive—but well. He was sitting up in bed, the fever gone, the eyes clear and bright, not a sign of any swelling in the leg. Later I learned from Alicky that Rasputin had not even touched the child but merely stood at the foot of the bed and prayed.[12]

Some argue that Rasputin used deception. They provide Rasputin accomplices in Anna Vyrubova, the empress's closest friend, and Dr. Badmaev, famous for the practice of Oriental root and herb medicine. Rasputin's enemy Iliodor believed if the conspirators needed money or saw their power waning, they gave Alexis "a yellow powder that made him ill without actually endangering his life." When the tsarevich became ill, Anna would remind his mother that Rasputin could restore his health. The powders were discontinued and Rasputin arrived just as Alexis began to improve. Rasputin's prestige would then be restored and he was given whatever he wanted.

Others explained Rasputin's "miracles" through coincidence. Alexandra's friend and biographer Baroness Sophie Buxhoeveden thought Rasputin had "his own sources of information and contrived to come in time for the recovery of the child to be attributed to him." Lili Dehn, another friend of the empress, concluded that luck was responsible for the tsarevich's recovery just at the time Rasputin prayed. Grigory always managed to come when Alexis was about to recover, and the empress believed his improvement was due to Grigory. Nicholas's mother and cousin Alexander were likewise certain that Alexis's recoveries simply coincided with Rasputin's visits to the palace.[13]

These theories are not convincing. Anna Vyrubova was far more loyal to Alexandra than to Rasputin, and she would not have acted dishonestly to advance his interests. It took Grigory's "holiness" and "powers" to win this honorable (if naive) woman to his circle of admirers. Badmaev knew Alexis was in bad health, but he did not know Alexis had hemophilia. The Buryat healer offered his medical services to the tsar, and during the crisis of 1912 sent potions to the palace, hoping they would be helpful. His services were rejected and the medicines ended up in a trash can. Rasputin and Badmaev were actually enemies until the war, when they formed a political alliance.[14]

Fortunate timing may explain some of Grigory's successes with the tsarevich. There were surely times during the decade in which Rasputin served Alexis when the boy was recovering just as "Father Grigory" appeared. This could not have been true in every case. The first few times Rasputin "healed" Alexis must have been least likely to offer coincidence. Rasputin surely had to "perform" in these early encounters.

Some suggest Rasputin used hypnotism. While he admits that hypnosis could not "alter the composition of [Alexis's] blood to replace the deficiency which prevented it from coagulating normally," George Katkov argues that "hypnotic influence can affect the vaso-motor system and cause a contraction of the vessels comparable to the effect of adrenalin and similar drugs." Robert K. Massie, the well-known writer whose own experience with hemophilia led him to study the Russian royal family and write its story, refers to the experience of Dr. Oscar Lucas at Jefferson Hospital in Philadephia. In a three-year period from 1961 to 1964, Lucas extracted 150 teeth from hemophiliac patients without a single transfusion of blood plasma. Charles Sydney Gibbes, the children's English tutor, thought that Rasputin used hypnosis to relieve the tsarevich's suffering.[15]

Rasputin's admirers hotly denied that he used hypnotism. They claimed that he commanded a power that comes only to a man of God. Maria Rasputin insisted her father thought hypnotism was satanic and never used it.[16] The director of the Russian police, Stephen Beletsky, also denied that Rasputin used hypnotism. Beletsky made it his business to read Rasputin's correspondence. "Several letters of one of the capital's leading mesmerists" attracted his attention in 1913. The mesmerist wrote his mistress to tell her that Rasputin approached him to learn his secrets. The mesmerist thought Rasputin possessed the qualities demanded in a hypnotist, and he expected to make much money giving him lessons. Beletsky discovered that the would-be teacher was also a "sort of speculator," and he forced him to leave the capital. "I do not know if Rasputin [took] lessons after this from someone else," Beletsky concludes, "for I soon left the service, and when I returned [in 1915] I was not provided with information about the surveillance of Rasputin" in the two-year interval.[17]

Rasputin might have turned to a master hypnotist to refine skills that impressed many eyewitnesses. People often commented on a *magnetism* Grigory possessed that struck them as "hypnotic." Alexis Khvostov, one of Grigory's bitterest enemies, claimed "not a single hypnotist could ever make an impression on me"; but "Rasputin was doubtless one of the most powerful hypnotists I have ever met at any time!" Rasputin's will "could be overwhelming and hypnotic, and it took a moment to recover from it." Felix Yusupov, Rasputin's assassin, also credited Grigory with magnetic force. The prince approached Rasputin to win his confidence and lure him into a trap. Yusupov claimed he needed healing.

Rasputin had the prince lie down. He gazed intently into Yusupov's eyes and began to stroke his head, neck, and chest. Grigory then kneeled, bowed his head and prayed with his hands on Felix's forehead. The starets leaped to his feet after some time and began to make "passes." Yusupov was now in a stupor, he felt a tremendous hypnotic force emanating from the strange man. Felix was paralyzed, he could not speak and was drifting to sleep as if under a "strong narcotic." Yusupov claims he finally rallied and resisted the hypnosis—but he willingly conceded that Rasputin was a man of tremendous spiritual force.[18]

If Rasputin knew hypnosis, that by no means indicates he used it to treat Alexis. Could a two-year-old child be hypnotised under any circumstances? And if hypnosis *under ideal conditions* can bring hemophiliacs through operations, we must admit that Rasputin did not work under ideal conditions. Alexis was suffering and exhausted when Grigory first came to his bedside; Maria Rasputin indicates he was dozing. Both versions of this episode claim that Grigory touched the bleeding area, prayed—and the bleeding stopped. Was this hypnosis? If so, observers would have realized the reason for Alexis's recovery. Nicholas and Alexandra would have been grateful; they probably would have credited the gift to God. But they—or less friendly witnesses—would have known that Rasputin used hypnosis.

It is doubtful hypnosis would have much effect under these conditions. Robert K. Massie thinks that no doctor "established in this field accepts the possibility that hypnosis alone could suddenly stop a severe hemorrhage." Tempting as it is to assume that Rasputin used hypnosis to stop Alexis's bleeding, Massie concludes that "[m]edically, it would not have been that simple."[19]

Rasputin's own explanation may be close to the truth: Grigory was a starets, a man of God, and he was entrusted with some important gifts. Among these gifts was the ability to relieve suffering through prayer—a gift referred to as "healing." It is true that Rasputin abused his gifts and strayed from his calling. But the evidence suggests that Rasputin commanded certain powers.

Rasputin might also have possessed a remarkable power that is apparently unknown in the West. This is the power "to parley with the blood," *zagovarivat' krov.* "We leave it to the scientists to discuss if such a thing belongs to the domain of material possibility," Poliakoff wrote on the matter. "We only say that the belief in zagovarivat' is widely spread in Russia, and that there are people who allege to have witnessed cases when it was accomplished." Baroness Sophie Buxhoeveden recalled such an incident when she was eight or nine years old. A horse on her grandfather's estate had cut his fetlock to the bone. The bleeding was so profuse that it seemed the animal would die. One of the people tending the horse recalled a certain "Alexander the horse-leech" who knew how to stop any kind of bleeding. Despite skepticism, they sent for the man.

Alexander removed the bandages and gently moved his fingers about the wound. His face was close to the stallion's leg, he stroked the animal and mumbled words no one could make out. To the amazement of the crowd, the bleeding stopped in a short while. Alexander now bound the leg to prevent a recurrence of bleeding. When the veterinarian arrived he admitted the horse was healing. The bleeding had certainly stopped.

The baroness noted that "blood-stilling" was a secret carefully passed from father to son. Recalling Rasputin handled horses from his early years, Bux-hoeveden concluded that he probably had this gift. She heard "parleying with the blood" was practiced on humans, though she never saw that.

Another case adds to this line of inquiry. A hunting party in Russian Poland came upon a woodsman who had almost amputated his foot with an axe. Someone fetched a peasant who was said to be a blood-stiller. Although the foot was nearly severed from its leg and the woodsman was bleeding profusely, a "miracle" took place when the peasant arrived. The blood ceased to flow. "I would never have believed it had I not seen it with my own eyes," an eyewitness concluded. De Basily cites this episode in her memoirs to explain Rasputin's success with hemophilia.[20]

Perhaps Rasputin had the gift of healing, or perhaps he knew "blood-stilling." Autosuggestion might also have become a factor once Grigory was established in the tsarevich's mind as the person who could bring his sufferings under control. Rasputin often relieved Alexis's sufferings over the telephone. Police General Komissarov was with Rasputin once when Tatyana called to say her brother was suffering from a terrible headache; the children begged the starets to come to the palace. Rasputin told the tsarevich a Siberian tale, then ordered him to bed. Rasputin was certain the headache would pass—and it did.

On another occasion a call came just as Rasputin was returning from a night "out." He was asked to hurry to the tsarevich's side. Grigory was drunk; pleading sickness, he claimed he could not come. The messenger insisted, saying nothing seemed to stop the flow of blood. Rasputin predicted that the bleeding would stop within an hour and promised to come to Tsarskoe Selo if it did not. The bleeding ceased instantaneously. Aron Simanovich, Grigory's personal secretary, noted on other occasions that Rasputin healed Alexis of insomnia and even fever over the telephone.[21] Much of this may be explained through autosuggestion.

While we may speculate about the "secret" of Rasputin's power, Alexandra had nothing to debate. She accepted Rasputin as a man of God with healing gifts. The empress believed in faith healing; she had little confidence in doctors. Baroness Buxhoeveden recalled a discussion with Alexandra well before Rasputin appeared about several children who died because their parents treated their illnesses with prayers, not medicine. "I expressed my indignation at such folly being possible with all the resources of science within reach." To the baroness's astonishment, Alexandra replied, "My dear, they did not pray hard enough. Had their prayers been fervent, the children would have recovered!" This was the key to the problem for Alexandra Fedorovna: to move God through sufficient prayer and devotion, to obtain His mercy.

Rasputin calmed Alexandra. "Don't worry about the child," he advised. "He doesn't need medicine, he needs as much a healthy outdoor life as his condition can stand. He needs to play with a dog and a pony. He needs a sled. Don't let the doctors give him any except the mildest medicines. Don't on any account allow them to operate. The boy will show improvement, and then he will get well."

Rasputin was rash to venture the last prediction. Hemophilia is a condition, not a disease, and those who have it do not "get well." But Rasputin insisted when the "child is twelve years old, he will begin to improve. He will improve steadily after that, and by the time he is a man he will be in ordinary health like any other man."[22] Someday Alexis would no longer need doctors—or even Rasputin.

In the meantime months passed and the relationship between Rasputin and Alexandra deepened. She called upon him when Alexis was ill; he prayed and God heard his prayers. Alexandra's own supplications brought no relief. Rasputin was different. He was a saint.

=== 4 ===
The Secrets of Father Grigory

The visitors began gathering before sunrise. They heard that Rasputin was an influential man who would help them with their problems. Rasputin saw as many as 200 of these people a day. Some were peasants requesting a prayer for loved ones. Businessmen sought contracts or government favors; officials hoped for promotion. Mothers and wives provided the largest group—women anxious to see a husband released from prison or a son kept from the army. If Rasputin had an unusually late night "out" he met this cross section of humanity on the landing outside his apartment. "You have all come to me for help," he would say. "I will help you all!"

Rasputin normally returned home just after midnight and rose at seven or eight in the morning. He took a leisurely breakfast, talked with friends and family members, then telephoned to learn what was new at Tsarskoe Selo. Rasputin "received" from 10 A.M. to 1 P.M. He was not bound by the order in which the visitors arrived. Beautiful young women enjoyed the highest priority. Rasputin was also partial to Jews—he often admitted them before important people who had waited longer.

Rasputin took these "interviews" seriously. People coming to him for help confirmed the fact that Grigory was an important man, a perception he encouraged. It is also true that petitioners touched the moral streak in Father Grigory, giving him an opportunity to display his finer qualities. Sometimes Rasputin had a secretary follow up a petition with the proper authority. More often he scribbled a note that began with a cross followed by a text that read, "Dear Friend, be so kind—do it for me. Grigory." These notes were not addressed to any particular person; bearers could hand them to anyone who could resolve their problems.

Rasputin often knew he could not help, but he hated to be the one to say "no." This would also be an admission that the visitor had an exaggerated notion of Rasputin's power.

Most petitioners brought gifts to win Rasputin's favor. Peasants presented cakes and fruit, chickens and ducks. The urban poor offered caviar and fish, fruit and fresh bread. More sophisticated guests bore icons or cases of wine. Businessmen usually had money. Rasputin took what was offered, but he was not by nature a greedy man. A wad of rubles just received as a bribe might end up with the next visitor. Or his price for a favor might be to "give all your cash to that person over there." Dishes of potatoes, sauerkraut (*kapusta*,) and black bread surrounded the samovar. Rusk made from black bread stood next to the salt. These "Rasputin rusks" (as they were called) were popular in the capital, even if their namesake was not.[1]

Rasputin's daughters lived with their father. Maria, the oldest, began her education at Kazan in 1908. She was then admitted to the Seiman Academy in St. Petersburg. Maria was homesick at this elegant boarding school and in 1910 was permitted to join her father. Grigory called Varvara to the capital soon after this; until the war broke out the two girls attended the prominant Steblin-Damensky Gymnasium on Liteini Avenue. The family's old friend Katya came from Siberia to oversee the household in Petrograd. Katya found a governess who could also tutor the girls and help them fill the gaps in their education.

Rasputin was a strict father—all the more so (perhaps) because his own life was so scandal-ridden. Hours of study awaited the girls when they returned from school. They were not permitted to go out alone and, even when escorted, were rarely treated to the cinema. Rasputin and his daughters prayed together every morning and evening. He carefully told them good-bye each night before going out. The girls were usually asleep when their father returned home, but occasionally they heard him trudging up the stairs. They then jumped into bed and pretended to be asleep when their father came into their room to bless them with a sign of the cross. Sunday mornings were spent in church, much of the afternoon was devoted to home worship. The girls found it tiring to be on their knees for hours on end. Fortunately the long skirts in fashion let them sit on their heels when their father was not looking at them.

Grigory was less successful in sharing his "big city success" with the other members of his family. He hoped that his son Dmitry might become a priest. Dmitry enrolled in a school at Samara but book learning failed to interest him. Dmitry was a strong lad, fond of horses and highly knowledgeable about them. Within a year he returned to Pokrovskoe to live with his mother, who also decided that city life was not for her. Praskovaya was brought to the capital at the expense of the Montenegrin sisters for a hysterectomy in 1906, but she decided to go back to Siberia to run the farm with Dmitry. She paid her husband and daughters a brief visit once a year. This in no way altered Rasputin's love

life. The women still came to his apartment. "He can do what he likes,"
Praskovaya said at such times. "Grigory has more than enough for everybody!"

Grigory's father Efim once visited St. Petersburg. The old man's journey wore
him out; he was not ready for the urban scene. Horseless carriages particularly
upset him; he made the sign of the cross over them as they darted about. Efim
soon returned home and stayed there for the rest of his life.[2]

One of the most important people in Rasputin's life was Aron Simanovich, a
jeweler who began his career as a diamond dealer in Kiev. He arrived in the
capital in 1902. Although Simanovich was Jewish he made a favorable impression
even upon anti-Semites, and within a few months the Princess Orbelian introduced him to the empress. Alexandra Fedorovna asked the value of various items
at their first meeting, and she was taken with his honesty and good sense. Aron
could see that the empress was cost-conscious, so he offered her "very low
prices." The tsarina compared Simanovich's prices with those of the court
jeweler Fabergé; she was usually satisfied. Alexandra brought Simanovich other
wealthy patrons.

Rasputin met Simanovich soon after settling in St. Petersburg, and they immediately formed a close friendship. Simanovich was amazed at what little sense
Rasputin had of planning for "the future." Rasputin struck Simanovich as "a
care-free person who lived only for the present day," Maria Rasputin confirms.
She also recalled that on some occasions they had no money. Grigory never
worried. He trusted in God, and some "gift" always came along to improve
the family's fortunes.

Simanovich had no patience with this attitude. Aron took on Rasputin's financial concerns and worried over the small details of Grigory's life. Simanovich
acted as "secretary, mentor, manager and defender." He was mixed up in all
his "business and secrets." Occasionally Rasputin rejected Simanovich's advice.
If the consequences were bad, Simanovich scolded the starets, and Rasputin
acted like a "guilty schoolboy." Grigory then accepted Aron's tutelage for a
time. Rasputin once gave Simanovich a photograph signed "To the best of the
Jews." Simanovich was enormously pleased.[3]

*   *   *

From the outset Rasputin was a "hit" in St. Petersburg. Feofan's support
opened even difficult doors. Grigory also profited from good luck. Nicholasha
and Anastasia discarded the "prophet" Elias, then his "student" Ilisei, just as
Rasputin appeared in the capital. Success at this court brought Grigory to the
salons of the countesses Kleinmichael and Ignatieva. Kleinmichael's gatherings
were social. Ignatieva was devoted to religion and politics; she belonged to the
"Star Chamber," a reactionary society that hoped to reverse the constitutional
gains of 1905. The hospitality of these women permitted Rasputin to expound
his teachings to large attentive audiences. The starets was soon established as
the exciting new figure on the religious scene.

Rasputin fascinated the capital's upper-class circles. Grigory acquired a taste for perfume and pomades, but to the end he dressed as a peasant. Grigory loved high-collared blue blouses and wore his velvet trousers puffed into high boots as polished as glass. Rasputin liked wide belts with bright, ornate buckles—or for contrast, colorful silk cords with large dangling tassels. The starets enjoyed dressing and devoted much time and thought to the task. A cross around the neck provided a final touch. Alexandra Fedorovna gave him the lovely gold cross that he usually wore. Women were physically attracted to Rasputin, a man of slender build and medium height with a thin face and a wispy beard with slight curls.

Rasputin knew the bored society folk he met would not be impressed with humility or flattery. Grigory's sole hope of victory lay in dictating the rules of their encounters. Rasputin artfully moved from one form of behavior to another. Sometimes he described the sex life of horses; he might pull a distinguished lady toward him and whisper almost threateningly, "Come, my lovely mare!" At other moments he drifted into a vacant gaze, as if a distant memory held him in a spell. In a melancholy voice he recalled Siberia: his farm, his village, or the scented flowers on the banks of the Tura river. From here the starets could easily pass into a lecture. He praised the dignity and virtue of a peasant's life of farming and hard work. "Look at my hands," Rasputin proclaimed. "Their horniness comes from hard work!" Rasputin did not hesitate to criticize his listeners for "fine clothes" and "useless manners." "You must be simpler, far, far simpler, only then will God come nearer to you. Follow me in the summer to Pokrovskoe, to the great freedom of Siberia. We will catch fish and work in the fields, and then you will really learn to understand God."[4]

Rasputin learned that even rudeness earned respect. As soon as he met the wealthy, influential socialite Varvara Uexküll, he descended upon her, saying, "What's this, little mother, pictures on the wall like a real museum. I'll bet you could feed five villages of starving people with what's hanging on a single wall. Just imagine how the peasants go without food!" Uexküll introduced Grigory to her guests. Rasputin fixed each person with a penetrating gaze; taking their hands, he plunged into the most personal questions. "Are you married?" "Where is your husband?" "Why did you come alone?" "Had you been here together, I could've looked you over, seen how you eat and live."

Even Rasputin's manner of speaking was well received. His words did not flow in normal fashion. While conversing with one person Rasputin suddenly turned to another. His speech consisted of jerky, disconnected phrases. Addressing Uexkull, for example, he was heard to say, "It isn't good, mother— it isn't good! Yes, it's possible to live like you do—it's necessary to have love— yes—well, what is here!" He also jumped from one theme to another while walking briskly about the room. Then he suddenly sat down, bent over, and rubbed his hands. All this made a strong and positive impression on the people who surrounded Father Grigory. They began to whisper that he had the key to life, that he spoke the truth and discerned much.[5]

Rasputin's poor table manners were likewise an asset. He rarely used a knife or fork. Grigory dipped pieces of bread in soup, picking out the solid food with his fingers. He was primarily a vegetarian, but also was partial to fish, fish soup, hard-boiled eggs, fruit, and tea. Grigory avoided vodka and other strong drink; he took madeira, also port, and on occasion champagne. Rasputin did not drink heavily in his early St. Petersburg years; at the end he was surely an alcoholic.

Rasputin was careful in his dress but careless about what eating did to his appearance. Grigory wiped his hands on his clothes and even his beard. Bits of food were liberally scattered throughout his whiskers; some claimed an inspection revealed what its owner had for lunch. We read that women were attracted to his dirty hands, to his grimy black fingernails.[6] This must be exaggerated. Nothing in Rasputin's routine would produce terribly unclean hands. He often visited the bathhouse. The image of Rasputin's blackened fingernails is probably a part of the mythology surrounding the mysterious starets. Grigory inspired both friends and foes to "improve" on the truth. There were always two Rasputins, the "real" Rasputin and the one who was said to exist. It is not easy to disentangle the two, as we see from the difficulty in deciding whether his fingernails were usually dirty or clean.

* * *

Successful as Rasputin was with the capital's socialites, a different group admired him as a religious teacher, a starets, a "man of God." They formed a long-term attachment to the master and looked to him for guidance in the smallest affairs. Smitten characterized Rasputin's female admirers as "nervous women with broken spirits and a certain sorrow they had not yet overcome. Their spirits thirsted for a religious consolation . . . which the official clergy could not provide, for typical priests did not possess spiritual fire; they were unable to excite the souls of people in general and the skeptically inclined intelligentsia in particular." But Rasputin had such an ability. Contact with him produced uplift—"and, in the sorrowful person, hope, yearning."

One of his female admirers was Olga Lokhtina, who saw Rasputin as the "Lord of Hosts," the "great God Sabaoth Himself." She and Grigory were lovers, and she invited him to live in her elegant apartment in the Peski district. Rasputin now had a base of operations and could come and go and receive people on his "own ground." Grigory also benefited from the social status of his new patron. Olga helped him with a growing correspondence and took dictation for letters that Grigory signed with a large awkward "G." Lokhtina often had tea at Tsarskoe Selo with the empress, regaling her and other guests with tales of Father Grigory. This too was helpful to Rasputin.[7]

Anna Vyrubova was another disciple of Rasputin. Her connection with Grigory and the royal family made her one of the most despised people in Russia by the time the tsar's government collapsed in March 1917. The hatred people felt for Vyrubova extended even to physical ridicule. Cantacuzène, for example, grants that Anna had a "fine complexion and teeth," but otherwise recalls her as "very fat" and afflicted with a "clumsy walk and figure, a pretty head, soft curly hair, blue eyes which always looked sleepy.'' The French ambassador described Vyrubova as "coarse and heavily built, with a round head, fleshy lips, limpid eyes devoid of expression, a full figure and a high color.''[8]

Yet this woman played a major historical role. She was born Anna Taneeva in 1884. Her mother was a Tolstoy, a grand lady whom the French ambassador Paléologue found ''well-informed and distinguished.'' Anna's father, Alexander Taneév, was a high official and amateur composer. Anna was a shy, withdrawn child. At 18 she came down with typhus. The Taneev estate outside St. Petersburg was near the home of the empress's sister Elizabeth. Elizabeth and Alexandra visited Anna, bearing flowers and warm wishes. When Anna was formally presented to the empress in 1903, Alexandra gave her a monogram and the court title of *fräulein*.

Anna met her future husband in December 1906. Alexander Vyrubov was soon coming to her house nearly every day. Vyrubov was so smitten with Anna that after a month he began telling people they were to be married, and she found herself showered with congratulations as his fiancée. Anna was presented at a bridal ball in February 1907, and in the swirl of ''dinners, presents, new gowns and jewels, I began to share the excitement, if not the happiness, of those around me.'' Anna's doubts about the marriage were swept out of the way by the approval of her parents, and especially the empress, who held that Anna had given her word and should not change her mind.[9]

At this troubled juncture in her life Anna met Rasputin. Anna recalled Grigory as ''an elderly peasant, thin, with a pale face, long hair, an uncared-for-beard, and the most extraordinary eyes, large, light, brilliant, and apparently capable of seeing into the very mind and soul of [a] person. . . . '.' Rasputin was wearing a long peasant coat, ''black and rather shabby from hard wear and much travel.'' Rasputin and Anna spoke of God. She wanted to ask about the wisdom of marrying Vyrubov. But ''when I was confronted with the close scrutiny of his piercing eyes I withdrew.'' ''He was so overwhelming—I'd never met anyone like him in my life.'' Anna finally asked Grigory's advice. He replied with a prediction: ''I would marry as I had planned, but I should not find happiness in my marriage.''[10]

Alexander and Anna Vyrubova were wed on April 30, 1907 in the palace church at Tsarskoe Selo. Neither partner was ready for marriage—least of all to the other. Anna left him in 1908 and they were divorced shortly after that time.

Anna Vyrubova, as she was still known, now drew close to Rasputin and to Alexandra Fedorovna. The empress recognized the extent of her responsibility for Anna's misfortunes, and she tried to repay her with the type of love and devotion domineering mothers reserve for weak, single daughters. Alexandra might have given Anna a salaried position, but each was anxious to make clear that material advantage was not the basis of their friendship. Anna was actually poor. What little came her way she often passed on to those who were still needier. Vyrubova's sole perquisite was a modest cottage some 200 yards from the Alexander palace where the royal family lived.

Anna's house was small, but it came to be an important place. The royal family usually met Rasputin here. As years passed and Anna gained a reputation for influence, shady businessmen and aspiring officials made their way to her address. Alexander Protopopov, the last royal minister of the interior and himself an adventurer of high order, described Vyrubova's humble dwelling as the "portico to power."[11]

Vyrubova saw Alexandra nearly every day. They conversed in English and read aloud from newspapers and books. "Then we took drawing lessons and sewed together as all the women" at court did. Alexandra was a contralto, and Anna sang soprano, so they performed duets. The two were crushed when separated; on such occasions they telephoned back and forth or exchanged messages and telegrams in English. Prince Michael Andronnikov once visited Anna at such a time. Vyrubova yawned through the entire hour, and nothing the witty prince could say interested her. In that brief time "they brought flowers from her highness, a telephone call from her highness, a note from her highness. And so it was all of the time!" On a few occasions, however, Alexandra could not lavish such attentions on Anna. They were parted for a day or more, and that was that. In such situations Anna pouted. This provoked good-natured teasing from Alexandra who coaxed a smile from Vyrubova by calling her "our little daughter," or even "our big baby."[12]

After dinner Anna Vyrubova often joined Nicholas and Alexandra at the palace. They and the children talked, did jigsaw puzzles, played checkers and patience, mounted stamps and post cards in collectors' albums. The adults chatted after the children were in bed, often until midnight. People who flourished at the court of the previous tsar suddenly had no access to Nicholas and his wife, and they resented Anna's position. Rumors held that Alexandra and Anna were lesbian lovers, which was as untrue as tales that Rasputin and Alexandra *and* Rasputin and Anna were lovers. Rasputin dismissed such talk with the terse comment: "Anna is not like that!" The Provisional Government investigated the matter. An extensive physical exam and some very direct questions—"I cannot here repeat even the least of them," Anna wrote in her memoirs— established her virginity if not her common sense.[13]

Anna thought of Grigory as "a saint who uttered Heaven-inspired words;" she believed he was infallible. The collapse of her marriage freed her to follow religious interests, and by 1909 Anna was a member of Father Grigory's circle. Anna later denied the obvious fact that she was Rasputin's "ardent admirer," but she did explain what she found so compelling about Rasputin. "He was an intelligent person, a person of natural gifts, and I loved to listen to him—I absolutely don't deny that," she told the Extraordinary Investigatory Commission in 1917. "I saw how he received every possible type of person, how he spoke with them. I loved to see that." Anna also noted that with no formal education Rasputin "knew all holy writing, the Bible, everything."

QUESTION: But really, wasn't he illiterate?

ANSWER: He knew everything, said everything, explained everything.[14]

* * *

Rasputin fascinated the citizens of St. Petersburg, but his power came from an ability to impress important people as a starets, a religious teacher, a man of God. Prince Nicholas Zhevakov, a keen observer of this scene, left a powerful account of Rasputin as a religious teacher. Zhevakov's memories are all the more valuable because at first he was not at all impressed with "Father Grigory."

Zhevakov met Rasputin in 1908 or 1909. The intermediary was Alexander von Pistolkors, a member of Grigory's circle who worked with Zhevakov in the state chancellory. Rasputin was using the aristocratic young man to meet influential people. Pistolkors invited Zhevakov to meet the starets. The prince accepted, but what he saw nearly brought him to tears. Rasputin looked like "a hunted rabbit." Grigory's eyes darted about the room, and he apparently feared offending the gathering. Yet these people were anxious to impress Rasputin. They clung to his every word, and extended their hands for the "prophet" to hold. Most were sincere, the prince supposed; most assumed their visitor was a man of God. "They were culpable only for lacking the least notion of what a true starets was."

Zhevakov's second encounter with Rasputin occurred after he had acquired a reputation as an excellent preacher. Pistolkors again brought the prince to the gathering. The starets was seated at a table when they arrived. Some of the guests were aristocrats, but others were "suspicious types"; one of this group was shouting about his "healing" from "Father Grigory." Olga Lokhtina added to the confusion. She sat in a corner, quivering in ecstasy as she read something or other.

"What have I fallen into?" Zhevakov thought. "An insane asylum, insane people?!"

Rasputin sat gloomily at the table, loudly cracking nuts. As soon as he saw Zhevakov and Pistolkors, he sprang to life, waving away a couple of young people so the newcomers could sit at his side. Then he began to speak.

"What did you come here for?" Rasputin asked. "To look at me or to learn how to live in the world so as to save your souls?"

"Saint! Saint!" cried Lokhtina.

"Shut up, fool!" snarled Rasputin.

Rasputin then explained that when he began his quest he realized he had to please God. Wondering how to do this he turned to the *Lives* of the saints. But the accounts began when these men and women were saints. "I thought to myself, that's wrong. Don't show me the lives of people who were saints, show me how they became saints. Then I will learn something. They committed great sins, misdeeds and evil acts. How did they forge ahead? What did they do? At which point did they turn to God? How did they attain understanding? Cruel and evil . . . suddenly they thought of God and came to Him! I wanted someone to show me how to do this.

"Salvation is in God," Rasputin continued. "Without God you will not take a single step. . . . Evil and sin—everything—shield God from us. The room in which you sit, the affairs you carry on, the people who surround you—all shield God because you do not live and think in God's way. What, then, should you do?

"After church, pray, and, on a Sunday or festival day, go out of the city to an open field. Go on and on until you cannot see the bleak cloud of factory smoke which hovers over St. Petersburg, only the pure blue horizon ahead. Then stop and think about yourself—how small, how insignificant, yes, how powerless you seem. And the whole capital will shrink to an ant hill while the people will become ants swarming all over it! And where, then, will your pride, self-love, awareness of power, rights and position go? You will feel pitiful, unneeded, useless. Then look up to heaven and you will see God. You will feel with all your heart that your only Father is the Lord God, that your soul needs God alone. And then you will wish to surrender your soul to Him alone. He alone will help and support you. You will find peace. This is the first step on the path to God.

"You may go no farther. Go back to the world, to your former tasks, cherishing what you have brought back.

"You carry God with you, within your soul. You will find peace in meeting Him and finding His shores. And through Him you will accomplish every thing which you will do in the world. Then every earthly thing becomes God's thing— not some heroic deed. And you will be saved through your labor in the glory of God. Labor is usually to your glory—but the glory of your striving will not save you. This is what the Savior said: 'The Kingdom of God is within you.!'

"Find God, live in Him and with Him. And on every holiday or Sunday, if only in your mind, leave your affairs, and instead of visiting or attending the theater, go to an open field, go to God."

Zhevakov admitted that Rasputin did not say anything new that day. Grigory expounded truths familiar to every Christian. But he expressed the "truth" in such a way as to give it practical application. Ordinary preachers served up philosophical reflections with a scattering of biblical references. Not Rasputin. He brought the ideal and the real together in a manner that was different.

"I have heard many sermons which were substantial and deep," the prince concluded, but "my memory has not retained a single one. Rasputin delivered his sermon fifteen years ago. I recall it even now."[15]

5
The Teachings of Father Grigory

Rasputin had just turned 14. He was in church one Sunday, listening to Luke, Chapter 17. At the twentieth verse, the priest came to the passage that years before made such an impression on Count Leo Tolstoy. Some Pharisees were asking Christ when the Kingdom of God would come. "The Kingdom of God does not come in such a way as to be seen," Jesus replied. "No one will say, 'Look, here it is!' or 'There it is'; for the Kingdom of God is within you."

Grigory pondered these words as he left the church that day. He had always thought of heaven as a distant place in the sky. Was this not the case? Perhaps the kingdom—perhaps God Himself—was within each human, even each animal? Young Rasputin decided the text that moved him so should be taken literally. "God was within him, Grigory Efimovich, and to find Him, one need only direct his search inward. God was not to be sought in a church; one did not address Him in some distant heaven. He was here, inside, this moment—and forever."[1]

Rasputin's later searchings confirmed this idea. Trips to monasteries showed that salvation was not necessarily found there. Vice might dwell in a cloister as much as in the secular world. Rasputin also decided that the clergy did not have the "keys to the Kingdom." Rasputin had little respect for priests and monks and was not awed by abbots or bishops. He often criticized and ridiculed the church hierarchy and its teachings. Grigory recognized that he was a humble peasant, but he was certain that God had spoken to him and communicated His will. Rasputin believed the spirit of God was within—and the Church was not relevant to that fact.[2]

Yet Rasputin also felt attachments to the Church. He was a Russian. The identity of the Russian people, their sense of unity and homeland, were all bound up with the Russian Orthodox Church. Even members of the radical intelligentsia often considered themselves to be a part of the Church. The splendor of the liturgy, festivals such as Easter and Christmas, an art and culture informed by the Christian message—all were bonds not casually broken nor easily replaced. One might see the Church's faults yet remain a voice in the "heavenly choir." Rasputin was strict in observing holy day obligations. He attended Mass on Saturdays and Sundays, and on Lenten Tuesdays and Fridays food in his home could not be cooked in animal fat.[3] Rasputin loved the Liturgies; relics and icons were significant for him. In this way, Rasputin expressed a love of Russia in the Church that Russians loved.

Rasputin also had a vision of the broader world and a sympathy for other faiths. This peasant who began with the anti-Semitism basic to his class became a friend of Jews and an advocate of their rights. Equally remarkable was Rasputin's opposition to nationalism and war. He opposed intervention to protect Russia's "fellow Slavs" in the Balkans. In an interview with a Russian journalist during this crisis of 1913, Grigory insisted that Moslem Turks were as close to God as Christian Slavs. This was the best reason (Rasputin went on to say) for all nations to live at peace. Grigory was not exactly a pacifist, and when the war that he opposed broke out, he prayed Russia would win. But had his views prevailed, peace would have endured, and the crisis that destroyed the Old Europe would have been contained.

The central element in Rasputin's Christianity was the search for salvation. So it is with every Christian. In Grigory's case the problem was complicated by an intense sexual vitality. As a young man he tried to contain his urges—and failed. The flesh and spirit were in perpetual conflict in Grigory Rasputin; biographers often fail to grasp his struggle for a moral life. Rasputin resolved the conflict by making his behavior a virtue and the basis of his religious outlook. "Since he was unable to control his conduct, he had to discover rational explanations, far-fetched as they might be, to make his behavior fit his view of a starets's life."[4]

His searchings led Rasputin to a sensational conclusion: If repentance wins salvation, we must sin to be able to repent. When God places temptation in our way, it is our duty to yield and secure the necessary conditions for penitence. "Besides, was not the first word of life and truth which Christ uttered to mankind 'Repent'? How can we repent if we have not sinned?"

Rasputin insisted that what keeps most people from yielding to temptation is not aversion to sin. If sin repelled, sin would not be tempting. One is not attracted by food one dislikes. What keeps us from sinning is the injury our pride would suffer with the repentance needed for forgiveness. "Absolute contrition implies absolute humility," an observer wrote summarizing Rasputin's thoughts. "No one likes humbling himself, even before God." Pride keeps us from temptation. But God is not deceived, not for a moment! "And when we are in the valley of Jehoshaphat He will know to remind us of all the chances of salvation He offered us which we have rejected."[5]

Rasputin dismissed much of what passes for "moral" behavior as pride, the first of the seven deadly sins. By keeping Christians from yielding to "temptation," pride keeps them from experiencing contrition, and without contrition there can be no repentance. Without repentance there is no forgiveness—and no salvation. Salvation comes from forgiveness. Forgiveness comes only to those who are repentant and contrite. But contrition and repentance come only from yielding to temptation.

Such teachings were heretical and fraught with difficulties. Are robbery and murder also paths to "salvation?" We have no reason to think that Rasputin approved of criminal behavior. It probably never crossed his mind that his doctrines could be so abused. When Rasputin spoke of "yielding to temptation," he was thinking of sex. He agreed that "the spirit must brand the flesh so that it might live," but he realized the "true pilgrim" faced danger here. He could easily fall victim to pride. Pride was the greatest sin, and the better a person tried to be, the greater the danger of falling into this sin. A Christian suffering from pride might never realize his pride—and his sin. Humility is the cardinal virtue. Only humility makes us realize what abject sinners we are and might become. The Christian must "commit a great sin in order to remind himself of the greater sin that awaited him in his pride, in his righteousness."[6] One might reach the depths of sin through sex. But from those depths regeneration may come, and then sinlessness. Pride comes before a fall, and sin precedes salvation.

Rasputin claimed true saints turned to sin so that in these depths their "aureole might shine with double brightness." Similarly Rasputin assured his followers that he drank to demonstrate the "hideousness of vice." He preached a life of purity not through "empty phrases," but by showing the "abject state in which the sinner perishes." Rasputin told the women who surrounded him they could do anything with him, for his mission was "to expose the ugliness of vice." Rasputin answered objections to this with another precept: "You have too much vanity, you must humiliate yourself."[7]

The women who crossed Rasputin's path needed no theology lessons to surrender to him. Many arrived with a request of some sort. Others were attracted by curiosity or scandal, and they yielded through physical impulse, not religious persuasion. But the members of Father Grigory's circle were impressed with the ideas he expressed at their table. Most of these women had led sheltered lives and had never committed terrible degrading "sins." They spent years admiring their own virtue. Now a man of God was telling them this was the wrong path. Prim and proper as they were, restlessness lurked in these women, and they wondered if they had been missing some tremendous experience. Sex and religion are a powerful mixture. One brings ecstasy, the other salvation. Rasputin was the master of both. To have him as a lover was to find marriage in the spirit. What appeared to be sin was really—in this case, at any rate—a path to salvation.

Perhaps Rasputin was a sinner; if cornered and pressed, he admitted it was so. On several occasions Rasputin disarmed interrogators by admitting: "I tried, I failed because I am a sinner, I will try once more." Grigory was actually sounding a familiar note in Russian spirituality. It is related to the unique Russian emphasis on the Suffering Christ. At issue is the question: Who is fit to approach God? "Breaking the commandments means for the Protestant breaking with God until repentance," the English student of Russian Christianity Stephen Graham notes, "but for the Russian peasant there is no such feeling of breaking with God. The drunkard, the thief and the murderer are just as intimate with God as the just man; and perhaps even more intimate." Rasputin was the master of this concept, and he could word it in a passionate moving way.[8]

The members of Rasputin's circle saw him as someone who had found the "truth," but Grigory never claimed that what he learned was the truth that his listeners would find. Rasputin taught the Kingdom of God is in *you*. "You carry God with you, within your soul." You will find peace in meeting Him, and through Him you will accomplish all of the things in this world which will be yours. Rasputin urged his listeners to undertake a voyage of discovery; he offered himself as an example of a person who was making that journey. "Enjoy me for a time," he seemed to say, "learn whatever it is I have to teach you—then be on your way."

It is difficult to identify the origin of Rasputin's ideas. His teachings were heretical from the Church's viewpoint, but Grigory did not fit into any particular heretical tradition.[9] Many claimed that Rasputin was a Flagellant, a member of the khlysty. The charge was based on the notion that the khlysty engaged in sex during worship services. Even reliable studies of Russian history sometimes claim that the khlysty mixed sex and religion. George Munro argues if this happened, it was rare. Such behavior would have been at odds with the values of this group. It is true that Flagellants sang and danced and whirled about, seeking an ecstasy that broke forth in glossolalia. Their mumblings were then accepted as inspired prophesies. After worshipping in this way, khlysty often lay on the floor, exhausted and sleeping. Contemporaries charged that group sex caused this depression. This was not true.[10] Allegations that Rasputin was a member of the sect were equally false.

Rasputin was often charged with using religion to impress gullible people and advance himself. Grigory certainly attracted credulous people and he was ambitious. But to dismiss him as nothing but a charlatan is to miss what made his sensational career possible. As much as he hated Rasputin, Iliodor stressed that "quackery" produces but brief victories. Thousands of "quack saints" thronged the highways of the dying Russian empire in Rasputin's day. They ended up as beggars and outcasts. "Rasputin was not of this kind," Iliodor wrote, "I wish to make that clear. In the beginning he was an honest, earnest man, a seeker after God."[11]

The serious strain in Rasputin's character appeared above all in his prayer life. Grigory prayed regularly, at length and with great intensity, this we know from several sources, not all of which were friendly to the starets. As a young girl Maria Rasputin saw her father spend hours in meditation, striking his head on the ground "until the skin became red." He fasted and prayed constantly, and forced his children—though not his wife—to join him in these devotions. The Russian journalist Sazonov who befriended Rasputin early in his career in Petrograd recalled the starets took little sleep and prayed a great deal. Sazonov's children once saw Grigory in the woods, locked in deep devotions. Their comments aroused a neighbor, a general's wife "who was unable to hear Rasputin's name without disgust." But she was "sufficiently curious to follow the children to the woods," Sazonov continues, "and indeed although an hour had passed, she saw Rasputin still immersed in prayer."[12]

Rasputin's "disciples" saw his qualities as proof that he was marked by election and grace. Grigory was a poetic man and travelled widely and saw a great deal. Maria Rasputin recalled the "tenderness" that came over her father as he told them of places he visited and experiences he had on the way. "Sometimes he mused over the deep silence of the Siberian forest and the wild beauty of the steppes." Maria noted Grigory's love of music, especially Gypsy music. Grigory believed he was as close to God dancing as in a monastery. "One praises Him in the joy that, in His goodness, He has created. David danced before the ark of the Lord."[13]

A young observer was impressed with this sensitive quality. Elizabeth Judas was nine when she first met Rasputin in 1906. Rasputin was waiting for Elizabeth and her travelling companions at Tobolsk to take them by wagon to their estate near Pokrovskoe. "Before starting our overland journey . . . we followed the Russian custom of sitting down for a minute or two. Later, as we stood up to leave, Father Rasputin made the sign of the cross, folded his hands, and, facing the beautiful Siberian sky, began to pray with the most wonderful words I have ever heard. He asked the Lord to bless our coming into this part of Russia, he spoke of the poor and the sick, and mentioned the name of my ailing Cousin Olga." But Elizabeth was upset over the fact that Rasputin did not mention the tsar or his family in his prayer. She recalled the discussion that ensued on this point:

"For whom do you pray, Lizochka?"
"For the tsar, of course."
"Why?"
"Because the tsar is God on earth."
"You are wrong, Lizochka," Rasputin said, smiling. "Everybody prays for the tsar, but they should pray for the poor people, the deaf and dumb and the blind. It is they who need your prayers."

The young girl was angry over Rasputin "telling me to pray so differently from the way I had been taught," and she moved to the back of the wagon to sit with her grandmother. But Elizabeth was soon sorry she had done this, for no sooner had she taken her place than Rasputin began telling "stories of his childhood and nature—such interesting stories that both my grandmother and I, trying not to miss a word, [twisted] around in our seats most uncomfortably."

Rasputin spoke of flowers and trees and the majesty of a stormy sky. He told his listeners "that it is not difficult for anyone to learn the language of Nature if he so desires." Her anger now quite gone, Elizabeth moved to the front of the carriage, "listening to every word spoken about the beauties of nature and how to speak to the Lord in prayer."

"I wish I could remember the exact words and all the examples that Father Rasputin used," Elizabeth Judas wrote a third of a century later. "No governess at home, no teacher or father or mother had ever explained nature so beautifully as did this so-called ordinary peasant of the village of Pokrovskoe in Siberia."[14]

Part II

Challenges and Setbacks

6
First Crisis

Rasputin did not win everybody. Nearly everyone at court and in the government disliked Grigory. Maria Fedorovna was struck by "his ponderous yet catlike tread" as they passed in a palace corridor. Rasputin bowed with insolent familiarity; he was aware of the dowager empress's identity though she did not know his until later.

Vladimir Kokovtsov was struck by the "repulsive expression" of Rasputin's eyes. "Deep seated and close set, they glued on me, and for a long time Rasputin would not turn them away as though trying to exercise some hypnotic influence." Palace Commandant Voeikov spoke of "knavish eyes which continually darted about, not looking one directly in the face." General Bonch-Bruevich thought Grigory's gaze was "cold, intelligent and vicious." Rasputin reminded him of "a member of a cheap Gypsy music-hall chorus," dressed as he was in a "bright red silk Russian shirt with a vest over it; black velvet trousers, lacquered boots and a black bowler hat." Rasputin reminded Kokovtsov of "an Armenian peddler with an ace of diamonds up his sleeve."[1]

These negative reactions exploded in 1908 in an attempt to oust Rasputin from the court. Grigory's antagonist was Peter Stolypin, chairman of the council of ministers. Stolypin was a tall strong man, a burly figure with handlebar moustaches, a protruding forehead, and receding hairline. He was born in 1862 into a noble family with a 20,000-acre estate. Stolypin entered government service in the ministry of internal affairs. Within two decades he was a provincial governor. Stolypin was admired for honor and ability—and for drawing inspiration from the countryside rather then the capital or the bureaucracy. By 1906 Stolypin headed the tsar's government as chairman of the council of ministers.[2]

Rasputin came to Stolypin's attention in 1908 through an investigation conducted by the secret police, the *Okhrana*. Police General Gerasimov recalled that "everyone was nervous" in the capital at this time; "every newcomer was feared and regarded negatively." The Okhrana was especially worried about adventurers who gained entree to the royal family and the court. They assumed "agents of certain foreign embassies" gained "detailed information" about Russian life through these people. Vladimir Dedyulin also asked the police to investigate Rasputin in 1908. The palace commandant described Grigory as "a peasant who is being sponsored by Anna Vyrubova"; he feared the newcomer was "probably a disguised revolutionary."[3]

These investigations led to a confrontation between Stolypin and Rasputin. Grigory learned that the police were inquiring into his life. He must have complained of this to an influential party, for Stolypin was ordered to halt Okhrana surveillance of Rasputin. A few days later Stolypin scheduled a meeting with Grigory. Stolypin asked his assistant, Paul Kurlov, to join him. Stolypin did not admit the tsar requested the meeting. The prime minister was continuing his drive to have Grigory expelled from the capital. Nicholas probably hoped if Stolypin met Rasputin, he would decide that Grigory was not such a terrible fellow and withdraw his opposition to a harmless peasant whose sole crime was to have befriended the royal family.

Kurlov found Rasputin to be "a lean ordinary individual with a wedge-shaped dark beard, and piercing intelligent eyes." Rasputin and Stolypin sat down at a large table. The peasant began by assuring the prime minister that there was no reason to be suspicious; he was a peaceful man with no political party. Stolypin frostily replied that if this were so, there was no need to worry about the police. At this point Rasputin tried to hypnotize Stolypin.

"He ran his pale eyes over me," Stolypin recalled, "mumbled mysterious and inarticulate words from the Scriptures, made strange movements with his hands, and I began to feel an indescribable loathing for this vermin sitting opposite me. Still I did realize that the man possessed great hypnotic power which was beginning to produce a fairly strong moral impression on me, though certainly one of repulsion. I pulled myself together, and addressing him roughly, told him that on the strength of the evidence in my possession I could annihilate him by prosecuting him as a sectarian." Stolypin ordered Rasputin to leave the capital at once "and never show his face there again."

Kurlov tried to calm Stolypin after Grigory left. Kurlov insisted Rasputin was only a sly peasant and that did not make him a menace. ("As they say, 'he carries himself on his head!' ") But Stolypin was determined to act. Two weeks later he asked Kurlov to prepare a police report on Rasputin. This material concerned Rasputin's personal life, his drinking, scandals, and the use adventurers were making of him. Stolypin also requested a Synod report on Rasputin's "religious" career. The plan was to bring a mass of derogatory information to the tsar.

"I advised Stolypin not to do this," Kurlov wrote in his memoirs, "for

Nicholas would conclude people wanted to discredit a person he liked.'' Stolypin ignored this advice, "but when he returned from Tsarskoe Selo that night, he said I was right.'' Nicholas heard the report without saying a single word. He then invited Stolypin to proceed with another briefing.[4] The royal displeasure was clear.

Stolypin persisted in his efforts. He was convinced that rumors linking Rasputin to the royal family were discrediting the tsar and weakening his government. Stolypin did not know of Alexis's hemophilia and Grigory's role in guarding the boy's life, so he did not realize he was on slippery ground. Nicholas's willingness to endure the pressure shows how highly he regarded his prime minister. Nicholas finally made a concession. After one of Stolypin's strongest attacks, the tsar promised *he* would not see Grigory again.

Stolypin apparently thought this gave him the right to dispose of Rasputin. He had a decree drafted returning Rasputin to Pokrovskoe; Grigory could not visit the capital for five years.

Rasputin was scheduled to return from Pokrovskoe to St. Petersburg in December 1908. An Okhrana detachment was waiting at the train station to serve him the papers. Grigory apparently knew a trap awaited; as his train pulled into the station, he leapt from the still-moving coach into a taxi. Rasputin sped to the home of Grand Duke Peter Nicholaevich and Militsa. An Okhrana guard stood at the mansion. Three weeks later the governor of Tobolsk announced that Rasputin had returned to Pokrovskoe. General Gerasimov asked Stolypin about the ban on Grigory's return to the capital. Should an Okhrana detachment deliver the order at Pokrovskoe? Stolypin had suffered enough humiliation. He recognized for the time that he was beaten and made a gesture which said, "Leave it be!''—and had the decree destroyed.[5]

Rasputin had survived his first crisis in St. Petersburg.

Rasputin won because the tsar supported him. The struggle attracted little attention, but those who saw it were amazed that a humble peasant could defeat the mighty Stolypin. The only explanation seemed to be that Rasputin fooled Nicholas and Alexandra. Apparently the tsar and his wife would not accept the proof that Grigory was a false starets. Thus a misconception was born.

Nicholas and Alexandra actually *saw* Rasputin misbehave. One instance involved the tsar's sister Olga. Grigory was greatly attracted to this beautiful woman, and the first time they met he plied her with the usual questions: "Was she happy? Did she love her husband? Why didn't they have children?'' Grigory was not discouraged by Olga's cold response. The next time they met, he took advantage of a moment when they were alone to put an arm around her shoulder and stroke her arm. Olga leapt up and quickly joined the others. Rasputin was showing that he assumed the right to treat women as he wished. "I am afraid Nicky and Alicky looked rather uncomfortable'' over Rasputin's manner, Olga recalled in later years.[6]

Nicholas and Alexandra probed Rasputin's personal life. They did not rely upon the police since they realized the Okhrana was against Grigory. They relied upon friends whose judgment they respected. Nicholas asked General Dedyulin and Colonel Alexander Drenteln to meet Rasputin and share their impressions. Dedyulin refused to make Grigory's acquaintance, but he used his position as palace commandant to collect evidence. He concluded that Rasputin was "an intelligent but crafty, lying peasant who exercised a certain hypnotic ability." Drenteln was equally negative.

The tsar also turned to Feofan and several clergy for an opinion of Rasputin. Their reaction was interesting—and perhaps influential—in shaping Nicholas's thoughts. They conceded Rasputin was sometimes possessed by "terrible evil," but he suffered such contrition for his sins that he became "as pure as a child washed in the waters of baptism." Rasputin was a "holy man," one "chosen of God." "I would all but guarantee his eternal salvation," Feofan declared. Bishop Hermogen's praise for Rasputin was even more strongly worded. "This is God's slave," Hermogen declared to someone who expressed doubts about Father Grigory, "You sin if you judge him even mentally."[7]

Alexandra launched her own investigations. Realizing that Feofan's impressions of Grigory came from what he heard and saw in the capital, the empress asked him to visit Rasputin's home. Feofan stayed in the home Rasputin had just built and furnished with gifts from the capital. Two weeks later Feofan went to Sarov, where he came upon negative information. When he mentioned the starets at the Diveev convent, for example, the mother superior threw her fork at the floor and shouted, "This is what should be done to your Rasputin!" But Rasputin behaved well at home and Feofan's positive opinion remained unshaken.[8]

Alexandra was still not entirely satisfied. She asked Anna Vyrubova and two other court ladies to visit Rasputin in Siberia during Lent of 1909. Anna did not think she was a good choice for the assignment, but the empress insisted, so she agreed. Rasputin boarded their train at Perm. When bedtime came the party agreed that Rasputin would share the coach of Madame "S," as she is identified in our sources. Grigory was to sleep with her maid Elena in the upper berth. This was too much temptation: The starets tried to seduce Elena who, after a noisy scene, ended up in the corridor.

Madame "S" returned home and warned Alexandra that Grigory did not deserve her confidence. She suggested that Madame Orlova, another person on the trip, could provide further information. The tsarina questioned Orlova and her maid Anyuta, but they did not actually see anything scandalous. Anna Vyrubova also witnessed nothing amiss; she dismissed any conduct to the contrary as a product of Rasputin's "naiveté and saintliness." Her memoirs celebrate a Rasputin household "almost Biblical in its bare simplicity"; their "plain meals" were of "raisins, bread, nuts, and perhaps a little pastry." Anna was impressed with the visitors who showed up in the evening, men who joined Father Grigory in singing prayers and psalms "with rustic faith and fervor." Vyrubova admitted that the clergy of Pokrovskoe disliked Rasputin, while most villagers ignored him.[9] This was scarcely devastating criticism. Rasputin survived another crisis.

Yet Alexandra did a reasonably good job of synthesizing information about the "real" Rasputin. Prejudice against the unfortunate woman has fostered the conclusion that she was ignorant about the seamy side of Grigory's life. Nicholas's sister Olga denied this, insisting that her brother and his wife were "fully aware" of Rasputin's background. "It is completely false to suggest that they regarded him as a saint incapable of evil," Olga continues, maintaining neither were "duped by Rasputin or had the least illusion about him." One might dismiss this as special pleading, of course, for Olga loved the martyred couple and was concerned to improve their image. But some evidence confirms her opinion. Feofan, for example, exonerated Rasputin but in the process admitted that Grigory often "sinned" with women. The empress seems to have accepted this at face value. She once lent the Countess Karlova a book about "Holy Fools" recognized as saints by the Russian Orthodox Church. Karlova was struck by the fact that Alexandra had underscored with a colored pencil those passages where this "foolishness for Christ" was accompanied by "sexual dissoluteness!"[10] Apparently the empress saw this as a tactful way to put Rasputin's behavior in perspective for the countess, to show her that sexual "lapses" did not prove a man could not be a starets—or even a saint. The empress was not ignorant of the "real" Rasputin.

But what were Nicholas and Alexandra to do with this knowledge? Admitting Rasputin's faults would force them to explain why they needed him. This would reveal deep secrets: Alexis had hemophilia, and only Grigory could safeguard his life. Perhaps Nicholas should have done this. Telling the truth about Rasputin might have saved his throne—and his life. But candor brings risks, in this case the possibility that Alexis would be excluded from the succession. The royal couple was determined that Russia would remain an autocracy and that Alexis in his time would be the autocrat.

Nicholas and Alexandra dealt with the charges against Rasputin by ignoring them. As aristocrats it was beneath their dignity to defend their relationship with Rasputin or anyone else. Alexis's health and their choice of friends were private matters. The tsar and his wife knew that Rasputin was a womanizer, and they realized that adventurers used him. At the same time they believed that Rasputin was a God-seeker. He could be a sinner and yet chosen. Even a starets might be flawed. Everything hinged on how the royal couple weighed the evidence. Their all-consuming need for Rasputin set the balance.

With the decision made to stand by Rasputin, Nicholas and Alexandra handled the continuing revelations about his "true" nature in what appeared to be an arbitrary, even obtuse, manner. Although they knew that Rasputin was generally guilty of the charges made against him, the tsar and his wife were cast in the role of insisting he was innocent. When told that Grigory kissed women, the empress retorted, "What of it, did not the saints of old greet their followers with a kiss?" Nicholas once made a great to-do over an error in a police report.

The document asserted that Rasputin behaved in a scandalous fashion in St. Petersburg at a day and time that the starets was at Tsarskoe Selo. The tsar dismissed the entire report and often referred to it to give Rasputin the benefit of the doubt when new charges surfaced. Voeikov, the last palace commandant, often tried to convince the emperor that Rasputin led a scandalous life. "I have already heard everything which you have told me several times," Nicholas unfailingly replied. "P. A. Stolypin carried out an investigation of this matter, and not a single one of the widespread rumors received confirmation."[11]

But Nicholas was tsar as well as father, and at times the "real" Rasputin burst forth in ways a ruler could not ignore. We shall see times in 1911 and 1912 when Nicholas dealt harshly with his starets. But the strongest force in the family's relationship with Rasputin was their need for him as a healer. As this force reasserted itself, Grigory returned to favor.

Grigory's enemies often cited a factor no one could deny: Rasputin was a peasant. This actually worked in Grigory's favor. Nicholas and Alexandra did not like nobles or bureaucrats, intellectuals or the bourgeoisie. In a strange inverted populism, their preference was for peasants. This attitude was not based upon ignorance, though it was colored by wishful thinking. The peasants they met were the "real" Russia; they were humble and devout, uncorrupted by wealth or status or urban life. These romantic ideas strengthened Rasputin's position.

Nicholas valued Rasputin's opinions as an indication of peasant opinion. Whether Rasputin exercised power is another matter. A tsar received advice from many people and groups. Nicholas's decisions did not conform to suggestions from any single source. Rasputin did not have much influence over the emperor's policy decisions before the First World War. Even at its zenith Rasputin's "power" consisted of the ability to control personnel changes rather than church or state policy.

Nicholas and Alexandra thought that Rasputin bridged the gap between the court and the peasants, the people they really wanted to represent. Rasputin also separated the royal couple from other elements of their world. People were puzzled over Rasputin's relationship with the royal family. Rasputin was apparently of some importance. What made this so? Alexis was known to be in bad health. Many supposed Rasputin was somehow relevant to his well-being. But such reliance upon Rasputin seemed strange—foolish, even—to those who did not know that the boy had hemophilia. Rasputin was also thought to cater in various ways to Alexandra's moody, mystical disposition. Gossips knew just enough truth to confuse themselves. Speculations over what went on behind the palace walls were unlimited.

As speculation flourished, the royal couple grew touchy about their Siberian friend. Nicholas and Alexandra resented people engaging them in discussions about Rasputin, especially when it was to attack him. On the other hand, the tsar and his wife made occasional efforts to change their friends' judgments about Father Grigory. Nicholas once asked Palace Commandant Dedyulin why he refused to meet Rasputin. He admitted he thought Grigory had an unsavory reputation that discredited the emperor. The tsar rejected this, maintaining that Rasputin was a simple, devout peasant who was able to calm his doubts and bring him peace. Nicholas believed that Rasputin was a man of "pure faith."[12]

Nicholas's comments sometimes confused his associates. Their ignorance about Alexis's hemophilia could make the tsar's words cryptic rather than clarifying. He seemed to hint that his wife was responsible for Rasputin's presence. Such was the impression Nicholas conveyed in his last conversation on the subject with Peter Stolypin, who observed that rumors linking Rasputin to the royal family were exposing the tsar and his wife to ridicule.

"I know and believe you are truly loyal to me, Peter Arkadievich," Nicholas quietly replied. "Everything you say may even be true. But I must ask that you never speak with me again about Rasputin. In any event, I can do nothing at all about it."[13]

=== 7 ===
Iliodor: Radical on the Right

The Don is one of Russia's great rivers. It rises near Moscow and meanders southward for 1,200 miles before splashing into the Sea of Azov. The river's gentle, almost lazy qualities earned it a special place in Russian hearts: Its nickname is the "quiet" Don. Peasants fleeing serfdom appeared along its banks in the fifteenth century. These "Cossacks"—the word comes from the Turkish for "free frontiersman"—prized freedom above all values. They raided their Tatar and Turkish neighbors, and lived by hunting, fishing, and raising cattle. The area was swept into the Russian empire in the following century, but the hardy Cossacks never accepted themselves as the *subjects* of any man. Two of their leaders, Stenka Razin and Constantine Bulavin, led uprisings in 1667 and 1707. Defeat changed the Don Cossacks. Most turned to farming, while others formed elite military units that Russian rulers used to conquer new lands. But the romance of freedom remained in the Cossack spirit—along with love for the stormy skies and the deep blue waters of the Don.

Serge Trufanov, one of Rasputin's great antagonists, was born a Don Cossack in 1880. He grew up in a peasant's hut, in poverty, thinking the tsar was like a god, though no better than a Cossack. Serge's radicalization began with the treatment he received at the local church academy. This fire of indignation grew hotter at the St. Petersburg Seminary, where he graduated in 1905. Trufanov went about the capital in laborer's clothes, seeing just how much reason there was to hate the established order. Iliodor (Serge's monastic name) hoped for an outpouring of Orthodoxy and a tsar who would rule for the poor.[1]

Iliodor was a seminarian when he met Rasputin in late 1903. "This is Father Grigory from Siberia," Feofan said shyly, introducing the visitor to Trufanov.

They kissed. Iliodor was not favorably impressed with the "unpleasantly sim-
pering peasant." Rasputin was dressed in a cheap, greasy coat, and his pockets
bulged as if often stuffed with food. Grigory's trousers were blackened with tar,
and the seat "flapped like a torn old hammock." Rasputin's hair was clumsily
combed in one direction; his beard was unattractive. Grigory's lips were "thick,
blue, sensual," and his moustache protruded like "two worn-out rushes." Rasputin's hands were pockmarked and unclean; there was dirt under his long nails.
He stank. Iliodor blamed the devil for this poor impression. He returned to his
cell, did 30 genuflections, and focused his thoughts on Grigory until Satan was
cast away.

Rasputin's reaction to Iliodor was entirely positive. Two years later, Feofan
told the young graduate that he was being appointed professor at the seminary
in Yaroslavl, making it clear that Grigory Rasputin helped him in this instance
and would continue to do so.[2]

Iliodor was unhappy as a teacher. He resigned after a year, returned to St.
Petersburg, and was driven away by nobles at court who thought he was a
revolutionary. Iliodor admitted that he *was* an "extreme revolutionist" who
rejected the left only because it denied God. Iliodor began to travel about Russia,
attracting followers and putting the final touches on his political philosophy. He
still attacked the nobles: "swindlers" who serve the devil, parasites with no
Russian blood and tongues that speak in every accent *except* Russian. Iliodor
called upon the tsar to restore the autocracy and establish the "Kingdom of God
on earth." Nicholas should turn on nobles and bureaucrats, Jews and capitalists;
he should become a peasant tsar, a communist ruler. This was a heady doctrine,
and it struck a resonant chord. Religious processions flocked to hear Iliodor.
Tales abounded of his fasting and his wood-block bed without mattress or pillow.
Followers called him a saint; revolutionaries tried to kill him.[3]

At this point Iliodor ran afoul of Stolypin. Violence flickered well after the
Revolution of 1905. Stolypin brought key landowners to the capital for a secret
meeting to help him bring the riots under control. He instructed them to appeal
to their peasants with patriotism—though if they continued their disorders, "I'll
shoot them all like so many dogs." Iliodor learned of this conference and exposed
it in a pamphlet. Although Nicholas admired Iliodor, this angered him. The tsar
punished the monk by sending him to the remote city of Tsaritsyn. Iliodor would
serve there as missionary to the pagan and semi-Christian natives of the Volga.[4]

The authorities were alarmed to see that Iliodor was more successful than ever
at Tsaritsyn. People flocked to hear him, and by the summer of 1908 his followers
had raised the money to erect a monastery. The Iliodorites did the work themselves— "Let one man bring a plank, let another bring a rusty nail!" their leader
intoned. "The church and monastery buildings were of the very crudest sort,"
an observer recalled, similar to "window display work."[5] But it was a stronghold
wherein Iliodor could rally his supporters and build a movement.

Iliodor's successes went to his head. At one point he claimed the right to
admonish not only officials, but also the tsar himself—if, in Iliodor's opinion,

Nicholas failed to act in accord with God's will and the Holy Scriptures. In March 1909, Nicholas ordered Iliodor to the Siberian town of Minsk where he would be observed by local authorities.[6]

Iliodor asked Feofan, now a bishop and confessor to the tsar and his wife, to intervene—but he refused. Rasputin agreed to help, but his motives are not clear. Rasputin might be described as a "conservative"; he was certainly a monarchist. But Grigory had no sympathy for the demagogy and anti-Semitism that characterized Iliodor. Nor was Rasputin pleased to see Nicholas II defied and humiliated. Perhaps Grigory simply liked Iliodor. They certainly had much in common, both being religious leaders of ordinary background who carved out novel roles. Iliodor later concluded that Rasputin and Feofan were approaching a break, which drove each to seek new supporters. Whatever Rasputin's reasons, Iliodor admitted that Grigory snared him at just the right time.[7]

When they next met, Rasputin again made a poor impression on Iliodor. Grigory leapt into the room, wearing a crimson-colored shirt and a belt with large silk tassels. His tight trousers were of expensive black cloth, and his patent-leather boots were highly polished. Rasputin grandly offered to support Iliodor, predicting that in three days he would leave not for Minsk but Tsaritsyn. Iliodor doubted his situation could be so easily resolved, but Rasputin stood by his prediction.[8]

A few days later Rasputin saw the tsar, and urged him to return Iliodor to Tsaritsyn. Nicholas wondered how he could do this after signing and releasing an order to send Iliodor to Minsk. As Grigory relayed the conversation to Iliodor, he assured the emperor this would not be difficult: If he wrote the instructions from left to right, he could take them back by rewriting the words from right to left. Nicholas granted the request, warning the fiery monk he was on probation and should expect no more favors. Iliodor feared he would be destroyed by the ministers. Rasputin dismissed this possibility—but he urged the unruly Cossack to have some sympathy for the tsar. Nicholas could not always undermine his own ministers.[9]

At this point Rasputin suggested that Iliodor meet the empress at Anna Vyrubova's cottage. The monk did not realize it at the time, but this was the opening gambit in a ploy to bring him under control.

When the meeting occurred, Alexandra began by scolding Iliodor for his immoderate behavior. The conversation then turned to Rasputin, who was not present.

"You listen to Father Grigory," Alexandra intoned. "He will lead you to the light." He was Russia's greatest living ascetic, a "saint," a "great prophet."

Alexandra then asked Iliodor to sign a pledge to never again attack the government. Anna Vyrubova had paper and pen ready, and the monk did as he was asked. But as he was writing, Iliodor prayed to heaven to bear witness that this promise was against his conscience—and thus a pledge he could not keep. He only wanted to be able to rejoin his followers at Tsaritsyn.[10]

Iliodor was supported by Hermogen, the bishop of his diocese. Most bishops soft-peddled anti-Semitism after the Revolution of 1905; not Hermogen. His attacks on the Jews kept Saratov in an upheaval. He clashed with local authorities and drove the provincial governor into early retirement. The bishop so angered the local *zemstvo* that it stopped printing his *Diocesan News* on the grounds that it sowed hatred and division. Hermogen certainly selected a broad field of enemies: "the intelligentsia, Jews, rich people and bureaucrats." Nor did he spare the Duma: "enemies of the Orthodox Russian people," "robbers and thieves who stop at nothing" to accomplish their goals. "Cast out this Mongol band!" he thundered, for "they, together with the revolutionaries, the Jews, the Poles, and other foreign races, are planning for Russia . . . a new, frightful . . . Time of Troubles."[11]

Rasputin took upon himself the task of making Hermogen and Iliodor more moderate. Grigory visited Hermogen in September 1909. Then they joined Iliodor at Tsaritsyn in November. A unique experience awaited Rasputin. For the first— and only—time in his life, Grigory was applauded by crowds. Iliodor's followers also greeted Hermogen.

Rasputin and Hermogen provided a sharp contrast. The bishop was a powerful man with delicate features and a full beard just beginning to turn gray. Grigory was of medium height and slender build; his beard was wispy and a bit disheveled. Many claimed that Rasputin was the greatest lover in all Russia. Hermogen spoke in a high-pitched voice; some said he had castrated himself in a fit of mystical ecstasy. A critic claimed the bishop's "bright, black eyes continually darted to the sides, leaving an unpleasant impression." His Judaic appearance was reminiscent of the prophets—ironic in one so distinguished by anti-Semitism.

The Iliodorites were grateful to Grigory for returning their leader to Tsaritsyn. Iliodor's good will was feigned; he was coming to hate Rasputin. The monk's followers wondered why their leader was "keeping company with such a scoundrel?"[12]

The two weeks Rasputin spent in Tsaritsyn added to his reputation. If some of Iliodor's followers were cool toward Grigory, others followed him, imploring his blessing. The ever-faithful Vyrubova supplied Alexandra with newspaper accounts of Rasputin healing the sick. The telegrams Rasputin fired off to Tsarskoe Selo sustained his reputation as an influential man. But Iliodor was troubled. He saw the starets kissing young women. By contrast Rasputin had little interest in the older women. "Mother, your love is pleasing," he told one such dame, "but the spirit of the Lord does not come down to me!"— implying Grigory thought the spirit descended upon him through his sexual organs.[13]

Rasputin made a mistake when it was time to return home: He invited Iliodor to accompany him. Rasputin thought the nine days required to reach Pokrovskoe by train, ship, and wagon offered an opportunity to impress Iliodor. Rasputin bragged of his sexual exploits while twitting his friend's monkish innocence. Grigory expounded his doctrine of "salvation through sin." Full of himself and not knowing where to stop, Rasputin began to boast about his relations with the royal family. He claimed Nicholas thought he was a new incarnation of Christ, while Alexandra kneeled before him, kissed his hands and pledged eternal friendship. At Pokrovskoe, Grigory showed Iliodor satin shirts the empress sewed for him. Iliodor asked for one or two of the garments; Rasputin kept two and gave him three. Iliodor pointed to a red shirt that had no collar, asking what became of the missing cloth.

"Papa had a sore throat and asked my help," Grigory replied. "I told him to smoke less and to wear the collar of this shirt on his neck and throat at night. He got well and took it as a miracle."

Rasputin tried to awe Iliodor in other ways. He fired off a telegram to "papa" and "mama" and received the usual prompt answer from Anna Vyrubova—but claimed it came from Nicholas. Grigory also bragged over his ability to reward his favorites. He claimed that Bishop Serge was promoted to archbishop of Finland upon his recommendation, and that Feofan was made bishop in his place for the same reason. Rasputin assured Iliodor if he were cooperative, he would also advance.

As a final touch Rasputin unlocked a large trunk and removed a packet of letters he claimed were from Alexandra, her children and various important people. Iliodor asked for a few. Grigory was delighted to grant the request.[14]

Iliodor took his pick as Grigory smiled, unaware of the risk. It was uncharacteristic of Rasputin to trust people so much. Although secretive and accustomed to intrigue, it seems that Grigory found Iliodor a kindred spirit, someone he really liked. Or was Rasputin intoxicated with himself and beyond control? This boastful generosity nearly destroyed Grigory's career. Iliodor soon turned on Rasputin, and two years later the letters appeared in a context suggesting that the empress and even her daughters were Grigory's lovers.

*   *   *

Rasputin lived quietly in the capital from 1905 through 1907. He was not well known at that time. Serge Bulgakov recalled that he first heard of Rasputin in 1907 from another churchman who was disturbed at the activities of this "phony mystic." The young theologian Bulgakov was alert to events in church circles; he learned of developments before the general public. Rasputin was still an obscure figure in 1907.[15]

Rasputin came to wider attention the following year. The Russian ambassador to Sweden, like so many others, learned of the mysterious peasant through chambermaids. Anatoly Neklyudov was visiting St. Petersburg in 1908 when he heard "strange rumors" of a "certain 'old man'—a man of the people, quite simple" who was received at court with a "great deal of fuss." Supposedly he is "quite intimate with the tsar and tsarina, who do everything that he tells them." The mysterious newcomer could get people appointed to government posts otherwise beyond their reach. Anna Vyrubova's maid also spread tales about Rasputin in 1908. The maid told a notorious gossip that her mistress befriended a "peasant who is [also] a monk." Anna kept his photograph in a

Bible, she sewed him a "white silk blouse with her own hands"—and "what is still worse," receives him with the tsarina. Someone who saw this photograph thought "this peasant [has] the eyes of a wild animal, an unbounded insolence and repugnant bestiality."[16]

Another important change came into Grigory's life in 1908. He was seized by the conviction that it was his mission to save tsar and nation. This feeling grew as time passed. Rasputin also learned he could become rich in the process. The royal family withheld income and favors—such material considerations would have compromised their vision of Grigory as a man of God. But others found value in a man with connections, and in 1910 the first group of businessmen involved Rasputin in a project to advance their interests. A bribe won his agreement to seek state financing for an irrigation project in Transcaucasia. As other "deals" followed, the impression emerged that Rasputin's support was worth a high price. As for his religious mission Grigory healed, counseled, and prayed to the end of his life. Whether he was a starets at the end is open to debate. It seems the spiritual search became increasingly less important to Grigory Rasputin beginning in 1908.[17]

Rasputin first came under press scrutiny in January 1910. These reports concerned the pilgrimage that Vyrubova, Orlova, and Madame "S" made to Pokrovskoe in 1909. This was nothing compared with another setback in January 1910: Feofan finally joined the ranks of Grigory's foes.

Feofan was disturbed over reports of the 1909 trip, but he reasserted his faith in Grigory through a now-familiar argument: Rasputin was a sinner, but he was contrite and making an effort to mend his ways. This line had worked so often. Feofan himself offered it to doubters. Then evidence appeared that Feofan could not ignore.

Chionya Berlatskaya and a woman identified as "Elena" came to the St. Petersburg Academy to present charges against Rasputin in January 1910. Chionya Berlatskaya had been a member of Grigory's innermost circle; she recorded his "Life of an Experienced Pilgrim." Berlatskaya claimed she was not Grigory's lover; their break supposedly came when he demanded sex. Chionya claimed that Grigory seized her in a railway carriage and treated her as his wife. She submitted, but was upset. Seeing this Grigory comforted her in his fashion. He claimed it was a sin for her to think he treated her badly. Actually—he claimed—he drove a devil from her through the window. Rasputin offered to pray with her, though she was apparently not pleased with the suggestion.

After sharing this experience with Feofan, Berlatskaya made the matter public. Gossips were delighted; Feofan's circle was devastated. Some of the bishop's friends were already turning against Grigory. Feofan now joined their ranks. It was painful to admit that Rasputin abused women and covered himself with a religious smokescreen. But Feofan became convinced that it was so.[18]

Yet the bishop did not act hastily. Feofan made additional efforts to persuade

Rasputin to mend his ways; then he began collecting evidence to brand Grigory a false starets. Feofan and Grigory now suddenly competed for Iliodor's support. Feofan tried to persuade the monk that Rasputin had hoodwinked them and was unworthy of their friendship. But Iliodor was not ready to break with Rasputin; he still praised Grigory to crowds of followers. Iliodor wrote out some of these sermons, and they delighted Nicholas and Alexandra.

Feofan found the Montenegrin sisters to be more willing allies. Their friendship with the tsarina had just collapsed. Anastasia and Militsia were jealous over the friendship that had developed between Alexandra and Anna Vyrubova after her divorce in 1908. Criticisms they levelled against Anna angered the empress. The sisters and Rasputin maintained good relations for a time, but as bonds between the princesses and Alexandra snapped the starets had to choose sides. Grigory chose the empress.[19]

The Montenegrins now shifted tactics and tried to restore their friendship with Alexandra. Thinking that Rasputin caused their difficulties with the empress, the sisters concluded that his removal would enable them to resume their ties to the empress. Anastasia and Militsa formed an alliance with Feofan, and the three prepared an offensive in the spring of 1910. The allies had supporters in the palace in Maria Vyshnekova and Sophie Tyutcheva. Rasputin seduced Vyshnekova, Alexis's nurse—and she brought the matter to Alexandra's attention. Tyutcheva was the girls' governess; she was angered by the access Rasputin enjoyed to Alexis and his sisters at bedtime. The coalition seemed powerful. Feofan was confessor to Nicholas and Alexandra; he would lead the attack. Anastasia, Militsa, and their husbands were the tsar's relatives by blood and marriage; they would expose Grigory as a womanizer. Vyshnekova could confirm the charges.

The press sprang to life as the conspirators launched their offensive. The church journalist M. A. Novoselov attacked Rasputin in the *Moscow News* as "A Spiritual Quack." The Kadet newspaper *Speech* speculated upon Grigory's political connections and activities. A torrent of hostility to Rasputin swept through the Russian empire during the spring and early summer of 1910.

Rasputin easily weathered the crisis. The press was not united in its hostility to Grigory. The progovernment *New Times* emphasized that the charges were not substantial, concluding that the campaign simply showed some important people were willing to resort to dangerous and unethical tactics to hurt Rasputin.[20]

The Montenegrins scurried to report their "sad discoveries" to the empress: Grigory was a false starets, an adventurer and wencher, and threatened the prestige of the dynasty. Alexandra had heard all this so many times! She received the sisters, listened silently—and never again treated them as friends. Their husbands maintained good relations with Nicholas II; Nicholasha commanded Russia's armies in 1914–15. But he broke all ties to Grigory and lamented that "Rasputin actually came to the tsar through my house."[21]

Vyshnekova and Tyutcheva posed a greater challenge than the Montenegrins or Feofan. Vyshnekova and Tyutcheva worked in the palace, and much of what they revealed was based upon personal experience. Sophic Ivanovna Tyutcheva came from a distinguished family. Her grandfather Theodore Tyutchev was an outstanding poet. His son and her father rose to high rank in state service. Opinions about Tyutcheva were divided. Alexander Mosolov, a court official, found her "a woman of exceptional personality and character, highly cultivated"—someone who made "an excellent impression on us all." Alexandra's friend Lili Dehn thought Tyutcheva was "not a very pleasant person"; Anna Vyrubova recalled Sophia Ivanovna as a "rather stupid" and "obstinate woman," the worst of all the "intriguing courtiers" she knew. Everyone agreed Tyutcheva was a strict disciplinarian who was convinced that young girls should not be exposed to certain topics of conversation. She did not hesitate to tell parents that their methods of rearing children were too permissive. Her domineering nature won her the reputation of being "a man in skirts."[22]

Tyutcheva objected to Rasputin's privileges at the palace. Sometimes he was there when Alexis and his sisters went to bed. Grigory told them stories and helped them with their prayers. The girls would be in their nightgowns. Laughter pierced the air, and pillows sailed about as Grigory lingered at their beds. All this was innocent by any reasonable standard. But Tyutcheva saw an insolent peasant exceeding his rights, and she wanted it stopped. Alexandra rejected the complaint. Tyutcheva then turned to others, such as Feofan.[23]

Gossips inflated Rasputin's behavior to wild proportions. Some claimed that he bathed the children and talked with them until they went to sleep. Nicholas was offended when his family's privacy was so violated. He also hated "scenes," especially when they concerned Rasputin. But the tsar realized Tyutcheva was dangerous, so he summoned her, listened to her complaints—and discharged her. As for Vyshnekova, it was announced she suffered a "nervous disorder" and was going to the Caucasus for treatment. Feofan was dismissed as confessor to the tsar and his wife. He was also reassigned to the diocese of Tavrida and Simferopol. Some would have relished living in this beautiful part of the Crimea. But Feofan was susceptible to tuberculosis; for him this approached a death sentence.[24]

Soon after Feofan's reassignment was announced on November 19, 1910, Rasputin encountered Iliodor. Grigory bragged of his victory over Feofan, gleefully predicting he would "rot away alive." Iliodor objected that it was not right to treat a bishop in such a manner. Rasputin made no apologies. Iliodor was now more convinced than ever that Grigory had tremendous power in the Church and the state.[25]

Nicholas II stood firmly by Rasputin in 1910. The tsar had his own reasons for wanting Grigory in the capital; only Grigory seemed able to safeguard Alexis's life. Rasputin also had a knack for saying the right thing. In 1910, for example,

Nicholas showed Grigory a large manuscript that the now-alienated Berlatskaya wrote about Rasputin and forwarded to the tsar.

"Grigory, shall I read this book or not?"

"Does it give you pleasure to read in the *Lives* of the saints how slanderers mocked godly men?" Rasputin replied. Nicholas admitted it did not.

"Well, do as you please," Rasputin concluded.

At this Nicholas took the book, stripped off its covers, tore the pages into four parts and threw the "truth" about Rasputin into the fireplace.[26]

Yet no relationship is beyond pressure. Strong as the friendship was between Nicholas and Grigory, events in early 1911 forced the tsar to send Rasputin away, if but briefly.

The first crisis came as an aftermath of the Vyshnekova affair. She went to the Caucasus to treat the "nervous disorder" that made her think Rasputin had seduced her. Vyshnekova happened to meet Metropolitan Anthony of St. Petersburg at Kislovodsk. She told Anthony of Rasputin's behavior and begged him to save the tsarevich from the "clutches of the devil." Anthony requested an audience with the tsar early in 1911. Nicholas maintained that the royal family's private affairs were none of his concern. Overcome by emotion Anthony expressed the thought that a tsar must live an exemplary life in plain view of his subjects.[27]

Nicholas obviously planned to ignore Anthony's complaints, but a new threat came against Rasputin. The blow was unexpected, and it came from a royal favorite who did not even know at the outset that "Father Grigory" existed. The episode developed from Iliodor's continuing political agitations.

Iliodor returned to Tsaritsyn by pledging that he would not embarrass the tsar or his ministers. But moderation was not in Iliodor's nature, and by 1911 his political agitations were more extreme than ever. Hermogen joined Iliodor at Tsaritsyn just before an army encircled the city. Both attackers and defenders braced for a struggle. The problem was complicated for Nicholas by the fact that he continued to hold Iliodor and Hermogen in high esteem. But Nicholas as tsar had to enforce the Holy Synod's command that Iliodor leave for a monastery at Tula, south of Moscow.

Rasputin advised Nicholas to send a friend to talk to Iliodor. The envoy might persuade the monk to leave Tsaritsyn; he could also get a feel for how the authorities should deal with the situation. Rasputin nominated Captain Alexander Mandryka for this mission because he was a "good man." Rasputin had other reasons for favoring the 34-year-old officer and commander of an imperial guards' regiment. Mandryka's cousin Maria was mother superior of the Balashevskaya Convent near Tsaritsyn. She admired Hermogen and Iliodor, and was part of the power structure that Grigory was building within the Church. Maria might pressure her cousin to persuade the tsar that Iliodor was not a threat and should remain with his followers. Rasputin sent the mother superior a telegram he would come to regret: "One of your relatives is on mission to Tsaritsyn on business which concerns us. Use your influence on him. Grigory."

Mandryka left the capital on February 2, 1911. Iliodor's followers received him with bread and salt and celebrated a *Te Deum* in his honor. They stressed a desire to see their leader remain at Tsaritsyn, claiming that they posed no threat to Nicholas or his government. Mandryka proceeded to the Balashevskaya Convent to pay his respects to his cousin. It so happened that Maria was in the capital, but the sisters made their visitor welcome. Before long the conversation turned to Rasputin. Mandryka had never heard of the starets, but the nuns knew him. Grigory often visited their cloister; the young sisters bathed him, and he seduced some and engaged in "orgies." Rasputin also boasted of his closeness to Nicholas and his family; the mother superior was obviously "under his thumb." The young officer was stunned. To prove their case, the nuns showed him the fateful telegram. Mandryka departed, profoundly troubled.

Mandryka presented himself at the palace on Shrove Tuesday, February 10, 1911. Nicholas was delighted to see Mandryka and asked him to lunch. Then they had coffee. Mandryka began a report that lasted two hours. The captain analyzed the situation at Tsaritsyn; he then took up his experience at the convent. With growing agitation Mandryka discussed the telegram and what he heard about Rasputin. "It is even said," Mandryka declared, "he enjoys the favor of Your Majesty!"

At this point the captain collapsed, sobbing. Nicholas rushed for water while Alexandra calmed the visitor. The captain pulled himself together, submitted his written report and left. The royal couple was disturbed at what Mandryka said and moved by his honesty. Rasputin was caught trying to deceive the tsar! The starets was two-faced: he pretended to lure Iliodor from Tsaritsyn while working to keep him there. Alexandra pleaded mitigating factors—but, ever-jealous of her husband's prerogatives, even she was offended. For the first time in his career as a royal favorite, Rasputin was out of favor.[28]

Low as Rasputin's fortunes were, they got worse. Ironically, Grigory's apparently unassailable position forced his enemies to yet more imaginative measures. Their efforts now bore fruit.

Rasputin's detractors were baffled over the apparent fact that Nicholas and Alexandra refused to recognize Father Grigory's "darker side." So his enemies hit upon a strategy to bring results that even the most naive partisans could not ignore. According to a general who followed the details of this conspiracy, "numerous photographs" were "taken by magnesium light at night revels in private houses." These prints were soon being "passed from hand to hand" throughout St. Petersburg.[29]

The photographs finally came to Rasputin. While entertaining court ladies one day, a messenger arrived with a parcel. Grigory looked at its contents and quickly closed the wrappers. After a brief intense talk with the messenger, he returned to his companions.

Later that night Rasputin told his servant and old friend Dunya that the package contained "some photographs of an obscene nature." The photographs showed Grigory "surrounded by a bevy of nude women—a fallen saint shown in the act of falling."

The man who delivered these photographs gave Rasputin a choice: "I must

leave St. Petersburg forever, or they will be shown to the royal family." Dunya
suggested a third alternative, and Grigory decided this was the best course of
action. Rasputin would not wait for his enemies to find their way to the tsar.
He would show the pictures to Nicholas. "I believe the Little Father will be
sympathetic," Grigory told Dunya. "If he is not, well, that will be God's will."

Nicholas granted Rasputin an interview. With bad luck, this might have been
their last meeting. As Maria Rasputin relates the episode, Nicholas looked at
each picture, frowned and shook his head as he fixed Grigory with a questioning
gaze. The tsar thanked Rasputin for coming to him with the incriminating evidence—and he pointed out the people behind it would continue their pressure.

"You have mentioned your desire to make a pilgrimage to the Holy Land. I
think this would be a good time for it. I will, of course, give you the journey
as a token of our esteem. The Lord knows you have earned it through your many
services to the crown."[30]

Rasputin fulfilled the tsar's command. Within a week he wound up his affairs
in St. Petersburg, placed the members of his household on a train for Pokrovskoe,
and in March 1911 set off on a pilgrimage to Jerusalem.

=====8=====
Jerusalem

Whatever happens to me on my wanderings over the world in the coming years, I have little doubt that even when I am old and gray I shall look back to it as the most wonderful thing I ever found on the road. . . .

> Stephen Graham, *With the Russian Pilgrims*, p.v.

Jerusalem stands on a 2,500 foot ridge west of the Dead Sea. It is one of the world's oldest urban centers. Jerusalem is significant for each of the three great Western religions: Judaism, Christianity, and Islam. David made it the capital of Israel; Solomon built the temple there. Jesus was crucified just northeast of the city. Mohammed was carried from Jerusalem to the Seventh Heaven to speak with the other prophets and draw strength for his own work. The Islamic conquests included Jerusalem. Christians seized Jerusalem during the First Crusade (1099), the Moslems took it back in 1187. Jerusalem was part of the Ottoman Empire when Rasputin visited the city during Lent of 1911.

A pilgrimage to the holy city was the highest act of devotion Russians could offer their faith in Rasputin's time. Trickles of Russian pilgrims made their way to Palestine even during earlier centuries. Some came by ship, others clambered over a more difficult route through the Caucasus Mountains to Turkey, Syria, and Palestine. A thousand such pilgrims appeared annually in Jerusalem by the 1840s, putting a strain on local monasteries and tourist facilities. Appeals to Nicholas I to relieve the situation were ignored. "Probably the Russian Court had not quite made up its mind as to whether it approved of pilgrimaging to Jerusalem," Stephen Graham wrote; "it generally objected to Russian subjects leaving their native land, being afraid of the infection of ideas of the corrupt west." But, in 1859, a brother of Alexander II made a pilgrimage to the Holy Land and became a fervent champion of the practice. The Russian government and private donors raised the money to buy ten acres of land for a cathedral, hostelry, hospital, and consulate. Within two decades 2,000 Russians were making the pilgrimage to Jerusalem each year. The Imperial Orthodox Palestine Society promoted pilgrimages and helped pilgrims once they arrived.[1]

We know little about Rasputin's pilgrimage. He claimed it was his second trip to the Holy Land, but he never said much about either journey. A brief book, which appeared under Rasputin's name four years later, is our major source of knowledge about the 1911 trip. Entitled *My Thoughts and Meditations— A Short Description of a Visit to the Holy Places and Meditations on Religious Questions Aroused Thereby,* it is the last and most ambitious of the six books published with Rasputin's name on the title page.[2]

Rasputin's *Thoughts* is a series of descriptions of what Grigory saw in such places as Kiev, Constantinople, and Jerusalem, each followed by devout ponderings caused by nature, churches, holy places, etc. This is a familiar genre in Orthodox literature, and Rasputin's effort is a success due to its simplicity and sincerity.

Rasputin began his pilgrimage in Kiev at the Monastery of the Caves. Grigory was glad to leave St. Petersburg, the center of "vain and worldly things," for a monastery where "the light of silence shines." He was impressed by the simplicity of the place, the absence of silver and gold, the "plain oak coffins" in which the saints rested. Rasputin saw the foolishness of youth and prayed to escape "earthly attractions" and "vanities." He praised his group of pilgrims as "true worshippers" gathering "the jewels of truth." "And I saw the Mother of God, and fear and a great trembling overcame me."[3]

From Kiev Rasputin went to Odessa. If Rasputin was like most Russian pilgrims, he boarded a crowded ship that spent 15 days lumbering to Jaffa. The English historian Stephen Graham travelled to Jerusalem with Russian pilgrims that same year. Graham paid 12 rubles each way for a third-class ticket. His vessel, the *Lazarus,* was designed to carry 21 passengers in the first class, 27 in the second, and 60 in the third; these numbers were merely theoretical. "Beyond the usual swarm of Turks, Arabs, and Syrians," he notes, there were 560 Russian pilgrims, nearly a third of whom slept on deck. This closeness gave the pilgrims unity. "The pilgrims all call one another brother (*brat*), father (*otets*), uncle (*dyadya*) or grandfather (*dedushka*). . . . " Their discomforts included two storms, a sun blazing on travellers so inexperienced as to wear sheepskin clothing, and a bathroom with three lavatories and no bolts on the doors. "Yet my dear old *dyadya* whispered to me on the morning before our arrival in Jaffa, 'We must not complain.' " Another called upon Graham to think of what Christ suffered. "What are our sufferings beside His! . . . It is good for us to suffer. I wouldn't take advantage of comforts. I wouldn't give up my share of suffering.'' A third pilgrim wondered, ''[W]hat good is it to come if we take no trouble over it?''[4]

The Black Sea brought peace and tranquility. ''My soul became one with the sea,'' Rasputin notes, ''and slept quietly.'' He meditated upon the ''boundless power of the soul'' and the beauty of the waves in the morning as they splashed on his ship. Grigory was also moved by the sun descending over the sea, the calm of night, and the joy he felt as he caught first sight of the trees of the coastline. Then there was Constantinople and the ''great and wonderful cathedral of St. Sophia.'' Grigory's heart melted as he contemplated ''how the Mother of God watches over all living creatures and prays for us all.'' He delighted at the thought that Mary ''knows all our needs, and we receive everything She asks of the Lord.'' ''Her whole concern is to forgive and console us.''[5]

From Constantinople Rasputin travelled to Mitylene, the ''small town where the Apostle Paul preached,'' then to Smyrna and the ruins of Ephesus. Rasputin was impressed by the last place, recalling that its history embraced John the Divine and the Virgin Mary, Paul and Timothy. He met numerous people along the way, ''but especially in the third class'' where he encountered ''many Christian women always at prayer.'' Stephen Graham was likewise struck by the intensity of the Russian pilgrims. There were no upper-class people in the group— all were peasants. ''Why did you come to Jerusalem?'' the Englishman often asked. Most could not answer, some would not. ''Some force deep in them urged them'' to this journey, he concluded, a force ''deeper than their power of articulation.'' ''The people travel here in fear and trembling,'' Rasputin agreed, for in this place ''it is oh, so easy to pray!''[6]

''My journey is finished,'' Rasputin declared when he arrived at ''the Holy City of Jerusalem by the main road.'' Grigory and his companions fell to their knees in prayer at this ''earthly realm of tranquility.'' From one side a pilgrim cried out ''Christ has risen!''—from the opposite a voice recalled Our Lord's agony. Sorrow filled Rasputin's heart as he walked the streets of the holy city, and tears flowed as he meditated on the fatal days of Christ's passion. But the greatest emotion came when Grigory visited what tradition marked as Jesus's tomb. ''I felt that the tomb was a tomb of love,'' he later recalled, ''for love finds no fault.'' By the time the pilgrims arrived at Golgotha, they thought they would never sin again, rescued as they were by Christ's suffering.[7]

''We unworthy ones prostrated ourselves'' in the garden of Gethsemane, Rasputin continued. They were all moved to realize that they were standing where Christ prayed. ''Some wept, others sighed; everyone had tears in his eyes.'' As Grigory ascended the slope of the garden, he thought he saw where the disciples slept, where Jesus came to awaken them. It seemed to Rasputin he was weak and fallen and incapable of rising to Christ's summons. ''We slumber and fall into evil ways,'' he exclaimed. ''Lord, awaken us!'' Then came the Blessing of the Great Sabbath.[8]

On this day the patriarch of Jerusalem takes off his robes and clad only in his undergarments, enters the chapel built around Christ's tomb. He finally emerges with a burning torch whose flame is greeted as a miracle. By now the faithful are exhausted from fasting and devotions, but the joyful occasion makes them forget weariness. "The joyful people gather in every corner of the temple," Rasputin notes, "and the Blessing comes upon them as they light their candles from the holy flame." Many took these burning candles home in glass and metal boxes.[9]

The Blessing of the Great Sabbath was the emotional crest of Rasputin's Lenten pilgrimage. But he still had to visit the Jordan River and the Dead Sea, several monasteries, the Inn of the Good Samaritan, the oak of Mamre, the towns of Bethany and Bethlehem—to mention only the more important places.

Toward the end of his *Thoughts,* Rasputin mixes religious feeling with the practical reflections of a seasoned traveller about the journey itself. He wished that arrangements would be made for more poor pilgrims to travel, fares would be cheaper, and people would not be shuttled about like cattle. The "simple faith" of the Russian peasants is "a great support to Russia," Rasputin maintained. "What could be better for simple people than to be able to tell people at home how they saw Christ's tomb?"

Rasputin witnessed the Catholic celebration of Easter a week before his own.[10] "I do not want to be critical," Rasputin wrote, and "I do not pretend to reach the depths of wisdom." Nevertheless, it seemed to him that the Catholic Easter had no joy "even within the church itself." The Catholics acted "as if someone had died," he adds, and there was nothing vivifying about their ceremony; they seemed to treat it as a commonplace event. The Orthodox, by contrast, were filled with joy on their Easter. Rasputin recalled the "ecstatic heights we True Believers reach when we celebrate these great events." I "do not wish for our faith to be under-valued," he insisted. "Even in perpetual winter it would shine upon the Faithful [such] as our Father John of Kronstadt and the many other luminaries of our Orthodox Church, thousands of God's people!"

Easter had come and gone; Rasputin's pilgrimage was done. He had been gone from Russia four months. The pilgrimage stirred feelings of devotion; at certain moments it seemed to Grigory that he could abandon pride, ambition, and sin. There may have been hypocrisy in this, but it is more likely that Rasputin stepped sincerely into the pilgrim's role and his soul was flooded with the feelings that characterized Russian pilgrims. But now it was time to return home. Rasputin's days of devotion were done, and a time of renewed ambition and calculation was at hand.

9

Again a Brilliant Star

Rasputin left Russia in disgrace in February 1911, but he returned in triumph four months later. Anna Vyrubova was critical to this astounding reversal. She gradually instilled doubts in Alexandra's mind about the accuracy of Mandryka's report. Anna also relayed news of the "saint's" experiences in the Holy Land. Rasputin sensed that the empress was returning to his fold, and he accelerated the process with a bold stroke that shows how astutely he understood Alexandra Fedorovna. The issue concerned Alexis—and Iliodor.

Iliodor's fortress-monastery at Tsaritsyn was under siege, and a bloodbath seemed inevitable. Grigory telegraphed Alexandra asking that Iliodor be allowed to stay with his followers. Otherwise God would be angered and Alexis's life endangered. This won Alexandra.[1] On the twentieth day of the siege, Nicholas issued a decree permitting Iliodor to remain at Tsaritsyn. Rasputin agreed to visit the firebrand as soon as he returned to Russia. Rasputin was using Iliodor to make himself valuable to the tsar.

Rasputin arrived in Tsaritsyn in June 1911 just after returning from Jerusalem. Iliodor had been reasonably friendly to Rasputin on his first visit in 1909. This time Iliodor had no time for Grigory. The crowds ignored Rasputin, and in the store he noticed he had been cut out of a famous photograph taken with Hermogen and Iliodor. The clerks insisted they could not sell the original even at give-away prices. The only people who honored Rasputin were his disciples Olga Lokhtina and Akulina Laptinskaya. But they did this so clumsily—they followed Grigory "like two walking mummies"—that it was embarrassing. When it came time to leave, they insisted that Rasputin must have a present. The collection scratched up 29 rubles for a cheap icon and tea set. Lokhtina and Laptinskaya quickly came up with 300 rubles to purchase a quality icon and tea service. Rasputin watched all this in anger—and predicted Iliodor's ruin unless he came to respect Grigory's power.[2]

When Rasputin returned to St. Petersburg, the capital was abuzz with rumors that Nicholas would soon dismiss Stolypin. Gossips swore that Alexandra was angry with Stolypin because he hated Grigory. The empress supposedly broke down her husband's attachment to his prime minister, and now Stolypin would be ousted from office. There was probably some merit to these reports. It is also true Stolypin had just handled an extension of local self-government into six Polish provinces so clumsily as to alienate the tsar's supporters in the Duma. Nicholas concluded that his chairman had lost the statesman's touch. Rasputin actually had little to do with Stolypin's downfall, but it was important to his career as a royal favorite. Grigory was about to be called upon for "advice" in appointing new officials.

The tsar was considering Serge Witte or Vladimir Kokovtsov as chairman of the council of ministers. Witte once held the office. He was widely admired, but Nicholas disliked him. Kokovtsov was not brilliant, but was serving well as minister of finance. Rasputin and his friend the journalist Sazonov were brought into the selection process. Sazonov was commissioned, almost certainly by the tsar, to sound out Witte about resuming the post of prime minister. Rasputin was asked, probably by the empress, to visit a third official, A. N. Khvostov, to evaluate his fitness as minister of the interior.

Alexis Nicholaevich Khvostov was born into a financially troubled noble family in Orlov province in 1872. The young man improved his situation through marriage to Catherine Popova and her million-ruble dowry. Popova retained control over her money. Despite skepticism she did permit her husband to invest in a pig farm. Khvostov was successful—and open to ridicule. He "left me irreconcilably repulsed," someone recalled, for "he was repulsively fat and singularly ingratiating."[3]

Even a harsh critic admitted that Alexis Nicholaevich was a "bright young man, energetic and enterprising," though "not when it came to matters of state." When Nicholas II asked A. A. Khvostov for an opinion of his nephew as minister of internal affairs, the uncle advised the tsar his nephew was "no stranger to intrigue," and "absolutely ignorant" of the affairs of that office; "[he is] an unsuitable character, quite bright but unable to criticize his own motives and thoughts." "His entire state service will be devoted not to business, but to considerations alien to it."[4]

Despite these negative qualities A. N. Khvostov rose quickly in the bureaucracy. In 1906, at the age of 34, he was made governor of Vologda province, and four years later he became governor of Nizhnyi-Novgorod. The last post was symbolically important because of the town's rich history. "When this governorship was awarded to a senior figure . . . it was a reward for a lifetime of devoted service. When given to a young man . . . it marked the person so honored as a man thought to have a great future." A. N. Khvostov certainly cultivated the future. He was frequently in the capital and befriended important people. Even by Russian standards he was extraordinarily anti-Semitic. Khvostov was a member of the Black Hundreds and proudly wore its badge.[5]

Rumors held that Stolypin would soon be dismissed. Khvostov wrote a memorandum attacking Stolypin's program as minister of the interior. The report outlined policies that Alexis Nicholaevich would follow. It was well timed, and Nicholas began to consider Khvostov for minister of internal affairs, a post second only to the prime minister in importance.[6]

Rasputin suddenly appeared at Khvostov's office in Nizhnyi-Novgorod in August 1911. Khvostov recalled that Grigory told him he was being considered "for a place in the ministry of internal affairs," and he had been sent "to gaze into my soul." Rasputin also wanted to visit Madame Khvostov and the children. Khvostov was bemused by his visitor. "Rasputin seemed naive and a bit amusing, and I spoke with him in a jesting manner. After a while I sent for a policeman to conduct him to the railway station."[7]

Sazonov was equally unsuccessful with Witte. Sazonov informed him in the summer of 1911 that Stolypin would be dismissed just after a trip to Kiev that he and the tsar announced for late August. Nicholas was considering A. N. Khvostov as minister of the interior. Would Witte serve as prime minister to give authority to the new government?

Witte was eager to return to power, but he rejected these overtures. "I did not know how valid this request was," Witte wrote in his *Memoirs,* nor did "I know who was more mad, someone who would suggest such a thing or someone who might accept it." Witte expressed the lowest opinion of Alexis Khvostov. "Among the current governors of the Stolypin epoch there is a mass of great hooligans, but Khvostov has first place in their ranks: no laws exist for him."[8] So the question of Stolypin's successors lay open as he and Nicholas set out for Kiev to dedicate a monument to Alexander II on the fiftieth anniversary of his proclamation ending serfdom.

Rasputin planned to join the royal family at Kiev. If we can believe Aron Simanovich, Rasputin had a premonition that some evil event would occur there. Grigory could not predict what the tragedy would be, only that something would happen—after which a terrible pogrom would sweep the city.[9]

Rasputin was standing on the sidewalk where he and the royal family could see each other as the procession passed. The tsar's carriage passed; then came Stolypin. Rasputin began to shake, he cried out, "Death is following him! Death is riding behind him! Behind Peter! Don't you believe me?"

"I was with him that night," an eyewitness recalled. "Rasputin slept in the next room and we were separated only by a thin wall. All night he kept me awake. He groaned, wailed, moaned, 'Oh, there will be a tragedy, a tragedy.'

"I asked, 'What's the matter, Grigory Efimovich?' "

"He would only say, 'Oh, calamity, death is coming.' And he carried on that way till daylight."[10]

Tragedy came the following evening, on September 1, 1911. The tsar and his minister attended the grand theater. A man shot Stolypin twice. He died on September 5. The royal family avoided Stolypin's funeral, and this provoked rumors that the empress, at least, was satisfied to see Rasputin's old enemy killed. This may not be fair to the tsarina. Spiridovich tells us that Alexandra suffered "nervous shock" over Stolypin's tragedy, though "she was calmed by [Rasputin's] presence." Nicholas was certainly moved. Nicholas returned to Kiev the day after Stolypin's death, coming straight from the steamer to the hospital. The tsar knelt and prayed at the body of his servant, repeating over and over, "Forgive me."[11]

Nicholas made Vladimir Kokovtsov chairman of the council of ministers. When the tsar asked his opinion of A. N. Khvostov as minister of the interior, Kokovtsov replied "He does not have a single quality one would expect from [this official] even in normal times." The new prime minister also cited Khvostov's extreme political views and lack of experience. The tsar's preference actually was Nicholas Maklakov. But Nicholas deferred to the new chairman's wishes and appointed Alexander Makarov.[12]

A. N. Khvostov now decided that it was a mistake to offend Rasputin. When he encountered Grigory in the capital, the relationship was reversed: This time Khvostov was friendly, but Rasputin was not. Rasputin told Khvostov that he sent a telegram from Nizhnyi-Novgorod to Anna Vyrubova just after their first meeting. Khvostov could not remember the exact wording of the telegram, but the gist of it was: "Tell Mama God is with him, but he still lacks something."[13]

Rasputin played a larger political role in 1911 than in earlier years, but he did not exercise real influence over events. Grigory wanted Stolypin removed, but Nicholas had his own reasons for arriving at this decision. Gossips noticed that Rasputin knew of Kokovtsov's appointment before it was announced; they took this to mean that the starets played a role in that appointment. Rasputin knew that Nicholas was considering *two* men for the chairmanship. When Witte rebuffed Sazonov, Kokovtsov was left as the choice. Grigory recommended against A. N. Khvostov's appointment as minister of the interior; so did his uncle and Kokovtsov. Whatever contemporaries thought, none of this suggests that Rasputin controlled these events.

Public opinion also credited Rasputin with toppling the head of the Church in 1911. This target was Director General of the Holy Synod[14] Serge Lukyanov, an ally of Peter Stolypin. Lukyanov aided Stolypin by preparing a report discrediting Grigory as a "holy man." Lukyanov was also at the center of the campaign against Iliodor. These moves made the empress and Rasputin his bitter enemies. Rumors that Lukyanov would be ousted showed that Stolypin was endangered. "I am exclusively responsible for the handling of the Iliodor affair," Stolypin wrote the tsar on February 26, 1911. "If it becomes obvious that Lukyanov was dismissed because of Iliodor, my conscience would torment me for having failed to defend him. For a statesman there is no greater sin, no greater fault than cowardice."[15]

These noble words did not change the tsar's mind. He delayed Lukyanov's dismissal until the Iliodor controversy died down lest the public get the notion that such a demagogue could end a minister's career. Rasputin had been demanding Lukyanov's head for nearly two years. Iliodor concluded the only reason Lukyanov survived for a time was that Rasputin had no suitable replacement. But on May 2, 1911, while Rasputin was in Jerusalem, Serge Lukyanov was replaced by Vladimir Sabler.[16]

Vladimir Karlovich Sabler was born into a wealthy noble family in the Tula region in 1845. The family was of German ancestry, and Vladimir Karlovich was often described as "Germanic." Young Sabler studied law and taught at Moscow University where he came to the attention of Constantine Pobedonostsev, professor of law and tutor of Alexander III and Nicholas II. Pobedonostsev anonymously published a newspaper article in 1873 "attacking Russian jurists [and singling] out Sabler as one of the less competent temporary members of the faculty. . . . " But when Pobedonostsev became director of the Synod, he made Sabler his legal consultant. Pobedonostsev was "privately quite critical of Sabler for his lack of organizing sense and discipline" ; and Sabler made "a large number of bitter enemies. . . . " Yet Pobedonostsev also "admired his young subordinate's energy," and he "relied upon him increasingly to help administer the Church." In 1892 Pobedonostsev elevated Vladimir Karlovich to the number two post, assistant-director general.[17]

When Pobedonostsev retired in 1905, Sabler also resigned his position. Sabler was appointed to the State Council, a dumping ground for bureaucrats forced out of high office, but he was anxious to find a more challenging position. Lukyanov's departure as director of the Holy Synod gave Sabler a new opportunity. Nicholas appointed him to follow Grigory's old foe.

Rasputin was held responsible for Sabler's fortune. Some claimed that he kneeled before Grigory to get the position. It was even said that Grigory lived in Sabler's home. Sabler was clearly a "Rasputin man." Most historians have not challenged this verdict. They should.

Iliodor is the source of the tale that has Sabler kneeling before Rasputin. Grigory was trying to impress Iliodor, and he made such claims about several people—including Nicholas and Alexandra. It is not likely that these people behaved in this way. Rodzyanko tells us some 500 citizens of Tsaritsyn wrote in 1913 to inform him that "Rasputin was staying at the house of V. K. Sabler." At this time Rasputin actually had his own apartment at 70 Nicholaevsky Avenue. The letter to Rodzyanko was probably from Iliodorites; by now their leader and Rasputin were locked in combat. Rodzyanko forwarded the complaint to Sabler, along with the demand that the director reply, giving his critics satisfaction. Sabler replied with a curt note insisting he did not even know Rasputin.[18]

Nicholas had his own reasons for making Sabler director of the Holy Synod—

reasons having nothing to do with Rasputin. Sabler had been assistant-director general of the Holy Synod for 13 years, and he was familiar with its tasks and willing to implement the tsar's program. "As far as Sabler's principles are concerned," Witte noted, "it seems to me he is [an example of those] government workers who always rise more or less to the top." Alexandra probably backed Sabler; he recently worked with her on a charity project. He also had the backing of some powerful bishops.[19]

As before Sabler made enemies. He ruled the Holy Synod with an iron hand, promoting churchmen whom many thought were pious rather than talented. Control over church academies was placed more firmly with monastic authorities who suppressed with heightened energy anything even faintly liberal. Professors in effect could belong only to parties of the far right. While many Russians were demanding increased authority for church parishes, Sabler actually found ways to reduce their powers. These and related policies disappointed liberals, plus a fair number of moderates and some conservatives. Guchkov complained that Sabler had turned the Holy Synod into a "holy mess."[20]

Sabler also had qualities many admired. He loved the Russian Orthodox Church and was a loyal friend of bishops, clergy, and especially monks. If some found Sabler cold and high-handed, others insisted he was warm and encouraging to subordinates. George Shavelsky, the last head-chaplain of the tsar's armed forces, called Sabler a "most original" director, a person who "left a definite imprint on church life in the pre-revolutionary period." Sabler took his tasks seriously; his hair and beard were gray when he was just over 30. Unlike his predecessors he often visited isolated towns and small villages. "What more could one want from a director general?" Shavelsky asked admiringly—to which one could reply, "Someone free of the Rasputin label." "The allegation was unjust but readily believed," an American historian notes of the charge that Sabler "was a sycophant of Rasputin."[21]

Rasputin caused Sabler difficulty at the outset of his career as director general. The issue concerned the elevation of one of Grigory's friends to bishop. He was the monk Varnava, born Vasily Nakropin near Olonets in 1860.

Olonets is a bleak region situated just south of Archangel where the Dvina flows into the icy White Sea. Vasily's father raised vegetables for the market. The boy was short and spoke in a high-pitched, feminine voice. As a youth he once donned women's attire for a costume ball; the governor took a shine to the young thing, kissed her hand, and tended to every whim. News of the charade brought Nakropin fame and the governor confusion.

Vasily managed to attend school in nearby Petrozavodsk. Charges that Nakropin was illiterate were untrue, but those who called him semiliterate were close to the truth. Shavelsky describes a letter Vasily Nakropin wrote him in 1913. "Each new word begins with a capital letter," Shavelsky recalled, "and a dot follows each word. The letter "yët" is absent. The letter is signed (in Russian, of course) "the Sinful Bis. Varnava."[22]

Vasily Nakropin became a novice at the Monastery of St. Clement near Olonets in 1897. As a monk he took the name Varnava (Barnabas) and became abbot of the monastery in 1899. He became famous for intelligence, insolence—and a knack for worming himself into situations that helped him advance. Varnava was promoted and transferred to important cloisters in Moscow. Like Rasputin he refused to modify his private life. "Varnava began to do in various homes what Rasputin did in the capital." The metropolitan planned a surprise visit to verify the rumors. Varnava's friends sounded the alarm, and his young male and female admirers put the cloister in order. When Vladimir arrived Varnava met him "with a modest face and polite bows."[23]

Varnava was a popular preacher. Stephen Beletsky stressed that Varnava had "an inquisitive mind, keen observation, and in the manner of an Old Believer teacher was well acquainted with holy writing and dogma." Varnava remained close to the people, and his speech was adorned with everyday sayings and references to holy texts. He won the admiration of Christians outside the Russian Orthodox Church. Many who were prejudiced against Varnava ended as his admirers when they came to know him better. "I do not mean to indicate [Varnava] did not have his shortcomings," the police director continues, "but they were absorbed by his very many good qualities."[24]

Varnava had important supporters. But at the time he met Rasputin he stood as high in the hierarchy as normally possible. Without an education Varnava could not become a bishop. Yet with Rasputin's help, who could say what was possible? Varnava was not deceived by Rasputin's "holiness." Varnava was a "strict monk," and some thought he despised the profligate Grigory. Yet Varnava set these feelings aside and began to accompany Rasputin to Tsarskoe Selo. Alexandra was not impressed with the monk at first. Varnava struck her as crafty and unctuous; the empress called him *suslik*, a squirrel-like rodent with a thick body and a bushy tale.

"The archbishops will feel insulted if a peasant is thrust among them," Rasputin conceded to Alexandra. "The academicians! So what? They'll get used to it. The suslik must be made a bishop. He stands up for me."[25]

Sabler shocked the Synod in July 1911 by proposing that Varnava be made an assistant bishop at Kargopol in the Olonets diocese. As "vicar-bishop" (the Russian title), Varnava would assist the presiding bishop while living in a different town with his own cathedral church. The title was important. It gave its holder a bishop's rank; with the least luck one would soon advance to full rank. An obviously reluctant Bishop Nikanor nominated Varnava. Archbishop Anthony begged Sabler to drop the matter, or to inform the Synod about Varnava's qualifications for advancement. "We would very much not want to be among those to blame for consecrating rascals."[26]

Sabler hoped if he ignored the issue it would disappear. But the tsar persisted.

"Why has Archimandrite Varnava not yet been elevated to the rank of bishop?" asked Nicholas.

"The Most Holy Synod does not agree," Sabler replied.

"Then tell the Synod that this is my will," the tsar insisted.

Sabler called the Synod into session and conveyed the tsar's message.

"Does this mean that even Rasputin will come to us for consecration?" Dmitry of Kherson asked sarcastically.

Sabler made it clear that he could not stand between the Synod and the tsar; if they would not endorse the appointment, he must resign. This put tremendous pressure on the bishops, given that Sabler stood so high in their esteem after a mere three months in office. But Sabler was also the tsar's representative, and this obligation was uppermost in his mind on the matter of Varnava.

"To keep you in your position we would even make a black boar bishop," Anthony of Volhynia conceded. In a letter he wrote "It has become clear Rasputin installed Varnava in the episcopate. The Synod placed him in the rank upon a written petition from Nikanor [which] was almost demanded by P. S. Damansky," director of Synod financial operations. Varnava would enjoy a yearly income of 2,000 rubles plus a generous housing allowance. "Rasputin was the one to blame for the Holy Synod's rascalish behavior," the archbishop sadly concluded, even though "he is a khlyst and takes part in their rituals."[27]

A few days later Rasputin visited Varnava to assess their victory. Bishop Anthony of Tobolsk happened to be spending the night with Varnava at the time. After supper he was placed in a bedroom next to Varnava's study.

"The door between the two rooms remained open," Anthony wrote. "The two friends were carrying on a conversation about church-state affairs, and I was an involuntary listener to it. For the most part they discussed who should be kept and who should be dismissed.

" 'Above all, it's necessary to get rid of Stolypin,' Rasputin said. 'He can't be endured.'

" 'Yes.' Varnava emphasized, 'he's mixed everything up with his land reform.'

" 'Vladimir has to be gotten out of the way,' Varnava added. 'His friend, archbishop Nikon of Vologda, should also be dropped. But Sabler should stay. He's ours, he listens and is a good man.' "[28]

Rasputin had good reasons for advancing Varnava's career. Grigory must have been attracted to Varnava's lack of education and polish; he was probably pleased by the monk's Old Believer touches. Like Rasputin Varnava had no interest in theology. Many found Varnava's sermons—so applauded by large crowds—to be nothing more than "vulgar witticisms." Detractors also thought that Varnava celebrated liturgies with a pompous touch.

The rogue in Varnava must also have appealed to Rasputin. Lieutenant Ivanov recalled meeting Varnava when he was still an archimandrite. Varnava invited the officer to visit his cell. Everything seemed suitably plain, until the monk opened a cupboard under the icons and took out rum, vodka, and cognac as well as sausages and dried sturgeon. Ivanov thought Varnava was a "rascal" who spent time in the drawing rooms of St. Petersburg, not in the religious life of his monastery. Did Rasputin realize this "rascal" despised him while using him to advance?[29]

If so this might have intrigued Rasputin most of all, given his approval of the other elements in Varnava's character. There was a dark force in Rasputin's personality, a malevolent restlessness. This often manifested itself as a drive to prove that the snobbish, upper-class people who staffed Russia's leading institutions were really no better than, . . . well, Grigory Efimovich Rasputin, the semiliterate starets from Siberia. Rasputin was pleased that such low-class upstarts as Varnava were—under his direction—taking over the Church. A demonic streak showed itself in Rasputin in connection with the suslik. The force reappeared and did not rest until it destroyed Rasputin and a great deal more in the bargain.

Rasputin recruited another bishop, Alexis, to his "faction" in 1912. Alexis was in disfavor because he sympathized with heretical followers of John of Kronstadt, and as bishop of Pskov interfered with efforts to win them back to Orthodoxy. The authorities transferred him to a less desirable post—Siberia. Alexis's son was travelling to visit his father in 1912 when he saw Rasputin on the same steamship. Leonid Molchanov introduced himself to Grigory and invited him to come along to visit Alexis at Tobolsk. Rasputin was grandly received. The bishop also did Grigory a favor: He squashed investigations into charges that Rasputin was a khlyst.

The friendship developed further in the autumn of 1913, when events showed just how powerful Rasputin was becoming in the Russian Orthodox Church. The exarch of Georgia died in August 1913. The disgraced Alexis could not imagine being appointed to this, the fourth most important position in the church hierarchy, but his son tried to arrange it. Rasputin promised to speak to the tsar. Grigory obviously did so; when Nicholas received Sabler to discuss the appointment of a new exarch, the tsar declared "your candidates have all gone by the board. The choice for exarch has fallen upon Alexis, bishop of Tobolsk."

Sabler was stunned. He insisted that Alexis lacked "moral qualities." The bishop lived with a woman who accompanied him and compromised him with the faithful. Seeing this argument was sinking, Sabler noted that Alexis was a crude unpolished man who lacked tact. Sabler reminded Nicholas that the bishop once offended him with a crude witticism in a welcoming speech. "I forgave him that," Nicholas curtly observed. The appointment stood.[30]

Alexis's departure for Georgia opened up the bishopric of Tobolsk and All Siberia. Who should be appointed to this position but Varnava! The nation buzzed over these developments. Grigory now had a representative on the Holy Synod (Alexis sat on the board *ex officio* as exarch of Georgia) and a "friend" as bishop of Tobolsk. Varnava could block access to the records that supposedly proved Rasputin was a heretic. Rasputin might now do as he liked in Pokrovskoe. Rasputin and Varnava "constantly went to Tsarskoe Selo together and were forced to be very close.'' The friendship was troubled, of course; Varnava hoped to offer himself as an alternative to the erratic, troublesome Father Grigory. His ambitions did not succeed, but they worried Rasputin.[31]

Varnava's behavior as bishop confirmed his critics' predictions. He divided his clergy into two groups: "Rasputinites" and the others. The first were rewarded, the second were not. Varnava's harshest treatment fell upon those in church education. He transferred people whom he actively disliked from one corner of the vast diocese to another. A particular priest with a large family was sent 300, 600, and even 1,200 miles to new assignments. When he begged Varnava not to do it again, the bishop scornfully insisted. The priest then turned to Father Vostokov, a church publisher whose journal often exposed the "Rasputin gang." The Holy Synod demanded an explanation from Vostokov after he attacked Varnava. Vostokov cited a mass of denunciations he had received from the Tobolsk diocese. Metropolitan Vladimir supported Vostokov, maintaining he had proved "Bishop Varnava is absolutely unprepared to direct an eparchy." Vladimir formally moved that Varnava be removed and exiled to a monastery, and he demanded that Nicholas be informed of his proposal.

"Excuse me from such a task," Sabler replied. "I am unable to struggle against the most august will." The members of the Synod fell silent and the affair remained unresolved.[32]

The full record of Varnava's misdeeds became known after the collapse of the Old Regime, when agents of the Provisional Government went through Varnava's office. "We discovered many photographs," Boris Smitten the chief investigator, wrote, "for Varnava like all ambitious people loved to be photographed." Smitten described two photographs that he claimed were "very characteristic." One showed him in bishop's attire, lying in a coffin on a bed. In the other the bishop is sitting, clasping a number of effeminate listeners, "while his forehead and lively eyes clearly indicate his native wit. The lower part of his face, with the features of a satyr or the god Pan, reveal the feelings which inevitably led him to the apartment of Prince Andronnikov," a notorious homosexual who—as we shall see—also had dealings with Father Grigory.[33]

10
Disgrace

Rasputin's enemies gained an important recruit in 1911. Hermogen finally admitted that Rasputin was a false starets and for the good of the dynasty should be returned to Siberia. Grigory probably sensed the change in progress during his visit that summer. The bishop reproached Grigory for his dissolute life, and he predicted that the scandals would eventually reach Nicholas and Alexandra. Grigory's defenses were uncharacteristically subdued, and the two men parted on an uneasy note. A few weeks later, Hermogen completed his transition to the anti-Rasputin camp.[1]

Hermogen could be a useful ally or a deadly enemy. He was an imposing figure and commanded a large following among both clergy and laity. Hermogen also had just been appointed to a term on the Holy Synod, so his voice would sound at the center of power. The bishop's weakness was a lack of political instinct. He railed against demands from "above"—Sabler's way of indicating the tsar and his wife. Hermogen was appalled at Varnava's elevation to vicar-bishop, and he kept the issue alive. But his biggest blunder was to attack a favorite project of Alexandra's elder sister Elizabeth.

Elizabeth felt an attraction to the religious life after her husband's assassination in 1905. In 1910 she took the veil and formed a special order of nuns to work with the poorest people of Moscow. Elizabeth advocated female deacons to assist Russian priests. Opponents noted deaconesses once existed in the Eastern Church, but were removed—and a council prohibited the vocation. But some influential bishops supported their restoration, and the proposal carried the Holy Synod in the autumn of 1911. Hermogen was vehemently opposed to the change and complained to Nicholas about this and other Synod actions. He also attacked

Rasputin's influence in Church and state. This created a scandal, for the bishop's grumblings were freely quoted about the capital.[2]

Nicholas and his family went to the Crimea after Stolypin's assassination. The tsar invited Rasputin to visit him on December 6, 1911, the day of the church calendar devoted to St. Nicholas and celebrated as the name day for Russian men with that name. Seeing his relationship with Hermogen deteriorating, Rasputin apparently saw a need to discredit him with the tsar. Grigory made much of Hermogen's opposition to deaconesses.[3] Rasputin must have been amused to see the bishop oppose a measure so close to the hearts of the empress and her sister.

December 1911 also found Iliodor in the final stages of turning against Rasputin. Despite some friendly moments at the outset of their relationship, by the summer of 1911 Iliodor was more than irritated by Rasputin's sexual escapades, his bragging, and his irreverent demeanor. In December he attended a meeting of key anti-Rasputinites in the capital, which heard Colonel I.A. Rodionov, a Cossack journalist and Duma member, deplore the latest rumors of sex between Rasputin and the empress. The dim-witted Mitya Kolyaba thought the tales were true and, in a rage, promised to kill Rasputin—or at least castrate him. Others in the group agreed it was time to act. Iliodor now admitted that Rasputin "was indeed the devil himself"—and apparently this was not meant as a mere figure of speech.[4]

The conspirators first went to Ivan Shcheglovitov, the minister of justice. They suggested that they hold Rasputin while agents removed the secret papers that they assumed were in Rasputin's residences at St. Petersburg and Pokrovskoe. Hermogen was certain these documents would lead Nicholas to see through "Father Grigory." Or would it be better to deliver Rasputin to Shcheglovitov and let him deal with the starets? The bemused minister agreed that Rasputin was a menace. But Shcheglovitov noted that it was no longer possible to detain Russians nor destroy their property outside the law. The conspirators now decided to take action on their own.

Alexandra once warned Rasputin that Iliodor might prove to be his most dangerous enemy. Events were about to confirm her prophecy; a trap was awaiting Rasputin as he returned to the capital.

Rasputin arrived on the night train from Moscow on the morning of December 16, 1911. He immediately called Iliodor to suggest they get together. Iliodor proposed a visit to Hermogen. Grigory readily agreed, and Iliodor soon came to fetch him in an automobile. Rasputin chattered away merrily until he arrived at the bishop's hostelry on Yaroslavsky Island; Grigory was suddenly uneasy, asking if his old enemy Mitya Kolyaba was there. Iliodor claimed he did not know. Rasputin was still more fearful to find a group awaiting him as he entered the vestibule. Hermogen now appeared, dressed in a stole and wielding a huge cross. He planned to confront Rasputin with proof of his scandalous life, then to extract promises in the presence of witnesses who included Rodionov, a merchant, a professor, and two priests. But before Hermogen began the service, Mitya attacked Rasputin. Shrieking and frothing at the mouth, Kolyaba grabbed Rasputin's penis. The conspirators finally separated Mitya and Rasputin. Hermogen now commanded Iliodor to speak.

Iliodor and others recounted Rasputin's various misdeeds.

"Is this true?" Hermogen finally asked.

"It's true," Rasputin replied after hestitating, "it's true, it's all true."

Rasputin was dragged to the chapel. The bishop demanded that Grigory swear never again to visit the tsar. Rasputin would go to the Monastery of the Caves at Kiev to ask its monks to pray for his sins. Then he would make a pilgrimage to Mt. Athos and Jerusalem.

"You won't return to Russia for three years," Hermogen thundered. "If I'm alive when you do, I'll investigate you. If you haven't obeyed me, I'll pronounce an anathema against you."

Grigory promised to do as Hermogen demanded. Snarling "Remember me!" he slipped away.[5]

Rasputin and his enemies now settled into furious intrigue. Hermogen and Iliodor bombarded Nicholas with telegrams. Rodionov approached V. M. Vonlyarlyarsky, a retired official with ties to Michael Rodzyanko, president of the Duma. Rodionov showed Vonlyarlyarsky the seven letters from Alexandra and her daughters that Rasputin had given to Iliodor two years before.

"Believe me," the fiery Cossack told Vonlyarlyarsky, "this is no simple peasant. He is a devil in the flesh. Persuade Rodzyanko to persuade the tsar it is impossible for such a person to have access to him and his family."

Vonlyarlyarsky arranged a meeting between Rodzynako and Rodionov. Until now the Duma president thought that tales about Rasputin were inflated rumors. Rodionov's tales made a big impression, as did the letters. Rodzyanko promised to take the matter up with Kokovtsov and other important officials.[6] Rodzyanko was a weighty addition to the anti-Rasputin faction and he would cause Rasputin considerable difficulty.

Rasputin was remarkably calm in this crisis. He first sought reconciliation with his enemies, not their punishment. Grigory asked Iliodor to intercede with Hermogen. Hermogen refused these overtures, turning his back as he fumed "never and nowhere."[7] Rasputin now wanted revenge.

Rasputin rushed to the palace to give his version of the affair. The next day a royal decree stripped Hermogen of his Synod seat. He and Iliodor were ordered back to their diocese. Pleading ill health, Hermogen begged Nicholas to withdraw his order, but in vain. The bishop and Iliodor defied the tsar by turning to the press, feeding what had become a major scandal. Hermogen claimed he was punished not for unpopular stands, but because he aroused the ire of his "unfriends." Synod denials called more attention to Rasputin's apparent ability to use Nicholas II to punish his enemies. Even ministers seemed powerless. Kokovtsov recalled speaking with Alexander Makarov on the same day that he intervened on Hermogen's behalf with the tsar. The interior minister told Ko-kovtsov "all sympathy was with Rasputin, '[whose enemies struck] as robbers in the forest after luring their victim into a trap.' "[8]

Hermogen and Iliodor defied Nicholas for two weeks. Then the tsar ordered Hermogen banished to a monastery in Russian Poland. As a bishop, Hermogen was entitled to a trial before 12 peers, but the tsar ignored this point of canon law. Seeing that Hermogen would not submit to banishment, Nicholas had the bulky bishop thrown into an automobile and taken to the railway station and exile. Hermogen remained at the Zhirovitsky Monastery until 1915 when it was evacuated in the face of a German offensive.

The fiery Iliodor proved more difficult to tame and control. The order for him to leave St. Petersburg came on January 17, 1912. The Holy Synod wanted to place him in the Florishchev Monastery near Vladimir. Iliodor went into hiding, then surrendered to the authorities. Changing his mind again, Iliodor gave his guards the slip and headed for Tsaritsyn, but was recaptured. Rasputin watched these events with cold malicious anger. One of his telegrams warned "Papa and my darling Mama" that the "tsar and tsarina are above all—and you must be so." "We must subdue the rebel Iliodor," another message thundered. "Otherwise the dog will devour everybody. He's a malicious dog; he doesn't care. It is necessary to break his teeth. Treat him more strictly. More guards. Yes. Grigory."[9]

Iliodor experienced an astounding transformation as winter turned into spring. On May 28, 1912, he petitioned the Holy Synod to unfrock him as a priest. On September 26 policemen cleared Iliodor's followers from their Tsaritsyn strong-hold. Iliodor renounced his faith in November, cutting his arm with a razor to sign the document in blood. The Synod unfrocked him—not because of Iliodor's request, the authorities claimed, but because he doubted the Resurrection. "I was a sorcerer and fooled the people," Iliodor spat back in a newspaper interview on January 1, 1913. "I am a deist," Iliodor concluded, "paganism is a fine religion."[10]

Rasputin's clash with Hermogen and Iliodor confirmed the public's conviction that Grigory was all-powerful and could defeat any foe. Subtleties, suggestions that Nicholas might have had several reasons for any particular action, were largely lost. Lev Tikhomirov, editor of the *Moscow News,* confided to his diary that "two terrible facts [were clear from this episode:] 1) Rasputin's strength at court; 2) an alliance between Sabler and Rasputin." Tikhomirov despaired over the drama he sensed was already taking shape, the growth of "terrible stories about the empress and the emperor which could have fateful consequences if spread about the people." This staunch monarchist was among the first to voice an increasingly common theme: Russia faced doom because of Rasputin. "Some terrible sort of fate is hovering over us, . . . the weight on my soul is terrible." "This ignoble Grishka—what is one to think, what is one to stand for, what is one to defend? When does something vile establish itself, through neglect, in place of the sacred?"[11]

Just after his clash with Iliodor and Hermogen, Rasputin suffered another blow from a different direction. This attack came from Michael Novoselov, lecturer at the Moscow Theological Academy and the publisher of an important church journal. Novoselov was an expert on the Russian sects and was aware of Rasputin as early as 1907. As an advocate of church reform, Novoselov hoped to use the "Rasputin affair" to discredit the authorities for ignoring the heretical ideas of a false starets. Novoselov published a pamphlet in January 1912 that "proved" Rasputin was a Flagellant. The police confiscated printed copies of this pamphlet, mixed the type, and destroyed the manuscript. This greatly "vexed" Alexandra's sister Elizabeth, who hoped the book would oust Rasputin from royal favor.[12]

The police action against Novoselov brought Alexander Guchkov into the fray. Guchkov was a colorful erratic politician who was born into a wealthy Old Believer merchant family in Moscow in 1862. Guchkov loved danger and adventure. He rushed to fight for his fellow Christians in Macedonia and Armenia when they rose up against the Turks. Guchkov also served in China during the Boxer rebellion. He believed Russia's greatest enemy was England, and with other Russians he joined the Boers in South Africa. A leg wound crippled Guchkov, but his treatment as a prisoner made him an Anglophile. He directed the Russian Red Cross in Manchuria during the Russo-Japanese War and was again captured by the enemy.[13]

Nicholas asked Guchkov's advice during the Revolution of 1905. Guchkov advised splitting the radical movement by cooperating with moderates in the local self-government councils known as *zemstvos*. Guchkov helped establish the Octobrist Party to preserve monarchy by adapting it to new conditions. He asked Nicholas to renounce autocracy and work with the center parties to consolidate a constitutional monarchy. As president of the Duma in 1910, Guchkov would report to the tsar; he hoped this position would let him function as a broker between Nicholas and his legislature. But Nicholas considered himself to still be an autocrat, and he refused to accept Guchkov's vision. Typically, if Guchkov did not have his way he might strike out—with equal passion—on a very different course. Guchkov turned on Nicholas for rejecting his leadership, and he constantly tried to bring turmoil to his reign. Alexander Guchkov impressed many as "an ambitious man who had become embittered and restless." Rasputin gave Guchkov an opportunity to show the "truth" about Nicholas: He was an inept ruler blocking what Russia most needed, a balance between strong monarchy and constitutional development.[14]

Guchkov retained two strong positions after his term as president expired: He was Octobrist leader in the Duma and edited the party's daily *Voice of Moscow*. Guchkov published Novoselov's suppressed pamphlet as a "Letter to the Editor" on January 24, 1912. Even more Russians now read of Grigory Rasputin, a "sly conspirator," an "evil corrupter of people's souls and minds . . . who impudently uses the Church itself as a cover."[15]

The controversy came at a time of renewed interest in Rasputin. The liberal *Russian News* and *Stock Exchange News* had just published articles showing

Grigory to be a behind-the-scenes manipulator who could defeat a bishop, the Synod—even a popular demagogue. The Novoselov affair confirmed all this. The press now exploded over Rasputin. Letters from ex-followers were published along with photographs of Grigory with current admirers. A Russian diplomat was amazed at the capital's mood when he returned in late March 1912. Everyone chattered about Rasputin's influence and Guchkov's attacks.

The post–1905 censorship had little power over the situation. Alexander Mosolov, as head of the court chancellery, could "rigorously [suppress] all issues of newspapers in which Rasputin's name appeared in connection with that of . . . the imperial family." But articles that did not mention its members by name were, "under the very precise text of the law, not liable to be submitted at all to the censorship of the court," Mosolov continues. "That made me completely helpless."[16]

Even appeals from top officials did not help. When the interior minister asked editors to moderate their attacks, they replied, "Remove Rasputin to Tyumen and we will stop writing about him." The prime minister approached two editors of *The New Times,* widely regarded as the government's unofficial mouthpiece. Kokovtsov complained that the newspapers gave Rasputin publicity that helped revolutionaries undermine the tsar. The editors insisted it was the liberal press that led in covering the "antics of the Rasputin crowd." Kokovtsov was amazed to realize "some evil hand" was working even in this conservative office, and "I could not count upon this paper or its editors to assist me." The censors could do no more than fine editors who went "too far" in discussing Rasputin and his influence. The articles proliferated, and the fines were chalked up as part of the cost of covering the story. Fines and confiscations only heightened public interest, and surviving copies of the offending newspaper changed hands at fabulous prices.[17]

Guchkov actually laid a trap. He was certain the authorities would confiscate issues containing Novoselov's expose. That would intensify speculation over Rasputin's apparent power. The next step was to force a Duma debate on the "Rasputin affair." The ill will this could be expected to generate would delay or defeat government measures in the legislative docket. Guchkov submitted an *interpellation;*[18] signed by 48 members, which the Duma passed on January 26, 1912. Guchkov's name was first on the list.[19]

Michael Rodzyanko now entered the battle. As president of the Duma, he was scheduled to report to the tsar on February 26, 1912. He decided to take advantage of the occasion to air his thoughts about the Rasputin affair. This was more than impulse. Since Rodzyanko would preside over the debate demanded by Guchkov's interpellation, he wanted to read Novoselov's pamphlet. When he requested a copy from the minister of the interior, Makarov replied "he had no copies of the pamphlet at his disposal, neither did he see any reason for circulating it." An "exceedingly angry" Rodzyanko rushed to the minister's office only to find several issues of the paper on Makarov's desk. The experience led Rodzyanko to a most subtle insight: Officials who "protected" the starets seemed to be his friends, but this was not necessarily true. Makarov despised Grigory. The favors he extended were to protect the tsar or his family or Russia— not Rasputin. Makarov was "perfectly honest," but he seemed to be servile "when it came to shielding Rasputin." It took a "stormy scene" for Rodzyanko to get a copy of the pamphlet.[20]

Rodzyanko was now deeply worried over the Rasputin affair and was determined to get to the bottom of it. He spent the time before his February 26 audience preparing a detailed study of Rasputin. Dr. Badmaev provided information from Iliodor and Hermogen. Rodionov produced the letters from Alexandra and her daughters that Rasputin had given to Iliodor at Pokrovskoe in 1909. Nicholas's mother, Guchkov, and the elder Prince Yusupov also helped in various ways. On the morning of the audience, Rodzyanko and his wife attended a special service at the Cathedral of Our Lady of Kazan; a century before to the day, the Russian commander Michael Kutuzov worshipped here before sallying forth to face Napoleon. Then the president of the Duma presented himself at the Alexander Palace for an audience with the emperor.

Rodzyanko began with technical matters and then moved to what he admitted was his "principal subject."

Rodzyanko told Nicholas he was worried about Rasputin's presence at court. If this offended the tsar, Rodzyanko would be silent, but as a loyal subject he felt he must be frank. The emperor was astonished, but with head bowed and gaze averted he mumbled, "Speak."

Rodzyanko spent nearly two hours recounting Rasputin's misdeeds. He accused Rasputin of being a khlyst and fornicator, and he read various letters, as well as passages from Novoselov's pamphlet. Nicholas struggled with his emotions and smoked one cigarette after another. At one point Rodzyanko offered a photograph of Rasputin dressed as a priest, forcing from Nicholas the admission, "Yes, this is really going too far. He has no right to wear a pectoral cross." Other photographs showed Rasputin with heretics and women.

Nicholas finally asked Rodzyanko if he had read Stolypin's report. He had not. They agreed that if Nicholas had heeded its message, the "Rasputin problem" would have been avoided.

Rodzyanko forced Nicholas to admit that Rasputin's Duma critics were loyal to the throne. Rodzyanko offered to resign if he had angered the tsar; Nicholas assured Rodzyanko he was obviously an "honorable man and a loyal subject." But Nicholas refused to promise that Rasputin, then in Pokrovskoe, would not be allowed to return to the capital.

The interview ended on an unexpectedly pleasant note. Rodzyanko had never met the tsarevich, and he asked for the favor of an introduction. The 20 stone president presented himself as "the biggest and fattest man in Russia," which made Alexis laugh. Rodzyanko was pleased that Nicholas was not stubborn or angry, nor did he suddenly end the conversation as many predicted.[21]

The Duma debates occurred just as a second anti-Rasputin group was launching *its* attack. One might think this court camarilla would have been pleased to see a parallel assault in the Duma, but it was not. The conservative men and women in this group were devoted only to Nicholas II and the monarchy. They despised the Duma, which they feared would use Rasputin to undermine the autocracy and defeat the government's program. The cabal did reach out to Kokovtsov, Makarov, and Shcheglovitov; as "servants" of the tsar they were appointed by and responsible to him alone. But the conspirators ignored possible allies in the Duma, though rightists there were the ones most appalled by Rasputin.

The conspirators planned to visit Nicholas individually, in relays, to warn of the danger that Rasputin posed to the tsar, his family, and the government. Alexander Makarov led off in mid-January 1912. Old Count V. B. Fredericks was the next to call. Kokovtsov suggested twice in February that Rasputin be excluded from the capital. The tsar listened cordially to these and other members of the cabal, but made no commitment. "This did not cause pessimism in the group, since they had not expected success with only one or two interviews."[22] But the conspirators were alarmed to see Michael Rodzyanko enter the picture. Palace Commandant Dedyulin learned that the portly Duma leader planned to air his thoughts about Rasputin when he reported to the tsar on February 26, 1912. The session made a big impression on Nicholas, and he decided to deepen Rodzyanko's involvement in the matter. This left the camarilla even more depressed. Ironically, the tsar chose one of its members—Dedyulin—to call upon Rodzyanko on February 28, 1912, only two days after the president's original report.

Rodzyanko was amazed at Dedyulin's visit. The palace commandant told him that the tsar had been "extremely taciturn and thoughtful" after their earlier meeting, that he said little and hardly touched his supper. Dedyulin made it clear that Rodzyanko's frankness in no way displeased their royal master. Nicholas could see that "Rodzyanko is a loyal subject who is not afraid of speaking the truth, [and he] told me much that I know nothing about." The tsar now wanted Rodzyanko to conduct an investigation into the familiar charge that Rasputin was a Flagellant. This was a daring gambit: Nicholas expected the evidence to persuade Rodzyanko that Grigory was Orthodox. This might quiet someone who could cause difficulty. If the emperor explained this tactic to the camarilla, they were not impressed. Years later, the memory of this episode still upset Spiridovich. Rodzyanko's involvement placed the matter in the hands of "the president of the Duma, not representatives of the government[!]," the general declared. It seemed the "emperor was indirectly showing his dissatisfaction with [me and my colleagues at court and in the council of ministers]."[23]

Rodzyanko was "astounded" by the tsar's request, but he gladly sprang into action. The next day he asked Peter Damansky to bring him the Synod's secret file on Grigory Rasputin. Damansky was known to be a "Rasputin man." He was born the son of a priest in Olonets province in 1859. (Bishop Varnava, another of Grigory's cronies, was born in the same area the following year.) Young Damansky attended the Siberian theological academy and joined the staff of the Holy Synod in 1886. Iliodor characterized Damansky as an opportunist who would do anything to advance his career. Damansky was Rasputin's friend, and he rapidly ascended the ranks of his bureau after Sabler became director general in 1911. Damansky had just become assistant-director when he clashed with Rodzyanko in early 1912.[24]

Damansky promptly brought the file to Rodzyanko's office. The president of the Duma pretended to be ignorant of Rasputin, wondering what Damansky would say about him to someone who was not a critic. Damansky assured Rodzyanko that Rasputin was a simple holy man who lived with the Sazonovs and enjoyed the friendship of some important people. Damansky kept a tight hand on the file and repeatedly assured the Duma president that the Rasputin "affair" was too trivial for concern. Rodzyanko realized that Damansky hoped to dissuade him from investigating the matter. Rodzyanko stood his ground and took the dossier. The next day Damansky asked Rodzyanko to return the documents, finally admitting the request came from the empress. Rodzyanko noted that Alexandra was no less a subject of the tsar than others; Nicholas gave him an order, and only a royal command could make him surrender the Synod file before he had completed his report.[25]

The fears of the court camarilla over Rodzyanko's involvement were well justified. Rodzyanko did nothing to strengthen the anti-Rasputin cause. He never even understood why Nicholas asked him to investigate Rasputin. An astute bureaucrat such as Kokovtsov by contrast grasped the point right away: Nicholas believed Rodzyanko's inquiry would refute Novoselov. Nicholas then expected Rodzyanko to help squash rumors that Grigory was a heretic. The obtuse Rodzyanko took everything at face value. He imagined that Nicholas really wanted his opinion as to whether or not Rasputin was a Flagellant.

Rodzyanko spread the news that Nicholas did him an honor; he was concerned to not miss an important witness or document. Kokovtsov reminded Rodzyanko that he had only been asked to study the matter not to conduct a full investigation. But nothing could shake Rodzyanko's conviction that he was called upon to save Nicholas and Russia. Rodzyanko actually formed a fact-finding committee that included Guchkov, now in deep disfavor with Nicholas II. The final blow was his conclusion: Rasputin was a khlyst! The evidence that acquitted Rasputin before Nicholas confirmed guilt to Rodzyanko.[26]

Nicholas was also angry over Rodzyanko's failure to control the Duma. The effort to tame Guchkov by making him an ally failed. When the Duma took up the state budget, Rasputin's enemies gained a chance to make more speeches about his ties with "certain high officials." These assaults reached a high point on March 9, 1912, when the Holy Synod's budget requests came to the floor. "How did this man acquire such a central position, how did he achieve such influence that even the supreme authorities of Church and state bow before him?" Guchkov thundered. He deplored "the monk's backers" who "prompt him on what to whisper next," ending with a sharp attack on Vladimir Sabler, director of the Holy Synod. The speech shocked the Duma and was applauded by every party and faction.

Sabler "looked at me, awaiting a word of defense," Bishop Eulogius recalled. The bishop was both a Duma deputy and a member of the Holy Synod. He admired Sabler and knew he was not a "Rasputin man." But Eulogius—like others at the Synod—was angry with Sabler for permitting Rasputin to meddle in their affairs through such officials as Damansky who were his "friends." The bishop sat there bewildered, recognizing that Guchkov was not entirely wrong. "I had to say something, but it was extremely difficult for me to defend [Sabler]. I said briefly I had no evidence for or against conviction, that I hoped the director general himself would defend his good name." Sabler took the rostrum and defended himself, some thought, "with great dignity." But Eulogius still admitted to himself that the attacks were "justified." The clash between the Duma and the Synod "discredited the Church, threw it into the mire and created a prejudice against everything related to it," he later wrote. "It was a terrible, tormenting situation." The Duma punished the government by rejecting credits to build new parish schools and to improve teaching conditions in those which already existed.[27]

The court camarilla also failed in its objectives. Events in the Duma left the conspirators aghast. Rasputin's critics there and at court agreed he must go, but the Guchkovs seized the issue to embarrass Nicholas and disrupt his legislative program. Rodzyanko might have been well-intentioned, but he was obviously unable to improve the situation. He probably made it worse; he certainly angered the tsar. Discouraged by these developments, members of the anti-Rasputin cabal ceased to function as a group. Most continued their efforts to discredit Rasputin with Nicholas II, but as individuals, not in concert. Rasputin again profited from disunity among his foes.

Rasputin no sooner celebrated his victory over the Duma than he fell from royal favor. The letters Grigory gave Iliodor at Pokrovskoe in December 1909 finally came back to haunt him. Five of the seven letters began circulating in hectographed form in St. Petersburg during late 1911, just as the confrontation between Rasputin and Hermogen–Iliodor was reaching a high point.[28] This fed the press's renewed interest in Rasputin in early 1912.

The letters were certainly mild by any reasonable standard. Alexandra referred to Rasputin as an "unforgetable teacher, savior and guide." She spoke of kissing his hand, sleeping on his shoulder, feeling the balm of his presence. The girls addressed Grigory as a "dear," "priceless," "true," and "unforgettable" friend. Maria and Tatyana wrote of kissing him, Anastasia—the youngest— spoke of problems with her brother. Olga confessed to sexual passion for a young man she had been seeing from afar at church. In any normal situation all this would be embarrassing, not compromising. But Rasputin and his critics had so lowered the tone of moral discourse that this "proved" his erotic relationship with the royal women. The government could take no legal measures because the letters "were not distributed in printed form."[29]

The minister of the interior finally tracked down the originals of the letters in late January. Kokovtsev recalled that the longest, from the empress, had been accurately reproduced in the hectographed copy. One of the letters that had not been circulated was a small note with a carefully written "A" from the tsarevich.[30]

"Makarov and I did not know what to do with the letters," Kokovtsov admitted. He finally recommended that his minister give them to the empress. Unfortunately for Makarov, he took another course of action. He brought the letters with him on his next scheduled report to the tsar. Seeing that Nicholas was in splendid humor, Makarov explained how the letters had been retrieved and then handed them over in an envelope. "The tsar turned pale, nervously took the letters from the envelope, and glancing at the empress's handwriting said, 'Yes, this is not a counterfeit letter.' Then [Nicholas] opened a drawer of his desk and threw the letters inside, with a sharp gesture unusual with him."

"Why did you ask me for advice only to act in the opposite way?" Kokovtsov asked Makarov when he heard of this episode. "Now your dismissal is certain."[31]

Kokovtsov proved correct. Nicholas was offended that the letters, a private family matter, were published by hostile forces. Nearly as embarrassing was the realization that his own people made the letters their business, negotiated for them, handled and read them. Alexandra was already hostile to Makarov for his opposition to Rasputin. Her anger against him was even greater now.

The return of the letters weakened Rasputin's standing with Nicholas and Alexandra. When the documents were in hectograph, Kokovtsov and Makarov assumed the letters were fabricated, being circulated to undermine the throne. The empress also seems to have believed this, probably because it was what Rasputin claimed. With the originals in hand, Nicholas and Alexandra could see that Rasputin's carelessness was actually the cause of the scandal. Alexandra—no less—fired off an angry telegram to Pokrovskoe (Rasputin returned there in February 1912) chastising the starets. Grigory claimed Iliodor stole the documents.[32] But this oily explanation did not mollify Alexandra Fedorovna.

The change in her attitude toward Rasputin became clear when Rasputin returned to St. Petersburg the following month. Alexandra refused to receive Grigory. When the royal family left for the Crimea on March 12, 1912, Nicholas made it clear that Grigory would not accompany them. But Anna Vyrubova could not resist stashing him on the imperial train. The tsar was angry at this disobedience, Rodzyanko notes with a touch of glee. The train was stopped, and the stowaway was removed.[33]

But Rasputin persisted. He arrived at Livadia several days after the royal family, accompanied by his wife and one daughter. Rasputin's sudden presence gave rise to endless gossip and extravagant talk. "Now I'm at ease," Prince Orlov sarcastically declared. "Rasputin has arrived—that means everything will go well."[34]

Rasputin was actually in danger at Livadia. A plot in the capital was being finalized at this very moment. General Bogdanovich and his ultra-right associates were discussing Grigory's murder with the leaders of the ministry of the interior. The governor of the Crimea was the point-man in their conspiracy. Ivan Dumbadze, a fiery Georgian who advanced through Bogdanovich's sponsorship, agreed to strike the blow. One plan had Dumbadze drowning the starets in the Black Sea; other possibilities were to hurl Grigory from a cliff or to kill him in what would appear to be a bandit attack. Dumbadze decided to murder Rasputin on the Yalta-Sevastopol ferry. He requested final permission in a cyphered telegram, which read: "Permit me to deliver Rasputin while he goes by cutter from Sevastopol to Yalta." Police Director Beletsky forwarded the communication to his superior, the minister of the interior. Makarov lost his nerve at the end and declined Dumbadze's request, claiming the plan was vague and dangerous. Grigory again profited from good fortune. Had his enemies been a bit more determined, the "Rasputin affair" might have ended in these days on the lovely shores of the Crimea.[35]

In the end Dumbadze could do nothing more than harass Rasputin. At least he did that. The governor expelled Grigory as "a person of no occupations and without visible means of subsistence." This shabby treatment threw Alexandra into a bout of "gloomy and nervous anxiety." Nicholas was also offended. Dumbadze did not understand that one did not strike out against friends of the tsar—not even if they were in disfavor. Nicholas asked the governor by what authority he sent the "excellent old man Grigory" from Yalta. Dumbadze replied that Rasputin seemed to be a suspicious and even dangerous person; the law and his duty dictated that Rasputin be expelled from the city.

Nicholas was not satisfied with this explanation and asked Dumbadze to permit Rasputin to return to Yalta.

"Sir," Dumbadze replied. "Your majesty is well aware that I would shed my last drop of blood for you and your august family. But I intend to preserve my honor as an officer up to the end, toward and against all. Moreover your majesty can at any moment relieve me of the post which you have graciously confided to me."

Nicholas took leave of General Dumbadze kindly. He remained the governor of Yalta, but rumors that Dumbadze would be appointed to a position at court stopped. Those who spoke respectfully of Dumbadze as a rising star now ridiculed his mannerisms and peculiarities. Alexandra was melancholy and withdrawn during the remainder of her stay. Only occasionally did people see her riding in a closed car with her daughters, "a set and sad expression on her face."[36]

Rasputin remained in disfavor. Grigory returned to Pokrovskoe; his career in the capital seemed to be at an end. No one in these days could have predicted that Alexis stood on the brink of his most terrible encounter with hemophilia.

=== 11 ===
"The Little One Will Not Die"

Tsar Nicholas II led celebrations of the hundredth anniversary of Borodino on September 7, 1912. The battle was reenacted in gala fashion. Engineers reconstructed some of the old redoubts and batteries; placards told of cavalry and infantry assaults. Detachments of soldiers stood in the same positions as their forebears, and at one dramatic moment the tsar rode a white steed across the battlefield. "A common feeling of deep reverence for our forebears seized us *all* there," Nicholas wrote, surprised perhaps by his feelings as he set foot "on the soil where the blood was shed of [so many] of our brave men." A few old-timers on hand actually remembered those bloody days. The tsar was most taken with Sergeant-Major Voitinyuk, then 122 years old.[1]

After further patriotic celebrations at Moscow and Smolensk, the royal family travelled on to Bielowieza, near Warsaw. The imperial grounds here spanned 4,300 acres and measured 130 miles in circumference. Bielowieza was one of the world's most fabulous big-game preserves. The king of the beasts in this forest was the auroch, or European bison, carefully kept to a herd of 770 animals. Nicholas enjoyed hunting as a way to relax and commune with nature, but he lacked the cold instinct of an accomplished hunter. Once on this trip the tsar took aim at a herd of stags, then reconsidered and dropped his rifle without firing a shot. When asked to account for his behavior, Nicholas explained that if it was proper to kill one beast, it seemed wrong to fire at a group and possibly wound others.

The tsar spent most of his two-week vacation riding horseback with the girls over picturesque woodland trails. Alexandra was rested and well, and even rainy weather did not spoil the general good mood. The family then moved on to another royal hunting lodge at Spala. Here Alexis suffered an injury, though it did not seem serious at the time. The boy hurt himself while jumping into a boat; the bruise was followed by a slight swelling to the left below the abdomen. Alexis fainted and was taken almost lifeless to bed. Dr. Botkin seemed sufficient for his care, however, and no specialists were summoned—a fact that shows how much suffering was accepted as normal for the tsarevich. But Alexandra wired Anna Vyrubova to join them at Spala. Did the empress sense that Alexis might take a turn for the worse? If so, it is still unlikely that Alexandra foresaw the horror about to descend upon her family.[2]

Anna Vyrubova described the imperial lodge at Spala as "one of the dampest, gloomiest places" she had ever seen. The windows were so poorly arranged that lights burned perpetually in the dining room while guests prowled about in an eerie gloom upstairs. Alexandra entertained the ladies in a cheerful sitting room. Nicholas and the local gentry hunted stag, proudly laying out the day's catch to flickering torches and the mournful calls of hunting horns. Anna Vyrubova did not care for this, having a "foolish love of animals" which kept her from enjoying the hunt. She favored the park and the little stream cutting through it. Anna particularly recalled a leafy patch where the family walked in the mornings. The scene was "remote and peaceful," and Vyrubova could understand the irritation that Nicholas and Alexandra felt as the police tramped around them on their outings.

Anna Vyrubova found the empress "greatly agitated" while Alexis was "pale and decidedly out of condition." Yet he seemed to be taking a turn for the better and was walking a bit. Alexis also complained of pain. One day the women took the boy for a drive. Alexis was soon suffering the most terrible agony in his back and stomach. That return trip was a terrible experience. Every movement caused Alexis great torment, and by the time he arrived home he was almost unconscious with pain.[3] Alexis had begun his most terrible encounter with hemophilia. The date was October 2, 1912.

Dr. Botkin realized that Alexis was suffering a severe lower left internal hemorrhage. Specialists who previously tended the boy began arriving at Spala on October 4. For the next nine days, Alexis endured incredible torture as swelling from the bleeding pressed against the nerves of his upper left leg. Pain spasms struck every quarter of an hour, his temperature kept him delirious around the clock. Alexis cried continually; those who worked around him held their hands over their ears as they went about their duties. Alexis's strength collapsed and the cries turned to wailing, then to a raspy, dull moaning. He kept repeating "Oh Lord, have mercy upon me!" The boy took no food; he could find no restful angle and could scarcely sleep. The sailor Derevenko carried him around when it seemed this might ease his suffering. Otherwise the tsarevich tossed about, growing paler, thinner, and more deathlike every day, "his great eyes looking like coals in his little, wan, drawn face."[4]

Alexis's condition was an agony to his family, especially Alexandra. She sat by his side for hours on end, soothing, praying, and doing what little she could to make him more comfortable. Nicholas relieved his wife periodically, but he admitted that Alexandra "bore the ordeal better than I." On one occasion Nicholas was so overwhelmed by his son's agony that he ran from the bedroom to the study, weeping bitterly. "But in my free moments I wanted only to go and sit by his bedside." Princess Irene hurried from Prussia to her sister's side. This was "a godsend to both of us," Nicholas wrote, for "she is so kindhearted, so level-headed and shows such composure in all circumstances." Irene had lost a son to hemophilia. But no one could really help Alexis or his mother, each bonded by the other's suffering. Alexandra knew her son was dying. At one point Alexis also saw this and welcomed it.

"When I am dead, it will not hurt any more, will it?" he asked. Alexis wanted to be buried "in the light" with the blue sky over him. "When I am dead, build me a little monument of stones in the wood."[5]

Fearing Alexis would be excluded from the succession, Nicholas and Alexandra were determined to keep his attack a secret. This imposed a routine that clashed incredibly with the grim reality of the sickroom. Pierre Gilliard recalled that visitors saw less of Alexandra than at first, but Nicholas "controlled his anxiety and continued his shooting-parties, while the usual crowd of guests appeared at dinner every evening." The empress had to entertain during the evening; it was part of the game she was determined to play. Maria and Anastasia performed two scenes from Moliere's *Bourgeois Gentleman*, while Alexandra sat at the front smiling and chatting with her guests. When the performance was over Gilliard saw her rush down the dark corridor that led to Alexis's room, with a "distracted and terror-stricken look on her face." The empress rejoined her guests after a few moments, the invisible mask again in place. Only later did Gilliard learn that the tsarevich suffered from hemophilia; for the moment he simply knew something was terribly wrong. "An hour later I returned to my room, still thoroughly upset at the scene which had suddenly brought home to me the tragedy of this double life."[6]

On October 6, 1912, Alexis's doctors informed Nicholas that the case was hopeless. Alexis's heart was scarcely beating; his temperature stood at 105° F. Blood poisoning and peritonitis now threatened his life; surgery to halt the internal bleeding would also produce a fatal hemorrhage. Alexis had reached the point of no return. Hemophiliacs at this stage simply did not recover. Only a miracle could save Alexis, Fedorov insisted. When asked what he could consider a miracle, he suggested spontaneous reabsorption of the tumor, but he cautioned that this would not occur as often as once in 100 instances. By this time rumors abounded. The *London Daily Mail* reported that Alexis had been injured by an anarchist's bomb. Even now Nicholas would not reveal the exact nature of his son's malady, though on October 8 he released the first bulletin about Alexis's failing condition. The tsarevich was popular in Russia, and prayers were freely offered on his behalf. Nicholas ordered a solemn service in Moscow before a miracle-working icon; crowds in the capital flooded into the Cathedral of Our Lady of Kazan.

"All the servants, the Cossacks, the soldiers, and all the rest of the people were wonderfully sympathetic," Nicholas wrote. A tent chapel was hastily erected in the garden and a *Te Deum* was celebrated each day. "Polish peasants came in crowds and wept while [the royal family's chaplain] read the sermon to them." Alexis's Cossack guard sang prayers. "What piles of telegrams, letters [and] icons with wishes for the darling's speedy recovery we received!" the tsar later told his mother. Nothing helped. Alexis received the last rites on October 10. The evening bulletin made it clear that the next would announce his death. Alexandra's golden hair was now tinged with gray, and Nicholas aged in a manner everyone noticed. At least the social life stopped once it was clear that Alexis was ill. Friends sat quietly in the empress's boudoir on the evening of the eleventh until Irene appeared, white and agitated, begging the company to retire as the "child's condition was desperate." Vyrubova and others remained, however, and at 11 P.M. Nicholas and Alexandra entered the room, despair written over their faces.[7] But Alexandra had not quite abandoned hope. There was still Rasputin.

Nicholas had enough control over his wife to keep Rasputin out of the picture so far. Alexandra now acted on her own. She asked Anna Vyrubova to telegraph the starets to ask him to pray for her son's life. What followed was a scene of remarkable drama.

Rasputin knew of Alexis's failing health from the bulletins that all Russians followed in these days. He had not been invited to intervene, and he did not; he may even have been angry over his recent treatment. The telegram Vyrubova sent on Alexandra's command arrived in Pokrovskoe on October 12, 1912, just as the Rasputin family was sitting down to lunch. Grigory read it and fell to his knees before the icon of Our Lady of Kazan, praying fervently and with all of the force at his command. Praskovaya beckoned the family to silence, not wanting the slightest noise to distract her husband. Onlookers froze like statues as Rasputin prayed intensely, his face covered with sweat. Grigory finally made the sign of the cross, rose, and dashed to the telegraph office. His future hinged upon what he would do. "For him this was a moment of great opportunity and great danger," historian Martin Kilcoyne notes. "If he was aware that he was a faker, his gall at this time was colossal; he staked his career" on the proper answer to Alexandra's telegram.[8]

On the morning of the following day, Alexandra entered the drawing room to be greeted by court and state officials. She was pale and drawn, but wore a most sincere smile. "The doctors notice no improvement yet," the empress replied to the questions, "but I am not a bit anxious myself *now*. During the night I have received a telegram from Father Grigory, and it has reassured me completely." When pressed for details Alexandra read the simple, powerful message: "God has seen your tears and heard your prayers. Do not grieve. The Little One will not die. Do not allow the doctors to bother him too much."[9]

At 2 P.M. the same day, the doctors declared "the hemorrhage has stopped." The good news instantly flashed about Spala, and at 3 P.M. a celebratory service was held to thank God for the mercy shown to this little boy. Alexandra left her private apartments for dinner that night for the first time since her son fell ill; She was exhausted but radiant. The doctors were astounded to hear her announce that the family would return to St. Petersburg in a week. This aggressive schedule proved possible. On October 14 Alexis's temperature fell to 38.9° (102°), and two days later the tumor in his groin began to recede. All were jubilant. Nicholas donned his Cossack uniform and returned to receiving guests and tending to state affairs. "Alexis's recovery will be very slow," Nicholas wrote his mother on October 20, 1912:

[H]e still has pain in his left knee . . . and has to be propped up on a pillow. But that does not worry the doctors, for the chief thing is that the process of internal absorption continues, and for this complete immobility is necessary. His complexion is quite good now, but at one time he looked like wax: his hands and feet, his face, everything. He has grown terribly thin, but the doctors are now stuffing him for all they are worth.

Alexis's left leg remained locked at a painful angle. Several months and much pain passed before massages and a firm use of the orthopedic "triangle" straightened the limb. The tsarevich was still lame when Russia celebrated the Romanov dynasty's tercentenary in 1913, and the boy travelled in the solemn procession to the Kremlin in the arms of a sturdy Cossack guard.[10] But he was alive.

Alexis's recovery has been much debated. The doctors clearly abandoned all hope for his recovery and admitted that there was nothing they could do. "I do not agree with my colleagues," Dr. Fedorov told Mosolov. "It is most urgently necessary to apply far more drastic measures; but they involve a risk. What do you think—ought I to say so to the empress? Or would it be better to prescribe without letting her know?"

"I could not possibly give an opinion on so delicate a question," Mosolov writes in his memoirs, though he did inform the minister of the court about Fedorov's enigmatic statement. Was Fedorov considering some experimental drug? Was he debating surgery, knowing the hazards but also realizing that in any case his patient was doomed? When Alexis began to recover, Mosolov asked Fedorov if he was responsible.

"Did you apply the remedy you spoke of?"

"If I had done so, I should not have admitted it," the doctor said, throwing up his hands. "You can see for yourself what is going on here," Fedorov added as he hurried away. Later that year he admitted that Alexis's recovery was "wholly inexplicable from a medical point of view."[11]

There *are* natural explanations for Alexis's survival. By definition every hemophiliac bout runs a course and recovery sets in—unless that attack is a fatal one. Alexis's recovery might not seem so remarkable. As for Rasputin's telegram, it may have calmed Alexandra who in turn may have dealt with her son in a different fashion, one that might have aided his recovery. Rasputin was offering sound medical counsel when he said that the doctors should not "bother" Alexis too much, though it is not certain that they were acting in that way or

that Alexandra could correct it if they were.[12] I have taken the position in this
book that some people have healing gifts through prayer, and that Rasputin was
one of their number. It seems that only this theory explains Grigory's earliest
healings of the tsarevich. It is conceivable that this gift might be exercised at a
distance, which in this case would be about 1,600 miles. The Spala episode
might be understood along those lines. On the other hand, it is possible that
Rasputin's prayers and telegram entered the picture just as Alexis stabilized.
Perhaps the boy hovered at the brink of death and recovered for reasons having
nothing to do with a Siberian starets named Grigory Rasputin.

   For Alexandra, however, the truth was clear. Her son had been ill, he had
approached death, and the doctors had been helpless. Rasputin prayed—and the
"Little One" did not die. Others might theorize, but Alexandra knew. This shy,
dedicated, self-confident woman was ever one to draw cosmic conclusions from
her experiences. Her son's recovery was a sign that their cause might yet prevail.
The royal family and the dynasty, Russia and the autocracy—all this could yet
be saved. With Rasputin again at her side, Alexandra would not fail.

=== 12 ===

"As Long as I Live, I Will Not Permit War"

Russia celebrated the three hundredth anniversary of the Romanov dynasty in 1913. Liberals emphasized that Michael Romanov was *elected* tsar on February 21, 1613 by the Assembly of the Land, a representative body whose members included free peasants and townspeople. Monarchists insisted that Russia's greatness was linked to her rulers. Nicholas was content to claim that the "Russian state was created and grew strong through the combined efforts of our crowned predecessors and all the faithful sons of Russia."[1] Plans were laid to use the tercentenary to boost the current ruler's prestige. Typically, Nicholas was handicapped by two obstacles: his wife and Rasputin.

Rasputin returned to the capital soon after the Spala episode, but the public was not aware of his presence until February 21, 1913. A service marking Michael's election 300 years ago on that day was scheduled in the Cathedral of Our Lady of Kazan. That morning, Rodzyanko learned that the Duma would be seated behind the State Council and Senate. The president of the Duma rushed to the cathedral to secure a better arrangement. Noisy exchanges no sooner got Rodzyanko's way than he learned of another crisis: Some peasant was sitting at the front of the area just given to the Duma, and the stranger refused to move. Rodzyanko rushed back into the cathedral, guessing at once whom he would encounter.

"Sure enough, it was Rasputin," Rodzyanko recalled in his memoirs. He was attired in a beautiful crimson silk tunic, high patent-leather boots, full black trousers and a peasant's overcoat. A pectoral cross dangled from a fine gold chain.

Rodzyanko ordered Rasputin from the church, but he would not budge. To the president's amazement, Grigory tried to hypnotize him. Rasputin ran his eyes over Rodzyanko's bulky frame: first his face, then his chest, and finally a direct stare into his eyes. Rodzyanko had encountered hypnosis, but never succumbed. This time he felt an unprecedented power of "tremendous force." He responded by staring into Rasputin's eyes. This broke the spell—and led to more argument.

"I was invited here at the wish of people more highly placed than you," Rasputin declared, producing an invitation. Rodzyanko did not relent, and Grigory fell to his knees and began to pray loudly.

"O Lord, forgive him such sin!" Rasputin finally cried, rising slowly to his feet. Throwing a final angry look at his tormenter, Grigory walked to the west door. A Cossack guard helped him into a car, arranged his splendid sable-lined coat—and Rasputin drove away.[2]

Alexandra also created difficulties for Nicholas. She had long proved unable to play a role that would endear a tsarina to Russians. The capital's festivities no longer included the gala balls so familiar under Alexander III. Receptions for the Russian nobility and diplomats were hosted by Nicholas and his mother, not the younger empress. The streets of St. Petersburg were gaily decorated for the royal procession to the Kazan Cathedral on February 21, 1913. But the crowds were strangely silent as the emperor passed, breaking into cheers only at glimpses of the four girls smiling under their broad, flower-trimmed hats. The service was splendid, though Alexandra's nervousness and her husband's gravity dispelled rejoicing. The news spread that Rasputin was in the cathedral. This was probably a distortion of the fact that Grigory had been there in the morning. But the rumor rippled through the crowd as people looked around for the Siberian starets, freely exchanging gossip and indignant remarks.[3]

Rasputin also made an appearance on Nicholas's spring tour of the provinces. The royal family passed through Moscow, then Vladimir, Suzdal, and Nizhnyi-Novgorod. Kokovtsov was struck by the "rather colorless" celebrations. The tsar was to relate directly to the ordinary people of Holy Russia on this trip. But Kokovtsov was impressed by the "lack of enthusiasm and the smallness of the crowds," which at best exhibited only "shallow curiosity." Small groups of peasants occasionally gathered along the Volga to see their tsar, but the late-spring winds were so biting that Nicholas did not show himself even at prearranged stops.[4]

Kostroma was more hospitable. Envoys from the Assembly of the Land came here 300 years before to beg the nun Martha to permit her young son to come to be crowned tsar. Crowds on the river bank followed the present ruler as his family left Kostroma. Many waded after the ship. "It seemed that the return of warm weather had thawed out the crowd," Kokovtsov wrote, pleased to see "anything approaching enthusiasm. . . . "

The only sour note was struck when Rasputin appeared at an important church service in the tsar's honor at Kostroma. The Romanovs and various important people were in the front at the right; Rasputin was to the left. A ripple of interest passed through the crowd as it took note of his presence. People were amazed that Rasputin was honored with such a prominent place, and Police Director Beletsky soon asked Grigory to take a less conspicuous spot. The starets moved but a few steps. As the crowd left to witness the laying of the tercentenary monument's corner stone, Rasputin took a perverse delight in grabbing a spot where everyone could see him. The ministers' wives asked Beletsky to identify the mysterious person sitting on the fence separating the church grounds from the construction site. After exchanging meaningful glances with the tittering ladies, Rasputin hopped down and left.[5]

Nicholas continued to Yaroslavl and Rostov, and in May he returned to Moscow. He was moved by his tour; it confirmed the assumptions that the tsar and his wife held concerning their place in the Russian land. Criticism was clearly confined to the capital; their task was to maintain the autocratic principles still cherished by the great mass of the Russian people. Overwhelmed to see loyal subjects swimming beside the boat as it left Kostroma, Alexandra declared to a lady-in-waiting, "Now you can see for yourself what cowards those state ministers are. They are constantly frightening the emperor with threats and forebodings of a revolution, and here—you see it yourself—we only need show ourselves, and at once their hearts are ours." Nicholas shared similar feelings with confidants. The more he learned of Russia's past, the more his love grew for this great land. The tsar spoke of taking more trips, perhaps to the Caucasus or even Siberia. "What peaceful plans! Everything seemed so calm and secure in those days!"[6]

Rasputin played a role in the "war scare" of 1913. The issue concerned Russian support for Balkan Christians. Bulgaria, Serbia, Montenegro, and Greece attacked Turkey in October 1912 and gained rapid victories. By March 1913 a party was demanding that Russia intervene, even at the risk of war with Austria-Hungary and her German ally. The pressures on the tsar were loud and direct. Militsa and Anastasia made a shrill case for supporting their Montenegrin homeland; their husbands also stood for military action. Nicholas saw advantages to war if, as many claimed was likely, the large powers would remain neutral, permitting Russia to score a quick cheap victory. Russia needed a success of some sort to erase memories of her recent humiliation by Japan. Russia might gain territories at Turkey's expense; war would stimulate the economy and cause Russians to rally around the tsar. For a brief moment it seemed that Russia might enter this struggle.

Rasputin sallied forth as a champion of peace during 1912 and 1913. We do not know the precise rhetoric he used with the tsar, but Grigory's views on the subject are well documented. A change in palace command also turned up an interesting fact: He was in regular contact with Nicholas throughout the crisis. Voeikov became the new palace commandant in late–1913, he now handled Rasputin's admission to the palace. Voeikov learned that Grigory was among the less-favored regular visitors who needed special permission each time they appeared at the Alexander Palace. Even though the tsar or his wife expected Rasputin, he was always held at the gate until the assistant-director of the court police telephoned permission to admit the starets. Voeikov saw that this "only served as an occasion for gossip. . . . " Rasputin was now to be admitted right away. When Voeikov asked how often Grigory appeared at the palace, he was told "once a month, sometimes twice."[7] This did not include Grigory's meetings with the tsar and his wife at Anna Vyrubova's cottage; Grigory and the royal family also exchanged many telegrams.

Rasputin's thoughts on war and peace show insight. Grigory had an intense, nearly mystical conviction that Russia must avoid war at all cost. In some respects this was an idealistic sentiment. Rasputin understood the cruelties of war; he pitied its victims and knew the havoc even a volunteer army brought to peasants. He also thought military experts were wrong to assume that war would be cheap in rubles or lives. Above all war would transform the Old Regime's problems into deadly crises. Rasputin told Iliodor Russia had sufficient trouble and enemies at home, she should not seek them abroad. Grigory's vision actually excelled that of the "peace party." Sensible as they were, they opposed war for specific parochial reasons. Few in the Russian elite grasped the danger that war held for the system. Only the revolutionaries matched Rasputin in this area. Trotsky, for example, understood that a war between the old empires—the Russian or the Ottoman, the Austrian or the German—would end in a common ruin regardless of who "won." This gave Trotsky little joy. "A sense of the tragedy of history which words cannot suggest was taking possession of me," he wrote of his moods in these months, "a feeling of impotence before fate, a burning compassion for the human locust." "A war between Austria and Russia would be a very useful thing for the revolution in all of Eastern Europe," Lenin held in a letter to Maxim Gorky dating from early 1913, "but it is not likely that Franz Joseph and [Nicholas II] will give us that pleasure."[8]

Rasputin discussed a Balkans war in two newspaper interviews in 1913. One appeared in the *St. Petersburg Gazette* on October 13. Rasputin began by ridiculing Russian journalists (he did not like the profession) for crying, "There will be war!"—and for urging Russia to "prepare for war and light the fire."

"I would ask . . . these writers, 'Gentlemen! Why are you doing this? Is this good?' We should do away with the fear and discord which a war [would bring] and not kindle discord and hostility. We Russians should avoid war and build a monument, a real monument, I say, to those who work out peace. A peaceful policy against war should be considered high and wise. What have our 'little brothers' [the Balkan Slavs] who the writers are screaming over and defending showed us? We have seen the doings of these 'little brothers,' and now we understand everything. Yes. As far as our allies there go, really, it is good to have allies there as long as there is no war. But as soon as war breaks out, where would [they] be?"[9]

"But are we not dependent upon foreigners?" another newspaperman asked in a second interview.

"That's not so bad," Rasputin replied. "Really, isn't [Russia's tie with foreigners] our strength? We won't lose anything. We'll remember something that used to be and isn't any more. It's good that foreigners come to us because the Russian people is good, its spirit's the best. The worst person we have has a better spirit than a foreigner. They have the machine. They feel this themselves and come to us for spirit. You won't survive with just the machine. It seems that everything around them is good, but there's nothing in the person himself. And that's the main thing."

The interviewer noted that Russia long defended ethnic groups from Turkey because that was the best expression of the "human spirit."

"Don't you think God knows this?" Rasputin replied. "But maybe the Slavs aren't right? Maybe they're being tested? I travelled to Jerusalem, I was at ancient Athos. There's a lot of sin there among the Greeks, they don't live like monks should. But the Bulgarians [the Balkan Slavs whom Russians were being asked to support] are even worse. How they jeer at Russians when we go there! They're a cruel nation, their hearts are puffed up. The Turks are more fair and peaceful on religious things. You can see how it is—but it comes out different in the newspaper. I'm telling you the real truth."

The interviewer asked Rasputin about a future war.

"Christians are preparing for war, they preach it, torture themselves and everybody else. War's not a good thing but Christians run straight to it instead of submitting [to what's right]. . . . In general it's not worth fighting, taking away life and good things from each other, destroying Christ's teachings and at the outset killing the very soul. What if I greatly offend you? Subjugate you? Then I'd have to be on guard against you and fear you—and you'd be against me anyhow. That's what happens if you use the sword. But if I always turn to you with Christ's love—then I'm not afraid of anything. Let the Germans and Turks take each other for friends, that's their misfortune and blindness. They won't get a thing out of it, they'll only bring themselves to an end more quickly. And we, lovingly and quietly, by looking at ourselves will again tower above everyone else."[10]

Rasputin had his way; Russia did not fight in 1913. This is not to say that Rasputin was the main factor. France failed to support Russia, while Germany seemed ready to back Austria-Hungary; this was certainly decisive. If Nicholas listened to his "hawks," he was never impressed with their views. He apparently agreed with Rasputin: Russia had more to lose than to gain in the Balkans.

Yet Grigory did think his views carried weight. "As long as I live, I will not permit war," he declared when the scare finally passed. He was ever-vigilant, as the following episode illustrates. An Italian journalist arranged to interview Rasputin, and she asked the prominent liberal leader Paul Milyukov what questions to ask. Milyukov thought war was imminent, and he suggested that she

seek Rasputin's opinion. "Yes, they say there will be war and they are preparing," Rasputin replied. "But may God grant that there will not be war. I am
troubled by this."[11]

Rasputin was prophetic on war and peace, and he reminds us that prophets
are often not well received by their own people. Russians broadly credited
Rasputin with preserving peace in 1913; some imagined that he almost single-
handedly guided state affairs. The *Bell*, a newspaper close to church leaders,
praised Grigory for this. "[D]eclaration of war with Turkey hung by a thread,
and our preserver from most senseless bloodshed is said to be an inspired 'holy
man,' a sincere prophet, who dearly loves Russia, and is . . . close to the helm
of our highest politics. . . . " Other Russians resented the situation. Paul Milyukov made the Duma ring with his criticisms: how could the Church reform
itself or present moral leadership when someone such as Rasputin exerted such
influence? The *Evening Times* reminded the *Bell* that "holy men" (startsy) should
not be directing foreign policy or appointing bishops; both tasks properly belonged to the tsar. Rodzyanko showed the two newspaper clippings to Nicholas
II, who professed to be puzzled at the attack. The tsar wondered which *startsy*
were so powerful in church affairs.

"Your Majesty," Rodzyanko replied, "there is but one *starets* in Russia, and
you know who he is. He is the sorrow and despair of all Russia."

Nicholas fell silent at this point and Rodzyanko tactfully moved on to another
subject.[12]

And so Russia, along with the rest of Europe, turned to the fateful year 1914.
Few at the time imagined important events were at hand. St. Petersburg's *Messenger of Europe* asserted "it did not take a prophet to see that the year 1914
promises nothing outstanding in our socio-political life." But other signs were
disturbing. The Reichstag's new military budget exceeded a billion marks; France
responded by restoring a three-year term of active duty, thereby increasing its
peacetime army by 50 percent. Those who held power were increasingly fatalistic
about war. Russian leaders especially seemed to think that war was unavoidable.
Minister of War Sukhomlinov, Foreign Affairs Minister Sazonov, Minister of
Agriculture Krivoshein—these and others fell into line one by one, admitting
that the crisis postponed in 1913 could not be contained if it should reappear.

Nicholas and Kokovtsov were among the few who really hoped to preserve
peace. The tsar saw the kaiser in the spring of 1913. Each assured the other that
he would be a force against war. Russia would leave Turkey as the "doorkeeper"
of the Straits of Constantinople, while Germany would restrain Austria and permit
the Balkan states to work out their own problems. But as days turned into weeks
and weeks became months, "Cousin Willi" increasingly turned to champions
of aggressive diplomacy. "Cousin Nicki" sent Kokovtsov to improve the situation. The results were not encouraging. Wilhelm thought that war was unavoidable, and it made "absolutely no difference who starts it."

Nicholas stood silent as Kokovtsov reported on the German situation. The tsar "was gazing out the window at the boundless sea in the distance," Kokovtsov recalled. "Then finally, as if waking from a reverie, he said, 'In all things is the will of God.' "[13]

=== 13 ===
Nearly Assassinated—War

Maria Rasputin was alone in her apartment in June 1914 when the telephone rang. A stranger was calling to confess that he had fallen in love with her and had followed her several times on Nevsky Avenue. He would not divulge his name until she granted him a meeting. Finding her admirer too insistent, the 16-year-old girl cut the conversation short. The caller tried his luck three times later. The Rasputins were about to return to Pokrovskoe, and Maria forgot her mysterious suitor in the excitement of departure. Toward the end of the journey a reporter by the name of Davidsohn introduced himself to Maria. She recalled him as a short young man, dark, witty, talkative—and apparently a Jew. Admitting it was he who called her on the phone, the reporter expressed pleasure at their meeting now. Maria's uneasiness turned to alarm when, as the ship approached Pokrovskoe, Davidsohn informed her that he planned to spend a few days in the town. Maria Rasputin should have been worried. Davidsohn was privy to a conspiracy that, within a few hours, nearly took her father's life.[1]

The next day was Sunday, June 28, 1914. (The dates in this chapter are "New Style," following the Gregorian calendar in use in the West.) The weather was balmy as the Rasputin family set out for Mass. During the liturgy, an ugly woman in rags approached Grigory and stared into his face. Her crushed and misshapen nose provoked loud comments from Dmitry, which brought a rebuke from his father. The woman was Chionya Guseva. She had been Grigory's lover. Syphilis so disfigured her face that Rasputin might not have recognized her in 1914. Guseva was now one of a band of Iliodor's female disciples who had been wronged by Grigory. Some wanted to castrate the starets; Chionya favored murder. With Iliodor's blessings she travelled to the Crimea to carry out her plan. Guseva learned that Rasputin was no longer there and returned to St. Petersburg, only to discover that her prey was in Siberia. By the time she arrived at Pokrovskoe, Grigory eluded her again. Learning that Grigory would return home in June 1914, Guseva arrived well before he did. Chionya lived in Pokrovskoe for ten days, disguised as a beggar. On June 28 their paths finally crossed.[2]

Several peasants greeted Rasputin at church and chatted with him as he strolled home for lunch. The postman presently delivered a telegram. Alexis had twisted his ankle in boarding the imperial yacht. Alexandra probably asked Grigory to pray for the tsarevich; she may even have implored her friend to return to the capital. Whatever the message it was serious enough to cause Rasputin, after some hesitation, to run after the mailman with a reply.

After a few yards Grigory encountered Guseva. She held out her hand as if begging a handout. While Grigory reached for some money, Chionya drew a knife from her shawl. She drove the blade into her victim's abdomen, then with a firm upward thrust drew a gash from Rasputin's navel to his sternum. When the bone stopped her knife, Guseva pulled out the blade and prepared to strike again. Rasputin ran back to his house, with Chionya in hot pursuit. She was about to strike again when Grigory struck her head with a piece of wood. Rasputin collapsed as some passers-by grabbed Guseva.

Maria Rasputin hurried home from a neighbor's house when she got the news. She saw Davidsohn at the door, wanting to enter yet looking about with indecision. Maria suddenly realized she had been duped. Davidsohn knew that an attempt would be made on Rasputin's life, and he wanted to be as near as possible to get a good story.[3]

Maria Rasputin found her father stretched on his bed, resigned to suffering. Praskovaya and Dunya sponged away the blood, revealing the damage done to Grigory's intestines. Praskovaya and Dunya continually wrapped Grigory with wet sheets to staunch the bleeding. The nearest physician was at Tyumen. Dr. Vladimirov took eight hours to cover the 55-mile trip in his troika. Rasputin refused an anesthetic when his wound was finally cleaned and patched. Vladimirov operated by candlelight; his patient was as pale as death. Grigory insistently predicted he would survive—and he urged the doctor not to worry.

Fortunately for Rasputin no vital organs were badly injured, and the treatment prevented infection. His doctor now faced a difficult decision. Was it better to hurry over rough roads in a springless troika or travel more slowly and risk the patient dying because he had not reached the hospital? Vladimirov chose the first alternative. Dunya and Maria Rasputin sat on each side of Grigory, cushioning him as best they could from jolts and bumps.[4]

Nicholas learned of Rasputin's misfortune on June 29. Fearing that Grigory might be the target of a conspiracy, the tsar tightened his security. ''A hunk of carrion struck me a knife,'' Rasputin telegraphed on June 30, but ''with God's help I'll live.'' ''Profoundly saddened,'' the royal family replied, ''praying fervently.'' Observers were uncertain of Nicholas's feelings. His bearing was stoical, and he showed no emotion at the thought that Grigory might die. The tsar's entourage was pleased to think that the "Rasputin problem" might be solved, though tact forbade celebrations. Alexandra was "invisible," closeted with Alexis who was only just beginning to recover from his most recent bout with hemophilia.[5]

Anna Vyrubova and other admirers were openly distraught at the news from Siberia. Akulina Laptinskaya rushed to Tyumen with letters and gifts from Rasputin's admirers; she kept constant vigil at Grigory's bedside. Alexandra sent Professor von Breden to tend Rasputin. It is well she did; the eminent surgeon reopened the wound to correct mistakes that might have taken the patient's life. Rasputin sent an artist's sketch made in these days. The picture reveals a chastened man, one who brushed against death and barely survived. Rasputin's head was bowed and his hands clasped. The inscription read: "What of tomorrow? You are our guide, Lord. How many Calvaries must we cross in life?"[6]

The Russian press was excited over Guseva's attack. It was not certain that Grigory would survive, and on July 2 several newspapers reported that he had died. But the starets clung to life, and news bulletins soon quoted Grigory repeating, "I'll pull through! I'll pull through!" Coverage now shifted to familiar political themes. *Russian Morning* reminded its readers that Grigory was a "political villain and a vile libertline." *Speech* lamented Rasputin's influence "in our Church and social life," as well as "secular and even political life." Rasputin was briefly in the limelight once more. But a world war was also getting under way, and Grigory was quickly forgotten in the crush of those events.[7]

Some of Nicholas's jurists wanted to try Chionya Guseva for attempted murder. Rasputin protected her. Perhaps he was motivated by chivalry or Christian forgiveness? Grigory also knew Chionya would explain to the court why she hated the "holy man" enough to kill him. Doctors who evaluated Guseva concluded she was "irresponsible," hence exempt from criminal punishment—and a trial. She was placed in an asylum at Tomsk pending recovery. Relatives soon petitioned for her release, claiming her mental health was restored. This forced the district court of Tomsk to investigate. The hospital director admitted his patient had no "specific form of mental illness," though she displayed "psychic agitation" and a "heightened religious disposition." The family's request was denied. They continued to press for her release, though this occurred only after the collapse of Nicholas's government in March 1917. Chionya Guseva then disappeared from the important place she held in Russian history for a brief moment.[8]

By an extraordinary coincidence, Rasputin was struck down in Pokrovskoe on the same day—June 28, 1914—and at almost the same moment as the Austrian Archduke Francis-Ferdinand and his wife were shot in Sarajevo. Guseva's blows forced Nicholas II to meet the crisis without Father Grigory.

Alexandra Fedorovna was opposed to war, and she wired Rasputin—some sources say daily—to gain his support. Grigory's first telegrams to Nicholas were oracular and ambiguous. "Don't worry too much about war," Rasputin advised on July 16, "when the time comes it will be necessary to declare it— but the time has not yet come; your sufferings will be crowned." "Don't despair, my kind, dear ones," he offered on July 19. "I believe [and] I hope for peace," he continued; "[T]hey [foreigners?] are preparing a great evil [,] but we aren't to blame. I know all your torments. It is very hard not to see each other. Friends are helpful secretly in the heart, can they help you?"[9]

Rasputin was so upset by the prospect of war, as days passed and the situation darkened, that he tore his bandages. He was especially appalled by talk of mobilization, an act that Germany and Austria would view as a direct threat. Grigory's telegrams now became bolder. "Do not declare war, evil will come to you and the tsarevich." Realizing this was having no effect, Grigory wrote a letter to the tsar. Grigory's primitive scrawl poured out an agonized vision:

Dear Friend:
I will say again[:] a menacing cloud is over Russia[:] much sorrow and grief [are approaching,] it is dark and no lightening is to be seen. A sea of tears immeasurable [is ahead] and as to blood? What can I say? There are no words, the horror of it is indescribable. I know they keep demanding war from you[,] evidently not knowing that this is destruction. Heavy is God's punishment[;] when he takes away reason[,] that is the beginning of the end. Thou are the Tsar[,] Father of the People[;] don't permit the madmen to triumph and destroy themselves and the People. Well, they will conquer Germany[;] and what about Russia? If one thinks[,] then truly [it is clear that] there has not been a greater sufferer since the beginning of time [than Russia, and] she is all drowned in blood. Terrible is the destruction and without end the grief.
                                        Grigory

Rasputin also tried to communicate through Vyrubova, another voice for peace. "Let papa not plan war," Grigory insisted, "for war will mean the end of Russia and yourselves, and you will lose to the last man." Anna conveyed this telegram to Tsar Nicholas; he tore it apart in anger. "Our domestic affairs are not subject to the [regulation of others]," the emperor declared. Nicholas threatened to put Rasputin on trial.[10]

Rasputin was always convinced that he could have prevented the war if only he had been in St. Petersburg in the summer of 1914. It is tempting to view this as groundless boasting. But the kaiser tried to resolve the crisis peacefully; cooperation from Nicholas II would have strengthened Wilhelm's hand. The tsar did not really want war. Rasputin's presence in St. Petersburg would not have guaranteed peace, but his absence certainly weakened that cause.

Rasputin's strengths in this crisis were recognized by Serge Witte. The ex-prime minister was in Germany at the beginning of the crisis. Witte favored peace, and he rushed home to serve this objective. He told Osmolsky, a friend, "there is only one man who would be able to help untangle the complex political situation at the present time": Grigory Rasputin.

"How could Rasputin be considered an experienced diplomat?" Osmolsky replied, astounded. "He is a totally illiterate person who reads nothing. How could he know the complex policy and interests of Russia, and the interdependence of all nations?"

"You do not know what a great mind this remarkable person possesses," Witte insisted. "He knows Russia better than anyone—her spirit, mood, and historical aspirations. He brings a certain flair to everything he knows, but unfortunately he is not here now."

Osmolsky conveyed this conversation to Grand Duke Andrew Vladimirovich Romanov, who entered it into his diary on September 17, 1916. The grand duke was struck by Witte's opinion, and he often thought about it. Andrew Vladimirovich wondered how Witte came to such an evaluation, especially since the former prime minister publicly disparaged Grigory. Perhaps Witte thought he could use Rasputin to return to high office? The grand duke doubted that Witte actually knew Rasputin, but he conceded that those who did seldom admitted it. Witte opposed war; Andrew Romanov concluded this made him and Grigory allies.[11]

So Alexandra was the sole important force for peace in St. Petersburg. When she learned of Russia's mobilization, she could scarcely believe it was directed against Germany as well as Austria-Hungary. The empress rushed into her husband's study, and for a half-hour Anna Vyrubova heard an excited exchange. Alexandra then rejoined Anna and collapsed wearily. "War!" she mumbled breathlessly. "And I knew nothing of it. This is the end of everything." They sat quietly until 11 A.M. when, as was customary, Nicholas joined them for tea. He was also gloomy and distracted, and the tea hour passed in nearly complete silence.[12]

Russians read about Germany's ultimatum on the evening of August 1, 1914. News of the German declaration of war came the following day. Enormous crowds before the Winter Palace affirmed the unity of tsar and fatherland. A week ago the city was torn with revolutionary demonstrations; most radicals were patriots now. Nicholas appeared on the balcony just after three o'clock, followed by the empress. An electric current shot through the crowd as it caught sight of their tsar; a mighty "Hurrah!" rang through the air. People fell to their knees before the ruler of Holy Russia. The front rows tried to hush the others so the tsar could speak, but the excitement was uncontrollable. After a few moments, the kneeling people began to sing the Russian national anthem, "God Save the Tsar." Nicholas stood for a time on the balcony, head bowed and overwhelmed by this solemn experience. He then turned and slowly returned to his apartments.[13]

July and August of 1914 left Europe's diplomats and statesmen exhausted. The French ambassador Maurice Paléologue returned to his embassy just short of midnight on August 9, 1914 to face another "bundle of telegrams which had arrived during the evening." It was nealy 2 A.M. when he got into bed.

"Too tired to sleep," Paléologue recalled, he took down the Bible, "one of the few books one can open in this hour of universal agitation and historical convulsion." He fell to reading Revelation; when he reached Chapter six, he stopped at the following passage:

"And out came another horse, bright red; its rider was permitted to take peace from the earth, so that men should slay one another; and he was given a great sword. . . . And then I saw a pale horse, and its rider's name was Death, and Hell followed him; and they were given power over a fourth of the earth, to kill with sword and with famine and with pestilence and by wild beasts of the earth."[14]

Grigory Rasputin at his Siberian home in Pokrovskoe. Photograph courtesy of V. M. Purishkevich, *The Murder of Rasputin*, edited by Michael E. Shaw, translated by Bella Costello (Ann Arbor: Ardis, 1985). Reprinted with permission of Ardis Publishers.

The royal family

The Empress Alexandra with Tsarevich Alexis in 1915

His Majesty Nicholas II, Tsar of All the Russias, 1894-1917

The Empress Alexandra

Rasputin surrounded by admirers

Anna Vyrubova

The Alexander Palace, residence of the royal family at
Tsarskoe Selo

Rasputin in a Siberian hospital, just after Guseva's attempt against his life in the summer of 1914. The inscription reads, "What of Tomorrow? You are our guide, Lord. How many Calvaries must we cross in life?" (p. 108)

Alexander Protopopov, Minister of the Interior

Pitirim, Metropolitan of Petrograd

Prince Felix Yusupov, organizer of the conspiracy that took Rasputin's life. Photograph courtesy of V. M. Purishkevich, *The Murder of Rasputin*, edited by Michael E. Shaw, translated by Bella Costello (Ann Arbor: Ardis, 1985). Reprinted by permission of Ardis Publishers.

Vladimir Purishkevich, Rasputin's principal assassin. Photograph courtesy of V. M. Purishkevich, *The Murder of Rasputin*, edited by Michael E. Shaw, translated by Bella Costello (Ann Arbor: Ardis, 1985). Reprinted by permission of Ardis Publishers.

PART III

AT THE HEIGHT OF POWER

=== 14 ===
Rasputin Returns

The capital was shrouded in gloom when Rasputin returned there in early September 1914. (The dates in this and following chapters are "Old Style," following the Julian calendar in use in Russia before the Bolshevik Revolution.) The jubilation that rocked the city when the war broke out was gone. Russia's armies suffered severe setbacks in East Prussia, and it was clear that the struggle ahead would be costly and difficult. Rasputin's friends gave him a rousing welcome. Otherwise the Venice of the North was now somber and discouraged.

Rasputin found the capital changed in other ways as well. The Germanic name "St. Petersburg" was officially changed to a more Russian *Petrograd*. Grigory's old enemy Kokovtsov was in retirement, replaced by the elderly Ivan Goremykin.[1] At 74 Goremykin could remember the days of serfdom and self-confident autocrats. He was a short slender man, furtive and fox-like with long side whiskers and a reputation for sleeping through committee meetings. (When he woke up Goremykin loved to note that the discussion was exactly where it was at the time he dozed off.) The old gentleman's mind and health were good, but Goremykin belonged to the past and people were amazed to see him assume such an important position in January 1914. Goremykin described himself as "an old fur coat taken out of mothballs." By the summer of 1915 he was complaining that the tsar "can't see that the candles have already been lit around my coffin and that the only thing required to complete the ceremony is myself!" Nicholas probably selected Goremykin because he was a blind advocate of autocracy and would execute orders with a minimum of friction or disagreement.

Rasputin was fortunate to see Goremykin head the government. Goremykin cultivated people with even small measures of power: his door was open to

Grigory and they often saw each other. Goremykin did not necessarily carry out Rasputin's "instructions," but the starets cared more for courteous receptions than obedience to particular requests. Goremykin advised other ministers who sought his advice to treat Grigory in the same way.[2] This further enhanced Rasputin's feelings of importance. Madame Goremykin and Rasputin were actually friends. This grand dame was known for her skills with the potato; her tasty imaginative recipes pleased the most fastidious palates. She often sent dishes to the vegetarian starets, taking measures to be certain that they arrived at his apartment piping hot and at the peak of good taste.[3]

Rasputin was concerned to repair his injured relations with Nicholas II. The tsar was angry with Rasputin's opposition to war in July 1914. Early defeats suggested that Grigory was right; this further irritated Nicholas. Rasputin did not apologize for his earlier views, but he agreed that every effort must now be made for victory. He felt certain that defeat would destroy Russia and topple the Romanovs. A "half-argument" is wasted effort regardless of who wins, Grigory thought, it will only lead to more conflict. Rasputin went so far as claim to be happy the war came, for it forced Russia to rid herself of "two great evils": alcohol and friendship with Germany. (Nicholas proclaimed prohibition to conserve grain.) Now Germany must be crushed at all cost.[4]

Alexandra was delighted to see Rasputin, but she had little time for him. The sufferings of the hour suited the empress's purposeful character. Her greatest need in life was to serve. The war shifted the expectations of a tsarina from the social to the serious. She showed administrative ability, plunging into the organization of military hospitals—some at Tsarskoe Selo at her own expense.[5]

Alexandra should have confined herself to such activities. But she, her two older daughters, and Anna Vyrubova trained as nurses and plunged into the most ordinary tasks of military hospitals. Not all of the wounded were pleased at such attention. Many soldiers wanted their empress to be a beautiful, remote symbol, not a menial woman tending the bedpan. Yet Rasputin encouraged Alexandra to be active in this way, and all who knew her were amazed to note her excellent spirits and appearance.

Alexis's good health during 1914 also put Rasputin at a disadvantage. The royal family did not need Grigory as much as before, and they saw him less often. Rasputin came to bless Nicholas on September 19, 1914, the day the tsar departed for his first inspection at the front. But when Rasputin telephoned a week later to see the empress, he was told she was busy and he would have to wait a few days. Grigory was so annoyed he slammed down the receiver. "In other days he wouldn't have even asked if he could go to the palace," someone noted, "he'd have gone straight there."[6]

A rift between Alexandra and Anna Vyrubova further diminished Rasputin's contact with the royal family. People long noticed that Anna Vyrubova flirted— perhaps unintentionally—with Nicholas; she sat at certain places at the table and used her eyes to catch his attention in various ways. They also played tennis and took long walks alone together. Alexandra refused to let this bother her.

She trusted her husband and her best friend, and justifiably so. But the empress grew "ill, very low-spirited, and full of morbid reflections" during early 1914. Nicholas now turned even more to Anna. Alexandra noticed this and became jealous. By spring the empress was describing Anna as "crude" and "unkind." The two ladies worked together on various projects once the war broke out, but warmth and intimacy were gone.[7]

The rift damaged Rasputin's interests. Although Grigory visited the palace, he usually met the royal family at Anna's nearby cottage. Vyrubova constantly chattered about "Father Grigory" ; if Alexandra's faith in him wavered, Anna shored it up. Anna brought him messages, and Grigory directed telegrams to the royal couple through her.[8] Vyrubova's eclipse showed how indispensable she had always been to Rasputin's career. Without Anna, Grigory would have healed the tsarevich, won his parents' admiration, and pulled an occasional string. But the Siberian peasant would not have become the powerful, behind-the-scenes character we associate with the name of "Rasputin."

Rasputin's disposition was also different after his return to the capital. According to Maria her father was now irritable and he lost his healing gifts and felt that his prayers were not being heard. The crisis began in the Tyumen hospital when Grigory recovered from Guseva's knife. He realized he had to win back the gifts he lost as if he were a beginner once more. Rasputin prayed and meditated, fixing his mind on biblical passages. He also began to drink more; Rasputin's daughters urged moderation, but he insisted on doing as he wished. "Why shouldn't I drink?" Grigory insisted. "I am a man, like the others."[9]

These changes were not important to Rasputin's circle. Its members looked up to him as much as ever. He still made the sign of the cross over Anna when they parted. Grigory "perform[ed] strange rites and mumbl[ed] incomprehensible words" over the Pistolkors as they "kneel[ed] before him." Laptinskaya's devotion was loud enough to be called "pathological." These and others—Olga Lokhtina, Munya Golovina and her mother, the elderly noblewoman Gushchina—kissed Rasputin's hand and addressed him as "Father Grigory." One follower compared Rasputin with a famous Russian saint, "but we have the joy to see him in this life and to obtain edification from him. God will bless him in death, and he will be glorified."[10]

Rasputin's disciples gathered at a new address. After living at seven different places in less than nine years at the capital, Rasputin finally found a permanent dwelling. In May 1914 he moved into apartment 20 at 64 Gorokhovaya Street.[11] Rasputin's neighbors in this working-class area were a porter, a young dressmaker named Katya, Utilnya the masseuse, and Neustein, a nosy fellow of no apparent occupation. The five-story building was fronted by a small courtyard and wall. People entered an archway, passed the manager's flat, and reached individual apartments via a wide staircase. A mass of steamy odors assaulted one's nostrils—odors ranging from sheep's cheese to cabbage soup and rancid butter. Rasputin occupied a five-room apartment plus kitchen on the third floor overlooking the courtyard. The flat had a large anteroom, an important feature when its resident expected dozens of visitors each day. The dining room was pleasant and bright, and baskets of flowers and fruit stood on the table next to a samovar; this was the reception room and the place where Grigory spent most of his time at home.

Boxes of provisions in the kitchen testified to the master's prosperity. Rasputin's bedroom was small and simply furnished; the red fox-skin bedspread on the narrow bed was a present from Anna Vyrubova; the walls were decorated with icons and biblical scenes, plus pictures of Nicholas and Alexandra. A writing table littered with papers stood in the study along with leather armchairs and a couch for lady guests. Some disparaged the massive oak furniture and cheap oil paintings, but the dwelling was suitable for Grigory. It was five minutes from the train station for Tsarskoe Selo. The block also gave easy access to Nevsky Avenue, the capital's main thoroughfare. An American visitor in 1980 found that the building still resembled photographs from Rasputin's time. The street itself has been renamed in honor of Felix Dzerzhinsky. The telephones were also probably different. Rasputin's number was 646–46.[12]

Nicholas ordered enhanced security for Rasputin after Guseva attempted to kill him. A team of 24 Okhrana agents watched over the starets day and night. They were supplemented by guards from the chairman of the council of ministers, the Petrograd police department, and certain banks. Detectives were posted on Gorokhovaya street, along the stairway to Rasputin's apartment and in the courtyard below. Rasputin had mixed feelings about the arrangement. Knowledge that his life was in danger made him grateful for protection. But Grigory disliked being followed, and he often gave his detectives the slip. Sometimes Rasputin darted down the back stairs to a side street, sometimes he lost his "tail" in restaurants or at homes. The bewildered agents then telephoned people to see if the "dark one"—Rasputin's code name was *temnyi*—was in their company. Russian security men simultaneously guarded their charge and spied upon him. The officer in charge of Rasputin's security attempted to tap his telephone. Petrograd's telephones were under control of the city government, and it would not grant the Okhrana's request. "But without a doubt," General Komissarov testified in 1917, "they were tapping my telephone!"[13]

The police accounts of Rasputin's life during the war leave one amazed that any man could continue such a pace day after day, week after month after year. It seems incredible that one person could consume such vast amounts of alcohol, make love to so many women, and survive so many wild parties. Some claim that Russians have a unique taste for carousing, which is more evident there than in other cultures. Even so Rasputin was in a league of his own.

The police records tell the story in a straightforward manner. Rasputin came home "very drunk" with Tatyana Shakhovskaya on November 14, 1915. "They left again directly," the report continues. He returned at two o'clock completely overcome with drink. On November 22, Rasputin arrived past 8 A.M. after an absence of 24 hours. The following day: "Rasputin has been away since yesterday evening; he returned this morning at dawn, absolutely drunk." "Rasputin came home at five o'clock in the morning" on November 25; the actress Varvarova spent the night in his flat. "Rasputin was absent from home the whole night" on November 29. December 3: Rasputin left in the company of Filippov and returned drunk. Two days later, Rasputin came home drunk at three A.M. "He has again been absent the whole night," we are told on December 7. The following day Rasputin dined at the fashionable Dondon and then accompanied two ladies to their lodging at the Hotel Russia. He spent the night with Varvarova and returned home with her the next morning. Two days later Grigory left someone's house at 2 A.M. accompanied by two women. They found the Villa Rode closed and were not admitted even though Rasputin banged on the door and pulled the bell. The group ended at Massalsky's Gypsy Chorus, where they remained until ten A.M. the next morning. The revelers—still drunk—moved "to Yachininskaya's flat, whence Rasputin departed at twelve [noon]. Towards the evening he left for Tsarskoe Selo." This was a typical month in the life of Grigory Rasputin. A month similar to any other month.

Brawls and public scenes marked Rasputin's life in these days. At 10 P.M. on May 14, 1915, Grigory suddenly exited an apartment, with two men in hot pursuit. On June 2 he returned home and made drunken advances to Utinya, then Katya, and then the porter's wife before Dunya dragged him away. On the morning of January 14, 1916, Grigory broke a large glass pane in the entrance door. Four days later he returned at 7 A.M. with two men and a lady "completely drunk"; he "sang loudly in the streets" and spent the rest of the morning "shouting and stamping about in his flat." Two women came to call later, but Rasputin sent them away. They were angry, called Grigory a "scurvy peasant," and told the detectives that once at the Villa Rode they saw Rasputin running about "dressed only in his shirt"; the restaurant was closed for this outrage.[14]

The common element in all of these episodes was drinking—drinking so vast and continual as to leave Rasputin's protectors stunned. Rasputin drank "about two quarts of monastery wine," we are told on June 15, 1915. July 11 found him consuming "large quantities of wine and beer." On August 10, 1915, Rasputin set new records and amazed himself: He came out of his house at Pokrovskoe at 10 A.M. and began questioning the police about the previous evening. He was puzzled "at having got so drunk" since he had "only three bottles of vodka." He continually repeated, "Ah my dear fellows, that was an ugly business!" By this time Rasputin's Okhrana guards had developed a terminology that classified their charge's drinking into stages. Their reports describe Father Grigory as being "slightly inebriated," "inebriated," "fairly drunk," "drunk," "very drunk," "absolutely drunk," "completely drunk," "dead drunk," and, finally, "completely overcome with drink."[15]

For all of Rasputin's carousing in the capital, the greatest scandal of his career broke in Moscow. Rasputin went to the old capital on March 25, 1915, to pray

at holy places in the Kremlin. The trip was calculated to shore up his image as
a starets. As usual the carnal elements soon surfaced. After his devotions Rasputin
went to the Yar, a famous gypsy restaurant, accompanied by two journalists and
three young ladies. They ate and drank in a private upstairs room to the sounds
of a gypsy band. This was Rasputin's favorite type of music; it never failed to
ignite his fire. He scribbled notes to the female gypsies and tried to grab several.
Their angry rejection triggered boasting about his amorous exploits. Drunk, full
of himself, and not knowing where to stop, Grigory began to rave about his
relations with the empress.

"See the belt?" he bellowed. "It's her majesty's own work. I can make her
do anything—Yes, I Grishka Rasputin. I could make [the 'old girl'] dance like
this if I wished!" (At this point Rasputin was making an obscene gesture.)

Rasputin attracted considerable attention by this time. Several people were
offended. When challenged to prove he was really *the* infamous starets, Grigory
dropped his pants and waved his penis at the spectators. The British agent R. H.
Bruce Lockhart was in the main hall with friends; he noticed a commotion
upstairs. "Wild shrieks of women, a man's curses, broken glass and the banging
of doors raised a discordant pandemonium." "Head-waiters rushed upstairs, the
police arrived"—and the racket continued. "There was more coming and going
of waiters and policemen, and scratching of heads and holding of councils. The
cause of the disturbance was Rasputin—drunk and lecherous, and neither police
nor management dared evict him."

Telephone calls to increasingly high officials finally reached the empire's
police director. Dzhunkovsky ordered Rasputin arrested. "Having disturbed
everyone's enjoyment for two hours, he was led away, snarling and vowing
vengeance." Grigory was released the following morning on "instructions from
the highest quarters." Rasputin left for Petrograd later that same day, March
17, 1915. A group of women accompanied Grigory to the station.[16]

News from the Yar shot through the capital's social circle. Grigory's enemies
were delighted: Rasputin actually had subjected the empress to public ridicule.
Even Alexandra must now realize this was not a holy man!

Nicholas gave Dzhunkovsky enthusiastic permission to investigate the Yar
episode. He submitted a formal report on June 1, 1915. For one of the few times
in their friendship, Nicholas was really angry with his Siberian starets. The tsar
summoned Rasputin and demanded an explanation. Grigory gave his usual excuse. He admitted that he was a "sinful man," a simple peasant lured to an evil
place and tempted beyond his limits. He denied the allegations that would give
a husband greatest offense. Nicholas was not very satisfied with this, but Grigory
was entirely exonerated in Alexandra's eyes. She poured out bitter wrath against
"my enemy" Dzhunkovsky and "that vile, filthy paper." "If we let our Friend
be persecuted, we and our country will suffer for it," she wrote her husband at
the front. Alexandra begged Nicholas to "get rid of Dzhunkovsky." On August
19, 1915, he was finally dismissed as assistant-minister of the interior. Predict-

ably this was taken as evidence of Rasputin's unlimited power, though Grigory himself maintained that he had nothing to do with Dzhunkovsky's ouster.[17]

Serious pursuits also played an important role in Rasputin's wartime years. People gathered in still larger numbers at his apartment each morning; the line trailed down the stairs and sometimes onto the sidewalk. A friend compared these scenes to "a movie, each time something new." The cast included "university students and school pupils, priests and society women, old people and military people from aristocratic regiments. . . . " A group of peasants one morning sought Rasputin's aid in a suit with a landowner. Next came a lady in mourning; she held Grigory's hand and wept as they spoke. Jews and Polish refugees waited next to a guards officer; dressmakers sat beside women in the latest fashions. Rasputin received each person in his study, leaving often to talk with someone or to use the telephone. Then back to his visitors.[18]

One of Rasputin's petitioners was a peasant woman who lost her husband and both sons in the early days of the war, leaving her to care for his mother and sisters. She came to the capital to see if she was eligible for a pension. The woman could not get an answer to this request. She finally turned in desperation to "Father Grigory."

"Have to make them listen to you," he mumbled. "All they do is scribble paper. They're fools, bulging with their own affairs."

"Do you have any money?" Grigory asked a gentleman.

"Just what's in my pocket," he replied.

"Give it all here," Rasputin commanded. "You can part with a little bit of money!" he barked, accosting each visitor one by one. At length Grigory returned to the widow, clutching a fist of money.

"Take this, dear lady!" he said respectfully, handing it over. Seeing that his visitor was entirely overwhelmed, he put his arm around her shoulder and led her to the door. "Go, farewell—don't lose it!" Reaching the street, the woman counted the money. "Father Grigory" had collected 23,000 rubles, more than a minister's salary for a year. "What a person!" she thought as she walked away.[19]

Rasputin also helped people by writing "notes." These slips of paper circulated and even developed a cash value—as if they assured the bearer a job, a contract, or a favorable military assignment. Each began with a little cross at the top. Then came one or two lines urging favorable attention to an unspecified favor for the man or woman bearing the note. The messages were unaddressed, and the owners might present them to several officials until they finally located someone with the authority to grant their requests. Later copies were typed.

The value of the notes differed according to the official approached. Foreign Affairs Minister Sazonov threw them into a trash can. The minister of education once upbraided a woman who offered him a "Rasputin note." P. N. Ignatiev claimed nothing could keep him from granting a just request—or refusing one

that was not. Other officials were frightened of Rasputin or anxious not to incur
the displeasure of his supporters, These messages might be quite effective with
them. The rumor mill told of a woman who approached a general requesting
that her son leave the front briefly to receive a blessing from his dying father.
She was not even admitted to the general's office; then she produced the ''pre-
cious paper square'' from Rasputin's hand. The scene immediately changed, the
woman was brought to the general's office. He received her courteously, agreed
to what she asked, and personally saw her out.

Few admitted that Rasputin's messages influenced them. An exception was
Heinrich Schlossberg, a Jewish businessman who was anxious to secure Grigory's good will. To Schlossberg's amazement, just after meeting Rasputin a
stream of widows and orphans appeared at his office with these ''little notes''—
scribbles that were ''barely literate, bearing the mark of a person who had never
studied writing.'' ''This went on for a time and cost me dearly,'' Schlossberg
sighed ruefully, ''since the people asking my help really did need it.'' Other
Jewish millionaires who befriended Rasputin—Manus, Soloviev, Kaminka—had
similar stories. When Grigory visited Moses Ginsburg, he usually took all the
money he had on hand to give the next group of ''visitors'' at 64 Gorokhovaya
Street.[20]

Those who wrote for help learned that one had to call upon Rasputin to get
his attention. Another peculiarity was a lack of curiosity as to the fate of his
requests. Once Grigory wrote a note, he apparently had no further interest in
the matter. Rasputin often knew his messages would not help; he might even
say as much. Even so, he could be persuaded to write a note. Perhaps he hated
to be the one to say ''no.'' Sometimes he may have hoped to impress—if but
briefly—the petitioner. A lady in a low-cut ball dress once handed Mosolov a
Rasputin note. The message urged him to ''fix it up,'' she's ''all right.'' The
woman wanted to become a singer in the Imperial Opera. The director of the
court secretariat did his best to explain that the position she was seeking had
nothing to do with him.[21]

Rasputin accepted a variety of ''gifts'' in exchange for his favors. An attractive
woman could expect Grigory to demand sex, probably on the spot. This usually
sparked no resistance, as it was taken for granted. Others were surprised and
decided that the prize was not worth its price. A woman visited Grigory in
November 1915 to ask him to see that her soldier-husband was kept in a Petrograd
hospital. The first thing Rasputin did was to ask her to undress. She did so. He
plucked at her face and breasts, begging her to kiss him. He finally wrote the
note requested, then returned to this flirting game. The woman rejected Grigory's
advances, he took back the note and told her to return tomorrow. As she left
she told the detective who recorded the episode that she would not come back.
Rasputin wanted money as well as sex, and she had neither for him.[22]

Rasputin had no regular means of support and depended upon gifts for a living.
Peasants brought him cheese and wine, fruit and bread. These presents added
up and kept the household well fed. His most interesting bribe was a magnificent

fur coat with beaver collar and hat. One of his followers admired this coat in Moscow in March 1915. "My dentists gave this to me," Grigory explained. He was referring to a famous scandal known as the "Smolensk affair." Several Jews from that area purchased dental degrees to gain the right to live in Petrograd while they actually pursued different professions. They were caught and ordered expelled—until Grigory intervened.

Other offerings were more substantial. Grigory rescued 300 Baptists from prison for resisting military service at 1,000 rubles per man. He charged 250 rubles to free a petty forger, 2,000 rubles to keep a man from the front, and 5,000 rubles to release a political prisoner. Rasputin received 20,000 rubles for expediting the sale of a house tied up in a disputed inheritance. N. A. Gordon gave Grigory 15,000 rubles to serve as "commercial consultant" to his factory. Dr. Badmaev offered Rasputin 50,000 rubles in October 1916 to facilitate a business deal. Apparently this was not the first time Rasputin and the Tibetan healer worked together: "Therefore, I and [my business associate] General Kurlov warmly ask you, dear Grigory Efimovich, to forward this most humble request *in ways familiar to you* [emphasis added], believing that our dear tsar, once he becomes familiar with its essence will present it to the council of ministers for action."[23]

The ultimate source of Rasputin's influence was his relationship with Nicholas II. Grigory brought petitions to release men from military service, front-line duty, and even prison. Nicholas approved enough of these requests to preserve Grigory's reputation as an effective wheeler-dealer. Business proposals were trickier, for Rasputin did not have the grasp of details needed to defend a project if challenged. Nicholas was especially suspicious of military contracts. Rasputin easily retreated, stressing that he was only carrying out another's request— seeking to be of service to the tsar, etc. Similar scenes occurred with ministers. Rasputin often brought "projects" to Khvostov and Beletsky when they headed the ministry of internal affairs. Rasputin "always emphasized he had no interest in the affair but was doing someone a favor from the goodness of his heart." Grigory had a dim comprehension of what he was seeking; while chattering away about one proposal, he might hand over the papers to another. "When Khvostov or I noted what he requested—a concession or an order—was not within our sphere of influence, Rasputin would fish another request out of his pocket."[24]

In the spring of 1914 Rasputin befriended one of the most powerful men in Russia. Dmitry Rubinstein was exactly the type of person who would appeal to "Father Grigory." Although he was a wealthy banker, there was nothing of the "stuffed shirt" about Rubinstein, a short vivacious man who radiated joy and good will. "Mitya's" origins were humble—though unlike Grigory he acquired an education and a law degree. Rubinstein directed a bank in Kharkov before arriving at the capital, where he soon emerged as head of the Russo-French Bank. Rubinstein was ambitious, and money was his instrument for advancement. He donated large sums to charities, and in time he attained the Order of

St. Vladimir Fourth Class. Then Rubinstein learned that his old rival Ignace Manus received the rank of actual state counselor. This entitled the railwayman to be addressed as "your excellency." Rubinstein got to work on securing the same honor. On one occasion he donated 250,000 rubles to build a sailors' sanatorium at Yalta. Dmitry also befriended the empress. Alexandra wrote her husband that Rubinstein "has given 1000's already [and is] willing to give 500,000 for this invention being made [an airplane?] if he receives the same as Manus."

Rasputin probably introduced Rubinstein to the empress. He used Grigory to meet Goremykin and donate 200,000 rubles to a hospital that his wife sponsored. Mitya paid Rasputin's rent and carried out certain undertakings with his help. The police learned from a female informer on February 5, 1916, that "Rubinstein has lately arranged an important deal to the amount of 300,000 rubles, and Rasputin has received from him a commission of 50,000 rubles."[25]

Rubinstein learned a short while later just how valuable a friendship with Rasputin could be. Mitya attracted increasing attention during the war as—it was rumored—a speculator and a spy. Rubinstein was finally arrested in the summer of 1916 for illicit financial dealings. Rasputin was frantic over the possibility of a trial; information that might become public in a courtroom could embarrass him. So the starets worked to get Rubinstein released. The free and grateful banker sent Rasputin 500 rubles worth of flowers. Grigory had other banker friends: Alexis Putilov, Alexander Vyshnegradsky, and Chaikevich. Spiridovich tells us that Rasputin was on good terms with Minister of Finance Peter Bark, though the minister denied knowing the infamous Rasputin.[26]

Despite rumors to the contrary, Rasputin never held a salaried position at court. Rodzyanko was wrong in thinking that Grigory was "entrusted with the office of the 'emperor's lampkeeper,' whose duty it was to tend the lamps burning day and night before the holy icons." There was no such office. Rasputin was too clever to ask for such favors. His pose at Tsarskoe Selo was that of a man of God. A mention of income would have sounded a discordant note, and Rasputin was sufficiently clever to avoid it. It was also unnecessary: Various people at court helped Rasputin with his expenses. The extent of Alexandra's aid is not clear. Rasputin often complained that she was stingy and not even willing to cover his taxi fares to and from Tsarskoe Selo. A. T. Vasiliev, the tsar's last police director, claims that Rasputin received 10,000 rubles a year from the empress's "private purse." Alexandra paid Grigory's rent before the war, when Rubinstein took over the honor.

Other officials also saw that Rasputin got money during the war, and they were generous. Rasputin was paid 1,000 rubles per month from the "discretionary fund" of the ministry of internal affairs during the fall of 1915. A knowledgeable observer estimated Rasputin's income at 12,000 to 18,000 rubles per year.[27] This probably does not include bribes—the best source of earnings for an enterprising starets.

Rasputin had no head for business, but he attracted friends who helped with these problems. His first "business manager" was Ivan Dobrovolsky, a corrupt ex-school inspector. Dobrovolsky collected Grigory's bribes, saw that his expenses were paid, helped with correspondence, and ladled out advice about how to get on in St. Petersburg. Aron Simanovich was determined to replace Dobrovolsky. He placed doubts in Rasputin's mind that led to a collaspe of their friendship. Grigory and Dobrovolsky restored relations, but their days of joint business ventures were in the past.

Another important person in Rasputin's business affairs was Ivan Manasevich-Manuilov. He was born into a poor Jewish family in 1869. His father was exiled to Siberia for counterfeiting postal excise labels. From early years his eldest son Ivan displayed charm and good looks. At seven he was adopted by Fedor Manuilov, a Siberian merchant who saw enough flaws in the boy's character to specify that he could not claim a 100,000 ruble inheritance until his thirty-fifth birthday. Young Manasevich-Manuilov converted to Lutheranism, moved to the capital, and borrowed against his future estate to pursue the "fast life." He befriended Prince Meshchersky, publisher of *The Citizen,* a conservative daily newspaper.

The young man also served the Holy Synod and the police. He went to Rome in 1899 to gather information about Catholic efforts to defend their church in Poland. He also spied upon Russian revolutionaries and bribed foreign journalists to treat Russia favorably. Nicholas II put up 10,000 francs of his own money to help organize *La Revue Russe,* which Manasevich-Manuilov edited in Paris. Ivan became interested in counterintelligence and during the Russo-Japanese War organized a Russian service modelled along the lines of the French Sûreté Générale. Manasevich-Manuilov was fired from this position for stealing from his agents' wages and for buying outdated and obviously false information.[28]

Manasevich-Manuilov served Beletsky as a paid informant during the war, and he was close to Pitirim and Dmitry Rubinstein. He handled Boris Sturmer's confidential affairs, which included acting as contact man with Rasputin. Paléologue met Manasevich-Manuilov at this time and was struck by his "beautiful tight-fitting frock coat," his "well-oiled hair and proud bearing," and an expression that was "hard, cynical, and sly." Sturmer called him a "vile person." Perhaps it was this that qualified him to serve on Rasputin's "staff." A. N. Khvostov investigated Ivan and three other men and a woman whom the Okhrana regarded as Rasputin's "secretaries." They were found to be pursuing two dozen of their own "most sordid schemes." Police General Komissarov also commented upon the "Rasputin company." "They managed their own affairs," the Okhrana general testified, and they formed "a totally unique group" in search of wealth. Komissarov supervised Rasputin's security for a time, and they became friends of a sort. Even so "I was not admitted to this holy-of-holies."[29]

Manasevich-Manuilov suffered a crisis in the summer of 1916, that also endangered Rasputin's interests. An officer of the Moscow United Bank informed Eugene Klimovich, the city's police chief, that Manasevich-Manuilov had just threatened to expose shady features of the bank's activity unless he was paid 25,000 rubles. Klimovich asked the bank to pay with marked bills. Manasevich-Manuilov was arrested with the money on him. The ensuing investigation threatened Manuilov's associates, including Rasputin. Gossips said that Grigory turned to Alexandra, requesting that she use her influence with the tsar to halt the trial. Minister of Justice Makarov insisted that Manasevich-Manuilov appear in court. Makarov already crossed Rasputin's path four years before in connection with the hectographed letters scandal. To the amazement of the nation, the tsar freed Manasevich-Manuilov and soon thereafter fired Makarov! Release of a culprit such as Manasevich-Manuilov caused a tremendous amount of talk and was taken as one further manifestation—if any were needed—of Rasputin's unlimited power. Manasevich-Manuilov was rearrested, tried, and sentenced to a prison term just before the Old Regime fell in February 1917.[30]

*   *   *

A tragedy restored Rasputin's contacts with the empress. The train Anna Vyrubova took from Tsarskoe Selo to Petrograd on January 15, 1915, wrecked. Anna suffered a dislocated shoulder, both legs were shattered, her head and spine sustained major blows. Nicholas and Alexandra rushed to Anna's bedside, but her mother asked that Rasputin be left out of the matter, and he did not learn of the accident until the next day. A white-faced, trembling Grigory phoned friends for a car. Madame Witte lent her chauffeured limousine. Rasputin found Anna in a hospital, tossing about, mumbling "Father Grigory, pray for me," as the tsar and his wife looked on.

Grigory came to Anna's side. He took her hand and cried, "Anushka! Anushka! Anushka!" She awakened to the third summons.

"Grigory, it is you—thanks be to God!" Anna whispered.

"She will live, but will always be a cripple," Rasputin said quietly. Shaking and perspiring he collapsed in a faint. Nicholas and Alexandra were moved; God again saved a loved one through "Father Grigory." The doctors still did not think she would live. But on the seventeenth, Anna improved sufficiently to undergo surgery. "I suppose I suffered as greatly as one can and live," she wrote. But survive she did, though her body was disfigured and she could move about "only slowly and with the aid of a stout stick."[31]

Vyrubova's accident restored the relations that once existed between Anna and the empress. For several terrible hours Alexandra faced the possibility of losing her friend. Whatever hostility the empress harbored toward Anna vanished; despair turned to joy with her recovery. Who could bear grudges after such an ordeal? The four—Nicholas, Rasputin, Alexandra, and Anna—were brought to still deeper friendship. But we now see a different Vyrubova. Anna was suddenly "all-powerful" with Alexandra; the senior lady gave her young friend's opinions increasing weight. Anna actually began to use the royal "we": "We do not permit" or "We do not agree"—meaning Nicholas II, Alexandra Fedorovna— and herself.[32]

Anna Vyrubova still revered Rasputin and saw his words as holy writ. It was indeed critical to his interests to see that Alexandra and Anna resume their friendship. Vyrubova was again in a position to squelch every criticism, to refute every charge, and place the great man's flaws—if there were any—in "proper perspective." Vyrubova sustained an endless chatter over Grigory Efimovich Rasputin, the modern saint. Anna Vyrubova was Rasputin's extra dimension, his fifth element, his best ally.

Rasputin was not blessed with similar fortune with other "loved ones." Although close to his daughters, he was still distant from his wife and son, and especially his father. The two had a terrible encounter in Pokrovskoe on September 9, 1915. Police records show that both Grigory and Efim were "exceedingly drunk." They came to blows and were separated with difficulty. The father received a " . . . large purple bruise which completely closed his eye." Efim now insulted his son even more harshly. "He threatened to tell everybody that Grigory was an ignorant old fool who only knew how to fondle Dunya's [the maid's] soft parts." "This time Rasputin had to be held down with force to keep him from assaulting his father again." Days later Grigory still walked "with a slight limp, the result of having damaged his hip in his fight with old Rasputin."[33]

Efim died in 1916. Grigory spoke of going home for the funeral and the traditional 40 days mourning. Soon after this Beletsky met Rasputin on the street and expressed surprise that he was still in town. Rasputin had hoped "to carry out this last duty to a relative he had always admired," but certain "highly placed people" asked him to sacrifice the "desires of his heart" and remain in the capital. Grigory spoke with "winsome sincerity" and Beletsky thought the man's conscience was in order. Beletsky assumed that Rasputin had "changed his style of life, if only in those first days which are so sharp for anyone who has lost a near one." To the police director's amazement, this was not the case. Beletsky's detectives informed him that nothing had changed in "Father Grigory's" personal life. "Everything was the same—the same drunkenness, the same carousing, the same relationship to women."[34]

===== 15 =====
A New Saint, a National Scandal

The tsar's telegram arrived at Tobolsk on the evening of August 27, 1915. At 11. p.m. the cathedral bell began to toll, summoning the people to church. The chimes aroused a tense curiosity. What demanded such immediate attention? Another Russian defeat? News of a victory? A hush fell over the congregation when Varnava appeared, clad in bishop's robes. He bowed to the congregation and, with his cocelebrants, approached the tomb of John Maximovich, a local holy man who died two centuries ago and was recently proposed for canonization. The purpose of this service was to recognize John as a saint. Varnava began the liturgy by singing a refrain to the beloved Greek saint, John Chrysostom.

"Saint John, Father John, pray to God for us!"

This invocation was clever; people who questioned whether John Maximovich should be a saint might conclude that the address was to John Chrysostom. But Varnava was fortunate that night; no one offered criticism, the mood in the church was solemn and elevated, and the people and their bishop were one. So Varnava proceeded with the beatification of St. John Maximovich. The doubts came the following day. "Did we act properly?" some asked, "Did we rush into this?" Such questions were in order. Varnava acted on the strength of a secret telegram from Nicholas II—and with the collusion of Grigory Rasputin. The controversy this produced would demoralize the Church and lead the nation to think that the "Rasputin gang" could behave however it wished. The theatrical ceremony in the Tobolsk Cathedral on the night of August 27, 1915 was a swan song, the "last event of its kind in imperial Russia."[1]

For a long time Nicholas was popular despite such scandals. Monarchy was still a powerful force, a tsar was a symbol around which a troubled nation could rally. Nicholas was well fitted to this role. He possessed remarkable charm and a regal bearing. He often visited troops at the front and in military hospitals. The soldiers appreciated such attention. Nicholas's presence created a "special atmosphere, grave yet uplifted." Despite his small stature, the tsar "always seemed taller than anyone else in the room, and he moved from bed to bed with an extraordinary dignity." Nicholas's eyes were "gray and luminous"; they "radiated life and warmth and established . . . an almost mystic sense of contact." As Nicholas proceeded to the next soldier, the man he was leaving often shut his eyes to impress the tsar's appearance on his memory. When Alexis joined his father the impact was still greater. The men were astounded to see their present and future rulers, and they were moved by their simplicity—Nicholas was a colonel, Alexis a private—and concern for their welfare.[2]

Nicholas's greatest problems came from the moderate opposition. Liberals and moderate conservatives were alarmed over defeats, arms shortages, incompetence, and even treason. By the spring of 1915 they were urging the tsar to call the Duma back into session. The demand for a "ministry of public confidence" also dates from this time. If Nicholas granted this concession, the ministers would answer to the Duma—and not him—for their policies and actions.

Nicholas refused to share power with the Duma. He regarded his authority as autocratic and indivisible; he regretted concessions made in 1905 that encouraged some to think Russia was moving toward a parliamentary system. Nicholas— supported by his wife—thought that his duty was to pass his father's power to his own son. By the summer of 1915, however, the tsar admitted that he should part with four widely criticized ministers. At their head was Minister of War Sukhomlinov, a man of such vast incompetence as to make some think he was a German agent. Public opinion had also shifted against Minister of the Interior Maklakov, Minister of Justice Shcheglovitov, and V. K. Sabler, director general of the Holy Synod.

Nicholas dismissed the first two in early June 1915. He also announced that censorship would be relaxed and the Duma reconvened. Moderates were delighted at these moves, as with the rumor that Shcheglovitov and Sabler would soon go the way of Maklakov and Sukhomlinov.

The Holy Synod was of particular concern to Rasputin. He was appalled by predictions that Alexander Samarin would replace Sabler as director of the Holy Synod. Even if public opinion was unjust in labeling Sabler a "Rasputin man," it is true that he ignored Rasputin's influence with other officials. But Samarin was among Grigory's harshest critics, and if he led the Synod, Rasputin's power within the Church would be severely attacked. It was not certain that Samarin would accept the post if it were offered. He was invited to Stavka (GHQ on the western front) in June 1915 to discuss the possibility. At first Samarin declined, but after repeated discussions a proud tsar was finally able to present him as the new lay leader of the Russian Orthodox Church. The celebrations at Stavka were open and heartfelt. People embraced and exchanged congratulations on Russia's good fortune.

Nicholas dismissed his minister of justice on July 6 in favor of A. A. Khvostov, another Rasputin foe. The emperor now had an able cabinet enjoying the confidence of liberal and moderate Russians. Observers were amazed that Nicholas stood up to his wife in making certain changes, especially at the Holy Synod. "I am sure that you will not like this," he wrote of Samarin's summons to Stavka, "but we must have an "honest, devout and well-intentioned man whose name is known to the whole nation and who is unanimously respected."[3]

Alexandra and Rasputin heard the same gossip as others, and they also wondered if "all the ministers were being changed." The empress described Grigory as being "most anxious to know" if Samarin was replacing Sabler. She advised her husband not to drop Sabler "before one has a very good one to replace him." As for Samarin, Alexandra predicted he "wld. go against our Friend & speak up for the Bishops we dislike—he is so terribly Moscovite & narrowminded." Then came the terrible news: Sabler was out; Samarin was in. Alexandra was thunderstruck. Nicholas actually made such an important decision without her agreement! Rage and frustration leapt from the pages of her next letter. Rasputin was "in utter despair" at the change, "& now the Moscou set will be like a spiders net around us. . . . " She reminded her husband that "our Friend's enemies are ours." "I beg your pardon for writing all this," the tsarina continued, "but I am so wretched ever since I heard it [the news] & can't get calm."[4]

Alexander Samarin was one of the most popular figures of the day, and Russians were delighted with his appointment. Alexander's father Dmitry was a prominent Slavophile who worked with the government to abolish serfdom in the 1860s. This gave the young man ties to both conservatives and liberals. Alexander grew up on a 4,700 acre estate surrounded by books, ideas and interesting visitors. He studied history and philosophy at Moscow University, then served in the army and as a local official. In 1908, at 31, Alexander was elected marshal of the nobility of Moscow province. Until he resigned to lead the Synod, Samarin was the spokesman for the most important group of nobles in the empire.

Alexander Samarin was extremely conservative. He opposed legislative powers for the Duma and characterized Milyukov as a "revolutionary" regardless of "what disguise he will assume." An admiring critic thought Alexander lacked "creative imagination." Perhaps Samarin was a "typical Slavophile of the 'sixties" (he was born in 1869) who dreamed of a spiritual alliance between tsar and peasant "which would justify and sanctify the power of the supreme authority." But his sincerity made him popular with liberals and some leftists. Samarin was devout; he belonged to reform groups that sought to free the Church from state control and improve the condition of poor parish priests. Samarin worked with the Red Cross during the war. The English observer R. H. Bruce Lockhart described Alexander Samarin as "one of the very best representatives of his class."[5]

Russians were pleased with the news of Samarin's appointment. "Among the clergy it was like Easter Day, one paper reported. "All joyfully congratulated each other." The *Moscow News* charged

Not one newspaper, Right, Left or Moderate, has uttered one single word of approval for [Sabler]. . . . This remarkable fact must be noted. Even those journals which were created by Sabler for his own personal ends are silent. Evidently it is necessary either to speak the truth [or] to keep silent. Positively, literally nothing good can be said [of V. K. Sabler].

Despair over the state of the Church exploded with Sabler gone. The *New Times* charged that church schools were disorganized, seminaries were losing students, and priests were abandoning parishes; worst of all, many noticed a "weakening of belief among the people and the growth of indifference to the Church." The clergy echoed these concerns. Priests in the Duma delivered a petition to Samarin in August 1915. They noted a "coolness to the Church" among even "simple people" with "a decline of the religious spirit [and] moral life" The clergy's authority had fallen so low that "even the best and the most energetic . . . sometimes fold their arms in helplessness and despair."[6]

The new minister of the interior cooperated with the attack on Rasputin by relaxing press censorship. Prince Shcherbatov forbade only direct references to Grigory's relations with the royal family. The *Stock Exchange News* ran a series from August 14 to 18, 1915 entitled "The Life of the Starets Rasputin." These articles outlined Grigory's career and portrayed him as an important figure who "plays a great role in the fate of the nation." "How is [this] possible?" one column asked,

How has an abject adventurer like this been able to make a mockery of Russia for so long? Is it not astounding to think that the official Church, the Holy Synod, the aristocracy, ministers, the Senate, and the numerous members of the State Council and the Duma have demeaned themselves before this low hound? . . . Only yesterday the political and social scandals which the name of Rasputin conjures up seemed perfectly natural. Today Russia means to put an end to all this. . . .

The press campaign in the capital became nationwide by August 16. Rasputin was so stung by the attacks that he tried to answer his enemies. The *Siberian Trade Gazette* was charging that he was a horse thief in his youth. "Quickly tell me where and when and whose horse I stole, as printed in the paper," he demanded in a telegram. "If you don't answer, I know to whom to complain." The editor ignored the challenge. Krylov reprinted Rasputin's message and called its author a half-educated peasant.[7]

Rasputin's fortunes plunged sharply in these days. Much of his power had consisted of meddling in the Holy Synod. Grigory was also concerned with internal affairs and justice; the first controlled his security, while the second could use his misdeeds for legal action. Enemies headed all three offices by July

1915. Alexandra still supported Grigory, but he must have wondered about the tsar. Samarin had been offered the Synod directorship in 1911, but he demanded assurances that Rasputin would not play a role in the Church. Nicholas was unwilling to give such a pledge, so the position went to Sabler. Now Samarin had the office. What did this mean?

Grigory returned to Siberia in June 1915 just after Nicholas announced Samarin's appointment. It seemed that Samarin drove Grigory from the capital. Rasputin actually planned his trip before Sabler fell. But Grigory's position was weaker than any time since 1912.[8]

As so often happened, events suddenly shifted in Rasputin's favor. Just after Nicholas shook up the council of ministers, he fired Nicholasha and assumed personal direct command of his armies. The implications of this development for Rasputin's power were breathtaking. It was at this juncture in the fall of 1915 that Rasputin began to play an important role in undermining the government of Nicholas II.

Nicholas had a mystical conviction that a tsar's place was with his troops, especially if they were losing. He longed to join his soldiers in Asia in 1904, and was just barely persuaded not to settle on the German front in 1914. As defeats mounted Nicholas increasingly felt he should be with his regiments. Perhaps this was a mistake, but Nicholas saw arguments in its favor. Assuming direct command would demonstrate that he was unshakably committed to victory; the tsar's presence would elevate—if briefly—the army's morale. The present commander was popular, but in truth the grand duke was an unimaginative general with no better plan than to throw enormous reserves of soldiers against the enemy. There were arguments against the bold move. Even the Germans respected Nicholasha. Would Nicholas or his generals do as well? Would the blame for difficulties and defeats now fall directly on the tsar?

The weight of the objections diminished in Nicholas's mind as the fighting progressed. In part this was a result of Alexandra's influence. She was intensely jealous of the grand duke. The empress feared that he might use his popularity to topple her husband and exclude Alexis from the succession. Alexandra fumed at the suggestion that her husband would be anything less than an excellent commander. She saw an expanded role for herself if her husband were at the front. Nicholas would continue to make key political decisions at Stavka, but his wife would be expected to handle routine business at the capital. Behind her stood Rasputin, a fact that made him favor the change. Indeed we may document Rasputin's involvement in this episode more precisely than is usually the case when he meddled with political issues.

The crisis peaked in July 1915. Grigory was still vacationing in Siberia; Alexandra summoned him back to Petrograd. Rasputin arrived at 10:30 A.M. on July 31, 1915. He met with the tsar that day, then again on August 4. Rasputin advised Nicholas to follow his wife's counsel and his own "inner feelings" by assuming the supreme command at Stavka. Nicholas agreed and Grigory returned to Siberia on August 5. Rasputin expected the tsar to waver, so he sent several telegrams in the coming days reiterating the correctness of this historic gamble.[9]

Nicholas's ministers flew into a panic when they learned of his plans on August 6, 1915. They foresaw countless problems and setbacks from this decision. Samarin and Shcherbatov stressed that Alexandra's influence—and Rasputin's—would be enhanced by these changes. Even loyal old Goremykin admitted that his master should not take this step.

The ministers decided to present their views. The tsar received them as a group on August 20, 1915. It was an intense encounter; Nicholas perspired and clutched a small icon. "I have heard what you have to say," Nicholas said at the end, "but I adhere to my decision."

Discouraged but not defeated, the boldest ministers decided on a different strategy the following day. Alexander Samarin already consented to act for the entire group in combating Rasputin's influence at the Holy Synod. He now took further, more radical steps—steps that ended in his downfall. He suggested that the ministers sign a letter imploring their royal master "not to remove the Grand Duke Nicholas from the High Command of the army." Samarin agreed to draft the letter. The text stressed that "your decision threatens Russia, your dynasty and your person with serious consequences." If Nicholas would not follow their advice, the petitioners asked to be replaced since "we do not believe we can be of real service to Your Majesty and to our country." Samarin's signature was the fifth of eight on the final draft. Military obligation prevented the minister of war and of the navy from signing the letter, but they endorsed its contents. The ministers of transport and justice did not sign; Goremykin was not even asked. Indeed the ministers complained about him, asserting that they could no longer work with him at their head.[10]

The letter was delivered on August 22, a few hours before Nicholas left for Stavka. The tsar was angry with the document and its spirit of independence. He instructed Goremykin to tell its authors of his "displeasure"; they were not permitted to resign.

Nicholas's determination to replace Nicholasha was one of his most momentous decisions. Not that it damaged conduct of the war; military affairs were in the hands of General Alexeev, the new chief of staff and an abler figure than Nicholas Nicholaevich. The tsar's presence was symbolic. A year later, he recalled the moment "when I stood facing the large icon of Our Savior [in our favorite little chapel, and] some inner voice seemed to persuade me to come to a definite decision and to write to Nic. immediately about my desire to replace him at Stavka." In the very next line, Nicholas assured his wife that he came to this decision "independently of what our Friend [Rasputin] said to me." "I beg you to thank Him for sending me the two flowers,"[11] the tsar added, flowers that Father Grigory used to extend his own congratulations of the day.

*   *   *

Samarin and the other ministers were shaken by their failure to persuade Nicholas to remain in Petrograd. A British observer thought they were men of "honest purpose and real ability," but without the "will to govern." Only Alexander Trepov "seemed to possess the will to power that every statesman should possess." The others appeared to be "searching for opportunities to get out of the government rather than to get control of it. . . ."[12]

Samarin in particular was dispirited and depressed. Even so he was determined to challenge the "Rasputin gang." The clash was not with Grigory Rasputin, but with his friend Bishop Varnava.

As soon as Varnava arrived at Tobolsk in 1913 he began to appoint clergy whom Rasputin approved. The bishop established an arrogant relationship with the educated clergy and preferred unlearned men for promotions and choice assignments. A stream of complaints flowed to the Holy Synod, but Sabler was at a loss to act. A Rasputin crony actually had a medal bestowed on Varnava in 1915. His position seemed unassailable. Varnava clearly depended upon Rasputin. He celebrated a Mass at Tobolsk after Guseva tried to kill Grigory, calling upon the faithful to "pray for the welfare of God's devoted servant."[13]

Popular anger against Varnava boiled up as soon as Samarin replaced Sabler. Dissatisfied people took advantage of a visit that Samarin made to Tobolsk to ask him to transfer Varnava, creature of the well-known "horse thief" and "heretic" Grigory Rasputin. Complaints were also aired about the bishop's lengthy sermons, some of which were so unbecoming that women and children had to be sent out of the cathedral. Varnava charged that Russia's sufferings were due to abortion, which he fancied had been introduced into the country by Germans. "We asked often: will this war soon end? But is it time to raise this question? Does the number of dead sons equal the number of innocent babes who have been killed by their foolish mothers in their wombs?"[14]

Few who knew John Maximovich thought of him as a saint. He was born into a Polish noble family in the Russian empire in 1651. John was a professor at the Kiev theological academy and in 1695 became a bishop in the Russian Orthodox Church. As metropolitan of Tobolsk, he forcibly baptized the native peoples of Siberia. The year 1915 would mark the two-hundredth anniversary of John's death. Holy men and women were often proclaimed saints on such anniversaries. Such recognition carried benefits to a diocese. Miracles at the tombs of new saints attracted national attention, for "new saints are fond of manifesting their magical powers, while old saints take no pleasure in it." Pilgrims customarily flocked to worship at the shrine of a new saint, bringing income. The bishop was traditionally elevated to archbishop. Many noticed Varnava's "limitless self-love" and his desire to link his name with some great event in the history of the Church and continue his path to the metropolitan's rank.[15] What ambition must have blazed within this peasant from Archangel? With so much talk of restoring a patriarch in the Russian Church, did Varnava even dream of eventually occupying that high throne?

Varnava asked the Holy Synod to have John Maximovich included in the canon of the saints on June 10, 1915, the two-hundredth anniversary of his death. The people of Tobolsk also petitioned the tsar, and he forwarded it to Sabler with a note asking that the request "be considered in the Holy Synod." The petition was probably Varnava's handiwork. The handwriting of the document was identical to that of his summons to the Holy Synod; Varnava's name was first, followed by clergy and officials.

The Holy Synod decided such requests by asking two questions. Was the body preserved from decay? Did miracles occur at the grave? On December 8, 1914, the Synod ordered Varnava to unwrap John's body. In a masterful effort to put the best face on a bad case, Varnava admitted "by God's will the body of Saint John was not preserved, but the entire skeletal frame was well preserved." On January 23, 1915, the Synod asked the bishop to provide accounts of miracles. Varnava had nothing to report. He simply repeated his petition. The ever-tactful Sabler offered a compromise: He suggested that a decision be postponed until peace. Seeing himself blocked in the Holy Synod, Varnava now turned to other "authorities."[16]

Nicholas had been at Stavka as supreme commander for only three days when the "John Maximovich scandal" was set in motion. Rasputin telegraphed the tsar on August 26, 1915, urging him to ignore the Synod and see that John was recognized as a saint. A wire from Varnava the next day assured the tsar miracles were occurring at the tomb, and that the people loved their ruler and were glad to have a new saint. Alexandra supported Varnava. "Bishop Varnava comes from the people, he understands them," she told Prince Zhevakov. "He knows the people's faith and is able to talk to the people; the people follow him and believe him." The empress was scornful of the Holy Synod. "Is one really able to measure saintliness arithmetically?" she fumed. Alexandra was scornful of Sabler's proposal to postpone judgment. "Is it really possible to categorize faith as 'well-timed' or 'not well-timed'? Faith is always well-timed." Alexandra was certain that a new saint would bring help to current difficulties. On August 29, 1915, she advised her husband to "give Samarin the short order that you wish *Bishop Varnava to chant the laudation of St. John Maximovich* because *Samarin* intends getting rid of him, because we like him & he is good to *Gr*[rigory]."[17]

Alexandra could have saved her trouble. Nicholas had already acted, and for once his actions were even less wise than those his wife suggested. Had the tsar followed her advice and compelled the Holy Synod to recognize John Maximovich as a saint, at least it could be said that the emperor and his Synod were acting together. A tsar customarily confirmed canonizations; occasionally they prodded an unwilling Synod into agreement. But a Russian ruler had never acted unilaterally, secretly, and in open defiance of church authorities. Nicholas was about to do all this for John Maximovich.

On August 27, 1915, Nicholas telegraphed Varnava: "You may sing the laudation but not the glorification." "Laudation" was a stage of canonization similar to the Roman Catholic Church's "beatification." It authorized public veneration of relics. If miracles followed, the Church proceeded to "glorification," recognizing the holy person as a saint. On the strength of this telegram Varnava sang the laudation of John Maximovich that night. "The first laudation has been sung," the local governor telegraphed Nicholas on September 2, 1915. "Not only the common people but a majority of intellectuals took it to be a glorification." To deepen the confusion, priests celebrated services at John's shrine in the cathedral as if he were a saint. For several days no thunder was heard in Tobolsk. Some claimed this was proof that the heavens rejoiced at Varnava's act.[18]

Varnava knew his "canonization" would cause controversy. By keeping the tsar's telegram a secret, the bishop was playing with his enemies, creating the impression that he defied the Holy Synod—knowing if necessary he could cover himself by producing the wire. Varnava rushed to Pokrovskoe to take counsel with Rasputin the morning after the laudation. A telegram three days later summoned Varnava to the Synod to account for his behavior. Millions were now chattering over the bishop's misdeeds. On the same day (August 31, 1915) Rasputin and Varnava telegraphed the tsar from Pokrovskoe, assuring him that the common people were moved by the laudation and wept joyful tears. And now Varnava was being summoned to the capital for punishment![19]

Samarin met Varnava the day before the hearing in an effort to win him over. According to Alexandra, Samarin praised Hermogen as the "only honest man, because he was not afraid to tell you [Nicholas] all against *Grigory* & therefore he was shut up." Samarin appealed to Varnava to turn on Rasputin and to go to the tsar and tell him the truth about Father Grigory. The bishop replied he would do this only if Nicholas so ordered.[20] The encounter ended without Samarin accomplishing anything constructive. But he put himself in a position where he appeared devious and calculating.

Varnava appeared at the Holy Synod on September 8, 1915. Samarin and the bishops were seated; Varnava stood. Samarin asked questions, "lolling back in his chair with crossed legs cross-examining a Bishop about our Friend." Varnava conducted himself bravely, this was conceded even by those who disliked him. He refused to admit guilt; he celebrated the laudation "by an order from above." Varnava finally produced the fateful telegram. The interrogation was accompanied by cynical laughter, especially from Bishops Agafangel of Yaroslavl and Serge of Finland. Serge called out in a half-voice that Varnava asked to kiss Rasputin's hand. Varnava told Samarin to mind his own business and "not to judge a hierarch." Nothing was settled by this. Varnava was warned to stay in Petrograd and expect a second hearing.[21]

Alexandra wrote Nicholas "[it's] abominable how Samarin behaved to him in the hotel & then in the Synod." What her husband read in the newspapers "is untrue, he gave exact answers to all questions and showed yr. telegram about the *salutation.*" Alexandra noted that "Peter the Great of his own accord also ordered a *'salutation'* it was at once done, in the place and round about." "Lovy, you must be firm & give the strict order to the *Synod* that you insist upon your

order being fulfilled,'' the empress continued. ''Your will and order count, make
them feel it. *Varnava* implores you to hurry with clearing out *Samarin* as he
and the *Synod* are intending to do more horrors and he has to go there again,
poor man, to be tortured.''[22]

Varnava had no intention of being ''tortured'' again by the Holy Synod. He
told the tsar of a list of nine questions he would be asked at the next hearing on
September 10, 1915. These questions ''made my hair stand on end'' as they
concerned ''my relations with Rasputin, all calculated to produce a scandal.''
Varnava claimed that he had to visit his sick sister at Petrozavodsk. The bishop
actually took refuge with Prince Andronnikov. Varnava benefited from Rasputin's continuing support. ''Metropolitan John Maximovich glorifies himself with
miracles,'' the starets told the tsar in a telegram. ''In vain do our fathers who
have sat so long [an ironic reference to the gray-bearded members of the Holy
Synod] hinder your intention. The Lord blesses our work for peace and good
will for all, and your arm subdues all [with] thunder and lighting.'' The Synod
invalidated the laudation and ''retired'' Varnava as a bishop. But time was on
his side. Rasputin soon returned to Petrograd, and he pressured Nicholas and
Alexander to support Varnava. As for Alexander Samarin, the tsar and his wife
were already seeking a replacement.[23]

Samarin in fact was unhappy as leader of the Holy Synod. He was typical of
a number of ''provincials'' elevated to high office during the war. If Nicholas
had directed and supported these men, they might have breathed new energy
into the state machine. As it was they foundered in a bureaucratic maze. Samarin
no sooner settled into his duties than it became clear that his background and
attitudes were severe handicaps. Popularity and brilliant beginnings were not
substitutes for experience. Samarin prided himself on not being a bureaucrat,
which is to say he could not bend his staff to his purposes. Vladimir Gurko a
veteran official and a fine memoirist, conceded the Russian bureaucracy had ''its
defects, but at least it knew administrative technique.'' Samarin for all his virtues
was a ''dilettante,'' and his ''dilettantism showed itself very soon.''[24]

Samarin irritated Nicholas. The tsar did not like to see his ministers constantly
in the news. He was even less pleased when the press ''took'' to new appointees.
They enjoyed, if but briefly, a popularity that Nicholas could not claim; fanfares
also suggested that the tsar showed poor judgement in appointing their predecessors. Nicholas particularly despised publicity about the Church.[25] Here at
least everything should be in order. An experienced bureaucrat such as Sabler
knew how to ''manage'' Nicholas. Sabler was honest; he argued his opinions,
but tactfully—and he learned when to back down. Sabler gave the impression
that everything was in order. Samarin by his very nature represented upheaval
and innovation.

Samarin's collision with Rasputin and Varnava probably hastened the end of
his term. So did Alexandra's shrill calls for his head. But Rasputin and the
empress were not the only factors working against Samarin. His role in suggesting

and drafting the ministers' letter of August 1915 was probably the last straw. Nicholas watched Samarin and Shcherbatov—another "dilettante"—founder in office for three months. Then he decided they must go.[26]

Nicholas's ministers came as a group to Stavka on September 15, 1915. This was their first collective meeting with the tsar since he assumed the supreme command. Samarin reported on the Synod's recent actions against Varnava. The emperor was exceptionally pleasant to his director general, chatting with Samarin about his family and service with the Moscow nobility and the Red Cross. The two men parted on a most cordial note. A meeting of the council of ministers was scheduled that evening. While it was in progress a letter came for Goremykin. The old man asked for a recess; then he took Samarin into the next room to convey its message: "Be sure to tell Samarin in a friendly way that he is being dismissed from the post of director general of the Holy Synod."[27]

Alexander Samarin returned to a rousing welcome in Moscow. The assembly of nobles happened to be in session, and it expressed regret that Samarin was ousted from the Synod. There was talk of reelecting him marshal, but Samarin squelched this out of deference to the tsar. The British historian Pares thought even now Samarin was "probably the most conservative and loyal of all [the tsar's ministers]." The nobility of Moscow province was also conservative. An observer called its angry support for Samarin the "first swallow of the revolution."[28]

Other classes of Moscow were shaken by Samarin's dismissal. Bruce Lockhart happened to be in the city just after Samarin's ouster, and he found public feeling was "very excited." Rumors held that the Duma would soon be recessed and it was. This—as well as the change in the supreme command—were blamed on the "court," a euphemism for Alexandra and Rasputin. Factories went on strike on September 17, 1915; the tram stopped in protest. "The feeling against the emperor and Goremykin is very bitter." Rumors abounded of a "revolution as a pretext for separate peace, Rasputin, assassination of Goremykin, etc., ..."[29]

Moscow remained tense for several weeks. General Spiridovich was amazed at the mood when he visited there in late October 1915. After the healthy attitudes of the front he discerned an "atmosphere of intrigue." "It seemed everyone and everything was aligned against the government. The people of Moscow really seemed to hate Alexandra Fedorovna, Anna Vyrubova and Rasputin." Spiridovich was alarmed to see that this anger was beginning to include Nicholas. Samarin was still "loved by the Moscow nobility, admired by the merchants and known to all Muscovites in the best way." The following month, Princess Paley noted that Samarin's disgrace made the nobility of Moscow a "hotbed of revolution." Samarin continued to serve Nicholas. More than a year later, the governor of Moscow wrote the prime minister that Samarin and his circle were again trying to rally the Moscow nobility to the tsar. But in his opinion the faith that Nicholas and Alexandra still showed in Rasputin were ruining these efforts.[30]

The entire Russian empire was indignant. The lessons of August and September

1915 appeared clear: Rasputin and his "gang" could do whatever they liked—
proclaim a saint, topple a minister, dismiss a supreme commander—anything!
Nicholas seemed to be their willing tool. With this came another devastating
development: the collapse of a sense of authority and an end to the feeling of
order, which is basic to a monarchy.

Knowledgeable Russians realized that Nicholas was more than an accomplice.
Giving Varnava secret permission to do what the Synod denied was shocking:
The emperor was sowing confusion within his own system. For the first time
the entire nation saw what only a few once knew. Nicholas possessed a "satanic
talent" for discerning the nation's "feelings on the issues of the day and then
going against those feelings with a sort of nasty joy."[31]

The damage worried thoughtful conservatives. The Russian Orthodox Church
had been a rock of authority for hundreds of years. Priests and bishops, monks
and nuns were beginning to turn against Nicholas in large numbers in the fall
of 1915. "All of Russia is talking about this [irregular canonization of John
Maximovich]," a member of the royal family fearfully confided to his diary.
"The mood everywhere is quite excited, and we will not have to wait long for
the nation to ask: either we or him [Varnava]." Grand Duke Andrew Vladimirovich was pessimistic; he knew that the end of the episode "will be bad."
"Priests are talking to the people in all the churches and saying such things as
I dare whisper only while dreaming."[32]

16
Rasputin and the Homosexual Prince

Michael Andronnikov was a notorious homosexual. His father was Armenian, the scion of an ancient Cahetian family. His mother was of German descent. Michael was born in 1875 and grew up on the family estate in Livonia. The boy enrolled in the Page Corps, but sickness forced him to resign just before graduation. Andronnikov entered state service the following year, in 1896. He was a poor worker and by 1900 still occupied the lowest of the bureaucracy's 14 ranks. High absenteeism brought a discharge in 1914. Michael managed to be assigned to the director of the Holy Synod as an "official on special assignment." This gave him the right to wear a civil servant's uniform, and attend receptions and social functions—but he received no salary.[1]

Andronnikov had no interest in a state career. He wanted to be a wealthy, powerful man. Beginning with little more than the title of prince, he was determined to become a manipulator. Such people moved in a world few Russians knew existed, a shadowy realm of bribes and illicit contracts, a place where fortunes were made and lost—and made again. Such a career would not come easily. If it could be had at all, it would be the product of great daring and effort.

Andronnikov's cousin, the Princess Dzhambakurian-Orbelian, presented him at court just before 1905. Andronnikov proceeded to take the capital by storm. He carefully monitored developments in government and high society. He visited ministers and chatted with them about their work. The prince with the large briefcase was soon bringing news of one office to another; he was clearly a "man in the know." Andronnikov also cultivated second-echelon officials, getting their cooperation by hinting that he was close to the "boss."

Andronnikov convinced many newly promoted officials that he was responsible for their successes. He did this by cultivating St. Petersburg's messenger boys. The prince lured these lads to his apartment, plied them with food and drink—perhaps a bit of sex—and encouraged them to take a nap. Going through their bags, he often guessed an envelope's contents from its address, the sender, the offices involved, current gossip, etc. Andronnikov wired congratulations to men whom he suspected were being promoted. He then visited his new "friends," intimating he was responsible for their good fortune. Andronnikov presented fine icons to the gentlemen; their wives received candy and flowers. Andronnikov was soon marked as an influential man, someone to please and cultivate.[2]

Andronnikov affected idealism if questioned about his interests. "I have no official post," he told Mosolov. "I might call myself an aide-de-camp to the Almighty," the prince chirped, warming to his theme. "In that capacity I have to know everything that is going on in St. Petersburg, that is the only way I have of showing the love I have for my country. I seek no other function, I follow Him Who makes justice reign or restores its reign when necessary."

The mask fell in 1917 when Andronnikov was dragged before the Extraordinary Investigatory Commission.

"I am a person," the prince began on that occasion, "a citizen who wants to be of greater usefulness." He ended by admitting that his real profession was "visiting ministers." His famous briefcase contained nothing but old newspapers, but a secret cabinet in his flat held records of dealings with hundreds of associates.[3]

Andronnikov took bribes for endorsing petitions, obtaining oil permits, expediting appraisals of property-securing loans, and performing other favors. During the war he secured promotions and arranged desirable transfers. The prince had manganese mines in the Caucasus. Later he was interested in state lands in Bukhara and Khiva that were irrigated at government expense and ready for cotton farming. Agriculture Minister Alexander Naumov learned that Andronnikov was obtaining control over the Khiva project through a joint-stock operation. Naumov was amazed that a leading official in his own bureau supported the application. With all his authority Naumov was just barely able to defeat the scheme.[4]

Andronnikov lived in the moderately fashionable Belvue Hotel for 18 years, in a suite that rented for 100 rubles per month. He then moved into an enormous apartment on the corner of Fontanka and Troitskaya Boulevards. The prince received church and society leaders in the parlor while gay parties raged in other rooms. Officers and students made themselves at home; "they ate, drank and slept two to a bed," a valet recalled. Andronnikov had his choice of lovers, escorting the prize to the bathroom or his bed. "I believe the prince had more than a thousand young men here during my two years of service," the former servant continued. Andronnikov also liked street boys. Some were amazingly dirty; the prince enjoyed bathing them. But his attachment to them lasted only a few hours.[5]

Andronnikov was devout; he was renowned for charity and having a sympathetic ear. Young men sought his counsel. After intense discussions the prince often brought men to his "chapel," a corner partitioned from the bedroom and furnished with icons, candles, and places to kneel. From here many a fellow ended in the bed. The prince's apartment was "off limits" for entire military academies. Yet the students still came.[6]

The prince spent money at a breathtaking clip. Rent on his new apartment was 600 rubles per month. Most meals included a guest—often more than one. Those who packed the flat were not bothered if the host was absent. The wine still flowed. A hundred bottles from the English Cellar barely lasted two weeks. Fruit came by the case; snack trays offered the costliest caviar, sturgeon, and sausages. At one point a servant was bringing Andronnikov 1,000 rubles daily from Putilov's Bank. After his downfall Andronnikov claimed he still had "several thousands" in the bank. On the other hand, he admitted "I really don't have capital. The tens of thousands I command are from bank credits." Money went through Andronnikov's hands, and he often had no funds. At times such friends as Beletsky "helped out."

Andronnikov had no political philosophy. Putilov recalled the "most liberal and conservative ideas swam about" in the prince's head. He took his thoughts from different people, fashioning a whole without sensing contradictions. Andronnikov expressed a certain idea one moment, a different one minutes later, yet a third in a few hours. The prince judged ideas in terms of his relations with the people who offered them; if they fell out of favor the ideas were discredited too.[7]

Rasputin introduced himself to Andronnikov in early 1914. The prince inquired repeatedly about Grigory's health after Guseva's attempt on his life. Rasputin answered each telegram. Andronnikov was struck at how sick Grigory continued to be several weeks after returning to Petrograd. Andronnikov met Anna Vyrubova at this time. Varnava's clash with the Holy Synod brought the prince into closer contact with the "Rasputin gang." The bishop was "very sick at that time," the prince later testified, "and stayed with me because he was in no condition to leave." "The whole herd moved in, and I was forced to feed and water them—and to doctor Varnava." Andronnikov was in legal difficulty when the bishop was discovered three weeks later. Varnava did not have the papers needed to stay in the capital. The authorities moved to expel Andronnikov. The prince managed to remain in Petrograd only by activating every source of influence at his command.[8]

Stephen Beletsky was another important member of the "Rasputin gang." He was a classic example of a good person falling victim to base instincts. Stephen Petrovich Beletsky was born in the Ukraine in 1873. He overcame his lower-class background through ability and an appetite for hard work. At the age of 21, Stephen was police captain of Kiev province. In 1911 he became assistant-minister of internal affairs. The man who held this position directed the empire's police. Beletsky fought the revolutionaries by infiltrating provocateurs into their organizations. These agents encouraged their comrades to engage in terrorist acts. The police then arrested the revolutionaries as criminals. Officials who opposed this policy argued that the government should stand for law, not encourage crime. Among these critics was Vladimir Dzhunkovsky, an ambitious young aristocrat who replaced Beletsky in January 1913. Beletsky took the blow personally. To him it seemed that a "courtier" was replacing a "man of the people."[9]

The tsar's welfare system cushioned a "retired" official's fall from power with an ornamental promotion. Accordingly Beletsky was appointed to the Senate. But empty honors had slight appeal for Stephen Petrovich. "Strong blood flowed in his veins and he sought activity," Andronnikov recalled. "He went to everyone seeking something to do." People had always spoken well of Beletsky. Kokovtsov characterized him as a "good worker, a human, energetic, good person." Shavelsky spoke of his "inner order and nobility which harmonized well with his great efficiency and seriousness." Friends now saw distressing changes. Stephen's "moral relationship" to people was different; he became "untruthful and false." Observers remarked on Beletsky's "buttery face and yellow hands" and that he spoke in an "ingratiating manner." The death of his oldest son in April 1915 was another blow. Beletsky was determined to be a success again. Virtually no price was too high to reach this goal.[10]

Beletsky met Rasputin at Andronnikov's apartment in late 1914. Beletsky had been Grigory's enemy; he had shared police information with enemies of the starets. Ambition now dictated new alliances. Beletsky asked for Rasputin's help in regaining power. Stephen Petrovich certainly knew how to pacify the starets: He pointed out that Grigory was safe when he headed the police. The "mistakes"—Guseva, the report on the Yar, etc.—had occurred under Dzhunkovsky. Rasputin agreed it was a shame that the ministry of internal affairs was headed by such people. With Rasputin's support, Andronnikov and Beletsky could began to seek a replacement for Prince Shcherbatov.[11]

Alexis Nicholaevich Khvostov was the successful candidate. He had been eager to become minister of internal affairs since 1911, when the reception he gave Rasputin aroused Grigory's ire. Nicholas had various reasons for rejecting the ambitious young governor, but Alexis Nicholaevich blamed his bad luck entirely on his encounter with Rasputin. Khvostov was determined to have the starets on his side when the next opportunity appeared. In 1915 Khvostov learned that Andronnikov was an influential man whose contacts included Rasputin. Khvostov approached the prince and proposed an alliance.

Andronnikov thought that Khvostov was an ideal candidate for minister of the interior. Although Nicholas passed over Khvostov for promotion in 1911, the tsar was interested in the young man and followed his later career. Business interests also demanded an understanding with Alexis Nicholaevich. Khvostov led a group in the Duma that blamed Russia's economic problems on German capital. Khvostov gave a fiery speech on the subject on August 3, 1915. He promised to focus next upon German interests in Russia's electrical industry. It so happened that Andronnikov was an investor in the Electrical Society of 1886, a large German company. When the war began, the prince issued brochures claiming the ownership was now Swiss. This pacified critics, but Andronnikov was anxious to avoid further controversy. He saw that an alliance with Khvostov was one way to control him.[12]

Andronnikov realized that Nicholas was seeking a strong statesman, a "new Stolypin." The prince approached Anna Vyrubova, offering Khvostov and Beletsky as a team capable of giving strong leadership to the ministry of internal affairs. Andronnikov's timing was superb. "Shcherbatov is impossible to keep," Alexandra wrote of the incumbent minister on August 28, 1915, "better quick to change him." The next day: "Beloved, A[nna]. just saw And[ronnikov] & Khvostov & the latter made her an excellent impression." Alexandra admitted that Goremykin was against Khvostov, but she was more impressed with Vyrubova's opinion. "He is most devoted to you, spoke gently and well about our Friend [Rasputin] to her."[13]

Andronnikov and Khvostov pressed Vyrubova to arrange a meeting with Alexandra Fedorovna. They certainly knew how to accomplish this goal. "He [A. N. Khvostov] wants very much to see me, looks upon me as the one to the situation whilst you are away (told it Andronnikov) & wants to pour out his heart to me & tell me all his ideas."

Alexandra finally received A. N. Khvostov on September 17, 1915. The empress was gracious and a bit reserved. She chided Khvostov for his rudeness to Rasputin at Nizhnyi-Novgorod in 1911, expressing the hope that his "eyes had been opened" since then about "Father Grigory." "She added the tsar often recalled me," Khvostov noted, "and there would not be any objection to my appointment as minister of the interior if only Rasputin's security would rest with Beletsky."

Khvostov impressed the empress. She telegraphed her husband about him twice the day they met. The next morning Alexandra poured additional thoughts into a lengthy letter. Here was a "man, no petticoats—and then one who will not let anything touch us, and will do all in his power to stop the attacks upon our Friend." Khvostov was the strong leader they were seeking. He stood for autocracy and had a definite plan for making peace with the Duma; he was even thinking about such postwar problems as demobilization.

Nicholas received Khvostov and was also impressed. The tsar dismissed Shcherbatov on September 26, 1915. Dzhunkovsky had been assigned a military post the previous month. Khvostov and Beletsky were appointed to their positions. Goremykin advised against these changes, but he was ignored.[14] Guided by Prince Andronnikov, the troika[15] had scored an astounding victory, a victory more intricate and impressive than outsiders understood at the time.

*   *   *

The purge in the ministry of internal affairs disturbed many Russians. Varnava's defiant canonization of John Maximovich had rocked the nation earlier the same month, September 1915, creating the impression that no force could resist the power of the "Rasputin gang." Alexander Samarin, the fiercely anti-Rasputin leader of the Holy Synod, was fired on the same day as Shcherbatov. They and Dzhunkovsky were popular, and each was seen as an enemy of Rasputin and a martyr in the struggle to free Russia of his influence.

Stephen Beletsky was something of a silver lining on these dark clouds. Everyone agreed that he was knowledgeable and experienced. Some thought he was the "only one at the present time who might retrieve this situation."[16]

Rasputin was vacationing in Siberia as these changes unfolded, but the telegraph kept him abreast of developments. Alexandra apparently asked Grigory's opinion of Khvostov before receiving him, for on September 16 she wrote Nicholas that Rasputin "made us understand that *Khvostov* wld. be good."[17] This does not mean that Rasputin was the main force behind the troika's success. Grigory learned to agree with Alexandra if he saw that her mind was set. Rasputin might have tried to block Khvostov's appointment if he thought he could do so. Seeing that he was powerless, he agreed with the appointment and claimed partial credit for it—if only to bolster his image as a powerful man.

The troika had Rasputin to supper at Andronnikov's apartment on September 28, 1915, just after he returned from Siberia. It was a tense meeting at first. Grigory reminded Khvostov of their first encounter in 1911, claiming that he did not even have the money for a return fare to the capital. Khvostov was all apologies; he would have given Grigory some money had he known that the starets was short of cash. The mood brightened when the men sat down to dine, and they began to discuss "business terms." Rasputin needed the troika as much as it needed him. The ministry of internal affairs maintained Rasputin's security and also controlled censorship. Shcherbatov had been permissive and Grigory had been much attacked. Khvostov and Beletsky promised protection in both areas. Beletsky would also pay Rasputin 1,500 rubles per month from police funds. The triumverate hoped this would free Grigory from the need to take bribes, which in turn led to disreputable relationships.

Rasputin agreed to behave in a reasonable way in exchange for these favors. Andronnikov would act as liaison between Rasputin and the ministry of internal affairs. The four would dine periodically. Grievances could then be aired and mutual goals discussed. The party ended on a happy note. Tensions would surface within the alliance, but its beginning was as good as could be expected.[18]

The most realistic view of the arrangement was offered by Beletsky's wife. She realized that ambition consumed her husband; she did not know he had befriended Rasputin. Beletsky dreaded facing his wife with the news. He told her of his return to power the day it was announced. "I cannot say the news surprised her,'' Beletsky later recalled. "[She saw] my tendency to trust people and be carried along. She understood the weakness and lack of balance in my character."

"Get out, plead sickness, even . . . ,'' she begged, "but resign before it's too late!'' Stephen Petrovich admitted he did not have the strength to do it. But he agreed to stay away from Rasputin's notorious flat. Future meetings would be arranged by Andronnikov.

Seeing that she could not detach her husband from his "friends,'' Olga Beletskaya offered a prediction. The affairs of the troika would become increasingly complex and Stephen Petrovich—willing or not—would soon be irretrievably committed to it. "My wife proved to be correct,'' Beletsky wrote in prison on June 24, 1917. Within a year, the Bolsheviks took Khvostov, Beletsky, and other ex-officials to Moscow to be shot.[19]

The troika assured Rasputin that he would reshape the Holy Synod. The four were soon discussing the best candidate for director. Gossip held that Sabler might be reappointed, especially since he had shed his Germanic surname in favor of "Desyatovsky,'' his wife's name. Rasputin was now opposed to Sabler, who had also moved—if belatedly—to combat Rasputin's influence in the Holy Synod. Sabler planned to fire Grigory's closest ally, Peter Damansky, and reduce the powers of other " Rasputinites'' such as Vasily Skvortsov and Peter Mudrolyubov. Sabler also persecuted some Russian monks at Mount Athos who held heretical notions about the meaning of God's name. Rasputin found these teachings attractive; he sympathized with the monks and was angry at their tormentors.

Rasputin became extremely agitated as he recalled these "misdeeds''; he shouted that he would in no way support Sabler's candidacy. Sly smiles were exchanged around the table; the troika had taken another step in advancing its candidate. Their man was Alexander Nicholaevich Volzhin.[20]

Volzhin was born in 1862 into an aristocratic family with 3,000 acres in Kursk province. He attended Moscow University and married Princess Olga Dolgorukaya, a member of a distinguished noble clan with estates in excess of 6,200 acres. Alexander entered state service and became governor of Khomsk province and then director of the ministry of the interior's department of general affairs. In short, his background was illustrious and his career reasonably distinguished. Volzhin was only a name to the public, and his appointment would not provoke indignation. Nicholas II knew Volzhin's sons from their service in the guards regiments. Volzhin hoped to become a minister. His love for church song and antiquities made him a plausible choice to lead the Holy Synod.[21]

Khvostov and Beletsky knew that Volzhin was "not prepared for this duty,'' but they could control him; so he was their choice. Nicholas wanted Goremykin to select the candidates; this would bolster his authority as prime minister. As it was, Andronnikov gave a list of "good men'' to Vyrubova. Alexandra insisted on evaluating the candidates, and Nicholas let her have her way. The empress wanted the new head of the Holy Synod to be a "man ready to have himself chopped to pieces for you," someone who would drive dissident bishops from the Synod and "think of his churches, clergy & convents & not of whom we receive." Rasputin was another important consideration. The Synod should be led by someone who "will stand up for our Friend." The search finally was narrowed to Alexander Volzhin.

"I received *Volzhin* with whom I talked for 3/4 of an hour," Alexandra wrote on October 8, 1915. He "made me a perfect impression"; he "seems the right man in the right place, very glad to work with energetic young Khvostov." Volzhin knew how to impress Alexandra Fedorovna: "In going away he asked me to bless him, wh. touched me very much—one sees he is full of best intentions & understands the needs of our church perfectly well." "God grant all his good intentions may be successful & he have the strength to bring them into life."[22]

The tsar's approval was the final step in getting Volzhin appointed. A.N. Khvostov broached the subject during a report at Stavka. Nicholas received Volzhin, was impressed with him and his plan to resolve the John Maximovich crisis. Volzhin thought that the controversy should die down and then the Holy Synod would approve the canonization and uncover John's relics for public veneration. Volzhin expressed a desire to meet Rasputin and enjoy his support. Volzhin truly did seem to be the "right man" at the right time. He was immediately appointed director general of the Holy Synod.[23]

The Russian public was numb from the controversies of September 1915 and showed little interest in Volzhin's selection. No one realized that this was a significant development. Even Rasputin must have been surprised to see how great his power in the Church would become within a matter of weeks.

17
Rasputin and the Homosexual Bishop

The metropolitan of Petrograd held the most prestigious throne in the Russian Church, followed by the metropolitans of Moscow and Kiev and the exarch of Georgia. Rasputin's dominion over the Church reached a high point in the fall of 1915, when an obscure bishop whom he had brought to prominence suddenly became metropolitan of Petrograd. This man was Pitirim, a renowned thief and homosexual. Pitirim's rise to power outraged the nation. It also solidified Grigory's grip on the Church. By the time Rasputin was assassinated in December 1916, Russians assumed—with only a degree of exaggeration—that their Church was very much under his control.

Pitirim was born Paul Oknov in Riga in 1858. His father was a distinguished priest at the cathedral, and Paul grew up in a cultivated, comfortable environment. His mother's influence was especially strong; Paul's final wish was to be buried next to her. He studied at Riga's gymnasium and the seminary at Kiev. Oknov became a monk under the name *Pitirim*. Church leaders in Russia were drawn from the monasteries, and Pitirim rapidly ascended the hierarchy as an educator. Pitirim became a vicar bishop at Chernigov in 1894; two years later he was made a full bishop at Tula.

Those who knew young Pitirim spoke of his "femininity," and his "large, thoughtful eyes bordered with eyelashes" and "marvellous black curls which fell right to his shoulders." This "very good-looking young man" was known for two characteristics: homosexuality and greed. Pitirim scandalized Tula by establishing a house for his lover, a lay brother. They plundered the bishop's estate and became quite wealthy. Just one property transfer netted 10,000 rubles.[1]

Pitirim was sent to Kursk as bishop in 1904. Pitirim engaged in a campaign of "petty fault-finding," which led his vicar bishop to suicide. But Pitirim suffered a setback at Kursk. He was interested in finding new saints, and laudation of a local holy man in 1896 had brought him bishop's rank at Tula. Pitirim tried to advance himself again in this way at Kursk. His celebrations in honor of "Saint" Joseph, a deceased bishop, were poorly organized. This angered Sabler, and he transferred Pitirim to the remote diocese of Vladikavkaz. Pitirim was an old friend of the Rasputin family, and he now turned to Grigory for help. In 1913 he was assigned to a better post as archbishop of Samara.[2]

Pitirim made a good first impression at Samara. He presented the city with an icon and worked to be an efficient pastor. On the sly he fostered his relationship with Rasputin. The local postmaster showed the governor a telegram that Pitirim had sent to Rasputin congratulating him on his name day. Pitirim also advanced the interests of the "Rasputin gang." A novice named Novoderzhkin arrived at Samara with a letter from Rasputin. The young man had been dismissed from his seminary; Grigory asked Pitirim to help him. The archbishop made Novoderzhkin a deacon, then a presbyter, and finally a priest at Samara's Iversky convent. This displaced a priest who had served for a decade in a position that his father had held for 30 years. Complaints followed and the Holy Synod demanded an explanation. Pitirim replied that Novoderzhkin was recommended "by a person who enjoyed the confidence of people in high places," and for this reason he had to be preferred.[3]

Rasputin was important to Pitirim when leadership of the Georgian Church became vacant in 1914. The presiding bishop there was known as "exarch," the equivalent of a metropolitan. When the exarch died, Nicholas considered Pitirim for the post. Sabler tried to prevent this by giving the tsar a list of qualified candidates. Nicholas studied the paper and then wrote "Pitirim" at the top. Gossips concluded that Pitirim's advancement was due to Rasputin's support. The tsar and his wife had not even met Pitirim at the time. An introduction came when they visited the Caucasus later that year. Nicholas and his entourage were impressed with Pitirim's piety, learning, and manners. The tsar told Alexandra he was interested in Pitirim for the still more important position of metropolitan of Petrograd.[4]

The death of Metropolitan Flavian of Kiev in November 1915 opened Pitirim's path to Petrograd. Pitirim's advancement would involve some "bishop's leapfrog" : Vladimir could be demoted to Kiev (the third most prestigious church office), and Pitirim could come from Georgia to the capital! No Russian metropolitan had ever been demoted. Vladimir's only offense had been to oppose Rasputin. This provoked indignation from both Alexandra and Grigory, who had long been urging Nicholas to punish the "offender."

The day after Flavian died, Alexandra wrote to her husband suggesting the transfers of Vladimir and Pitirim. Nicholas agreed and Vladimir was assigned to Kiev. Synod Director Volzhin was appalled to think that Pitirim might follow Vladimir at Petrograd. He forwarded a report on Pitirim's ethics and personal life to the tsar. Nicholas insisted on Pitirim. Not one of the 13 bishops on the

Holy Synod that fall approved of Pitirim or the way he joined their group. Tension also surrounded Pitirim at the Alexander Nevsky Monastery, the metropolitan's official headquarters and residence. The monks here admired Vladimir and were in no mood for an intruder.[5]

Political figures also disliked Pitirim. Some displayed open contempt. It was the custom for leading officials to attend services at St. Isaac's Cathedral on certain festival days. The minister of agriculture refused to do this because the metropolitan officiated. Naumov had also snubbed Pitirim in earlier years when both were in Samara—Naumov as governor and Pitirim as archbishop.

Michael Rodzyanko predictably offered the sharpest reaction. The new metropolitan came to pay his respects to the Duma's president. Rodzyanko was cold and Pitirim felt ill at ease. The conversation drifted to change in the Church.

"Reform is absolutely necessary," Rodzyanko agreed. "If you, your eminence, wish to earn the gratitude of the Russian people, you must spare no effort to purify the Orthodox Church. . . . Rasputin and men like him must be expelled, and your own name cleared from the opprobrium of being looked upon as a nominee of Rasputin."

"Who told you that?" Pitirim replied, turning pale. He asked Rodzyanko if he had ever spoken to Nicholas about Rasputin.

"Yes, many a time," the president conceded. "As for you, eminence, your very looks betray you."[6]

Pitirim was determined to be a good leader. He toured his diocese, giving speeches and celebrating Liturgies. Pitirim often visited military hospitals. He broke with the traditional routine of Synod members. They showed little initiative, limiting themselves to activities that the director suggested. Pitirim displayed energy and initiative. He advocated higher pay for parish priests, and one of his commissions raised the pensions of retired clergy. Pitirim hoped to codify church law, and streamline the Synod courts and their administration. He was the only member of the Synod's governing council who favored an "Orthodox offensive" in Western Europe. Pitirim wanted the Russian Orthodox Church to establish missionary dioceses in Western Europe and translate key works into those languages. Plans were fixed in 1917 to build a cathedral in London that spring. But the revolution intervened to bring these plans, and others, to ruin.[7]

Despite his efforts Pitirim was not popular. His enemies insisted that he was "entirely colorless and undistinguished," was "neither learned or pious," and possessed of "no gifts or special activity." He "celebrated Mass in a very theatrical way," Shavelsky continues, "no one on the staff at Tsarskoe Selo liked it." Pitirim's voice and movements were artificial. His beard was wispy, he did not look people in the eye, and his speech was ingratiating. At 58 he seemed to be an old man. "He was short and moved about in a singular way, . . . his figure was pitiful rather than authoritative and certainly uncongenial." Pitirim "was always unsure of himself," he "seemed to fear something and to live under the threat of some grief or ordeal." Zhevakov adds that his friend "expended great effort to seem calm, he spoke with difficulty because of torturous throat spasms."

"I never had friends," Pitirim lamented to Zhevakov, "I was never able to blend with those around me. I didn't belong anywhere, no one ever understood me. The environment is a tyrant, she demands sacrifices I can't give without betraying vows I made to God."[8]

Some loved Pitirim. He had a handsome companion in Ivan Osipenko. Pitirim claimed that the young man was his illegitimate son—or that he had raised Ivan from childhood. Osipenko's father was actually a hearty Cossack; as a student Ivan studied church song. Pitirim and Ivan Osipenko probably met at Kursk when Pitirim arrived there as bishop in 1904. Ivan Zinovich Osipenko became Pitirim's secretary in 1912. The young man was devoted to the bishop and tried to shield him from questionable people. But neither was familiar with Petrograd and each made mistakes. Osipenko was even more greedy than Pitirim. Beletsky—ever a judge of corruptable people—handed Osipenko 300 rubles at their first meeting, promising the same amount each month if he would accept Beletsky's advice. Beletsky got little for his money. Osipenko heightened the impression that the new metropolitan was a man of scandal and impropriety.[9]

Rasputin was Pitirim's friend and was delighted to hear that he was coming to the capital as metropolitan of Petrograd.

"Do you know Pitirim?" the starets asked Andronnikov.

"I don't," came the reply.

"Then you should go to see him," Grigory continued. "He's a very good fellow. He's one of us."[10]

Pitirim's feelings for Rasputin were complicated. He considered Grigory a friend. But he wanted to shake the image of being a "Rasputin man," and this made the metropolitan skittish in dealing with the starets. Osipenko was Grigory's constant companion, but Pitirim never went to Rasputin's apartment. When Grigory came to the Alexander Nevsky Monastery, the metropolitan acted as if they were engaged in some conspiracy. This amused A. N. Khvostov, and he arranged a test to see how the two would react if caught together.

Khvostov made an appointment with Pitirim at the monastery. He had Komissarov bring Rasputin there at that time. Pitirim was just telling the minister that he had no dealings with Grigory when he was told an "eminent Georgian"— Rasputin's code name—had arrived to see him. When Rasputin phoned or visited, Pitirim dropped what he was doing in favor of the starets, and he did so now. The metropolitan received Grigory in another room; they embraced, kissed, and addressed each other with the familiar "you." Pitirim then noticed a stranger.

"Who are you?" the metropolitan asked.

"I am Adjutant-General Komissarov," he replied.

Pitirim was stunned. Rasputin was amused to see Pitirim so upset at being seen with him. Grigory walked to the study, shouting at the top of his voice. There sat Khvostov, laughing. A sullen Pitirim eventually joined them. The metropolitan scurried to Tsarskoe Selo the next day to complain against General Komissarov.[11]

Despite such snags, Rasputin and Pitirim enjoyed a close (platonic) relationship. The starets was a frequent and welcome guest at the metropolitan's mansion, and his visits took on something of an official character. Rasputin built the "Salvation Church," put it under Pitirim's pastorate, and went there when the metropolitan celebrated the Liturgy. The priests on Pitirim's staff greeted Rasputin at the door and treated him as if he were a dignitary. Pitirim favored Grigory in other churches too. At the end of one service, he once waved Grigory to the front to be first after the royal family to kiss the cross. Rasputin was often present when the faithful presented their metropolitan-celebrant with ceremonial gifts of bread and salt.[12]

The rogue in Rasputin and Pitirim also brought them together. Pitirim surrounded himself with people whose only place in other monasteries would have been the confessional. He gave the Alexander Nevsky Monastery a new father superior, Filaret, a crude man expelled from another house for fighting with the novices. Filaret lived in the cloister with his mistress, who was also a friend of Rasputin. Contractors learned that Filaret expected a 10 percent kickback, and if they were slow in settling he abused them in public with vile language. It would have done no good to complain to Pitirim. He milked the cloister for 100,466 rubles in 1916 alone. Rumors held that he paid Rasputin 75,000 rubles for his post and other favors.[13]

Rasputin and Pitirim gleefully defiled the once-proud Nevsky Monastery. Gypsy musicians entered through the Church of St. Valdimir. Rasputin used a secret lane at the back. Alcohol flowed to the beat of tambourines and gypsy music. Mock processions weaved drunken paths through the cloister. Brother Afanasy fell afoul of one such cavalcade as he was locking up late one night.

"What are you doing here?" Osipenko screamed. "Spying on us? You won't be at the monastery any more tomorrow!"[14]

Pitirim charmed Nicholas and Alexandra. No metropolitan was ever closer to the royal family than Pitirim. Others visited Tsarskoe Selo twice or three times a year; Pitirim travelled there weekly. Alexandra enjoyed Pitirim's Liturgies and found him to be an engaging conversationalist. She also hoped that Pitirim would improve Rasputin's position. Nicholas and Alexandra pretended to ignore hostility to their "Friend"; in truth they regretted it. Pitirim saw this and praised Father Grigory. It was mutual. Rasputin knew that Pitirim was useful to him and supported the metropolitan whenever his name came up at Tsarskoe Selo. Alexandra Fedorovna was pleased at the relationship, and she hoped that Pitirim's "authority would paralyze the suspicion, blame and ill-will attached to Rasputin."[15]

Rasputin and Pitirim were interested in power, not reputations. Their goal was to control the Holy Synod *and* the Russian Orthodox Church. They weeded out their noisiest critics while installing their followers at every level from the capital to remote parishes and monasteries. This was an unprecedented power play and ultimately it failed. Grigory was murdered, the Old Regime fell, and the Church ousted the "Rasputin gang" from positions procured when their leader was alive. But the attempt, the dimensions of the plan, and its daring all form a remarkable chapter in the Russian past.

=18=
Rasputin—Master of the Russian Orthodox Church

Alexander Volzhin was not a successful leader of the Holy Synod. "It's difficult to be director general after Samarin," Volzhin admitted just after taking office. "Samarin was too direct. *Est modus in rebus!*" he added, quoting Horace on the point that, even in good things, temperance is a virtue.[1]

Volzhin's style of leadership was different. He tried to be a practical politician. The new director won Rasputin's friendship. He accepted Beletsky's advice on the John Maximovich controversy. Although Pitirim was the only Synod bishop to support Varnava, Volzhin settled the affair on his terms. The Synod withdraw its censure of Varnava and even gave new ground. Varnava actually took only the first step in recognizing John as a saint. Full proclamation of sainthood came the following June. The Synod dispatched Metropolitan Makary to Tobolsk for the solemn ritual. Anna Vyrubova and Lili Dehn also trekked to the "saint's" tomb. By telegram Grigory assured Nicholas that the "new-found Saint John Maximovich was gloriously proclaimed among us in Tobolsk. He is in glory in his beloved house and is not to be diminished." Varnava received the Order of Vladimir Second Class and was promoted to archbishop in October 1916.[2]

Volzhin accepted Beletsky's direction on another key matter: the need to advance men agreeable to the troika—Beletsky, A. N. Khvostov, and Andronnikov. Khvostov suggested that Nicholas Zaionchkovsky be made assistant-director of the Holy Synod. Volzhin endorsed the nomination. Zaionchkovsky was not a "Rasputin man." As a wealthy aristocrat and able official, he did not need Rasputin, though he was evasive when asked his opinion of the starets. Grigory had open supporters in Synod Treasurer N. V. Soloviev and Chief Secretary Peter Mudrolyubov. The latter was cunning and able, as well as a fine writer, but had a bad reputation. Rasputin and Pitirim fought to secure major promotions for Mudrolyubov before and after he entered the Synod. Each battle was a contest of strength and a victory for the "Rasputin gang."[3]

Father Vasily Skvortsov was another Rasputin ally at the Holy Synod. Skvortsov began his career as a missionary to the sects. He became a landowner and edited various journals and the *Bell,* a conservative church newspaper. Skvortsov attended the Tobolsk celebrations in honor of John Maximovich and published a series of articles praising the starets Grigory Rasputin.[4]

The "Rasputin gang" at the Holy Synod not only tended the master's wishes, but also spied for him and their allies. Soloviev kept Rasputin and Varnava informed of news and rumors. Soloviev's wife actually brought police reports to Grigory at Pokrovskoe. Natalya Prilezhaeva was another key "Rasputinite." She was Varnava's sister and wife of a minor Synod official, a simple but cunning woman with a large ear for important facts.[5] With these and others tending his interests, Rasputin gained a reputation for having a "friend" in every office, corner, and social gathering.

Thirteen bishops were Rasputin's "friends." At the top of the list were Metropolitans Pitirim, Makary of Moscow, and Alexis, the new exarch of Georgia. Isidor was the most unsavory member of the group. He was convicted of sodomy and other crimes in 1911, and was imprisoned at a monastery. Isidor was rehabilitated in 1916 and placed at the head of a monastery in the Tobolsk region. Varnava then made him vicar bishop. Isidor even rejoined his lover Flavian; the affair with this lay brother had caused Isidor humiliation five years before. Alexandra told her husband on October 1, 1916 that she spent "a quiet, peaceful evening 8 ½–10 ¼ with our Friend [Rasputin], Bishop Issidor—Bish. Melchizedek—talked so well & calmly—such a peaceful, harmonious *atmosphere.*" Beletsky confessed to disliking Isidor at first "because of his particular closeness to Rasputin and his contribution to Rasputin's behavior." "But now I am unable to condemn Isidor because . . . [u]nderstanding Rasputin's weakness, he loved Rasputin in his own way. The rest of us disliked Rasputin and were negative towards him, but for various reasons we tried to make him think we loved him."[6]

Rasputin's power at the top was reflected in lower levels of the Church. "Many important church leaders took him into account," Beletsky wrote, as did the "middle clerical ranks which sought—as human weakness often does—the benefit of his power." But not all of Rasputin's "friends" realized their goals. Abbot Anatoly hoped to become a vicar bishop though he was barely literate and could not name one Old Testament prophet. Anatoly knew Rasputin, calling him "a great ascetic sent down from on high for the salvation of sinful Petrograd." Not only was the abbot rejected for promotion, but also his qualifications to lead a monastery were ridiculed in the Duma.[7]

The rogue in Rasputin made him partial to other rogues. He was friendly to a peasant by the name of Vasily who solicited donations at the Kazan Cathedral. Vasily claimed to be building a church. He stood hatless and barefooted in a monk's garb displaying the insignia of the Union of the Russian People. Vasily passed out picture postcards of himself and a church that he claimed to have erected. The archbishop of Vasily's diocese advised the police that the beggar was an extortionist and should be stopped. "But he enjoyed Rasputin's protection," Beletsky noted, "hence we could not fulfill the archbishop's demand, even though [Vasily] was also down with the local police as a suspect in other crimes."[8]

Rasputin's power was also felt in the courts. The courts repeatedly found against a woman in a lawsuit with a prominent church. She repeatedly appeared at the ministry of justice, insisting that an official who tried to discourage her was "too young to know how these things go." An imperial order finally resolved the matter in the lady's favor. The woman explained that "she befriended Rasputin when he was poor and unknown; he remembered this and repeatedly helped her when she needed it."[9]

The Duma's anger over Rasputin's power exploded in November 1916. A priest-deputy warned that the "Orthodox Church is in danger: brothers, protect it!" A lay delegate saw in Rasputin and his followers a "frightening, gaping ulcer that threatens to infect the whole church organism." V. N. Lvov, who would head the Holy Synod under the Provisional Government, wondered if a "schism would not occur, a split of the hierarchy into two parts—one, composed of those who stand for the Most Holy Synod [voice from the Left: "For Rasputin!], and the other of those who [may withdraw and legally form another Church]."[10]

The government tried to keep this controversy out of the press, but editors ignored their restrictions, daring the tsar's officials to touch them. The newspapers "openly called Metropolitan Pitirim a Rasputinite, they spoke of his sympathies for the 'holy man.' " The conservative *New Times* was as indignant as any other paper. A leading article entitled "The Voice of the People" on December 2, 1916, lamented the fact that "laymen—ordinary Orthodox persons—have been forced to defend the Church" from its leaders.[11]

Monarchists were especially troubled. Vladimir Kokovtsov lamented the fact that the church leadership was "completely under the heel of the Rasputin clique." The ex-prime minister doubted that the religious forces in Russia could take much additional strain. Priests were underpaid, demoralized, and bitter over their treatment by the "authorities." Revolutionary propaganda was beginning to enter the seminaries; students there were impoverished and the socialist gospel struck resonant chords. "And to complete their perversion, agitators fan them into fury against the higher clergy by telling them of the Rasputin scandals!"[12]

People imagined that Rasputin and his allies were about to attack their enemies. The French ambassador reported a "lively agitation in the bosom of the Holy Synod" in February 1916. The "whole Rasputin gang rejoices exceedingly"— Pitirim, Varnava, and Isidor would soon announce the "elimination of all prelates, abbots and archimandrites who still refuse to bow the knee to the erotomaniac-mystic of Pokrovskoe." Lists of clergy to be dismissed or demoted were said to have been published; some would even be exiled "to monasteries in the depths of Siberia, from which there is no return."[13]

Rasputin and his "gang" did lash out at some enemies, but fitfully and with little energy. The list of people whom Grigory considered to be "enemies" suggests that for all his supposed power, he was insecure—paranoid, even. Rasputin was quite agitated over a certain Oleg, a barefoot "fool in Christ" who had just appeared at Tsarskoe Selo and was about to be presented to society at an eminent home. Rasputin had Oleg expelled from the capital. He also saw a rival in Father Mardary, a Serbian monk stranded by the war. Mardary was a teacher and a "hit" with prominent women who looked to him as a religious guide. Grigory had Pitirim assign Mardary to the Caucasus.[14]

Rasputin used the police against his enemies. Archbishop Anthony of Kharkov was expelled from the Holy Synod when the police found criticism of Grigory in his mail. Rasputin's influence was also felt in Irkutsk, nearly 3,000 miles east of Petrograd. The city was a dynamic place, boasting two daily newspapers plus a famous museum and theater. The people of Irkutsk particularly resented Grigory's interference in the Church. The stage was set for trouble then when the police intercepted a letter from Archbishop Innocent decrying Rasputin's influence. He was immediately "retired." Stormy demonstrations marked Innocent's departure—demonstrations that the authorities discouraged but chose not to prevent.

Rasputin was alert to his interests in Siberia and was involved in selecting a new bishop for Irkutsk. For a time, it seemed the post would go to Rasputin's friend John Vostorgov. Father John had hoped to become a vicar bishop in Moscow under Makary, but Pitirim feared an uproar. Irkutsk seemed an ideal assignment. Paganism was still strong in this region, and Vostorgov was a missionary and even served in Siberia in 1906. Just before his assignment was announced, Vyrubova came across a critical statement that Vostorgov once had submitted to a church commission investigating "Father Grigory."

"Vostorgov's done for now," Rasputin growled as he read the document. "He won't get a thing!" Vostorgov apologized for his indiscretion, and Beletsky even intervened on his behalf. The efforts were futile. No promotions were in store for John Vostorgov.[15]

Rasputin and his allies struck out at other churchmen. One of their sharpest critics was Vladimir Vostokov, a liberal idealist who edited *Responses to Life* while pastoring a large working-class church near Moscow. Father Vladimir often opposed Rasputin and Varnava. He published a petition from his parishioners attacking the Siberian starets. Metropolitan Makary closed *Responses* and assigned its editor to Kolomna. Hopefully Vostokov would now slide into obscurity. Then came the end of Alexander Samarin's term at the Holy Synod. Vostokov was Samarin's friend, and he prepared an address welcoming him back to Moscow. Alexandra was furious: "[T]hat horror *Vostokov* has sent [Samarin] a telegram in the name of his two *'flocks,' Moscou & Kolomna*—so the dear little *Makari* wrote to the [Synod] *Consistory* to insist upon a copy of *Vostokov's* telegram to *Samarin* & to know what gave him the right to forward such a telegr.—how good, if the little Metropolitan can get rid of *Vostokov*, its high time, he does endless harm."[16]

Makary demanded that Vostokov stop his attacks on Rasputin. When the priest refused he was charged with heresy. Such cases were normally pressed to the end. Proceedings against Vostokov were dropped as soon as he left Moscow, suggesting that their purpose was to drive him away. Bishop Andrew invited the priest to join him at Ufa, 700 miles east of Moscow. Andrew was a liberal on both social and religious matters, and he had been as troublesome for the authorities as Vostokov. Grigory, Pitirim, and Vyrubova wanted the Holy Synod to discipline Andrew and Vostokov, but Beletsky persuaded them that such a controversy would damage their interests. Even so Rasputin scored a victory. A priest lamented these events to his fellows, insisting the case put Moscow's clergy to shame.[17]

Andrew was remarkably bold in defying Rasputin. Most bishops took Samarin's downfall as a sign to not antagonize the starets. Only Synod members Vladimir, Serge, Arseny, and Shavelsky continued to oppose Rasputin and Pitirim. Arseny's office at the Alexander Nevsky Monastery was next to Pitirim's, but Arseny never visited his neighbor. Shavelsky presented his card when Pitirim arrived; otherwise he ignored the upstart. "Chief Chaplain Shavelsky puts on airs," Pitirim fumed, "but I'll wring his neck."[18]

*   *   *

Rasputin's reign in the Holy Synod blackened Volzhin's reputation. He became director by pledging to "consult" the empress and Rasputin. He did so at the outset. This practice encouraged people to think that Volzhin was commonplace—an "obscure, servile official." The truth was more complicated. If Volzhin had been servile, he would have survived by caving in to pressure from the Rasputin clique. Few realized that Volzhin took a stand against Grigory and his allies. A power struggle gripped the Synod under his leadership.[19]

Volzhin was supported by Zaionchkovsky and such key officials as Victor Yatskevich. Shavelsky claimed that the director "took the straight path: with facts in hand he denounced [Pitirim] before Nicholas." The "false metropolitan," by contrast, played a more subtle game. Pitirim was polite with Volzhin while undermining him with Rasputin.

Pitirim's camp had a different view. Prince Nicholas Zhevakov denied that he or Pitirim ever criticized the director with Nicholas or Alexandra. Zhevakov claimed that Volzhin was a "good person," but "limited" and *"insincere* in his work." "A. N. Volzhin lived in an atmosphere of lies," the prince continued. "[T]hey surrounded him and he absolutely did not believe in people." Nor did he probe into the problems and work of the Holy Synod. Alexandra Fedorovna also became a harsh critic of the Synod leader. Volzhin was barely in office six weeks when the empress warned her husband that *"Volzhin* will need a good deal of 'picking up' from you, he is weak & and frightened." A short while later, Alexandra decided that he was "too pompous" for his office "where simple, modest believing people are needed." At the end, the tsarina came to think that Volzhin was a "handsome man of the world" and "quite unfit for this place."[20]

Volzhin and Zaionchkovsky were replaced by Raev and Zhevakov, two of the oddest characters to taste power under Tsar Nicholas II.

Prince Nicholas Zhevakov was ugly; he had a hoarse voice and a head resembling a black radish. Shavelsky dismissed him as a "princelett" seeking a "rapid career." The prince was interested in the history and life of the Russian Orthodox Church. The intense, naive young man approached several new directors, hoping to secure a transfer from his secular bureau to the Holy Synod. He was rejected every time. Zhevakov met Rasputin when he was just beginning his career in the capital. Zhevakov admits that he was impressed with Grigory's spiritual gifts, but their paths then diverged. Zhevakov sought Grigory's support during the war, when leading positions suddenly opened to "friends" of the starets. Zhevakov also sought a scholar's image by publishing a *Life* of the newly canonized St. Ioasaf. This book plus a word from Rasputin brought Zhevakov to Alexandra's attention a few days after Alexander Volzhin took over the Holy Synod on September 30, 1915.

Zhevakov asked to see the empress: A vision told him to score a victory for the Russian army by bringing "an unwieldy but very holy icon" to the front. The idea appealed to Alexandra Fedorovna. "I am going to see *Zhevakha* tomorrow—to hear all about the Image," she wrote Nicholas on October 9, 1915. The empress heard that Zhevakov was "quite young, knows all about the Church questions, most loyal & religious"; she was already certain that "it would be good to draw him to the *Synod* as a worker." "*Zhevakha* is charming and we had a thorough talk about every thing," she bubbled on the following day. "[H]e knows all Church questions and the clergy and Bishops à fond, so he would be good as a help to *Volzhin*."[21]

Volzhin did not want Zhevakov's help. The prince was marked as a "Rasputin man" and Alexandra's pet. But the empress was quite taken with this aspiring young bureaucrat. The tsarina spent nearly two hours with Zhevakov at their first meeting and admitted that if they had met a few days earlier he—not Volzhin—would have been appointed to lead the Synod. Volzhin was appalled to hear that Zhevakov might replace Zaionchkovsky and, in several stormy meetings, made clear his disdain for the prince. This was a challenge to Rasputin, disputing his right to have his way in the Church, the one area in which he expected to reign undisturbed. Alexandra soon advised her husband that Rasputin "finds you ought to tell *Volzhin* you wish *Zhevakov* to be named his aide—he is well over 40, older than *Istomin,* whom *Samarin* took, knows the Church far better than *Volzhin* & can be of the very greatest help."[22]

Nicholas had just dazzled the nation with "bishops' leapfrog": Vladimir was demoted from Petrograd to Kiev, and Pitirim was advanced from Georgia to the capital. Contemptuous as they were of "public opinion," the royal couple decided to delay replacing Zaionchkovsky with Prince Zhevakov. Rasputin suggested that a number three position be created for Zhevakov—a "second assistant-director general." The Duma was about to go into session, and Volzhin protested that this would create difficulties for him before he had a grip on his office. Beletsky backed him. Nicholas decided that Zhevakov must wait.[23]

Not for long. Alexander Volzhin informed Nicholas on August 1, 1916 that "frail health" forced him to retire. Volzhin's foes were already seeking a suitable successor. Rasputin and Pitirim identified five candidates; Alexandra screened each man. One was the elderly General Shvedov; with no experience in church service, he had enlisted Rasputin's support last time, when Volzhin got the nod. Shvedov's reappearance shows how small the pool of talent had become for such an important office! Rasputin now favored Nicholas Kulchitsky, a 60-year-old physician who taught histology and served in the ministry of education. Pitirim found Kulchitsky satisfactory, but his name was finally withdrawn and the two power brokers settled upon Nicholas Raev. It was inconceivable that such a candidate—Raev was the principal of a girls' school—would have been viable even a year before. But even a harsh critic admitted that of the candidates available, Raev was the best.[24] The next step was for the man of the hour to meet Alexandra Fedorovna.

"Raiev made me an excellent impression" she wrote of their first meeting on June 27. Yet the empress continued her search. Then came Volzhin's resignation on August 1. Alexandra suggested that her husband "see *Raiev* to have a good talk with him and see whether he suits you—I believe that he with *Zhevakov* as aid wid. really be Godsend for the Church. . . . The other candidates I find quite unfit and knowing next to nothing about the church."

Nicholas made Raev director general of the Holy Synod on August 30, 1916. But the tsar still admired Zaionchkovsky, who administered the Synod in the midst of these changes, and planned to keep him in office. This displeased Rasputin who insisted that Zhevakov take the position. Nicholas revived the earlier idea of making Zhevakov a "second assistant." This pleased no one. Raev did not want Zaionchkovsky on his staff, while the Duma was incensed to see a sinecure suggested for a notorious "Rasputinite." Zaionchkovsky was "promoted" to the senate, and Zhevakov assumed his position on September 30, 1916. Volzhin was "advanced" to the state council.[25]

Nicholas Raev's background was reasonably distinguished. His father was a metropolitan of St. Petersburg who advanced Pitirim's career by making him the seminary's rector. Young Raev also cultivated Pitirim. But Nicholas did not choose a church career. He entered service in the ministry of education and then moved to the state council; he was a member of several state commissions during the war. Raev was 60 when he met Alexandra; he wore a wig and was considered comical. His 30-year-old wife was beautiful and well educated; her dowry also included a 2,500-acre estate. Alexandra heard that Raev was "an excellent man, knowing the Church by heart since his childhood." The empress jarred her husband's memory of the candidate by writing: "[Y]ou probably know him—has the *ladies high school* under him, and when there were [disorders] in all the schools and universities [during 1905], his girls behaved beautifully." Rasputin's business manager also knew Raev. Simanovich organized the Scientific-Commercial Society, with Raev as its president. "Despite the impressive name, this was an ordinary card club where high-stakes playing went on day and night."[26]

The Synod purge greatly advanced Rasputin's power in the Russian Orthodox Church. Pitirim and Zhevakov were old friends of Rasputin, and they continued to enjoy his support. Raev was not Rasputin's first choice as director, but they easily came to terms. Rasputin "spoke with *Raiev* over an hour," Alexandra wrote a month after he took office, "says he is a real God's send, & spoke so well about all Church questions & in such a *spiritual* way." Raev also learned how to manipulate the empress. "Had *Raiev* for nearly an hour" she wrote, "interesting & understanding so well with all the necessary questions." Twelve days later, Alexandra noted in a chronicle of her recent activities: "*Raiev* (good talk). . . ."[27]

But the struggles in the Synod diminished the victor's prize. The Synod was so divided and politicized by September 1916 that "misunderstandings and conflicts brought normal work to a halt." Zhevakov presented himself and his friends as victims; he insisted that historians did not treat them fairly. Zhevakov found the much-maligned Raev to be "gentle," "shy," and "kind"; he recalled their stimulating discussions over a host of issues. Zhevakov claimed that Raev's primary objective was to improve conditions of the village clergy. The prince also praised Pitirim for not striking back against his enemies; Zhevakov regretted that the "Synod opposed N. P. Raev and me simply because we were friends of Metropolitan Pitirim, and the Synod still regarded him with extreme displeasure." The atmosphere reeked of "carbon monoxide"; the intrigue created difficult conditions and prevented fruitful beginnings.[28]

At least the "Rasputinites" celebrated their power. The Synod decided to present Alexandra an icon and a tribute for her work with the wounded. The anti-Rasputin members had no enthusiasm for the demonstration, but they did not dare oppose it. So the governing board gathered at the Alexander Palace on September 25, 1916. Pitirim was obviously anxious to please Alexandra; Raev's behavior "made the eyes hurt." The empress seemed bewildered; she uttered a few stilted phrases, then bade each visitor farewell. Shavelsky was lost in thought, asking himself, "Why did we come?"

A mishap occurred at the end. Bishop Michael understood that a person should withdraw without turning his back to Her Majesty. He did his best with this difficult maneuver, but bumped into a pedestal with a costly vase. The vessel shattered. "This accident left the superstitious empress in a depressed mood."[29]

19

The Troika Shatters

Rasputin's behavior threatened his usefulness to the troika. Beletsky put Grigory on a subsidy of 1,500 rubles per month, thinking that a generous allowance would keep him from shady business deals. Beletsky hoped to keep Rasputin's name out of the news, especially since the Duma would go back into session on November 1, 1915. The triumverate saw the need for an Okhrana officer to oversee "Father Grigory's" daily routine. Khvostov, Beletsky and Andronnikov sought a man who was "experienced and worldly, capable—considering Rasputin's personality—of handling all sorts of difficult, unpredictable situations."[1]

Michael Komissarov was selected for this assignment. At the time, he was a 45-year-old colonel in line for the next important police promotion. Komissarov was experienced and able, but he had a checkered past. Rumors held that he misappropriated police funds for personal use. Komissarov once received 10,000 rubles for inciting anti-Jewish riots. Stolypin did not like him. But even critics admitted that Komissarov was loyal to those who advanced his career, and this was a quality that Beletsky valued in a subordinate. Komissarov's wife played a role in his advancement. She was anxious to see her husband get ahead and for health reasons had to leave Vyatka, their current assignment. Madame Komissarov pressed Beletsky for the needed promotion. She also met and charmed Rasputin. Grigory liked Komissarov and his wife from the moment they met.[2]

Komissarov quickly adjusted to Rasputin's routine. He arrived early each day, sometimes before Grigory. Komissarov listened to Rasputin's end of the conversation when Anna Vyrubova called at 10 A.M. noting things that would be of interest to Khvostov and Beletsky. Komissarov also used Rasputin to relay information that he wanted the gullible woman to bring to court. Komissarov then talked with Grigory, stressing "themes, considerations and projects of interest to us," while assuring Rasputin that the troika was devoted to him and the royal family. Komissarov noted places and people Grigory should avoid. Rasputin then received petitioners of the day. He handed many of these requests to Komissarov who forwarded them with his daily report to his superiors. "Komissarov joked that Rasputin and he settled affairs of state and made needed changes in the cabinet." Grigory and his household soon trusted their guest. Komissarov was blunt and unpretentious—exactly the type of official who would appeal to Father Grigory. Early on, one of Rasputin's discourses annoyed the colonel and he showed it. "Cut the God stuff, Grigory," he snapped, "talk straight and make sense." "Rasputin always respected the direct approach," the British historian de Jonge notes, "and had more than a little scorn for anyone fool enough to be taken in by him."[3]

It was not easy to supervise Rasputin. He knew his life was in danger and he wanted protection; in edgy moments he invited his guards to tea. But Grigory knew that these agents also spied upon him and realized that Komissarov's goal was to make him behave. At times the rebel in Rasputin gained the upper hand. He enjoyed commandeering automobiles from state agencies. Rasputin and his friends would jump into a car and pull away, laughing as the detectives scratched their heads. When Beletsky stationed a car on the street, Rasputin searched for a still faster vehicle.

Komissarov sometimes accompanied Rasputin when he went out. On one occasion, Rasputin was drunk at the Tsarskoe Selo railway station and began to stroll on the platform. Komissarov argued that the empress would be upset if Grigory was seen in such a condition. "Rasputin's reaction was that of a drunk who kicks against authority because when sober he has to address that authority with deference," de Jonge notes of this episode. Rasputin cursed the tsarina in terms so vile as to shock even the worldly Komissarov. He shook Grigory and told him the next time that happened would be the last.[4]

Rasputin enjoyed probing his relationship with Khvostov and Beletsky. Grigory was offended to hear that Khvostov denied knowing him, so he began calling "potbelly" both at his office and home. Such calls were screened and deflected, but one evening during a social gathering, an Okhrana officer not aware of procedure loudly informed Khvostov that "Grigory Efimovich" was calling on "pressing business." Madame Khvostov knew that name, and she was shocked. The woman was confined to a wheelchair. She was a good wife, proud of her husband, and tended him to the point of self-neglect—but this was too much!

Rasputin also called Beletsky, and one day his wife answered the phone. Grigory invited the couple to tea. Madame Beletsky frostily declined, pleading poor health and work at a military hospital that the ministry sponsored. In the next three days, five women seeking work arrived there with notes from Rasputin. Mmes. Khvostov and Beletsky were furious, and their husbands made Rasputin realize that future calls must be addressed only to Beletsky or Prince Andron-nikov.[5]

Greed and ambition soon caused the troika to unravel. Andronnikov was the first to fall. The prince entered into "business deals" with Grigory; Rasputin believed that Andronnikov cheated him. After a stormy argument, Rasputin told Beletsky that he would not reappear at Andronnikov's apartment. Beletsky rented a "conspiratorial flat" on Italian Street for future meetings.[6]

By this time Khvostov was trying to persuade Beletsky that they no longer needed Rasputin. After a few more days Khvostov suggested that Beletsky have Grigory murdered. When the Extraordinary Commission investigated Khvostov in 1917, he claimed that he was motivated by a warm, if excessive, devotion to the royal family. The episode that supposedly turned Khvostov against the starets concerned Olga, the tsar's oldest daughter.

A. N. Khvostov had the impression that Olga did not care for Rasputin. Grigory certainly subjected her to scurrilous talk. Police reports showed that Grigory regaled visitors to the capital with tales of sexual relations with Alexandra and her oldest daughter.

"Mama loves me," he once bellowed, "but with her daughter Olga, I . . . [Rasputin was making obscene gestures]."

Khvostov learned one day that Rasputin was actually in the midst of such a tale. "Do you want me to get Olga here?" he shouted at one doubter. "She's in Petrograd, she'll come to me," he claimed as he reached for the telephone.

"Olga" appeared; "Olga" was arrested. She proved to be one of Grigory's friends, a prostitute whose fur coat suggested royalty. This charade was sufficient to impress the provincial rubes. Khvostov swore the "incident convinced me that to save the motherland Rasputin had to disappear."[7]

Khvostov almost certainly had additional reasons for turning on Rasputin. His rapport with Nicholas convinced Khvostov that he did not need anyone else. Khvostov knew how to "handle" his master; he stressed material that Nicholas found interesting and reassuring. Khvostov noticed the emperor relished disa-greement; it suggested that the young man was honest and capable of bold leadership. Nicholas soon awarded Khvostov the Order of Anna First Class.

Early success fed Khvostov's ambition. Although he enjoyed only five months of power, Khvostov moved to weed out some officials in favor of men who (hopefully) would follow his leadership. A. N. Khvostov's ultimate ambition was to replace Goremykin as prime minister and to emerge as the tsar's "strong right arm." Khvostov believed that he could reconcile throne and Duma, and then manipulate the 1917 elections to produce a more conservative group of legislators. Nicholas and Alexandra had similar dreams. For years they had been seeking a "new Witte," a "second Stolypin"—but a fresh face, someone who would not injure their pride. Khvostov's plan might have worked had he moved cautiously, showed more principle, and not fallen afoul of Grigory Rasputin.[8]

Grigory angered Khvostov by refusing to support him as chairman of the council of ministers. Grigory liked Goremykin and thought he should continue as prime minister for a time. By late 1915 Nicholas wanted a younger man in the office, someone who would work with the Duma. To the tsar it seemed that his choice was between A. N. Khvostov and Boris Sturmer. Khvostov was supposedly Rasputin's ally, but the men shared no warmth or trust. Sturmer, by contrast, promised to fulfill all of Rasputin's "requests." Sturmer also expressed his esteem for Grigory to the empress. Rasputin felt that Nicholas could find a better candidate than Sturmer to head the government. but confronted with this choice, he thought a "senior fellow is needed on top." Sturmer's appointment was announced on January 20, 1916. Khvostov's anger deepened with the news that Rasputin and his friends laughed at him, "saying 'potbelly wants a lot!' "[9]

Khvostov suggested that Grigory tour some famous north Russian monasteries while the Duma was in session. Khvostov believed the Duma would take Rasputin's disappearance as a sign that his power had declined. Even Vyrubova and Varnava thought the plan was in Grigory's interests. Such a trip would prove that Rasputin was a holy man devoted to the religious life. Grigory agreed for an 8,000-ruble bribe, plus Khvostov's promise to make a supporter governor of Tobolsk. Khvostov planned to have Grigory murdered on the trip. But Rasputin was only having fun at "potbelly's" expense. Grigory took what was promised, then breezily announced that he had changed his mind. Khvostov was not discouraged. He simply admitted he must take stronger, more direct action to get Rasputin out of the way.[10]

Khvostov first asked Komissarov to murder Rasputin in late January 1916. The minister offered his subordinate 200,000 rubles plus expenses in hiring collaborators. Khvostov showed Komissarov the money, taking it from the ministry's safe. Komissarov replied that he and his men would do this out of duty, not for a bribe—if they did it. The request actually angered Komissarov; it offended the code of the Okhrana. He turned to Beletsky for advice.

Beletsky was in a difficult position. Khvostov tried to win his support by assuring him that higher office and rewards were also in store for him if Khvostov became prime minister. Yet Khvostov must have lacked confidence in Beletsky if he turned to Komissarov with this plot. Beletsky shared Komissarov's reservations. Beletsky decided the best way to protect Komissarov and his own interests was to approach Khvostov and ask to be included in his plans. Khvostov agreed, but Beletsky and Komissarov still faced unpleasant alternatives. If they tried to expose their superior, he would deny everything; they had no proof of his guilt. If they murdered Rasputin, Khvostov could turn on them, professing outrage that top policemen could engage in such a criminal act. So Beletsky and Komissarov stalled. They agreed to kill Rasputin but postponed action by presenting Khvostov with various plans, hoping the course of events would rescue them from their situation.[11]

Khvostov took an active part in plotting Rasputin's murder. Even small details thrilled him, and he expressed a desire to participate in the deed. Khvostov suggested strangling Grigory in a car and packing the body in snow near the seashore where it would be carried out to sea. Beletsky wanted to poison Rasputin's madeira. Komissarov was asked to study poisons. He made his report in late January 1916. Komissarov lectured "like a professor" on potions, describing the characteristics and traces of each. Khvostov was in ecstasy. Komissarov finally tried one brew on Grigory's cats. He described how the animals thrashed about and expired in deep agony. Khvostov was so pleased that he had Komissarov repeat the tale several times. Rasputin was furious—and he blamed the wrong person. "That Andronnikov killed my cats!" he shouted at the pitiful scene. Rasputin had the prince exiled to Ryazan for the crime.[12]

Khvostov soon realized that Beletsky and Komissarov did not intend to kill Rasputin. This drove the minister to his own double game. He continued to talk murder with his colleagues, while turning to others for action. Khvostov finally approached Iliodor through Boris Rzhevsky, a Red Cross official who had embezzled funds from his organization. Rzhevsky travelled to Norway and enlisted Iliodor's support. Beletsky got wind of the plot and had Rzhevsky arrested at the customs station as he returned on February 7, 1916. Investigation of Rzhevsky gave Beletsky evidence of Khvostov's guilt. Petrograd now buzzed with the news that a high official was plotting to kill Rasputin. Grigory learned of Khvostov's involvement from the woman who accompanied Rzhevsky on his visit to Iliodor.[13]

Khvostov and Beletsky were now open enemies; their clash rocked the ministry of internal affairs. "Both were intriguers to their fingertips and walking invitations to caricature," the American historian Harcave notes. Khvostov had a "face so broad and cheerful as to suggest unbelievable goodness," whereas Beletsky sported the "turned-up mustaches, elegant beard, and general mien of a middle-aged roue." The nation was stunned by their charges and counter-charges, a "preposterous game of betrayal and counter-betrayal." Khvostov actually hoped to survive as head of the most vital ministry in Russia. He rushed to Anna Vyrubova and "on bended knees offered his explanations." He claimed that he approached Iliodor to keep him from publishing a book that would discredit Rasputin and the royal family. If assassination entered the picture *Beletsky* was to blame! Khvostov invited Rasputin and Anna Vyrubova to dine; he was respectful of Grigory and even kissed his hand. Khvostov persuaded Nicholas to fire Beletsky and to send him to Irkutsk as military governor. Olga Beletsky was glad. She had long urged her husband to abandon intrigue, to return to the provinces, and live with new honesty and simplicity. By now Beletsky admitted she was right.[14]

Nicholas gave A. N. Khvostov an unusually cordial interview on March 3, 1916, an interview that put worries about his future to rest. Within a few hours he was dismissed as minister of the interior. Beletsky's appointment to Irkutsk was canceled 12 days later. Rasputin and Anna Vyrubova intervened with Nicholas and Alexandra on his behalf, but in vain. Beletsky was appointed to the senate and granted a stipend of 18,000 rubles.

For once in her life, Alexandra admitted that she had been wrong in judging people. She even offered something of an apology. "Am so wretched that we, through *Gregory* recommended *Khvostov* to you," she wrote on March 2, 1916. "[I]t leaves me not peace—you were against it and I let myself be imposed upon by them." But the empress did say a few words in her defense. She told Anna Vyrubova from the very first that she admired A. N. Khvostov's "great energy," but she also noted his "self-love," which was "something not pleasing to me." As for his attempt to murder Rasputin, Alexandra thought the "devil got hold of him, one cannot call it otherwise."[15]

20
Rasputin—Master of the Russian State

Grigory and the prime minister enjoyed a close relationship. As soon as Goremykin was appointed to the position, he agreed to meet the starets. Andronnikov brought Rasputin to Goremykin's elegant office.

"Well, what's up, Grigory Efimovich?" the chairman asked.

Rasputin tried to hypnotise Goremykin.

"I'm not afraid of your gaze!" Goremykin insisted. "Speak up, now—what's your business?"

Grigory slapped Goremykin on the knee and said, "Tell me, Old Man of God, do you tell the tsar the whole truth?"

"Yes, I say everything about what I'm asked," Goremykin replied, throwing a questioning glance at Andronnikov.

Rasputin now came to the point. The Russian press had been criticizing the shortage of supplies in the cities. Grigory believed that Siberia could help, and he had some specific suggestions. Goremykin was defensive and skeptical. At one point the chairman fell silent and the two stared intensely at each other.

"Well, Old Man of God, that's enough for today!" Rasputin finally declared.[1]

Rasputin and Goremykin often saw each other in coming weeks. Goremykin received the starets and carried out requests he thought proper. Grigory loved to awe hangers-on by phoning the prime minister day or night, making it clear that they had business with each other. Rasputin and Madame Goremykin were also friends. His prayers relieved her ailments; many of Grigory's conversations with Goremykin concerned her health. Madame Goremykin understood the power of food to win a man's good will. She prepared fabulous potato recipes, rushing her latest triumphs to Grigory's apartment. Rasputin served as intermediary to people who wanted to meet Goremykin. Dmitry Rubinstein forwarded 200,000 rubles for a hospital to Goremykin and his wife through "Father Grigory."[2]

Nicholas and Alexandra also liked Goremykin, but were coming to see that he could not continue in office. When Nicholas assumed command at Stavka, he tried to strengthen the "old man's position" with the ministers, but it was futile. "Yesterday's [conference] has clearly shown me that the ministers *do not wish* to work with old Gor., In spite of the stern words which I addressed to them. . . . "

Goremykin's relationship with the Duma was worse. The prime minister still considered Russia to be an autocracy, which made the deputies upstarts. They hissed Goremykin, and he admitted that he dreaded further scenes of this sort. The Duma was scheduled to resume its deliberations in November 1915. Goremykin asked Nicholas to postpone the date, which put the tsar in an awkward position. Nicholas also despised the Duma, but he had to deal with it. Goremykin was a liability—and increasingly so.

Rasputin and other members of Nicholas's circle agonized over these issues. Should Goremykin be kept? Should the Duma meet as scheduled or continue in recess? Grigory "cannot bear the idea of the Old Man being sent away," Alexandra wrote on November 13; he "has been worrying & thinking over that question without end."[3]

Rasputin was growing less hostile to the Duma at this time. His early contacts with rightists had strengthened Grigory's feelings for autocracy. Rasputin then dismissed the Duma as a "landlord's club," "a pack of dogs collected to keep other dogs silent." He assured the tsar that the Duma did nothing for the peasants, and they did not support it. But Rasputin's vision matured during the war, and he reevaluated the Duma's place in the tsarist system. He remained a monarchist. The subtleties of politics eluded Grigory, and he never grasped the aims of Russia's parties and newspapers. He felt the ministers—and all Russians—should support the tsar. Rasputin worked himself into "visible excitement" over this question. He paced about, raising his hands in despair and crying out, "Why do the members of the Duma not like the tsar?" "Does he not live only for the well-being of Russia?" He was puzzled at the attacks on Alexandra; he insisted that all who knew her realized she loved Russia. Even so, Rasputin was coming to think that Nicholas should improve his relationship with the Duma—and soon.[4]

The troika deserves some credit for improving Rasputin's attitude toward the Duma. Beletsky warned Grigory that "all Russia and the army would blame him" if Nicholas did not reconvene the body. "On the other hand if he could facilitate its convocation, this would [impress] certain deputies." The Khvostov–Beletsky program hinged on reconciling throne and Duma; they hoped Rasputin would help them. Only then could they guarantee Rasputin's security—or so they said.

Beletsky introduced Rasputin to A. A. Kon, a journalist with contacts in the Duma. Kon was a student of religion; he was impressed with Grigory and agreed that he should meet certain deputies. Beletsky was upset to learn that this was known and discussed in the Duma, and he persuaded Rasputin to draw back. But the campaign ended on a successful note. Grigory saw that the tsar could win friends in the Duma and not just among the rightists. (Rasputin called them "blockheads.") On November 15, 1915 Grigory told Alexandra that the prime minister was "quite wrong" to oppose reconvening the Duma. Rasputin "of course . . . loathes their existence (as do I for Russia)," but he insists "one cannot again uselessly offend them."[5]

Rasputin urged Nicholas to improve his relationship with the Duma by paying it a surprise visit. The tsar resisted such a gesture at first, but by November 1915 he was rethinking the matter. The obstacle now was Goremykin. Alexandra and Rasputin met at Vyrubova's cottage on November 4, 1915 to discuss the problem. Grigory advised Nicholas to "see the old Gentleman & gently tell him [that] if the *Duma* hisses him, what can one do, one cannot send it away for such a reason." Alexandra did not mention Goremykin in her next three lengthy, newsy letters to the tsar dated November 7–9, 1915. Such silence was not characteristic, and it may indicate that the empress was undergoing some crisis with the old prime minister. A letter stolen from Rasputin's desk at this time indicates that he was writing "highly placed people," testing their feelings about seeing Goremykin retire. By November 10, the tsar decided to replace him with the minister who most closely shared his views, A. A. Khvostov.[6]

A. A. Khvostov was the uncle of A. N. Khvostov. Khvostov senior had opposed his nephew's advancement, saying the young man was an opportunist. Nicholas heeded A. A. Khvostov's advice in 1911, but he rejected it in 1915. Uncle and nephew both sat on the council of ministers in November when, by an ironic twist of fate, Grigory was again asked to pass upon a Khvostov's qualifications for higher office. Only now the candidate was A. A. Khvostov, and the position was chairmanship of the council of ministers. There was another important difference. Nicholas had several reasons for not making A. N. Khvostov minister of the interior in 1911; this time the decision about A. A. Khvostov was entirely in Grigory's hands.

Rasputin asked Alexandra to persuade Nicholas to not inform the old man of his dismissal "until he [Grigory] has seen Uncle *Khvostov* on Thursday [to see] what impression he will have of him."

The plan was for Grigory to appear as an ordinary petitioner at the ministry of justice and ask to see its head. A. A. Khvostov would see Alexandra the same evening. Depending upon Rasputin's recommendation, their conversation would be on routine matters or Khvostov would be asked to head the government.

Grigory's evaluation was negative. He found A. A. Khvostov to be "honest" and that—"one good thing [is] that he is devoted to the old man—" Ivan Goremykin. But Rasputin also concluded that the senior Khvostov was "obstinate," "very dry & hard," and "not to be compared with *Goremykin.*"[7]

So Goremykin obtained a reprieve, probably without realizing his job was ever in danger. Nicholas honored his prime minister's wishes and announced that the Duma would not meet until February 1916. Most Russians accepted the news with little comment. The government's critics were furious. Goremykin intensified their anger by announcing that the Duma would only meet for three weeks, and its deliberations would be confined to the civil budget.[8]

Goremykin was so unpopular that he endangered the entire government. The problem was to find a replacement who would be strong and willing to carry out the tsar's orders, but without angering Duma moderates. It was not easy to find such a person by late 1915. "I keep on racking my brains over the question of a successor for the old man," Nicholas wrote on January 7, 1916. He did have a candidate, though he wondered if he was "young enough or sufficiently up to date."[9]

The man of the hour was Boris Vladimirovich Sturmer. He was born of a noble family in Tver province in 1848, which made Sturmer nearly 68 when he was appointed chairman of the council of ministers. Boris's father was a cavalry officer of Austrian ancestry; his mother was a Panin. With landholdings of nearly 1,900 acres, the Sturmers were comfortable but not distinguished. Young Sturmer graduated from St. Petersburg University and entered government service in 1872. He became governor of Novgorod in 1895. Unlike most governors Sturmer got along well with local legislatures; this gift won his promotion to prime minister in 1916. But Sturmer was pompous and not well liked. He was not given a farewell party when he left, the only governor in Novgorod's memory to be so snubbed. "No one bade him farewell except the fireman's orchestra," Rodzyanko testified in 1917, and "it performed various operetta marches."[10]

Sturmer served as governor of Yaroslavl Province from 1896 to 1902. As before, he got along well with the local zemstvo while implementing orders from the capital quickly and without argument. He now came to the tsar's attention. In 1901 Nicholas wrote "I wish other governors would understand things so well and give as good an account in fulfilling requests. . . . " But there were continued rumors of avarice; people spoke of Sturmer's banquets, servants, and costly trips. Nevertheless he was nearly appointed minister of internal affairs after Phleve's assassination in 1904.

Sturmer was in eclipse after 1905. Nicholas was forced to make concessions to progressive opinion: Ultramonarchists such as Sturmer were "promoted" to the State Council. Sturmer slid into obscurity. He tried and failed to become director of the Holy Synod in 1911 and mayor of Moscow in 1913. Then came the war. The increasingly low caliber of people appointed to office made Sturmer wonder if he could also return to power.[11]

Sturmer seemed impressive. Standing a full six feet, he was broad-shouldered and solidly built; his hair was white, and his long thin beard was strikingly well groomed. Sturmer held himself majestically, spoke little, and cut a fine figure in a green-gold court uniform. But the man's manner bespoke his character. People described his eyes as "sly and shifting," and his expression "lacked dignity." Sturmer's critics spoke of his "cringing manner" and a "somewhat over-flattering" style of conversation. The American ambassador called upon

the new prime minister to pay his respects. David Francis chatted away with
Madame Sturmer while the "baron paced up and down the room, and every
now and again stopped in front of a large mirror in which he surveyed himself
with evident satisfaction [as] he turned up the ends of his moustaches which
were in the style of a German kaiser." The Germanic touch had been part of
Sturmer's problem. German surnames handicapped ambitious Russians during
the war. Sturmer tried to assume his wife's name, but all the Panins had to
approve the change. This was not forthcoming, and Sturmer seemed doubly
ridiculous for the setback.[12]

Sturmer mounted a quiet but energetic offensive to gain high office. He presented himself to friends and associates as a man worthy of an important position.
Pitirim was the link between Sturmer and Rasputin. The metropolitan worried
over Goremykin's plan to reconvene the Duma for only three weeks. Pitirim
was convinced that the tsar needed a younger man who would work with the
Duma. Pitirim met Sturmer in late 1915; Rasputin and he apparently had a slight
acquaintance dating from 1914. Pitirim suggested Sturmer might be the man
they were seeking as chairman of the council of ministers.

Rasputin was not as enthusiastic over Sturmer as Pitirim. Grigory renewed
his acquaintance with Sturmer; the most he could say was that he would like to
get to know him better. Their next meeting produced an agreement. Sturmer
assured Rasputin that he was devoted to the throne; he frankly asked the starets
to help him become prime minister. In exchange Sturmer promised to be Grigory's "friend" and carry out his requests. Grigory assured Sturmer that the
only problem was to bring his name to Nicholas's attention in the best way.[13]

Pitirim now visited Alexandra to put in a good word for Sturmer. Pitirim was
already scheduled to report on Synod business at Stavka on January 12, 1916.
He used the occasion to urge Nicholas to replace Goremykin with Sturmer. This
was a false move, and it showed how Rasputin excelled Pitirim in manipulating
the tsar. The emperor liked Pitirim and received him cordially, but he resented
a churchman meddling in state affairs. Nicholas admitted to his wife that he was
"surprised" at the metropolitan's interest in the Duma; "I should like to know
who influenced him in this matter."[14]

Rasputin, by contrast, knew that the way to Nicholas was through Alexandra.
If Rasputin persuaded her that someone was fit to hold an office, she would
recommend the man, and he was often appointed. Boris Sturmer provides a
striking example of this interaction. Alexandra first wrote Nicholas about Sturmer
on January 4, 1916. He was a "right man" who "will work well with the new
energetic ministers." Three days later, she thought Sturmer's "head is plenty
fresh enough"; he "would do for a bit, & then later on if you ever want to find
another you can change him." "He very much values *Gregory* wh. is a great
thing." A third letter on January 9 delivered the ultimate pronouncement: Rasputin advised the tsar to make Sturmer prime minister. "Our Fr. said about
Sturmer not to change his name and to take him for a time at least, as he is such

a decided loyal man and will hold others in hand,—let one scream if one wishes, they [the critics] always will at any nomination."[15]

Nicholas was now sympathetic to Sturmer's appointment. He knew if Sturmer came to Stavka "various rumors and suppositions" would follow. The tsar preferred to hold the interview a few days later, when he would be in the capital. If he appointed Sturmer, Nicholas wanted it to come "like a clap of thunder."[16] And that is exactly what happened.

Russia and her allies were amazed to hear that B. V. Sturmer would head the tsar's government. Goremykin's retirement was no surprise. He was elderly and wanted to step down. He actually enjoyed a final burst of popularity. Whatever his faults, Goremykin was honest and principled and had served in key positions for decades. Sturmer was forgettable and forgotten—and the memories one could conjure up were not flattering. One minister thought the new chairman's "gifts were strictly rationed," and he "suffered from acute sclerosis due to old age." Another maintained that Sturmer "never could formulate his thoughts" freely; to express himself he "had to write the simplest things down on paper." Some recalled his knack of sleeping through committee meetings while seeming to follow what was being said. Paléologue spent three days gathering information about Sturmer, and he found nothing pleasing. Sturmer was "worse than a mediocrity," the French ambassador concluded; he was a man of "third-rate intellect, mean spirit, low character, doubtful honesty, no experience, and no idea of state business." Rasputin had a similar opinion of his new "friend." Their relationship was a matter of mutual convenience. "He's old, but that doesn't matter," Grigory declared contemptously. "He'll make do!"[17]

Rasputin's first conference with the new prime minister came on January 21, 1916, a day after Sturmer's appointment. Unlike Goremykin, Sturmer was not willing to receive Grigory openly. On two occasions Rasputin visited Sturmer secretly, in Pitirim's office at the Alexander Nevsky Monastery. They usually met at the residence of the commander at the Peter and Paul Fortress. (The general's daughter Lidiya was a member of Grigory's circle and Sturmer's good friend.) On January 21 Rasputin and Sturmer got together in the apartment of Elizabeth Lerma. She was the mistress of Manasevich-Manuilov, the man whom Sturmer engaged to act as his agent in situations where a breach of secrecy would compromise a prime minister.[18]

Sturmer arranged the meeting at Lerma's apartment to assure Rasputin that his requests would be carried out as promised. Grigory realized something was wrong. Rasputin suddenly saw Sturmer was a perfect example of the "landlord in government." He "suspected that the man was not to be trusted, that behind the facade of fawning obsequiousness" lurked a desire for independence. Rasputin was the first to see that the new chairman would betray his promises. Sturmer had just returned from Stavka; the reception made him feel powerful.

Sturmer used Rasputin to become prime minister, but now it seemed that he had no need of his Siberian ally. Sturmer was also serious in seeking good relations with the Duma; ties to Rasputin would be nothing but a liability here. Sturmer also turned against Pitirim. He called to inquire about the metropolitan's health, but somehow never got around to fulfilling his "requests." Sturmer even gave Volzhin unexpected support in fighting the "Rasputin gang" in the Holy Synod. Pitirim needed several weeks to see through Sturmer. Rasputin was more alert. He confronted Sturmer only ten days after he became chairman of the council of ministers.[19]

The dramatic scene occurred at the Peter and Paul Fortress. Rasputin arrived to find Pitirim and Osipenko chatting with Sturmer. They left so that Grigory and the chairman could talk. To the amazement of the listeners, Rasputin began screaming at the top of his voice.

"You won't laugh about going against mamasha's wishes!" Grigory shouted, referring to Alexandra Fedorovna. The noisy exchange went on for a while, and then Rasputin and Manasevich-Manuilov left.

"What were you yelling at the old man about?" Manuilov asked.

"He's not obeying mamasha," Rasputin bristled. "He's begun to hop around on his own. The little man better stay on his string. If he doesn't, his neck will get broken!"[20]

Seeing his alliance with Rasputin slipping away, Sturmer was even more attentive to the empress. Their relationship continued to be warm for several months. Sturmer also tried to pacify Grigory.

"I can't do everything he wants," the chairman lamented. "He wants an automobile, and I see to it. I show him a lot of courtesies." But Rasputin was still displeased with Sturmer.

"The dog, the filthy little old man!" Grigory fumed when he heard that Sturmer rebuffed petitioners with Rasputin's now-famous notes. "He crosses himself, promising to do everything—but he doesn't do a thing!" the starets raged. "He probably thinks mama will always indulge him—and that he can get along without me," Rasputin fumed on another occasion. "All I have to do is say a word, and they'll drive the old man out!"[21]

Rasputin was disappointed with Sturmer, but he still hoped that the new prime minister would improve relations with the Duma. One morning, after an evening of unusually heavy drinking, Grigory invited his police guards to join him for tea.

"Why are you melancholy, Grigory Efimovich?" one of the men asked. "What are you so pensive about?"

"I've been told to think about how to deal with the Duma," Rasputin replied, nursing a headache. "I just don't know. What do you think?"

"It's out of the question for me to think about this," came the reply. "Or do you want me to get into trouble with my superiors?"

"Know what?" Rasputin cried. "I'll take him to the Duma myself. Just let him walk in and open the door—no one can do a thing about it."[22]

The Duma met at the Tauride Palace at 2 P.M. on February 9, 1916. Court carriages appeared and Nicholas II strode into the hall where Potemkin's parties once dazzled Catherine the Great. A *Te Deum* began as soon as Nicholas reached the altar in the hypostyle chamber. It was a moving scene and tears flowed. Nicholas was pale and ill at ease; his right hand tugged at his collar while the left perpetually opened and closed. The tsar spoke briefly on patriotism and unity, addressing the deputies as "representatives" of "my people." Despite a stumbling delivery, the listeners responded with loud cheers. Their emperor took the initiative in launching what promised to be a new chapter in relations between the tsar and his legislature.

"Your majesty," Rodzianko cried at one point, "do make the most of this joyous occasion and proclaim here, at once, your will to grant a responsible ministry. You cannot fathom the full magnitude of such an act which will have the beneficent effect of pacifying the country and bringing the war to a victorious end."

"I will think it over," Nicholas replied as he left.[23]

Sturmer now gave the main address. It was a rambling speech emphasizing the historical foundations of the Russian state. Sturmer cut a poor figure. His listeners found him "less decrepit than Goremykin, but nevertheless decrepit, [speaking in] a weak voice which was not able to keep control even of the calm and silent audience."[24]

But Sturmer was not responsible for the rapid collapse of these new relations. Nicholas and the Duma differed in their view of what these relations should be. Nicholas hoped—as his wife put it—that his visit would be a "stimulant & make all work hard & in unity for the blessing & grandeur of our beloved country."[25] The Duma hoped for more. It expected the tsar to abandon his pretensions to autocracy and appoint ministers agreeable to the Duma. None of this materialized; quite the opposite. Nicholas returned to Stavka, while Sturmer remained in the capital to "discipline" the legislature. Nothing had really changed.

Indeed a new scandal rocked the Duma and further discredited the tsar's government. The news broke that A. N. Khvostov tried to murder Grigory Rasputin. By early March 1916, Khvostov and Beletsky were exchanging charges in newspaper interviews. Bewildered Russians were not accustomed to seeing their officials behave "like the Mafia," as Beletsky put it. Ministers were Olympian figures, remote and majestic. As celestial bodies reflect a portion of the sun's light, so the tsar's ministers radiated a part of his own glory. Nicholas made Khvostov a minister and gave the nation a criminal. "This revolting tale of Khvostov and Beletsky . . . is without example in the history of the ministry of the interior," a shocked nobleman wrote. Dr. Badmaev warned Nicholas that the Khvostov–Beletsky affair was "very serious" and damaged the throne. "Gloomy impressions have arisen around this matter as well as many lies concerning Grigory Efimovich [Rasputin]."[26]

The tsar's mystique began to erode at this time. Reform-minded Russians had thought it best to not push their demands until the war ended. The Khvostov scandal persuaded many that Nicholas was the "main obstacle to the country's successful pursuit of the war"; a sense of duty now made some think an "unworthy incumbent" was on the throne. Conservatives in the armed forces and the bureaucracy were equally bewildered. The Khvostov scandal lowered the tsar's prestige in circles where he had not been criticized before.[27]

Khvostov's downfall might have brought a change in Nicholas's method of government. Alexandra admitted that she was "so wretched that we, through Grigory recommended Khvostov to you." The empress recognized "you were against it and I let myself be imposed upon" by people she does not name. This was a good time for the tsar and his wife to stop and take stock of how they were handling power. They showed no interest in such a reevaluation. The very letter containing Alexandra's "apology" goes on to remind her husband "to keep our Friend's Image near you as a blessing." Nor do Nicholas's comments on the fiasco suggest that he learned anything about the wisdom of relying upon Alexandra and her circle.[28]

Rasputin was as active as ever in meddling with state affairs. Just after Khvostov's dismissal Anna Vyrubova asked Grigory, "Who is to be [the next] minister of internal affairs?"

"I don't know myself," Rasputin answered. "Shcheglovitov wants it—but he's a rogue. Kryzhanovsky's pushing me to have dinner. He wants it—but he's a swindler. And then Beletsky wants it. If I'm not murdered yet, he's the one who'll kill me for sure. Well, since the old man [Boris Sturmer] is already sitting [as prime minister], let him stay alone [hold both posts] and rule."[29]

Rasputin was leaving his apartment for Tsarskoe Selo at the time of this brief conversation. A few days later, Sturmer was indeed made minister of the interior as well as prime minister. Rasputin's advice on this point was not the only factor leading the tsar to this decision. Stolypin and Kokovtsov also combined the two posts; it gave a forceful man a firm grip on vital parts of the Russian state machine. Alexandra and Rasputin did not know it at the time, but Nicholas was considering a wartime dictatorship in which Sturmer would be the "strong man" to direct civilian affairs. Would Sturmer show himself to be a "strong man?" Nicholas was giving him a chance to prove himself. Sturmer got the same vote of confidence as two illustrious predecessors. Sturmer quickly proved that he was no Stolypin—nor half a Kokovtsov.

═══ 21 ═══
"Our Friend's Opinions of People Are Sometimes Very Strange"

Dr. Badmaev was a well-known figure in the upper-class circles of the capital. His elegant clinic on the outskirts of the city offered "Tibetan medicine": healing through a variety of herb and plant concoctions. Badmaev was actually Mongolian. He was born into the Buryat tribe near Lake Baikal in eastern Siberia in 1851. The boy, named Zhamsaran, tended his father's large herd of cattle. At the age of 12, he left the windswept steppes and enrolled in the gymnasium at Irkutsk. Meanwhile, an older brother, Siltim, established a thriving practice in Tibetan medicine in St. Petersburg. Siltim was anxious to see his younger brother advance. He brought Zhamsaran to the capital in 1871 and enrolled him as a student in eastern languages at the University of St. Petersburg. Zhamsaran converted to the Eastern Orthodox Church as Peter Alexandrovich Badmaev.[1]

Badmaev championed Russian expansion in Asia. He served in the Asian section of the foreign office and taught Mongolian. Power came his way through the Tibetan medicine that he began to practice in 1875. By the time the war broke out, his patients included the two leaders of the Duma, President Rodzyanko and Vice-President Alexander Protopopov. Protopopov first came to Badmaev in 1903, claiming—so he said publicly—to suffer from a "tubercular ulcer" on his leg. Protopopov probably contracted syphilis as a young grenadier officer; Badmaev treated him with the "arousing powders" that made him popular with the social set. By 1915 Protopopov's behavior was extremely erratic. He lay in Badmaev's clinic six months from late 1915. Protopopov impressed the Buryat healer; it seemed that he should occupy a high post in the government.[2] To accomplish this Badmaev needed Rasputin.

Badmaev and Rasputin were enemies before the war. Then they set their differences aside and cooperated in business deals. (Just one of these transactions, if successful, brought Grigory a 50,000-ruble bribe.[3]) Protopopov's advancement marked the high point of their collaboration.

Rasputin and Protopopov certainly came from different worlds. Alexander Dmitrievich Protopopov was born into a noble family in 1866. Alexander Dmitrievich was educated in the cadet corps and served in the guard. He retired in 1890 to direct a large cotton factory plus 19,600 acres of family lands. Protopopov organized a "brotherhood" of landlords to crush the local peasant movement in 1905. Protopopov was a dreamer; his mind ranged widely over key social and political issues. He was too conservative to win election to the first two Dumas, but he won a seat in the Third Duma. Protopopov was a member of the liberal wing of the moderate Octobrist Party and was elected vice-president of the Fourth Duma. He also directed a bank and was president of the Union of Cloth Manufacturers.[4]

Rasputin and Protopopov first met in 1913. Grigory was taken with the elegant gentleman from Simbirsk, and he declared that Protopopov would someday be a minister. Rasputin was not what Protopopov expected. Grigory was "pleasant and meek"; if he did not have "full common sense," neither was he a fool. They got reacquainted during Protopopov's convalescence during the war. Rasputin often visited his new friend in the next few weeks. At one point Grigory declared that Protopopov should be prime minister. Badmaev laughed along with others, but secretly he was quite pleased. Rasputin did not realize it, but the "root and herb doctor" was organizing a new trolka. As with the earlier triumverate of Khvostov–Beletsky–Andronnikov, the object was to capture the ministry of the interior. Protopopov would head the bureau, and Kurlov would be his assistant. As the architect, Badmaev would control appointments and profit financially at every turn. Rasputin's support would reassure Nicholas and Alexandra. Badmaev smiled as events moved according to his plan.

Rasputin had his own plan. Just then he was turning against Goremykin because of his terrible relations with the Duma. Protopopov was vice-president of that body; surely he would establish good will between crown and legislature. Grigory was always on the lookout for promising statesmen; we could easily underestimate his idealism and desire to "help" in this way.[5] Again we see how well the Siberian peasant manipulated his tsar. Grigory simply mentioned Protopopov to Nicholas in the winter of 1915. The emperor replied he had not met the man. The matter rested there until Protopopov's career came to a major turning point in the summer of 1916.[6]

Protopopov led a Duma delegation to Western Europe in July 1916. The visit was to reassure England, France, and Italy that Russia would remain in the war until victory. Protopopov had great charm, and he impressed Europeans as being one of their own. "He talked the commonplaces of the allied cause, but with a conviction and warmth of imagination which made his speeches by far the best made by any foreign visitor to our [British] shores since the outbreak of [the] war," the British historian George Buchan observed. The king of England openly wondered if "Cousin Nicki" was making full use of this man's obvious abilities. There were a few disconcerting touches. Protopopov suffered from insomnia; his talk on occasion was wild and strained. Sometimes he would launch into some amazingly off-color tales about Rasputin and the royal family. These episodes were dismissed as unimportant. A. D. Protopopov's performance as a whole fetched rave reviews.[7]

Protopopov's mission also brought him before Nicholas II. The vice-president briefed the tsar about his trip. "Yesterday I saw a man I liked very much, Protopopov, vice-president of the state duma," the emperor wrote on July 20, 1916. All the necessary elements were now in place for Protopopov's advancement. Rasputin persuaded Alexandra of his merits, and Nicholas had no doubts. Rodzyanko's endorsement reflected Duma approval.[8] The problem was to find the position best suited to Protopopov's experience and interests.

Protopopov's ambitions were modest at this point. He expressed an interest in the ministry of trade and industry, then headed by Prince Shakhovskoi. This was also Rodzyanko's hope. Shakhovskoi was an ultramonarchist, hostile to the Duma and the special councils, and Rodzyanko was his unsparing critic. Nicholas also thought this ministry matched A. D. Protopopov's background.[9] Then Rasputin intervened to carry events in an entirely different direction.

Rasputin was angry over certain changes on the council of ministers in the summer of 1916. These reassignments weakened his power, though as usual the Russian public imagined the innovations were due to his influence. People spoke of "ministerial leapfrog": ministers came, went, and on occasion traded offices. Russia saw four different prime ministers, five ministers of the interior, four ministers of agriculture, and three ministers of war from September 1915 to March 1917. Five other ministries each had three different heads. This "bewildering gallery" of office-holders was "allured by the illusory glamor of power." Some maintained their positions for several months, others for a few weeks; Alexander Trepov, one of the prime ministers, did not last 50 days. The historian Michael Florinsky called this chapter an "amazing, extravagant, and pitiful spectacle, and one without parallel in the history of civilized nations."[10]

Rasputin's interests were damaged by the "double shuffle." Sturmer gave up internal affairs for foreign affairs in July 1916, while A. A. Khvostov traded justice for internal affairs; Alexander Makarov became minister of justice. Foreign affairs was of no interest to Grigory, and whatever influence he might muster with Sturmer would be wasted in this office. But internal affairs and justice were of great importance to Rasputin. The first saw to his security and regulated the press. The minister of justice brought indictments and tried cases. Khvostov senior and Makarov were old foes of "Father Grigory" and could be expected to fight him. They might be doubly effective working together! Rasputin was influential but not all-powerful, and for a moment he lost control over the situation.

"This little old man [Sturmer] has lost his mind," Grigory shouted when he heard the news, banging a table with his fists. "He doesn't understand a thing about those [diplomatic] matters. Mamasha cried out against it—how could he be selected for this work? Besides which, he still has a German name!"[11]

Rasputin might restore his power through Protopopov. But he would gain nothing if Protopopov were minister of trade and industry. The incumbent Prince Shakhovskoi was already in Rasputin's corner, even if he denied it publicly. Protopopov would be far more useful at internal affairs. Rasputin persuaded Alexandra that Protopopov was the right choice for this post, though—incredibly—she had not even met the candidate and was operating entirely on the strength of Grigory's recommendation. ("He likes our Friend since at least 4 years & that says much for a man. . . . I don't know him, but I believe in our Friend's wisdom and guidance.")

Alexandra wrote three letters in these four days urging her husband to make Protopopov minister of the interior. The empress reminded her husband that A. A. Khvostov is "nervous & feels ill" and that he "wants to leave & Protopopov is a suitable man." Each letter stressed that Protopopov was Rasputin's choice. Protopopov wanted Paul Kurlov as his number two man, so Alexandra also demanded the ouster of "Klimovich, who is a bad man, hates our Friend & yet comes to him pretending and cringing before him." "Shakhovskoy too good to be changed," she added, remembering (perhaps) that Nicholas originally thought of Protopopov as a candidate for his position.[12]

This barrage on Protopopov's behalf bewildered Nicholas and provoked a testy response, which deserves to be quoted in full.

Stavka. 9 September 1916.

Thank you with all my heart for your dear, long letter in which you pass on Friend's message [urging me to appoint Protopopov minister of the interior].

It seems to me that this Protopopov is a good man, but he has much to do with Factories, etc. Rodzyanko has for a long time suggested him as the Minister of Trade, instead of Shakhovskoy. I must consider this question as it has taken me completely by surprise. Our Friend's opinions of people are sometimes very strange, as you know yourself—therefore one must be careful, especially with appointments to high offices. I do not personally know this Klimovich. Would it be wise to discharge them at the same time? That is, I mean to say, the Minister of the Interior and the Chief of Police? This must be thought out very carefully. And whom am I to begin with? All these changes make my head go round. In my opinion, they are too frequent. In any case, they are not good for the internal situation of the country, as each new man brings with him alterations in the administration.

Alexandra would not listen. "Please take Protopopov as minister of the interior," she persisted; "he is one of the Duma, it will make a great effect amongst them & shut their mouths."

Nicholas could not prevail when his wife's feelings were this strong. "It shall be done," he wired tersely the following day. He also noted that the weather was clear and cold.[13]

Nicholas II spent the war seeking a strong figure to head his government. Three high points stood out. First were the four ministers brought into the cabinet in June–July 1915. Then came A. N. Khvostov as minister of the interior that September. Nicholas's third major effort was tapping Boris Sturmer to lead the cabinet in January 1916. Each of these "new beginnings" brought failure and a still weaker government.

A. D. Protopopov was the tsarist regime's last "strong man," its final attempt to rally its forces and solve the nation's problems. To his credit Nicholas knew Protopopov was no Stolypin. But at fleeting moments perhaps Nicholas hoped that Protopopov could at least bring peace with the Duma. Protopopov was the first member of that body to enter the council of ministers. Some expected more appointments of this type. This might lead to a semblance of the "government of public confidence" that the Duma's progressive block was demanding.

Protopopov's promotion actually made the situation worse. Rodzyanko had been urging Nicholas to replace Sturmer with a more liberal popular figure such as Grigorovich, minister of naval affairs. If the tsar followed this course of action, Protopopov might have represented an effort to build bridges from the throne to the Duma. But Sturmer remained at the head of the government; Protopopov would serve Sturmer, and Sturmer's program would be Protopopov's program. In this context Protopopov seemed greedy for power, and to his surprise his friendships in the Duma quickly collapsed.

Protopopov was amazed when a colleague demanded that he step down.

"How can you ask me to resign?" he asked in amazement. "All my life it was my dream to be a vice-governor, and here I am a minister!"[14]

Protopopov's allies celebrated his appointment.

"I did this," Rasputin boasted. "The State Duma needed some little thing, it was necessary to take [somebody] from the State Duma. We made a mistake with fat-belly [A. N. Khvostov] because he was one of those fools from the right. All rightists are fools, I tell you. Now we took somebody here from between the rightists and leftists—Protopopov."

"God bless yr. new choice of *Protopopov,*" Alexandra wrote. "Our Friend says you have done a very wise act in naming him."

Nicholas continued to be fearful; he made Alexander Dmitrievich *acting* minister of the interior. "God grant that he may turn out to be the man of whom we are now in need!" he reflected on September 23, 1916. Three weeks later Nicholas was still uneasy. "Protopopov spent nearly two hours with me last night," he wrote on October 17. "I sincerely hope that God will bless his new work of responsibility! He has firmly decided to carry it through to the end, in spite of all difficulties. But I am afraid that the difficulties will be great, especially for the first two months!"[15]

Protopopov's astrologer told him that Jupiter (his planet) was passing over

Saturn, which meant the moment was right to become a minister. This prediction was not justified. Protopopov was probably suffering from advanced syphilis, and his behavior became increasingly erratic. A lady who dined with him was struck by his "unhealthy yellowish skin" and his "restless hands" with their "aimless movements." "I will save Russia," he proudly proclaimed one moment, "I feel that I was chosen to rescue Russia from misfortune—to save her." The next instant he was so "nervous and excitable . . . it was difficult to catch him at any fixed address."

Alexander Kerensky also had a strange encounter with the new minister. Kerensky noticed an easel in Protopopov's office holding a famous image of Christ: Jesus's eyes appeared shut from a distance, but open as one studied them more closely.

"I see you are surprised, aren't you?" Protopopov remarked. "You have been looking at Him intently all the time. I never part with Him. Whenever there is a decision to make, He shows me the right way."

Kerensky was aghast. He knew Protopopov as a normal man; these changes were mystifying. Protopopov was now raving about his plans to save Russia. Kerensky suddenly rose, smiled, and almost ran from the office.[16]

Rasputin also expected Protopopov to save Russia. The great issue in the fall of 1916 was feeding the cities, and the government launched a "preparedness campaign" to solve these difficulties. The sown areas fell a quarter or more as a dozen million peasants donned uniforms. Even so food was abundant; the problem was getting supplies to their destination. Russia's railroad system was weak when the war broke out; rolling stock and rails deteriorated as the nation went on military footing. The army had top priority, so the cities suffered. The urban population grew 10 percent by 1916, but its grain supplies were only two-thirds of the prewar level. Prices spiraled upwards. Rents in Petrograd doubled and then tripled. Industrial wages rose 142 percent but when adjusted for inflation actually fell more than 70 percent. Rationing began in the summer of 1916, and the supply system still deteriorated.[17]

Rasputin was worried about this situation. Grigory had become wealthy, but his peasant background made him understand ordinary hardships. Nicholas and Alexandra also appreciated the problem, in part because Rasputin harped on it so much. The question was what to do. Rasputin suggested that the way to eliminate the "tails" (waiting lines) in front of shops was to build "through entry ways" to counters where preweighed food packages could be quickly handed out as people came through. Grigory also argued that food supply should be transferred from the ministry of agriculture to interior, where the police could enforce rationing. The minister of the interior already had more power than anyone else on the council. Rasputin's plan would give him still more authority. The person who held that office, if successful, would indeed be the savior of Russia.[18]

Protopopov assured everyone that he would solve the supply-rationing problem if given the necessary authority. His fellow ministers were not impressed: They voted eight to six against transferring this jurisdiction from agriculture to interior.

But Nicholas and especially Alexandra believed in Protopopov. The emperor had Sturmer ask the Duma to place supply matters within the ministry of the interior. If the Duma did not agree, Sturmer would enact the measure through Article 87 giving the government the power to secure emergency measures. A tsar could not back a minister more strongly than this.

Protopopov panicked. For all his brave talk he was a weak man. He also ignored his work. Protopopov attended few meetings of the ministers, but he spent hours with the empress talking about the Physiocrats. "I must admit I had not thought about [supplies and rationing] sufficiently or gotten acquainted with it," he later testified. "I had never even been in the statistics section of the ministry of the interior, and I did not know what data were there concerning supply of the population." "Nor would I have brought useful qualities to the situation," he sadly concluded.

His bluff called, Protopopov rushed to the tsar and his wife. He made much of the ministers' opposition to giving him control over supply functions. Protopopov suggested that a council of three ministers wield this authority: Trepov, Shakhovskoi, and himself. Nicholas glanced anxiously at Alexandra and smiled as Protopopov droned on. The empress was quiet—and displeased. Nicholas and Alexandra were "dissatisfied with my indecisiveness," Protopopov subsequently recalled; they insisted "I should stop wavering now that I had obtained the tsar's agreement to direct supply activity."

Rasputin was furious when he learned of the weakness of his new Joan of Arc. "He himself ran up to me and asked me to give him the rationing question—and when mamasha and papasha agreed, he chickened out. If a minister's a coward, he's out of place!"[19]

Other Russians were disillusioned with Protopopov. He was clearly a creature of Rasputin, a supporter of Sturmer, and incapable of improving the political situation. The first issue of a newspaper that Protopopov had created to manipulate public opinion called upon him to resign! Sturmer supported Protopopov about half of the time; the only minister who did better was Dobrovolsky, a notorious Rasputinite. The others "openly rejected his plans, treated him with undisguised hostility and carried on an underground war of bureaucratic intrigue."[20]

This opposition bothered Protopopov. He clung to those who supported him: Nicholas and Alexandra, his wife and two daughters, and his coconspirators. Protopopov still needed Badmaev's "cures"; he rushed to the clinic at stressful moments to talk to Badmaev and Rasputin. Grigory was disappointed with Protopopov, but their friendship endured. Protopopov and Kurlov soon parted company. Kurlov actually ran the ministry, but his scandal-ridden past made him a liability. Kurlov also took Protopopov for granted; he shouted at him and treated him as a child. Nicholas finally discharged Kurlov in early December 1916.[21]

* * *

Nicholas journeyed to Kiev in late October 1916 on what fate decreed would be his last encounter with his mother. Alexis came along. The tsar's loved ones were shocked at how "Nicky" had changed. Olga found her brother "pale, thin and tired," and the dowager empress worried over his "excessive quiet." Gilliard noted that Nicholas was "usually very self-controlled, but on occasion he showed himself nervous and irritable, and once or twice he spoke roughly to Alexis Nicholaevich." Maria Fedorovna and her circle begged Nicholas to make some changes. He was urged to dismiss Sturmer and Protopopov, and to break with Rasputin. The fact that the Duma would reconvene on November 1 must have doubled the weight of this advice.[22]

In fact, Nicholas did dismiss Sturmer. "All these days I have been thinking of old St[urmer]," Nicholas wrote on November 8, 1916, reminding his wife of the prime minister's great unpopularity. He went on to say that the situation was "much worse than it was with Goremykin last year." The empress and Rasputin mounted a hasty campaign to save the old man, but it was no use. Sturmer's final act was to advise his tsar to make Trepov, the minister of communications, prime minister. Nicholas agreed.[23]

The new chairman of the council of ministers was unusually able. One wonders if Nicholas did not have in Trepov a last chance to save his regime. The left's hatred of Trepov suggests it feared as much.

Alexander Trepov was born in 1864 into a wealthy noble family, which won the hatred of "progressive Russia." His father, as governor of St. Petersburg, ordered a political prisoner flogged, and was shot and wounded by the revolutionary terrorist Vera Zasulich in 1878. Alexander's older brother Dmitry held the same post during the Revolution of 1905; he became famous for the celebrated order, "spare no bullets!" Alexander Trepov was an energetic minister of communications, though the deterioration of Russia's transport system brought criticism.

Trepov had strength and vision. Although a staunch conservative, Trepov favored close relations with the Duma. He was booed so loudly on his first appearance there as prime minister that he could not speak—but that did not change his program. Trepov saw that even the conservative State Council had come to agree with the Duma: The power of the "dark, irresponsible forces" must end, and the tsar should grant a "cabinet which would rely on the Duma and carry out its majority's program." This situation was serious and Trepov used it for his ends. If he served as prime minister, he would replace the four most incompetent, unpopular ministers with men of his own choice.[24]

Trepov's biggest target was Alexander Protopopov. Nicholas knew this change would infuriate Alexandra, and a letter tried to soften the blow. The tsar felt sorry for Protopopov; "he is a good, honest man, but he jumps from one idea to another and cannot make up his mind on anything." Alexander Dmitrievich was "not quite normal after a certain illness," and it was "risky to leave the ministry of internal affairs in the hands of such a man in these times." Then the most revealing line: "I beg you, do not drag our Friend into this. I wish to be free in my choice."[25]

Alexandra was furious. She did not "drag our Friend [Rasputin] into this," but her next two letters bombarded Nicholas with appeals to change his mind. The empress arrived at Stavka on November 14, 1916. Nicholas and Alexandra discussed Protopopov's fate so the documentation their letters sometimes offer on interesting issues disappears. We know this: The tsarina won and Protopopov stayed. Rasputin sent Nicholas at least four telegrams in these days. One protested changes that Trepov was making on the council of ministers: "No one [else] has authority on your ship!" Another reminded the tsar Protopopov was "ours"—"support him!" A third urged Nicholas to pass the autocratic power he received from his father on to his son.

"Yes, those days spent together were difficult," Nicholas wrote after his wife left, and "*only* thanks to you have I spent them more or less calmly. You were so strong and steadfast—I admire you more than I can say. Forgive me if I were moody or unrestrained—sometime one's temper must come out!" Massie characterizes this letter as the "only evidence in the whole of their correspondence of a serious quarrel."[26]

Alexandra's 13 letters in the next dozen days blazed with a heightened sense of crisis and a conviction of what Russia needed to survive the test. "You have spoilt [people] by yr. kindness and all forgivingness," she warned her husband, "[you are] so kind, trusting and gentle" that such people as Trepov and Rodzyanko "try to ennervate, frighten and prick at you." Alexandra admitted her shortcomings; she was "always so shy without you, my Lovy dear"; some of her letters were "impertinent." But the empress felt a sense of urgency; only she could save her husband. "Why do people hate me?" "Because they know I have a strong will & when am convinced of a thing being right (when besides blessed by *Gregory*) do not change my mind." "Those who are affraid [sic] of me . . . or are up to some wrong, never like me," she insisted, "[they] don't look me in the eyes; . . . but those who are good and devoted to you honestly & purely—love me."

Alexandra feared that her husband would surrender power or turn on those who were really devoted to them. The empress pleaded with Nicholas to "keep" Protopopov, the "truest friend; . . . stick to him, be firm, don't give in." Above all the tsar should hold the "deepest faith in the prayers & help of our Friend." Rasputin "is praying so hard for you," "his dreams means [sic] so much." "He has kept you where you are," Alexandra flatly declared at one point, "only be as convinced as I am & . . . then all will be well."[27]

The saddest note in Alexandra's song was sounded in Petrograd in the fall of 1916. The tsarina had a secret staircase built that led to a small chamber next to the tsar's receiving room. She could now listen to all conversations. Rodzyanko "noticed, or rather felt, the presence of the empress" here during one of his reports to the tsar. "But this did not trouble me, and I continued to state the truth openly about Sturmer and Protopopov and Rasputin."[28]

Trepov was furious to learn that Nicholas was keeping Protopopov, and he tried to resign.

"Alexander Fedorovich," the tsar replied in an imperious tone, "I order you to carry out your duties with the colleagues I have thought fit to give you." Trepov left, choking with anger.

Trepov now resorted to a desperate gamble. His brother-in-law Alexander Mosolov knew Rasputin. Trepov asked Mosolov to offer Rasputin a bribe if he and Protopopov would "retire." Grigory would receive 200,000 rubles and a house in Petrograd plus expenses—including bodyguards.

"I want him to refrain from meddling further in appointments of ministers and high government officials," Trepov told Mosolov. "As for the clergy, I leave him a free hand if he wants it. No personal interviews with me; if he wants to say anything to me, he must do it through you. You know the man. Try to make him listen to reason."

Mosolov thought this was a "great mistake" and indeed Grigory angrily refused the offer. Mosolov tried to defend the proposal. But after an hour and two bottles of wine, the answer was still "no." "After this fiasco I went back to Trepov," Mosolov wrote. "He realized that he was done for."[29]

Trepov was dismissed as chairman of the council of ministers on December 27, 1916. He had served in his office for 47 days. By then Rasputin had been dead for 11 days.

Prince Nicholas Golitsyn was Nicholas's last chairman of the council of ministers. The Golitsyns were one of Russia's leading families. Vasily Golitsyn was the lover of Princess Sophia in the 1680s; he campaigned against Turkey while dreaming of reforming Russian society. Another Golitsyn foiled Sophia's plot to set her half-brother Peter aside and rule in her own right. A third Golitsyn chose the ruler of Russia in 1730. The *Soviet Historical Encyclopedia* has articles on eight different Golitsyns. A ninth article is devoted to Nicholas Golitsyn, last in an illustrious line.

This Golitsyn was old, in poor health, and semiretired. The prince served honorably as provincial governor, senator, and until recently a member of the far-right faction in the State Council. During the war he worked with the Red Cross, heading a commission that helped Russian prisoners of war. Alexandra cooperated with Golitsyn in these efforts. When a message summoned the prince to the royal palace on the evening of Christmas Day 1916, the prince assumed that the empress needed to confer with him on some aspect of their work. Golitsyn was not even surprised to be brought before the tsar. Nicholas explained that his wife was busy, he asked the visitor for a chat. The emperor noted that Trepov was leaving the cabinet. Who would be a suitable replacement? After a brief discussion silence set in.

"I have been sly with you," Nicholas confessed. "It is I who summoned you, not the empress. I have been thinking for a long time about who to appoint chairman of the council of ministers. My choice has fallen upon you."

Golitsyn was stunned. He was not fit to head the tsar's government, and he admitted it. He told the tsar he had "very little experience with political matters";

he was 66, in poor health, and needed a rest after 47 years of active service. Golitsyn was a man of limited ability and boundless honor. He told the tsar the truth, and he left assuming that reason would prevail. Three days later he received official notification of his appointment. As a monarchist who loved his tsar, Golitsyn had to respond to Nicholas's appeal for help.

Golitsyn did not do badly as chairman of the council of ministers. He failed to save the tsarist regime—but who could have done that at this time? "Yet he deserves to be remembered, if only for this story: asked by a friend why he, a man with no political ambitions or experience, agreed in the evening of his life to assume so hazardous a post, the elderly nobleman replied, 'Ah, to have yet another pleasant memory.' "[30]

PART IV

THE END

"The Rivers Will Flow with Blood"

Alexandra was the most hated woman in Russia by early 1916. Popular opinion held that she was leader of the "dark forces" driving the nation to destruction. Millions of Russians assumed that the German-born Alexandra favored peace with the kaiser; some swore she was a German agent. According to one rumor, she transmitted military secrets over a line from the Alexander Palace.

Rasputin was also considered part of the "dark forces," second only to the empress in usefulness to the German cause. Grigory had often stood against xenophobia and war, which probably sparked the idea that he was pro-German. Rasputin was actually patriotic: Once the struggle was joined he urged Nicholas to press for victory. Grigory did try to keep his son from being drafted. The tsar ignored the request, but Anna Vyrubova got Dmitry assigned to medical service. Rumors of this favoritism reinforced the notion that Rasputin was the real power in Russia, and the empress's lover.[1]

Russians constantly talked about Rasputin. In the summer of 1915 "one man's name was on everyone's lips," the Poet Marina Tsvetaeva noted, "that of Grigory Rasputin." By New Year's Day, she marvelled that none of the friends who gathered with her to greet the new year, 1916, "said the word 'front,' nor . . . was the name of Rasputin uttered." Six months later the situation was even worse. "Russia became an insane asylum holding both the sick and the well," Prince Zhevakov recalled. "People did not understand each other, they did not have a common language but rather tore at each other, inflicting blows and charges and blame." Exasperated hosts and restaurant owners finally posted signs that proclaimed: "No talking about Rasputin here!"[2]

Popular hostility toward Rasputin was not confined to the capital. A third-class coach leaving Voronezh, peasants in the provinces, women in line in the cities—all took Rasputin as a topic. The Bolsheviks sold "obscene pamphlets of the empress and the monk [while] exhibiting a series of disgusting and faked pictures at the local cinematograph," showing Grigory's intimacy with Alexandra and even her daughters. In late 1916 the authorities withdrew a recently released cinema news clip showing Nicholas presenting himself with the St. George Cross. When it was shown voices shouted "the Father-Tsar is with Igory, but the Mother-Tsarina is with Grigory."[3]

The rumblings extended to Stavka. A German cartoon caused widespread laughter there in February 1916. The kaiser was aiming a shell while the tsar measured a projectile, which was Rasputin. "All laughed, none thought it was necessary to refrain. Total disintegration." Zeppelins soon showered Russian lines with a similar cartoon and a demoralizing caption. Privates asked officers how the tsar could "stand for such a nuisance in his own house?" They could only shrug their shoulders and wonder: "Is he worth it?"[4]

Rasputin was often assaulted during the war. One night at the *Villa Rode* he fell to boasting of his relations with the royal family. Showing off his richly embroidered silk shirt, he declared "It's Shashka's work," using a diminutive form of Alexandra's name, which insulted a lady of her station. An officer stood up for the empress's honor and Rasputin was wounded in the fight that followed. Another time Rasputin claimed to be familiar with the royal girls. "If you like, I'll call Tatyana and tell her to join us." Three officers promptly sent the starets to a hospital.[5]

On another occasion two officers broke into a gathering at a restaurant. Grigory took his party elsewhere, with the officers in quiet pursuit. A shot rang out, women screamed and Grigory was dragged unwillingly to a car. "They don't love me," he said as the car pulled away with more gunfire. The officers were arrested. They claimed that they had been ordered to murder Grigory. Rasputin's face yellowed when he heard the news; he seemed to age suddenly by years.[6]

Serious attempts were made to kill Rasputin. A troika at full speed tried to run Grigory over as he strolled on Nevsky Avenue one night. He suffered a minor head wound. Rasputin and Anna Vyrubova were sleighing when a car attacked their vehicle and flipped it over. Rasputin was only bruised, but Vyrubova was said to be seriously injured. Another evening oak logs suddenly appeared in front of Grigory's automobile. The would-be assassins escaped except for an accomplice. She named the others. They were peasants from Tsaritsyn, which was still a place where Iliodor was loved and Rasputin hated. Grigory refused to press charges, and the peasants were rounded up and sent home.[7]

Rasputin was increasingly gloomy at the end. He still believed in his religious mission and never doubted that he should be at the royal family's side. But Rasputin and Simanovich often spoke of retiring to Palestine after the war. Friends, especially women, began to see a new troubled Grigory Rasputin.

"Some power he wanted to control was carrying him somewhere," the Russian writer Teffi recalled. She thought Rasputin had been "blown off his feet and carried away by a whirlwind."[8]

Rasputin found comfort in friends: Simanovich and Vyrubova, Beletsky and Protopopov. He was also close to Nicholas and Alexandra, though he never took the relationship for granted. Grigory still spent an entire day getting ready to go to Tsarskoe Selo. Kon observed one such preparation. For hours Rasputin's energy seemed concentrated in his face and body. He did not touch alcohol; he went to the bathhouse and then to church. Vasiliev thought that fear was behind these rituals: Grigory supposed his misdeeds had reached the royal couple, and they were summoning him to a final meeting. Maria Rasputin insisted that her father was a simple peasant who had been reared "to view the tsar as God on earth."[9]

Rasputin's relationship with the royal family took on a poignant character in their final months. Spring came, but the days were gray and windy, and a last blanket of snow fell and then quickly melted. The ice on the Neva cracked as the river rose, breaking the chains of winter imprisonment. Grigory and Nicholas took communion in March 1916; the tsar was moved by the experience. He told Rasputin "[I] will not be separated from you for anything in the world." But Grigory sensed that parting would come. At one of their last meetings, the moment arrived when the starets would ordinarily bless the tsar. "This time it is for you to bless me, not I you," Grigory said quietly.[10]

Alexandra and Grigory celebrated their final Easter in April at Tsarskoe Selo. When Alexandra took the bread and wine, she glanced at Grigory, inviting him to follow just after her. Paléologue heard that "they exchanged the kiss of peace, Rasputin kissing the empress on the forehead and she returning the kiss on his hand." It was the custom in Russia for a junior person to kiss the hand of the senior person who returned the kiss on the forehead. In this case, the roles were reversed—by the tsarina's choice.[11]

Rasputin told Alexandra that their Easter communion gave him new energy to fight their enemies. Grigory was certain that God had sent him to save the imperial family and Holy Russia. The empress certainly needed an arm to rest upon in November 1916. In a speech to the Duma, the Russian liberal leader Paul Milyukov attacked the "dark forces" around Rasputin and the empress. He cited instances of government incompetence, asking at each point, "is this stupidity or treason?" This produced a flurry of activity around the tsarina. Grigory saw Alexandra six times in eight days. As usual their meetings took place at Anna's house near the Alexander Palace.[12]

Rasputin's heightened self-confidence was mixed with despair. His disciples noticed a "melancholy, brooding air" in their leader during the 1916 Easter season, though he put on a brave face for the empress. "Do you realize before long I shall die in terrible agonies?" he asked, calling himself a "Christ in miniature." On another occasion, he was strolling by the Peter and Paul Fortress with two women. "I can see many persons in agony there," Grigory suddenly declared. "I can see heaps, masses of corpses, several grand dukes and hundreds of counts. The Neva will be all red with blood."

Rasputin realized that Russia's leadership could not cope with the crisis. "Papa doesn't know what he wants," Grigory moaned, "he's no good"—"he can't tell left from right"—"he's got no guts!" One moment he praised Alexandra as a "new Catherine the Great," but at another he admitted "something's wrong with mama." "Sturmer makes a mess." "Protopopov doesn't rule, he just dances around, telephoning everyone, asking advice!" "Nothing is any good," he concluded, "it's the devil's work. My soul is restless all the time."[13]

Rasputin saw his son for the last time in the fall of 1916. Dmitry was on leave in early November. He came from the capital for a brief visit, then boarded the train for home. "Good-bye, Mitya, I shall never see you again," Grigory sadly declared. Later that month Rasputin wrote—or dictated—a final letter to his wife. Grigory predicted "great misfortunes"; he quoted the Scripture that tells us the Son of Man will come when least expected. "The night is dark with the suffering that is before us," he lamented. "I shall not see it. My hour is very near, but though it is bitter, I do not fear it." Grigory assured Praskovaya that she and the children would survive if she would "pray and be strong in your affliction." "There will be many martyrs for the Faith," he continued, and "brother shall meet death from brother. The evil will be so great that the earth will tremble with it, and with famine and sickness; and miraculous signs will appear throughout the world."[14]

Rasputin composed another letter shortly before his death entitled "The Spirit of Grigory Efimovich Rasputin–Novykh of the village of Pokrovskoe." Aron Simanovich claims that Grigory gave this letter to the empress with a plea that she not show it to her huband.

I am writing and leaving this letter at St. Petersburg. I feel that I shall leave this life before January 1. I wish to make known to the Russian people, to Papa, to the Russian Mother and to the Children, to the land of Russia, what they must understand. If I am killed by common assassins, and especially by my brothers the Russian peasants, you, Tsar of Russia, have nothing to fear. Remain on your throne and govern, Russian Tsar, you will have nothing to fear for your children, they will reign for hundreds of years in Russia. But if I am murdered by boyars and nobles[,] and if they shed my blood, their hands will remain soiled by my blood and for twenty-five years they will not be able to wash their hands. They will leave Russia. Brother will rise up against brother, and they will kill each other and hate each other, and for twenty-five years there will be no nobles in the country.

Tsar of the land of Russia, when you hear the sound of the bell telling you that Grigory has been killed, you must know this: if your relatives carried out the murder, then not one of your family—that is none of your children or relatives—will remain alive for more than two years. They will be killed by the Russian people. I am leaving and feel in me the divine command to tell the Russian Tsar how he must live after my departure. You should be concerned for your salvation and tell your relatives that I paid for them with my life. They will kill me. I am no longer among the living. Pray, pray, be strong, think of your blessed family. Grigory.[15]

Rasputin was in a state of deep depression during the last three days of his life. But he did take one positive step. Grigory and Aron Simanovich went to a bank and Rasputin opened up accounts for his daughters, Maria and Varbara, depositing "several thousand rubles" in each. When Grigory returned home—despite Maria's pleas—he burned every letter and telegram he had saved from the most prominent people of Holy Russia.[16]

=== 23 ===
Conspiracy

We are not certain why Felix Yusupov murdered Rasputin. He said he feared that Grigory was undermining Nicholas's government and opening the path to revolution. Friends assumed that Felix was fascinated by the mystery and intrigue—that he enjoyed a titillating new adventure. Family pressure and an affection for Nicholas and Alexandra clearly played a role in setting Yusupov against the starets. Maria Rasputin claimed that Felix made sexual overtures to Grigory; she thought he craved revenge for being rejected. Each of these explanations is plausible, yet none satisfies. Yusupov's motives remain a mystery.

The prince met Rasputin in 1909. Grigory was very taken with Felix, but the feeling was not mutual and they parted for the next seven years. During this time Yusupov studied at Oxford and married Irina, the fabulously attractive daughter of the tsar's cousin Grand Duke Alexander Michaelovich. As an only son Yusupov avoided the draft. The need for new recruits eliminated this exemption, and the prince was promptly called up. Yusupov stalled for time by enrolling in an officer's training program. Somehow the Oxford graduate failed his final exams and had to repeat the entire course. At this point, Felix became concerned with Rasputin and the "dark forces."

A family setback made Felix question Nicholas and Alexandra—and their friend Grigory Rasputin. Yusupov's father was governor-general of Moscow during riots in June 1915 against Russians with Germanic surnames. The senior Yusupov was dismissed for ineptitude, but the family claimed it was because he found "treason and espionage everywhere. . . ." Felix's parents retired to their estate near Yalta. From here Princess Zinaida bombarded her son with letters critical of the court. Zinaida thought it "imperative to remove the manager

[their code name for Rasputin] and to depose Valide [Alexandra Fedorovna]."
It is not likely that Madame Yusupova wanted either killed. But her son might
devise another solution to the problem.[1]

The idea of killing Rasputin first occurred to Yusupov at this time. The family
was discussing Grigory's influence. Felix thought that Nicholas and Alexandra
could be persuaded to break with Rasputin. His parents pointed out that such
appeals had been made and failed. Murder now took an increasing hold over
the prince's thoughts.

Felix came to believe "not a single important event at the front was decided
without a preliminary conference" between Alexandra and Rasputin. Grigory
and the empress actually had no influence over military decisions. Nicholas
briefed his wife on war plans, but not their friends. On several occasions the
tsar warned Alexandra "[do] not communicate these details to anyone; I have
written them only for you." When Nicholas told her of plans for the 1916 spring
offensive, he added "I beg you not to tell *anyone* of this."[2]

Nicholas had good reason to be secretive—and hopeful. His generals spent
the early months of 1916 organizing what would be the high point of Russia's
war effort. In the spring General Alexis Brusilov fielded an assault in the south-
western sector that took the enemy by surprise and cost him a million casualties
and 400,000 prisoners. The Brusilov offensive also pulled 18 German divisions
from Verdun and kept the Austrians from exploiting a major success over the
Italians at Caporetto. Sensing an allied victory, Romania finally gave in to
Russian pressure and entered the war. But the cost was terribly high: Not counting
prisoners, the tsar's army suffered 1.2 million casualties in Brusilov's relentless
drive.[3]

Alexandra apparently heeded her husband's plea; she did not tell Grigory
about the Brusilov offensive. But Grigory was brimming with "advice" for the
tsar once it began. Yusupov and other Russians were thrilled by their army's
success, but the empress and Rasputin were shaken by the carnage. "He finds
better one shld. not advance to obstinately as the losses will be too great,"
Alexandra wrote on July 25, 1916. "Our Friend hopes we wont climb over the
Carpathians and try to take them, as he repeats the losses will be too great
again," she added on August 8. By September 9, the tsar's generals conceded
that they could not sustain the offensive. Nicholas again asked his wife to keep
this information from "Father Grigory." This time the tsarina refused to keep
him in the dark. "Our Friend says about the new orders you gave to *Brussilov*
etc.: *'Very satisfied with father's orders, all will be well.* He won't mention it
to a soul, but I had to ask His blessing for yr. decision.'"[4]

The Brusilov offensive marked a turning point in Yusupov's thinking. He
blamed Rasputin for the costs of the attack and its end. At this point the prince
did not think that Grigory was a German agent, but he was convinced that
Russian military secrets passed from the starets and his circle. Yusupov also
decided the peasant was discrediting the monarchy and dragging it to destruction.[5]

Yusupov approached senior statesmen with his plan to murder Rasputin. Surely these long-time critics would help rid Russia of such a menace. To Yusupov's surprise, they suddenly thought Grigory's importance had been greatly exaggerated! Rodzyanko admitted that the only solution was to murder Rasputin. He would do it himself if he weren't so old! Felix concluded that these men craved a quiet life; they were incapable of action that would disturb and threaten their happy lives. They did not recognize the danger Russia faced. Yusupov must act without them. But first he had to renew his acquaintance with Rasputin.[6]

A mutual friend arranged a meeting. Felix was amazed at how Rasputin had changed in the last seven years. Grigory's face was "puffy," he seemed to have become "lax and flabby." The starets no longer wore an "ordinary peasant's coat"; now he sported a pale blue silk blouse and wide velvet trousers. His appearance was "extraordinarily repugnant." "Yet he seemed very much at ease."[7]

Yusupov appealed for Grigory's aid as a healer. The prince claimed that he was in bad health and his doctors were unable to help him.

Rasputin promised to cure Felix. Grigory disparaged doctors: They stuff people with medicine that did nothing to help the patients. "But I know better," he proclaimed. "With me everybody gets well. I heal in God's way, and in God's name."[8]

The prince and the peasant now saw each other frequently. Yusupov grew even more frightened of Rasputin's power as their relationship deepened. Felix became convinced that Badmaev and Grigory had "doctored" Nicholas and his son with "various herbs" and "remedies unknown to European science." People noted that the tsar's powers of concentration were dissipated and that he was apathetic; his eyes grew weak, he rambled, and was often incoherent. Rumors held that Alexandra's letters insisted her husband take the "drops prescribed by Badmaev." "The sinister Tibetan and the still more sinister starets" were indeed a "formidable alliance."[9]

Yusupov claimed he feared for Nicholas's welfare. "The empress is a very wise ruler," Rasputin said. "She is a second Catherine [the Great]; but as for him, well, he is no Tsar Emperor, he is just a child of God." Yusupov concluded that Grigory was privy to a plan to remove Nicholas and install Alexandra as their son's regent.[10]

Vladimir Purishkevich was a short bald man with a full black beard. He was born into a wealthy noble family in Bessarabia in 1870. Purishkevich was a harsh anti-Semite and advocated absolute monarchy and Russian nationalism. He despised the Duma as a dangerous import from Western Europe, a concession wrested from the tsar in a moment of weakness. Vladimir Mitrofanovich joined the Duma only to ridicule it, to weaken it from within. He disrupted its proceedings with catcalls, insults, and comical faces. Purishkevich once threw water on a speaker; another time he sported a bright red carnation laced through the buttons of his fly. He was often expelled from the floor only to return as immoderate as ever.[11]

During the war, Purishkevich advocated cooperation among all factions committed to victory. He was no longer obstructionist. Vladimir Mitrofanovich's speeches now sparkled, and the Duma quieted respectfully when he rose to address it. Purishkevich also expressed his patriotism in deeds. He bought a locomotive and toured army lines with food and hot drinks, books, blankets, and medical supplies. Purishkevich received thousands of letters, many with contributions to help his work. Maria Rasputin praised him as a "man of integrity" and a "relentless worker," though she also saw him as "weak," "uneasy and ill-balanced."

Purishkevich hated Rasputin for undermining the tsar's government. He matched Milyukov's "Treason" speech with his own blistering attack of November 19, 1916. Purishkevich charged "all evil proceeds from those dark forces, from those influences . . . headed by Grishka Rasputin." Referring to the tsar's ministers as a "dozen sleeping beauties," he called upon them to awaken and act. "If duty is above career for the ministers, if they form a truly united cabinet, then let them go to the tsar to tell him that things can no longer continue in this way. . . . Go there to the tsar's headquarters, throw yourselves at the tsar's feet and ask him to open his eyes to the terrible reality."[12]

Purishkevich's audience repeatedly cheered. The applause reached a stormy height as he left the rostrum. But a thin young man in the gallery was strangely silent. He listened intently; then he turned pale and trembled as if in the grip of some "uncontrollable emotion."[13] He was Prince Felix Yusupov.

Impressed as he was at Purishkevich's speech, Yusupov's next effort was to involve a prominent liberal in his plans. Later the same day he called upon Vasily Maklakov, a distinguished journalist and a moderate member of the Kadet Party. Yusupov asked Maklakov to join him in killing Rasputin. Maklakov refused, though he expressed support and would serve as defense attorney if needed. Yusupov now turned to Purishkevich. The prince was granted an appointment on November 21, 1916.

Felix praised Purishkevich's speech but doubted it would help.

"Then what is to be done?" Purishkevich asked.

"To dispose of Rasputin," Yusupov quietly replied, smiling and fixing Vladimir Mitrofanovich with an unblinking stare.

"It's nice to say that, but who will undertake it when there are no decisive people in Russia? The government should do it—and cleverly—but it guards Rasputin like the apple of your eye."

"Yes," Felix conceded, "it is impossible to count upon the government. All the same, such people are to be found in Russia."

"Do you think so?" Purishkevich asked.

"I am certain of it, and one of them is standing before you."

Yusupov and Purishkevich talked for over two hours that morning. Both recognized the difficulties involved in killing Rasputin. Vladimir Mitrofanovich actually had entertained the idea of murdering Rasputin in 1912. Purishkevich was even more convinced of the need for this now, and he gladly extended his hand in cooperation. Yusupov proudly informed his new colleague that he had recruited two other men to the enterprise. The four would meet at Yusupov's house to plan the assassination of Grigory Efimovich Rasputin.[14]

At 8 P.M. the following evening, Yusupov introduced Purishkevich to Grand Duke Dmitry Pavlovich and Lt. Ivan Sukhotin. The men were eager to rid Russia of Rasputin, but they feared that an open murder would seem to be a demonstration against the tsar. Rasputin had best "disappear," and those responsible would keep silent. But if they were captured, it should be clear that the assassins were devoted to Nicholas. Dmitry Pavlovich was a member of the royal family, son of Grand Duke Paul. Yusupov stood for the nobility, and Sukhotin the junior officers. Purishkevich represented the Duma monarchists. It might be difficult to punish such men if they were caught.[15]

Yusupov knew that Rasputin's disappearance would devastate Alexandra Fedorovna, but he felt it was in her interests. "Only Grigory's death would free her from his spell, and permit Nicholas to emerge as a constitutional monarch."[16]

The conspirators decided to act at Yusupov's mansion. Felix would lure Rasputin there and poison him while the coconspirators stood close at hand. The assassins would put Grigory's body in a sack and stuff it under the ice to be carried out to sea—or at least concealed for the duration of the winter. Purishkevich's associate Dr. S. S. Lazavert was brought into the plot: A physician can be as useful in taking a life as in saving it.

The would-be murderers were anxious to finish their deed, but several factors dictated a delay. Felix's wife was wintering with his parents; he was living with her brothers. A suite of rooms—including the now-famous cellar where the murder finally took place—was being prepared for his return. But the work could not be completed until mid-December 1916. Dmitry Pavlovich's social calendar did not have a free spot until then; rearranging it might attract attention and would certainly compromise him if an investigation ensued. The date finally selected was December 16, 1916.[17]

Yusupov admitted that murder was a sin; offering the victim hospitality would make the deed even more dastardly. Felix prayed for guidance at the Cathedral of Our Lady of Kazan. He concluded that all personal considerations were insignificant if the object was to save Russia. The prince was now in a state of religious ecstasy. This helped Yusupov cope with the most difficult problem of all: to spend time with Rasputin, to pretend to be his friend, and to draw him into a fatal trap.[18]

=== 24 ===
Murder

Petrograd sparkled with snow on the morning of December 16, 1916; "wee pink clouds" dotted the sky, and the thermometer stood at − 10°. Rasputin rose early and, under heavy police escort, went to church and the bathhouse. He began to receive callers about 11 A.M. Then came an anonymous call threatening his life. Rasputin had so much wine at lunch that he could not take a telephone call from Tobolsk. A nap revived him sufficiently to receive Vyrubova in the early afternoon. Rasputin told Anna that he was to meet Yusupov's wife Irina that night. Vyrubova knew that Rasputin and Felix had been seeing a lot of each other recently, but the late hour seemed odd. Rasputin explained that Yusupov did not want his parents to know of the visit.

Alexandra agreed that the late-night engagement was curious. "There must be some mistake," the empress remarked. "Irina is at the Crimea and neither of the older Yusupovs is in town." "There is surely a mistake," the tsarina repeated thoughtfully. But she and Vyrubova temporarily put Rasputin's plans out of their minds.[1]

Strong forces acted the day Rasputin died to keep him home—and alive. The conspirators were scarcely tight-lipped, and the capital had been buzzing for days that Grigory would soon be murdered. Simanovich was so alarmed that he stayed with Rasputin throughout the day. He finally left near midnight just before Protopopov was to appear. Protopopov stayed ten minutes. He also cautioned Grigory to be careful, which may explain why Rasputin said nothing to him about his late-night plans.[2]

Grigory's daughters tried to keep their father home. At 10 P.M. they noticed he was wearing the light blue blouse and velvet breeches reserved for the most special occasions, and they asked if he was going out. Grigory offhandedly admitted that he was invited to the Yusupov mansion; Maria and Varbara hid his boots. Their father lay down for a nap and the girls went to bed. The bell at the servants' entrance announced a caller at midnight. It was Prince Felix Yusupov. Katya helped Rasputin find his boots, and then she retreated into the shadows to observe the situation.

"It's those children again," Rasputin grumbled as he put on his footwear. "They don't want me to go out." Grigory then put on his coat and slipped down the back stairs to face whatever the night would bring.[3]

Yusupov and his cohorts made careful preparations. Felix was to bring the guest to a corner of the wine cellar partitioned and decorated as a bachelor's den. Suspicions might be aroused if the room betrayed a stark, uninhabited character, so the prince spent the day selecting curtains and rugs, antique furniture, Chinese vases, ebony cupboards, tables covered with fabrics, and *objects d'art*. A large Persian carpet stood before the fireplace; a white bearskin rug guarded the labyrinthine cupboard. The room now exuded a cheerful comfort. The stillness "lent an air of mystery, a sort of detachment from the world. It seemed that whatever might happen here would be hidden from mortal eyes and buried forever in the silence of these stone walls." A spiral staircase led to Felix's study. The others would wait here while Yusupov entertained their victim.

A samovar with pastry and hors d'oeuvres were on the table; wines and glasses stood on a sideboard. Yusupov gave Dr. Lazavert a box containing the poison. Lazavert crushed the potassium cyanide crystals into a fine powder. He then removed the tops of the six cakes reserved for Grigory, giving each a strong dose. The potion was placed into wineglasses only at the last minute so the cyanide would lose a minimum of strength through exposure. The amount of poison applied was enormous; Lazavert assured his colleagues that the dose would cause death many times over.

The watchman at 64 Gorokhovaya demanded that Felix identify himself when he appeared at the back stairs. Yusupov avoided this by explaining that Rasputin was expecting him. But the secrecy Felix sought was breached. Although the detective guard was lifted at midnight, a single Okhrana agent remained on the scene. He discreetly followed Rasputin to Yusupov's home and remained there, watching.[4]

The strains of "Yankee Doodle" on a gramophone upstairs greeted Rasputin as he alighted at the side entrance of the Yusupov palace.

"What's going on?" Grigory asked. "A party?"

"No, my wife has friends with her," Felix replied. "They will go away soon, so for the time being let's go down to the dining room and have some tea."

Rasputin removed his wraps and took a seat. After a half-hour Yusupov came up the stairs to brief his friends on the situation. "Nothing's happened," Felix whispered. "That animal hasn't drunk or eaten. He won't accept my hospitality in any form."

After some hushed counseling Yusupov returned to his guest. Grigory now took tea, but still refused food. Then he changed his mind and ate two poisoned cakes. The cyanide should have taken effect immediately, but to Yusupov's amazement Rasputin simply chattered away. Felix finally got a glass of wine into Rasputin, then another. The poison still had no apparent effect. Grigory now asked the all-but-hysterical prince to sing some gypsy songs. It was 2:20 A.M. and Rasputin was quite alive.[5]

"What's all the noise?" Grigory asked, noticing a racket from the other conspirators, who were frantic at the delay and wondering what had gone wrong.

"Probably it's the guests going away," Felix replied. "I'll go up and see."

Yusupov conferred with his cohorts. All were amazed that the poison was having no impact. Felix told them that Rasputin was impatient with Irina's failure to appear. Their guest might well leave. The group decided that Felix should return and give Rasputin another five minutes. If he was still alive at that time, Yusupov would come back and they would find another tactic.

Felix reappeared and admitted nothing had changed. The discussion now favored trying another time. But Purishkevich, the oldest and most resolute member of the group, made it clear that was unacceptable. They had come to do a deed—and it should be done.

After various methods were proposed and rejected, Yusupov stepped to his desk, took out a small Browning, and with firm steps returned below. Felix's first preference had been poison. If all goes well poison is quick, clean, and silent. Alex de Jonge notes a successful poisoner need never reveal his intentions to the victim. Events follow a natural course. "He thereby avoids the terrible moment of naked embarrassment when both parties know what is about to happen and look one another in the eye."[6] Poison apparently failed on the night of December 16–17, 1916. Rising to the occasion, Felix settled upon a different approach.

Yusupov found Rasputin seated, head bowed, and breathing heavily. "My stomach is burning," Grigory complained. "Give me another glass of Madeira," he continued. "That will ease me."[7]

Rasputin and Yusupov talked on for a while. Although the hour was late Grigory suggested going to the gypsies. Felix was amazed that even now Grigory, for all of his much-touted "instinctive knowledge and insight," should still be "so utterly unconscious of his approaching end."

Rasputin praised the crystal crucifix; he then began to examine the elegant cupboard. The decisive moment was at hand.

"Grigory Efimovich, you had better look at the crucifix and say a prayer before it."

Rasputin stared at Yusupov in amazement, a trace of fear spread over his face. Gentle submission showed in his eyes as Grigory approached his host. Felix fired one shot, and Rasputin fell backwards onto the bearskin rug. The other conspirators now came stumbling down the stairs. The bullet struck the region of the heart; there was remarkably little bleeding. Rasputin was obviously dead. Dmitry Pavlovich pulled the body from the rug onto the stone floor. The conspirators turned off the lights, locked the door, and went upstairs convinced they had just saved Russia.

It was now 3 A.M. and the assassins rushed to complete their plan. Sukhotin donned Rasputin's coat, hat, and gloves. Dr. Lazavert would chauffeur him to Grigory's flat; there the imposter would exit the car and pretend to enter the apartment. Sukhotin would actually join Dmitry Pavlovich in a crouching position on the floor of the automobile. The car was to proceed to Purishkevich's train at the Warsaw Station where Mmes. Purishkevich and Lazavert, planned to burn the dead man's clothes. Dmitry Pavlovich, Lazavert, and Sukhotin would take a taxi to Dmitry Pavlovich's automobile and return to the Yusupov mansion. The assassins would then bring the body to a hole in the ice that Dmitry had found earlier that day near the Petrovsky Bridge.

Yusupov and Purishkevich remained behind in the prince's study. A vague feeling of alarm suddenly came over Felix; he was seized by an overwhelming desire to see his victim's body. Leaving Purishkevich upstairs, Yusupov returned to the cellar. Felix felt for a pulse; there was none. Yusupov suddenly grabbed the corpse and began to shake it. He then let the body fall back to its former position, the head dangling lifelessly. As the prince was leaving he noticed that Grigory's left eyelid was trembling ever so slightly. Then its movements became pronounced. The left eye suddenly opened! Then the right eye stirred. In a flash both eyes, "greenish and snake-like—fixed themselves upon [Felix] with an expression of devilish hatred."[8]

Rasputin sprang to his feet and lunged at Yusupov. With a mighty roar he took the prince by the shoulder and tried to seize his neck. Felix fought free and Rasputin again fell backwards, tightly clasping an epaulet torn from Yusupov's jacket. Rasputin lay motionless on the floor and then again stirred to life.

Felix clambered up the stairs shouting, "Quick! Quick! the revolver! he is alive!" In an instant the prince was in the study, his blue eyes bulging and his skin so pale that he seemed to have no face. Yusupov dashed into his parents' section of the mansion, leaving Purishkevich to deal with Rasputin alone.[9]

Purishkevich hurdled down the staircase just in time to see Rasputin running across the courtyard toward an open gate on the other side.

"Felix! Felix!" Grigory was shouting, "I'll tell the tsarina everything!"

Purishkevich fired once, twice—and missed both times. Rasputin was about to reach the gate to the street and freedom. Purishkevich made a tight fist with his left hand as if to concentrate all of his energy in the hand holding the revolver. A third shot hit Grigory in the back, a fourth in the head. Purishkevich ran up to Rasputin and kicked him in the temple. Purishkevich was finally convinced that Grigory Efimovich was dead.

Two soldiers were passing by the gate during the shooting. They followed Purishkevich to the house and knocked on the door.

"Young fellows," Purishkevich stammered, "I killed, I killed—I killed Grishka Rasputin, enemy of Russia and the tsar!" One of the soldiers kissed Vladimir Mitrofanovich as the other cried out, "Glory be to God, it should have been done long ago!"

"Friends, Prince Felix Yusupov and I are hoping for your absolute silence," Purishkevich continued. "You understand that the tsarina isn't going to reward us for this. Are you able to keep silence?"

"Your excellency," came the reply, "We are Russians. Have no doubt, we won't betray you."

The soldiers then carried Rasputin's body to the house as Purishkevich went looking for Yusupov. He found the prince in a bathroom, leaning over a wash-basin, holding his head with his hands and spitting repeatedly.

"What's wrong with you, my lad!" Purishkevich exclaimed triumphantly. "Relax, he's no longer with us. I put an end to him. Come with me, my dear, come to the study with us."

Yusupov stumbled along, repeating aimlessly, "Felix! Felix! Felix!" When he saw the body he flew into a rage. Rushing to his desk, Yusupov grabbed the two-pound, rubber fist-knuckles that Maklakov gave him and began to assault Rasputin's body. Purishkevich studied the macabre scene with a wry detachment. Yusupov seemed in "some sort of wild rage," a state of "absolutely unnatural excitement." Purishkevich guessed that something had passed between Yusupov and his victim when the two were together in the cellar, something that made an impression on Felix.[10]

Purishkevich and one of the soldiers bound Rasputin's body, wrapped in a large cloth, with stout cords. A policeman now appeared, asking about the commotion. A servant was insisting events at such an important home did not concern the police. But Yusupov decided to see the officer.

"Your highness, I heard shots. Has anything happened?"

Felix's plan had not allowed for the possibility of gunfire, much less that the police would appear to investigate. The prince obviously panicked, and under pressure tried to improvise a new story. Yusupov's first "new" tale—the one he delivered at this moment—claimed that some of his friends were tipsy and someone fired a weapon. Felix assured the officer that everything was in order.

Officer Vlasyuk left to exchange thoughts with Tikhomirov, the Okhrana detective who followed Rasputin earlier that evening. They agreed that Yusu-pov's explanations were not satisfactory, and Vlasyuk reappeared for additional information. This time Purishkevich took charge of the situation—and in his own honest fashion. Guessing that Vlasyuk was a "servant of the old type," Vladimir Mitrofanovich inquired into his patriotism, opinions about Sturmer, Rasputin, etc. Purishkevich finally took the policeman into his confidence.

"Well, little brother, [Rasputin] is no more!" Purishkevich dramatically pro-claimed. "We shot and killed him just now. You heard this—but if anyone asks say, 'to know is not to know, to be in charge is not to be in charge.' Are you able to not betray us and keep quiet?"

"I won't say anything if I'm not under oath when questioned," the policeman replied carefully. "But if I'm under oath, I'll have to tell the truth. It is a sin to lie."

Dmitry Pavlovich, Purishkevich, Lazavert, and Sukhotin stashed Rasputin's body in the limousine along with chains and two 72-pound weights. One of the soldiers accompanied them to the hole in the ice. Purishkevich noticed that Rasputin's fur coat and boots were still in the automobile. Asking why they had not been burned, he was told that his wife decided these items would not go into the stove without being cut to pieces, and—despite objections—she insisted that was out of the question. "We'll throw them into the water with the body," Purishkevich mumbled irritably.

Dmitry Pavlovich drove slowly to minimize attention at such a late hour. The assassins reached the spot near the Petrovsky Bridge located earlier. They heaved Rasputin's body over the guardrail into the Neva. The murderers then realized they forgot to use the chains and weights that would carry the body to the bottom and, if all went according to plan, out to sea. They placed the chains in Grigory's fur coat and tossed it in along with a single boot. Fortunately for the assassins, the sentry was asleep while all this was in progress.

The conspirators discovered Rasputin's other boot in the car when they returned to the Moika palace. They also noticed blood on the floor rug of the car. Yusupov had retired by this time, so Dmitry Pavlovich instructed a servant to burn these last pieces of evidence. The men now bade each other farewell. Purishkevich and Lazavert reached the Warsaw station at 6 A.M. In three hours a group of Duma deputies was to inspect Vladimir Mitrofanovich's famous train before it left on another trip to the front. "No one noticed us," he confided to his diary. "Everyone about us was sleeping in a dead sleep."[11]

25
The Reckoning

Katya was alarmed to see that Rasputin was not home on the morning of December 17, 1916. The girls called Anna Vyrubova. Alexandra received the news silently, with a grave face. By midmorning reports about the commotion at the Yusupov mansion came to Protopopov's attention. Vlasyuk told his superiors about Purishkevich's "confession." But aristocrats were continually joking about Rasputin and the police did not take the matter seriously at first. More was known by early afternoon. Workers crossing the Petrovsky Bridge reported traces of blood. The boot tossed after Rasputin's body missed its mark and was resting forlornly at the edge of the ice. Grigory's daughters tearfully identified it as their father's.[1]

Suspicion instantly fell upon Prince Yusupov. Unexpected developments of the previous evening drove Felix to improvise a new story. Continued questioning caused further improvisation—and a tale that could not bear much scrutiny. By the morning of December seventeenth, the prince was claiming that Rasputin phoned about 12:30 A.M. to suggest they find gypsy entertainment. Felix had guests and declined Grigory's invitation. About 2:30 the ladies wanted to leave. (As a gentleman he could not give their names to the police.) Dmitry Pavlovich was tipsy; he shot and killed a dog as he escorted the ladies through the courtyard. This explained the gunfire and traces of blood. If Purishkevich babbled something about killing Rasputin, he also must have had too much to drink! Now came the ultimate bluff: "The people who organized Rasputin's murder—if that has actually occurred—planned carefully and deliberately to connect the crime with me and my party."[2]

By afternoon Yusupov and Dmitry Pavlovich were desperate. Dmitry Pavlovich phoned the empress to ask her to receive him for tea. She refused. A few minutes later the telephone rang again; Yusupov was now on the line with the same request of Anna Vyrubova. (It was "almost as if the two men were in the same room," she notes.) Anna explained that the tsarina asked her to decline visitors. Felix now demanded an audience with the empress to "give her a true account of what had occurred[!]" Alexandra left the following message: "If Felix has anything to say, let him write it to me."[3]

The murderers swore they knew nothing of any harm that might have befallen Rasputin. No one was fooled. Relatives and friends accepted their guilt, admired the deed, and began organizing a campaign to spare them punishment. The police also thought the "boys" were guilty. Felix actually shot a dog on the morning of the seventeenth and had the beast dragged around the courtyard, hoping to confuse Grigory's bloodstains with those of the animal. The detectives inspected the dog and exchanged knowing glances; no animal could account for all the stains. Nor did the trail conform to what one would expect of a wounded canine. Events stood suspended as everyone waited for the body to be recovered.[4]

*   *   *

The news of Rasputin's disappearance shot through Petrograd. The press was under heavy censorship where Grigory was concerned; newspapers referred to him under such circumlocutions as the "person living on Gorokhovaya Street." The *Stock Exchange News* boldly defied the censor by announcing the "Death of Grigory Rasputin in Petrograd" in its evening edition of December 17, 1916. The story was at the bottom of page two, and every word of the brief announcement was in headline type: "This morning at 6 o'clock Grigory Rasputin suddenly passed away at one of the most aristocratic houses in the center of Petrograd after a party."[5]

Within an hour this edition was sold out or confiscated by the police, "and the streets were filled with people rushing from one newsboy to another looking in vain for a stray copy which might have escaped notice." The police reaction seemed to confirm the tale, and the news spread like wildfire. Friends congratulated each other on the telephone. People at the Imperial Theater shook hands indiscriminately, called for the national anthem, and ignored the play in their concentration on the amazing news. The mood was similar the same evening at a concert at Tsarskoe Selo.

Joy was also widespread on the streets. Strangers embraced; cabbies refused tips. People hoped the "dark days were at last at an end, and [with Rasputin] gone the military as well as the political situation would improve." Portraits of Felix Yusupov and Dmitry Pavlovich were widely exhibited and applauded.[6]

Other Russian cities also rejoiced. The audience at Moscow's Imperial Theater applauded and sang the national hymn when the news arrived there on the evening of December 17, 1916. The monks at the Zosima Monastery cheered. In Kiev a crowd angrily asked a member of the Duma "[w]hen are you finally going to run [the rest of the gang] off?" In Yalta some openly hoped that Rasputin's murder was the first in a series that would finally include Vyrubova, Protopopov, and Alexandra herself. Newspapers in Irkutsk could not report Rasputin's murder; but a detailed mimeographed account—some said it came from the office of the governor-general—freely circulated. This document featured a cartoon showing the Neva "covered with ice and snow . . . ; a large hole in the ice [was] in the foreground with tracks of a sleigh and footsteps around it; and the legend, "Farewell, Dear Friend!"[7]

Rasputin's death was celebrated where opinion was against Grigory: among aristocrats and officers, in cities and church circles. The mood was different elsewhere. A society lady who did volunteer work in a military hospital was shocked to see that her patients did not share her pleasure. When she tried to explain the significance of the deed, a soldier replied, "Yes, just one peasant reached the tsar, and the nobles killed him!" A nobleman from Kostrovna reported that peasants in his region of the Volga thought Grigory was a martyr.

"He was a man of the people; he let the tsar hear the voice of the people; he defended the people against the court people, [so they] killed him. That's what's being said in all the *izbas*." The source of this information thought that it reflected the opinion of "all the [peasants] of Russia."

Maria Rasputin claims that the peasants of Pokrovskoe "spontaneously decorated" her father's oratory. This may be true. A young army officer who passed through Pokrovskoe in 1918 was shocked at the praise for Rasputin. Markov had heard only criticism of the infamous starets from his class. But the peasant who drove him through Pokrovskoe believed that Rasputin "took the side of us peasants with the tsar. That's why the *burzhuis*[bourgeois] killed him."[8]

Government critics reacted in different ways. Milyukov welcomed the news, but Kerensky warned "this murder strengthens the monarchy." The revolutionaries were making good use of Grigory: Street-corner cycloramas at this time showed Grigory making love to the empress; it was scarcely in their interests to see him pass from the scene.

But some radicals sympathized with the assassins. The Okhrana intercepted a letter from the very type of proletarians who would soon overthrow the tsar's government. They sent congratulations to Yusupov from Lower-Novgorod on January 3, 1917.

What was done was what the people thirsted for. The rot has been uncovered, the first vermin has been disposed of. Grishka is no more, only his sinking body which presents no danger remains. . . . But there are still many dark forces partaking with Rasputin, building their nest in Russia in the person of the tsarina and other trash and degenerate animals of human refuse.

Nicholas was warned not to deprive the assassins of "life and freedom." Otherwise, the letter continued, "the entire nation will rise up as one and punish the tsar as it punished Myasoedov," the army officer who was unjustly convicted of espionage and hanged in March 1915.[9]

The tsar's attitude toward Rasputin's disappearance is difficult to fathom. Nicholas fired off a telegram to his wife on December 18: "Am horrified and shaken. In prayers and thoughts I am with you. Am arriving tomorrow at 5 o'clock." But those who attended the tsar did not think he was sorry to hear that Rasputin had disappeared. "I rather received the impression that the emperor experienced a feeling of relief," one wrote; another observer was struck by the "look of serenity and . . . happiness on the emperor's face." The atmosphere at Stavka was festive. Champagne flowed, toasts were exchanged, and cigars lighted up.

Gilliard accompanied Nicholas on his return. He was stunned by Alexandra's "agonized features" and her "inconsolable grief." "Her idol had been shattered. The only person who could save her son was killed. Any misfortune, any catastrophe was possible now that he was gone. The time of waiting began, that terrible waiting for the disaster which could not be escaped."[10]

Divers promptly went to work searching for Rasputin's body. On December 19, a river policeman noticed what seemed to be the sleeve of a coat frozen into and under the ice near the hole. Efforts to crack the ice here brought the body near the surface. Hooks took hold of the corpse and dragged it to the surface.

The victim's "face was almost unrecognizeable, clots of dark blood had coagulated in the beard and hair." The grappling-irons had inflicted damage on Grigory's head. One eye was "almost out of its socket." Incredibly Rasputin was alive when he hit the water: His wrists bore deep marks from a struggle to free his arms from their bonds. His right hand "lay beneath his chin [as if] contracted in a last sign of the cross."[11]

An autopsy was carried out but not published, and one reads contradictory accounts of its results. All versions agree the victim suffered three gunshot wounds, but the locations differ according to the writer. Some say one or more of the shots was mortal; others assert that Rasputin would have recovered had he escaped. His lungs contained water. This embarrassed those who considered Rasputin a saint, for the Orthodox tradition holds that a saint will not die by drowning.[12]

Protopopov feared that Rasputin's body would attract crowds and even provoke riots. So the corpse was taken to the Chesmensky almshouse just outside the capital on the road to Tsarskoe Selo. Limousines once whisked Grigory past this building to and from the palace. He was now thawing in the chapel. Protopopov hoped to keep the location of Rasputin's body a secret, but Grigory's daughters and friends promptly arrived to mourn their loss. All could see the powerful struggle raging within Anna Vyrubova. If Rasputin had been clairvoyant, how was he taken in by Yusupov? Was "Father Grigory" nothing more than a false starets? Few of his followers now believed in his "spiritual gifts." Vyrubova and some of the others would eventually find their way to a modified belief in Rasputin as a "man of God." But for the moment disappointment prevailed.

Yet they gathered. Akulina Laptinskaya prepared the body for burial; she dressed it in white clothes. Pitirim was too shaken to sing the Liturgy. This task fell to Bishop Isidor.[13]

The authorities discussed returning Rasputin's body to Pokrovskoe. But Protopopov still feared crowds and disorders, and he pressed for a secret burial in the capital. Anna Vyrubova had donated a tract of land at Tsarskoe Selo where a church and hospital were under construction; she suggested Grigory rest here on a spot that would be under the center aisle of the new church.

Rasputin was buried at 8 A.M. on Tuesday, December 21, 1916. Lili Dehn recalls it was a "glorious morning, the sky was a deep blue, the sun was shining, and the hard snow sparkled like masses of diamonds." Vyrubova was also present; a palace limousine brought Grigory's daughters and two other members of the household. The royal family was dressed in mourning. Alexandra was pale but composed until the coffin was taken from the police van; the empress then began to weep. The plain oak coffin had no inscription; a simple cross showed that its occupant had been Orthodox. Alexandra and her daughters signed the back of an icon and placed it on Rasputin's chest. Nicholas and Alexandra threw dirt on the coffin when it was lowered into the grave. The tsarina divided her flowers among the mourners and they scattered them on the coffin.[14]

"When the last solemn words had been uttered," Dehn writes, "the imperial family left the church. Anna and I followed them. Anna got into her sledge, I into my carriage. It was barely nine o'clock." By now incredible rumors were flying about Petrograd. Some said that Rasputin had been buried in the dead of night. Others swore that he was alive and had been seen about Petrograd! Protopopov spread a tale suiting his purposes, which was to put distance between the royal family and the late starets. Protopopov reported that Rasputin was being returned to Pokrovskoe for burial.

Nicholas II entered his thoughts in his diary. "My family and I witnessed a sad scene" this morning, he wrote, "the burial of the unforgettable Grigory, assassinated by monsters at the home of Yusupov on the night of the 16th and 17th of December."[15]

*   *   *

Rasputin's murder was a blow to Alexandra Fedorovna. Rumors that she gave way to violent hysterics were not true. Protopopov, in fact, was surprised at the composure Nicholas and his wife displayed in those days. "I saw no tears," he later testified, "I received no rebukes"—as well he might since he had been responsible for Rasputin's security. The commander of a naval guards unit at Tsarskoe Selo recalled that the royal couple took Grigory's death simply, calling it a "sad fact," but nothing more.[16]

Alexandra's faith in Rasputin was undiminished. She still believed that he had been a starets and a voice of the common people. She continued to trust his teachings and prophecies. Grigory had often told the tsar and his wife, "If I die or you desert me, you will lose your son and your crown in six months."

Alexandra must have worried over this prophecy. She certainly knew she could not trust anyone beyond her immediate circle.

Alexandra was active and vigorous; she continued to "help" Nicholas govern Russia during the seven weeks that he remained in the capital. But the days were melancholy. The empress often slipped off to Rasputin's grave with fresh flowers; she sat there praying and remembering happy times. Occasionally the strain broke through. One evening Alexandra was sitting close to the fireplace, absorbed by the music of a chamber group. The empress was unusually downcast as she stared into the crackling fire.

"Oh, Madame, why are you so sad tonight?" Lili Dehn whispered.

"Why am I sad, Lili?" Alexandra replied, turning to her young friend. "I can't say, really, but I think my heart is broken."[17]

Nicholas II had to deal with the possibility that Rasputin's assassination marked the first stage of a palace coup. For some time British diplomats had been discussing the "future" with key leaders of the opposition. Might the royal couple be forced to leave Russia? Could they be sent to a monastery? Would another Romanov lend legitimacy to such moves by serving as regent to Alexis? Was assassination conceivable?

It was. Among the many plans under discussion was that of a group of officers who considered "bomb[ing] the tsar's motorcar from an aeroplane at a particular point on its route." A celebrated ace offered to crash his plane into Nicholas's car. Many believed that General Alekseev was the center of a conspiracy to depose the emperor. Protopopov briefed the tsar on rumors of danger—some real, some imagined. Nicholas had the information. His problem was to act.[18]

Lazavert and Sukhotin were junior accomplices, but practically nothing was said about punishing them. Purishkevich was most responsible for killing Rasputin, but he was a member of the Duma. Vladimir Mitrofanovich was also at the front where his popularity with the army rose to unprecedented heights. It would be risky for even a popular monarch to act against Purishkevich. The question of punishment focused on the two remaining culprits: Felix Yusupov and Dmitry Pavlovich.

Nicholas also faced difficulties with these culprits. If they were tried, which court would have jurisdiction? Petrograd was then on a military footing; an army tribunal could be expected to acquit the defendants or give them a token punishment. Nicholas might create a special court, but the defense in a trial would discredit the tsar and his government. Many argued that only the tsar could punish a member of the royal family such as Dmitry Pavlovich. Prince Yusupov might claim the same privilege as the husband of one of Nicholas's nieces. Felix and Dmitry Pavlovich enjoyed great popularity. Flowers and letters came from every direction. When Felix confessed, admirers in Moscow bought him a gift. It would not be easy to punish such "heroes," angry though Nicholas was once he learned the details of their crime and its effect on his wife.[19]

The tsar's "punishment" was minimal. Nicholas exiled Yusupov to his estates at Kursk in central Russia; Dmitry Pavlovich was transferred to the Russian army in Persia. Even this was too much for some. A number of prominent Romanovs asked Nicholas to pardon Dmitry Pavlovich. "No one is allowed to indulge in murder," Nicholas wrote at the top of their petition. "I know that the consciences of many [of those who signed the statement] are disturbed," he continued, referring to their discussions about the need to dethrone the tsar. "I am surprised at your approach to me."[20]

The Romanov support for Dmitry Pavlovich was a political act, a demonstration against the emperor. Nicholas's rejection of their petition was equally political: He admitted that he did not have his family's support—and would not pay the price for it. "I am filled with shame that the hands of my kinsmen are stained with the blood of a simple peasant," the tsar lashed back in disgust. Letters intercepted by the police and the reports they submitted to the emperor showed that he could count on the loyalty of only two first-cousins once-removed. Rasputin alive had separated Nicholas from his kin; Rasputin dead sealed the breach. Another prop was crumbling. Few others now remained.[21]

Paranoia was common to both friends and enemies of the late starets. Dmitry Pavlovich was convinced that "partisans of Rasputin"—"adventurers" who "had nothing to lose and were capable of anything"—tried to enter his mansion on several occasions. These "suspicious-looking men" followed him to Persia, "intent on avenging the death of their powerful benefactor." Grigory's friends heard their names were on a list marked for execution. Anna Vyrubova received such threatening mail that Alexandra insisted she move into the Alexander Palace for better security. Stephen Beletsky believed that his name was second on the list.

The paranoid mood also appeared in "signs." If many Petrogradites celebrated Rasputin's murder, others were "full of terror"; they whispered of "terrifying events" and expected the "hand of doom." A taxi driver crossing the Petrovsky Bridge soon after Grigory's death pointed out the fateful hole to his English passenger. Then he crossed himself and cried out, "It has not frozen—he was a saint!"[22]

One of the oddest legends surrounding Rasputin asserts that he died poor. It is true that 3,000 rubles disappeared from Grigory's bureau once visitors and investigators descended upon the apartment. For a time the household was short of cash. But Grigory commanded a handsome estate. We know that he had 150,000 rubles on deposit in the Tyumen department of the State Bank. Simanovich told Protopopov that Rasputin's assets in Petrograd came to 300,000 rubles. Rasputin was comfortable when he died.

Rasputin's daughters found loyal support from their friends. Simanovich claims that Alexandra gave him 12,000 rubles to find the girls a new place to live; he supposedly added 13,000 rubles of his own money and they moved to an elegant apartment on Kolomenskaya Street. But—the tale continues, and one wonders if it is true—Maria and Barbara felt "unimportant" at this new location.

Since the tsarina had changed her mind about converting their old flat into a chapel-museum, they were permitted to return there.[23]

Nicholas and Alexandra offered Rasputin's daughters what they needed most: love and reassurance. The girls had been to court only three times when their father was alive. They now visited the empress and her daughters each Wednesday and Saturday. The tsar himself was present at the first of these meetings. "He was very emotional and tender with us," Maria recalled. " 'I will try to replace your father,' he told us. When we met the grand princesses on that occasion," she continues, "they cried a great deal and mourned our father." Nicholas's daughters insisted that Maria and Varbara address them by name— Olga, Tatyana, Maria, and Anastasia—not as "your imperial highness."[24]

The two Siberian peasant girls were moved when one of the most powerful men in the world offered himself as a humble substitute for their father. Within a few days Nicholas was unable to protect himself—much less others. He returned to the front for the last time on February 21, 1917. A few days later the Rasputin girls made their last trip to the palace. They were amazed at the angry crowds they saw on the way. Maria and Varbara succeeded in reaching Tsarskoe Selo, though not without difficulty. They were alarmed to learn that Anna Vyrubova was again staying in the Alexander Palace for safety. Anna, Olga, and Alexis had come down with measles. This was the last time that Rasputin's daughters saw Alexandra Fedorovna. "I can still see her in her white nurse's costume," Maria wrote, "at once preoccupied and confident, reassuring us in spite of her own anxiety with that sad smile hiding her tears."[25]

"What can I do?" Alexandra lamented as she bade the Rasputin girls goodbye. "Pray, and pray again. Our Friend in the other world also prays for you, and so he is nearer than ever to us. But how one longs to hear his consoling voice!"

A few days later Nicholas abdicated. He hoped that Michael would follow him as tsar. Nicholas's younger brother declined the throne. He knew that the days of monarchy in Russia were gone forever.

The revolution settled accounts with Grigory Rasputin on March 9, 1917, the same day Nicholas rejoined his family at Tsarskoe Selo. At midnight a band of soldiers broke into the church under construction around his grave. They opened the coffin. The embalming of Rasputin's body made it seem as if he were still alive, though the disfigured face made a fearsome sight. The soldiers stripped the dead man and "took measurements" of his penis with a brick. The body was brought to the imperial stables in the Pargolov Forest just outside Petrograd, placed on a pine-log funeral pyre, drenched with gasoline, and set on fire. The cremation lasted over six hours, until 7 o'clock on the morning of March 10, 1917. Several hundred peasants crowded around, undeterred by the icy wind and fetid smoke. "Silent and motionless, they gazed in horror-stricken stupor at the sacrilegious holocaust . . . slowly devouring the martyred *starets*. . . ." The soldiers stole the icon and a medal that had been lovingly placed on Rasputin's corpse. An American collector supposedly bought the icon for a large sum. The soldiers finally gathered Grigory's ashes and buried them under the snow.[26]

Reporters soon learned that Rasputin's grave had been desecrated. The American journalist Robert Crozier Long and colleagues rushed to cover the story. Long found Grigory's burial site "desolate and forbidding"; he was amazed at the revelry in progress. Soldiers were singing, shouting, and making foul remarks about the man who recently occupied the grave. Rude drawings of Rasputin scrubbing Alexandra in her bath now lined the walls. An inscription over the earthen pit proclaimed: "Here lies Grishka Rasputin, shame of the house of Romanov, and shame of the Orthodox Church." A "very ugly little Siberian soldier" squatted at the bottom of the grave. Encouraged by spectators, he jumped out and danced the *trepak*. Soldiers joined in as others spat into the cavernous hole.

Soldiers "assured us the tsarina a day before had secretly left the palace carrying a wreath of flowers; and that she had then first discovered what everyone else knew—that the revolutionaries had disinterred the body. . . . " This was a rumor, a crude parody of Mary Magdalene discovering Christ's empty tomb. The empress and her family were prisoners in the palace. Confinement spared her the humiliation of witnessing Grigory's end, though greater indignities would come her way soon enough.[27]

So ended the remarkable career of Grigory Efimovich Rasputin. Dmitry Pavlovich's stepmother suggested an epitaph.

It was Rasputin's lot to pass through the four elements. He was born and died in water; his body was committed to the earth. Fire consumed his corpse. Spring came, the snows melted, and his ashes were carried away by the wind.[28]

26

The Fate of the Others

Nicholas managed to reach Tsarskoe Selo on March 9, 1917. "Citizen Romanov" and his family remained there for five months, tended by a dozen faithful friends such as Lili Dehn and Anna Vyrubova, Gilliard, and Dr. Botkin. The new minister of justice visited the Romanovs to tell them their rights and obligations under the Provisional Government. Alexander Kerensky was rude at first, but he softened and then began to worry about the prisoners' safety. Kerensky wanted to send the royal family abroad, perhaps to England, but the public's increasing radicalism made this impossible. Kerensky made a fateful decision by the summer: The former tsar and his circle would be exiled to Siberia. If all went well, from here they could escape to Japan. By now Dehn, Vyrubova, and other friends had been forced from Tsarskoe Selo. Nicholas, his family, and those who remained departed for Tobolsk on August 1, 1917.

The Bolsheviks overthrew the Provisional Government on November 7, 1917.[1] The Bolsheviks decided to bring the Romanovs to Moscow (now the capital), but Alexis was still stricken from his latest bout with hemophilia. Nicholas, Alexandra, and their daughter Maria began the journey with the understanding that those left behind would join them as soon as Alexis's health permitted.

Nicholas passed through Pokrovskoe. The horses were changed at a spot directly across from Grigory's home. Praskovaya happened to be outside, and Barbara was at the window. The two women made the sign of the cross to their visitors as Maria Romanov quickly sketched their house. Rasputin once predicted that Nicholas would see Pokrovskoe. The emperor probably did not take the prophecy seriously then, but it was being fulfilled now.[2]

The commander of the tsar's party, Vasily Yakovlev, was alarmed to learn that the Romanovs were to be detained at Ekaterinburg. Yakovlev had become attached to the royal family; in time he would turn on the Communists and join Admiral Kolchak's anti-Bolshevik Siberian government. Yakovlev made the dramatic decision to travel in the opposite direction, to Omsk—then farther east, to freedom. He was stopped and forced to proceed to Ekaterinburg. Here the tsar's party was imprisoned in the house of the merchant Ipatiev. In May, Alexis and the remainder of the household were also brought to the "House of Special Purpose," as the Ipatiev dwelling was ominously called. Twelve people were crammed into five rooms. The prisoners suffered many indignities. Obscene pictures of Alexandra and Rasputin decorated the walls of the bathroom. The guards reminded the girls to notice the scenes when they entered the lavatory.[3]

The "Soviet of the Urals" at Ekaterinburg was determined from the outset to execute Nicholas and his party. The timing of their execution was fixed by the approach of an anti-Bolshevik army. Omsk fell to this force in early July 1918. The Red commander at Ekaterinburg estimated that he could hold the city only until July 15. The Ural Soviet decided that the Romanovs must be executed right away; their bodies would then be destroyed.

Ten efficient Cheka agents began their preparations on July 13. Plans specified that the bodies of the victims would be chopped into pieces and destroyed by 150 gallons of gasoline and 400 lbs. of sulfuric acid. The final remains would be dumped in an abandoned shaft at the Four Brothers Mine.

The royal family and its four remaining friends were awakened at midnight on the night of July 16–17, 1918. Nicholas and Alexandra, the children, Dr. Botkin, Trup the footman, Kharitonov the cook, and Demidova the maid were taken to the basement. They were told that an anti-Bolshevik force was approaching and automobiles would soon arrive to move them to a secure location. Nicholas was seated, holding his son who was not able to walk at that time.

"Your relations have tried to save you," the Cheka commander proclaimed, suddenly reentering the room with his heavily armed men. "They have failed and we must now shoot you."

Nicholas rose from his seat, moving to protect his wife and son. "What . . . ?" he stammered before a single bullet ended his life. The others now began to fire. Alexandra was also dispatched by one shot. Olga, Tatyana, and Maria died quickly, as did Botkin, Trup, and Kharitonov. Demidova burst into an adjoining room, pursued by the executioners who dropped their empty pistols and seized bayonet-ready rifles. Demidova tried to defend herself with a pillow containing some of the imperial jewels. More than 30 bayonet thrusts ended her torment. Alexis was wounded but still alive. One of the agents kicked him savagely; then his commander finished the boy with two bullets. Anastasia had only fainted. She now awakened and began to scream until bayonets and rifle butts ended her life. Similar blows crushed the skull of Jimmy the spaniel.[4]

*   *   *

Fate was also hard on the prime ministers who crossed Rasputin's path. Peter Stolypin was gunned down in 1911. Only two of the others—Kokovtsov and

Trepov—escaped the revolution. Boris Sturmer died in the Peter and Paul Fortress on August 20, 1917. Ivan Goremykin fled to the Caucasus and died there at the age of 78 on December 11, 1917. For a time it seemed that Prince Golitsyn eluded his captors. He simply disappeared. Golitsyn was finally discovered in a Leningrad cellar in 1925, eking out a living cleaning boots. The 75-year-old man was carried away on a stretcher and shot.[5]

The Provisional Government threw Stephen Beletsky into the Peter and Paul Fortress for interrogation. The once-mighty police director cooperated with the new authorities, supplementing four sessions on the witness stand with six lengthy depositions. After the Communists came to power, several foreign journalists visited the "notorious" prisoner. Albert Rhys Williams found Beletsky to be a "large-framed man with gray hair and shrewd brown eyes." Williams was told that Beletsky first "inform[ed] on his former pals, the most extreme reactionaries. Now he made it plain he had no use for Kerensky [whom he described] as 'sickly' and a 'hysterical man not able to run the country.' " "When we left his cell Beletsky shook hands, bowing over Beatty's ceremoniously. [T]he two Russians in our party put their hands behind their backs."[6]

Beletsky's obsequiousness did him no good. He was taken to Moscow along with others marked for execution. By a fine twist of fate, Beletsky briefly shared his death cell with A. N. Khvostov, his former boss and another person who had much to do with Rasputin's career. They refought old battles in the ministry of internal affairs, though without bitterness. Then came the morning of August 23, 1918—the day of their execution.

Death sentences in Moscow were carried out at Khodynka Field, the very spot where hundreds of people were trampled to death at Nicholas's coronation in 1896. The victims were brought here in trucks. Ditches the width of a man were waiting. (The length of the trench depended upon the work planned for the day.) The other members of the Khvostov–Beletsky group included Father John Vostorgov, Nicholas Maklakov, Ivan Shcheglovitov, a bishop, and two priests. The executioners permitted the men to pray and bid each other farewell. They knelt, prayed, received final blessings, and heard Vostorgov urge faith in God and the coming salvation of Russia.

"I'm ready," Father John declared as he boldly walked to the edge of the trench. The others quietly moved forward and took their places. An executioner behind Vostorgov took his left hand, brought it behind his waist and fired a single shot at the back of his neck while pushing him into the ditch. The remaining killers approached their targets. Beletsky suddenly bolted and ran several paces until two bullets brought him down. Then he was dragged to the grave, given a fatal shot, and thrown in with the others.[7]

Alexander Protopopov fell victim to a yet greater holocaust 11 days later. The Provisional Government had also imprisoned him in the Peter and Paul Fortress, summoning him to testify before the Investigatory Commission. The ex-minister rambled; at times he was incoherent. Syphilis had probably driven Protopopov mad by this time, but he faced his tormenters with courage and dignity. He

insisted that Rasputin had virtues—and no influence in the government. Protopopov claimed that he saw the starets only "fifteen or sixteen times," and he
denied visiting him socially or attending his burial.

Protopopov apologized for his behavior in power. "My entering the ministry
was more than a mistake," he admitted, "it was a tragedy." "My moral scruples
faded," he lamented at another point, "then things happened which led me to
misfortune." When Protopopov was reminded that he turned down the ministry
of finance for the greater power of the interior, he mused, "that was the evil of
my life."[8]

Protopopov's position improved when the Bolsheviks came to power. He was
released from prison and entered a clinic. Protopopov was failing, but he rallied
to a final courageous act. The Communists were just beginning to persecute
church leaders in Petrograd. Protopopov implored prominent Jewish visitors to
form a united front of believers against fiercer attacks that the ex-minister (cor-
rectly) predicted would occur in the future. This suggestion would have seemed
opportunistic from most Christians, but Protopopov was a longtime advocate of
Jewish rights, and his appeals had weight. Jewish leaders who were appalled at
Protopopov's insanity as a minister were now impressed with the "clarity of his
judgments."[9] The Reds did not tolerate such threats. Protopopov was again
arrested.

Protopopov's fate was sealed by one of the bloodiest episodes of the Russian
Revolution. The "Left-SRs" turned against their Communist allies on August
30, 1918, launching a bloodbath that—with better leadership and luck—might
have toppled the Bolshevik government. The Communist leader in Petrograd
was assassinated; Lenin was shot and almost killed in Moscow. Monarchists
were not involved in these acts, but the Reds took advantage of the provocation
to eliminate the leaders of all oppositionist groups and to frighten their rank-
and-file sympathizers into submission. Protopopov and 500 other leaders of the
old regime were taken to Moscow and shot on September 3, 1918.

Some Russian politicians managed to escape the Bolsheviks. Alexander Kerensky ended up in the United States, engaging in a lengthy campaign to exonerate
the Provisional Government and his own role in the struggle for a democratic
Russia. Milyukov and Guchkov went to France. Rodzyanko made his way to
Yugoslavia where he died in poverty in 1924. Some Russian émigrés faulted
him for undermining Nicholas's government, while others attacked him for not
turning against the tsar. All credited Rodzyanko with a noble character. His
memoirs are a scathing indictment of Rasputin, but his love for Nicholas was
strong to the end. The feeling had been mutual. "Only Rodzyanko told me the
truth," the former tsar told General Ruzsky after abdicating.[10]

* * *

Rasputin's allies in the Church continued in power until the February Revolution. Nicholas Raev made a surprisingly bold effort to shore up the tsar's

tottering government. The director general called the Holy Synod into emergency session on February 27, 1917, just as the struggle in the streets was turning in favor of the crowd. Raev demanded that the Church condemn the revolution. The Synod graybeards refused. Their stance was an eloquent comment on the "reign of Rasputin" now coming to an end. The Synod favored a constituent assembly to determine the future government. A statement in July 1918 celebrated the February events as the "hour of universal freedom for Russia [when] the country . . . rejoiced over the bright days of its life."[11]

New hands were steering the Russian Church in these days. Vladimir Lvov followed Raev as director of the Synod. Lvov championed high ideals when he thundered in the Duma against Rasputin and the "dark forces." Lvov was actually a man of small principles and a large appetite for power. Many suspected as much. Grigory's other critics thought that Lvov was "pathologically unbalanced"; they resented his exaggerated tales of Rasputin's "reign" at the Holy Synod. Once in power, Lvov struck out at anyone whom he suspected of being a Rasputinite. He was generally tyrannical, and bishops called to account for their actions were horrified at their treatment. Some actually turned to the Petrograd Soviet with their complaints!

Lvov was purged from the government when the "June crisis" forced the Provisional Government to drop all ministers to the right of the Kadets. Lvov now turned against Kerensky and became involved in a double-game that led to the "Kornilov uprising." Lvov presented himself to Kerensky as a spokesman of General Kornilov, and to Kornilov as an emissary of Kerensky. In fact he was neither. But Kornilov concluded that he had an agreement with Kerensky to crush the Bolsheviks and "restore order." The Petrograd Soviet halted Kornilov's offensive of September 7, 1917 by sabotaging the railways while spreading propaganda among the general's troops. This further undermined Kerensky and helped the Bolsheviks overthrow the Provisional Government two months later.

Lvov made his way to Paris in 1920. Here he switched sides again, praising the Reds for defending Russia's historical traditions. Lvov returned to the Soviet Union in 1922 to work with atheist organizations and newspapers. Lvov died in the Soviet Union, apparently in 1930.[12]

Four other directors of the Holy Synod survived Rasputin. Alexander Samarin continued to be active in church affairs. The patriarchate was restored in February 1918, and Tikhon was elected to the office. Recent assassinations of church leaders suggested that the patriarch was also in danger. Samarin organized Tikhon's security and helped to create the "Moscow Council of United Parishes" to keep Tikhon under constant observation. If danger appeared—for example, Chekists might take the patriarch into custody for "questioning"—the "Council" was ready to ring church bells and assemble crowds to follow Tikhon wherever he might be taken. The Soviet authorities were furious at Samarin; his work complicated their "plans" for the patriarch.

Alexander Samarin and others were arrested and subjected to a sensational mock trial in 1920. Samarin was sentenced to death, though the court recommended a stay of execution. Samarin finally made his way to the West and died there in 1932.[13]

Alexander Volzhin escaped to southern France. In Nice he befriended Alexander Naumov, the stern critic of Rasputin who briefly served as minister of agriculture. Their friendship fell victim to an argument that tore apart the Russian Orthodox Church after the Civil War. The issue was Tikhon's neutrality during the recent struggle. White émigrés were furious over this "betrayal"; some concluded that the patriarch was a tool of the Bolsheviks. Dissidents held a church council at Karlovci, Yugoslavia, in 1921 to organize a church independent of Moscow. Volzhin supported the Karlovci movement, Naumov recognized the patriarch of Moscow. The schism divided many émigré families and friends, including Volzhin and Naumov. But Naumov's memoirs are respectful of Volzhin. Naumov was concerned to set the record straight: "Volzhin was not a Rasputinite."[14]

Vladimir Sabler died impoverished in Moscow in 1923.

Pitirim's ties with Rasputin made him the most despised leader of the Russian Church. When the tsar's government fell, he was imprisoned in the Beshtai Monastery in the Caucasus. Pitirim and Prince Zhevakov, the former assistant-director of the Holy Synod, spent 1918 and 1919 in Pyatagorsk. When the White movement collapsed there in January 1920, they fled to Ekaterinodar and took refuge with Metropolitan Anthony Krapovitsky. This created an ironic situation. Anthony had been a Rasputin foe, and he often clashed with Pitirim and Zhevakov. They had used their power against Anthony. But Anthony forgave his enemies and took them in. Pitirim bitterly repented of his sins against Anthony. Reconciliation came at the end.

But not safety. As soon as Pitirim and Zhevakov arrived at Ekaterinodar, it became clear that the Whites were losing this stronghold as well. Pitirim was ill; he begged his colleagues to take him with them to freedom. They reluctantly agreed. No one noticed that Zhevakov made an early unexplained departure.

The next day Georgy Shavelsky brought Anthony some news.

"That Zhevakov is a son-of-a-bitch!" the former head chaplain raged. "He left without paying my [servant] Fedka for tending him and cleaning his boots. He didn't even pay for the shoe polish Fedka bought with his own money. And Zhevakov robbed Pitirim. He took two or three gold watches plus 18,000 rubles sewed in Pitirim's cassock. He tore the cassock and took the money from it!"

Pitirim died in Anthony's arms at Ekaterinodar on January 20, 1920.[15]

The Provisional Government restored Hermogen to favor and gave him an assignment he relished. The fiery Hermogen was made "Bishop of Tobolsk and Siberia." His investigation documented Varnava's abuses in the office. The pile of unopened envelopes that he discovered in an otherwise empty room included important directives from the Holy Synod. The Cheka arrested Varnava. But his experience was fortunate. Lenin's police released the ex-Rasputinite and received his thanks for the "civilized" way that he was treated in prison.[16]

Hermogen's fate was tragic, but also shows his noble character. If anyone in Russia had cause to despise Nicholas, and especially Alexandra, it was Hermogen. They expelled him from the Holy Synod and imprisoned him for attacking Rasputin. The Romanovs fell, but Hermogen returned to power. Yet his driving objective was to secure the safety of the royal family. Hermogen helped persuade Kerensky to send the prisoners to Siberia, thinking that from there they might escape to Japan. When the Provisional Government collapsed, Hermogen shifted tactics. The bishop of Tobolsk now worked with monarchists who streamed to Siberia with plans to save the Romanovs.

Hermogen's end came a few hours before the royal family was martyred. A White army approached Tobolsk in the same offensive that aimed at rescuing the Romanovs. The Bolsheviks took the last steamship from Tobolsk on June 16, 1918. The prisoners on board included Hermogen. The Bolsheviks bound each captive and threw him from the ship. Hermogen prayed for his tormenters. The Red Guards silenced him with a blow to the jaw. Then they threw their victim into the water with an 80-pound weight.[17]

Fate was kinder to Iliodor. In Norway he published *The Holy Devil* (1917), a best-seller that did much to shape the public's perception of Grigory Rasputin. Iliodor renounced the Russian Orthodox Church in favor of his own religion, the cult of "reason and the sun." Iliodor returned to Russia after the Bolshevik Revolution and tried to develop a church whose teachings reconciled Marxism and religion. The Communists were not interested in these efforts, nor did the people of the Volga turn to the demagogue they once cheered. Iliodor came to New York in 1921, joined the Baptist Church, and worked as a janitor in the Metropolitan Life Insurance Building. Iliodor went about music halls "pouring out slop" about Russia, the "government, the tsar's family—particularly the empress." He trotted out the famous letters that he swore Alexandra had addressed to Rasputin. The historian John Stephen imagines that if fate had so smiled upon Rasputin, the two old foes "might have spent their dotage reminiscing on a Central Park bench." But one perished under the Neva in 1916, and the other died of a heart attack at Bellevue Hospital at the age of 71, in 1952.[18]

*   *   *

Manasevich-Manuilov was in prison at the time of Grigory's murder, having been convicted of extorting money from a Moscow bank. The Extraordinary Investigatory Commission grilled him at length. The Bolsheviks freed Manasevich-Manuilov and he tried to flee abroad in 1918 with forged papers. Just as Manasevich-Manuilov was cleared for crossing at Beloozero, an ex-guard at the Peter and Paul Fortress asked if he had been a prisoner there. He denied the charge but was detained. After several hours, two women identified the culprit as *the* "notorious" Manasevich-Manuilov. The prisoner was shot. He took death calmly, dividing his few pitiful possessions with those around him "in memory of Manuilov."[19]

Separation from the royal family matured Anna Vyrubova. She was held under harsh conditions in the Peter and Paul Fortress, testifying before the Investigatory Commission. Anna was released after five months, then reimprisoned and freed several times. Anna and her friends reluctantly supported the Provisional Government; when the Bolsheviks came to power, she and Lili Dehn blossomed into crafty counterrevolutionaries. They and their confederates did what they could for the Romanovs, maintaining a secret correspondence with the empress and smuggling books and items that people in confinement so appreciate. Vyrubova and Dehn also raised money and recruited people who hoped to free the royal family. Lili escaped but Anna remained in Petrograd. Vyrubova befriended Maxim Gorky who urged her to write her memoirs. She went to Finland in 1920 and published her *Memories of the Russian Court*. Lili Dehn brought out *The Real Tsaritsa* in 1922. Anna Vyrubova died at 80 in Finland in 1964.[20]

Pierre Gilliard remained in Siberia for three years, working with the Kolchak government to document the fate of the royal family. He married Anastasia's nurse and returned to Switzerland by way of Japan. Gilliard had come to Russia as a young man in 1904, expecting to stay a short time before resuming his education for a career as a university professor. These plans were fulfilled. Gilliard became a professor at Lausanne University and received the Legion of Honor. He often lectured on Russia and the royal family, and in 1921 published his memoirs. Gilliard granted the faults of Nicholas and Alexandra; he also insisted upon their virtues. He died at 83 in 1962.[21]

Aron Simanovich was arrested after Nicholas's government fell. In time he managed to reach Kiev, then Odessa, and finally Novorossiisk on the northeastern shore of the Black Sea. There Simanovich encountered V. M. Purishkevich. Vladimir Mitrofanovich was a leader of the White movement. In fact, he was the first to be tried by the Bolshevik tribunal at the Smolnyi Institute in Petrograd. Purishkevich admitted that he was guilty of the charges: working with General Kaledin, who was then advancing on Moscow. The death sentence was taken for granted. But Purishkevich delivered such a powerful speech that soldiers in the audience rose to testify on his behalf. The jury wanted to find Purishkevich "Not Guilty!" After six hours a compromise was reached: The fiery monarchist was sentenced to 11 months of public work—nine if he stopped working against the Reds.

Purishkevich would not do this. He joined General Denikin and published a conservative journal at Rostov-on-the-Don. His relationship with Aron Simanovich was paradoxical. Purishkevich was violently anti-Semitic; he had murdered Aron's best friend. But he approached Simanovich for financial backing to publish his *Diary*. A partnership developed, but no friendship. Purishkevich was even party to a failed attempt to kill Simanovich. Then Purishkevich came down with typhus in Novorossiisk.

"By coincidence he lay in the same hospital as my son who was also ill with

typhus,'' Simanovich wrote. ''But no one thought any more about ancient en-
mities.'' Yet the paradoxes continued. The hospital was Jewish. The nurses
forgave Purishkevich's anti-Semitism, but as staunch monarchists they condemned him for crossing over to the Provisional Government after Nicholas's
abdication. Purishkevich seemed to prevail over his sickness; at one point he
and two nurses celebrated their ''victory'' with champagne. Then he died. ''I
must admit I received the news with considerable relief,'' Simanovich conceded;
Purishkevich ''was entirely capable of killing me one fine day.''[22]

Simanovich ended up in Paris. He approached Moses Ginsburg, Heinrich
Schlossberg, and other Russian Jewish émigrés with a threat to release his
memoirs unless they paid him large sums of money. They refused and Simanovich
published *Rasputin and the Jews, Memoirs of the Personal Secretary of Grigory
Rasputin* in 1928. Much is valuable in this little work, but much is fiction.
Rasputin and the Jews was quickly translated into French, German, Dutch, and
Spanish. Simanovich presents Rasputin as a willing instrument of wealthy Jews
who used him to approach Nicholas II and his officials to improve the position
of Russian Jews. This pleased the Nazis, and a lavish new German edition was
published in 1942.[23]

Felix Yusupov and Dmitry Pavlovich fled Russia after the Bolsheviks came
to power. Ironically, the ''punishment'' they suffered at Nicholas's hand put
them at places where flight was easier than it would have been from Petrograd
or Moscow. Yusupov escaped with two Rembrandts, a million dollars in jewelry,
and a collection of antique snuffboxes. He converted these assets into cash and
continued the aristocrat's life in the West. Felix often recounted the events of
December 1916. A writer who attended one of his dinner parties in 1922 recalled:
''[T]the room was lit by candlelight with Thespé the Abyssinian [servant] standing impassively behind him in the shadows. The effect was overpowering. When
Felix finished there was a long silence. Then the Duchess of Portland, one of
our guests, said softly, I felt I was there.''[24]

Dmitry Pavlovich was disgusted over Yusupov's delight in Rasputin's murder.
At the outset each promised the other that he would never discuss the deed.
Dmitry kept his pledge. He also rebuffed Felix's numerous attempts to reestablish
their friendship. Yusupov's ''presentations'' became increasingly theatrical. As
the years passed he favored even casual listeners with his ''show.'' Yusupov
read from notes; he loved to see female visitors tremble as they gazed at the
white bearskin rug that he claimed had been drenched with Rasputin's blood.
Dmitry Pavlovich's silence made his sister think he ''never lived down this tragic
and resounding affair [which he hoped would avert] an impending revolution.''
Dmitry married an American heiress and weathered the Great Depression as a
champagne salesman in Palm Beach, Florida. Tuberculosis claimed the grand
duke at the age of 50 in Switzerland in 1941. Yusupov died at 80 in Paris on
September 27, 1967.[25]

Maria Rasputin married Boris Soloviev in the fall of 1917. This young officer
presented himself to Maria and her circle as a monarchist who wanted to rescue

the royal family. Soloviev went to Siberia in January 1918 to establish contact with the royal family. Nicholas and Alexandra trusted him on the strength of his marriage to Maria Rasputin.

Soloviev established himself as the man through whom others communicated with the Romanovs. He claimed to have a plan to free the prisoners. In fact, neither he nor anyone else attempted a rescue at Tobolsk, and by the time the Romanovs passed under heightened security at Ekaterinburg it was too late. Some concluded that Soloviev was a Communist agent; others decided that he was inept or unlucky. All noticed that he was interested in collecting money. He and Maria made their way to Vladivostok and Western Europe. Soloviev died at Montmartre in 1926, leaving Maria with two little girls. The 27-year-old widow became an entertainer, singing and dancing in a Parisian cabaret. She later developed a big-cat act in the circus. Maria published three books on her father, which were designed to minimize his faults and defend his religious character. Maria Rasputin died of a heart attack in Los Angeles at 78 on September 28, 1977. She described her father's assassination as the "Watergate of Russia."[26]

The other members of Rasputin's family were not as fortunate as Maria. Aron Simanovich made arrangements for Varvara to come to Germany in 1923. When Soviet authorities searched her at the Moscow railway station, they found a detailed account of the royal family's life in Ekaterinburg. Varvara was detained and mysteriously died of poisoning. Praskovaya and Dmitry were exiled beyond Obdorsk in the early 1930s, apparently because they resisted collectivization. Maria concluded that her mother and brother "doubtless" died of want "in that Siberia that is so unfriendly to exiles."[27]

Pokrovskoe still exists, but it is a far different town from the one Rasputin knew as a boy. Yet in some respects Pokrovskoe has not changed. It is still in the midst of the "marsh beyond the Tatars," surrounded by barrens of lonesome pine where wolves prowl and legends grow. A miraculous type of hunter was once thought to fly from one part of the forest to another on broomsticks; today it is said they sail through the sky by teleportation. For those with imagination there is magic here even now, long after the death of Pokrovskoe's most famous son, Grigory Rasputin.[28]

Notes

Chapter 1, "Siberian Childhood"

1. Smitten, 10: 119; Amalrik, 15–16; M. Rasputin, *My Father*, 27, 29; Spiridovich, *Raspoutine*, 9.

2. Spiridovich, *Raspoutine*, 10; M. Rasputin, *My Father*, 27, 29; Iliodor, 115; Smitten, 10: 119.

3. *Padenie*, 4: 147; also *Encyclopaedia Britannica* (11th ed.) 26: 1042–43.

4. de Jonge, 29; Marsden, 31–35; Preston, 48–49.

5. Rasputin and Barham, *Rasputin*, 13–14.

6. M. Rasputin, *My Father*, 43–44; Fülöp-Miller, 14–15.

7. Smitten, 10: 119.

8. M. Rasputin, *My Father*, 45; M. Rasputin, *Rasputin*, 58–60.

9. Smitten, 10: 119–120.

10. Smitten, 10: 120; M. Rasputin, *My Father*, 44, 45.

11. Spiridovich, *Raspoutine*, 15–16, 17; Kilcoyne, 17–18.

12. Smitten, 10: 120; M. Rasputin, *My Father*, 44, 45.

13. Smitten, 10: 120, identifies Nicholas Raspopov as Grigory Rasputin's brother-in-law; other sources make Nicholas Rasputin his brother. But Grigory seems to have been an only child after his older brother's death. Katya and Dunya were Grigory's lovers at various times and lived with him in the capital during the war.

14. Rasputin's enemies also encouraged groundless rumors that Grigory and his father were horse thieves. The notion that neighbors tagged Grigory with the surname "Rasputin" is equally silly. It is true the verb *rasputnichat'* means "to lead a dissolute life" or "to be drunken and dissipated," so to Russian ears "Grigory Rasputin" suggests "Grigory the dissolute," the "debauched," etc. But "Rasputin" is a familiar Russian name. Siberian surnames often come from nature and topography. "Rasputin" probably

derived from *na rasput'e*, a fork in the road. The name might also be related to *rasputitsa*, the time in early spring when roads turn to mud. The name is widespread in Siberia. Another prominent "Rasputin" in later years was the Siberian writer Valentine Rasputin.

Weighty evidence indicates Grigory's family bore the name long before his time. Sergei Markov's investigations in Pokrovskoe prompted him to "affirm that there were fore-bearers of Rasputin [in this area] almost from Catherine's time . . . " (The young officer was there in 1918 in connection with a conspiracy to rescue the royal family. Since Markov despised Rasputin for undermining the tsar's government, he had no apparent reason to lie to improve Grigory's reputation (20).) Maria Rasputin recalls her grandfather told her that "when Ermak sent his ships along the Tura [during the sixteenth century] we were already Rasputins" (*My Father,* 29–30).

If Rasputin's name had no special connotations, it amused his contemporaries and bothered him. He actually signed himself "Rosputin," and in 1907 adopted the name "Novyi," the Russian adjective for "new." But Grigory did not succeed in shedding "Rasputin." He even continued to use the old name, spelled in his own peculiar fashion (Kulikowski, 54). Rasputin told Iliodor the tsarevich Alexis gave him the name "Novyi" (Iliodor, 111–12).

15. Concerning the khlysty and sex, see Klibanov, 52–54, 80–82; F. C. Conybeare, *Russian Dissenters* (Cambridge: Harvard University Press, 1921), 350–53; and George Monro, *Modern Encyclopedia of Russian and Soviet History* 16: 152–53. Concerning khlyst elements in Rasputin's first circle of religious followers at Pokrovskoe *ca.* 1885, see Spiridovich, *Raspoutine,* 35–36, and especially the same author's much-overlooked "Nachalo Rasputina," 2. Denisov, 660–61, discusses the Verkhotur'e monastery in 1908.

16. Smitten, 10: 120; M. Rasputin, *My Father,* 45; Rodzianko, 5.

17. M. Rasputin, *My Father,* 26–27.

18. Simanovich, 19–20, 23.

19. M. Rasputin, *Real Rasputin,* 19–20; Spiridovich, *Raspoutine,* 10. The sketch was by Maria, the third oldest of the four girls.

20. Iliodor, 109.

21. Timothy Ware, *The Orthodox Church* (Penguin Books, 1963), 47, 141; M. Rasputin, *My Father,* 47. The quote is from Kilcoyne, 17–18.

22. *Padenie,* 4: 499–500.

23. Maevskii, 38. In saying that he had been looking for God in monasteries and "in ships" (*v korabliakh*) Rasputin was making a reference to his undoubted fellowship with the khlysty—which does not prove that he was a member of the group. The khlysty called each of their congregations a "ship" (*korabl'*).

24. M. Rasputin, *Real Rasputin,* 10–11.

25. Spiridovich, *Raspoutine,* 36–37; Maevskii, 39–49; Chernov, 20; M. Rasputin, *Real Rasputin,* 22.

Chapter 2, "From Kazan to St. Petersburg"

1. The quote is from Spiridovich, *Raspoutine,* 38. M. Rasputin, *My Father,* 49; Kilcoyne, 33; Curtiss, 366; de Jonge, 73.

2. Iliodor, 163.

3. Iliodor, 163. On Feofan's prestige, see Rodzianko, 4.

4. Rasputin and Barham, *Rasputin,* 105.

5. Compare the accounts of Rasputin's encounter with John of Kronstadt in M.

Rasputin, *My Father*, 49, with the (apparently) less reliable account in Rasputin and Barham, *Rasputin*, 105. See also Iliodor, 109.

6. The quote is from Radziwell, *Rasputin*, 34. See also Witte, 3: 565; Maevskii, 131.

7. Dostoevskii, *Brat'ia Karamazovy* (Petrozavodsk, 1970), 30–39.

8. Zhevakov, 1: 264–65.

9. Smitten, 10: 120.

10. Spiridovich, *Raspoutine*, 38–39; Radziwell, *Rasputin*, 46.

11. Smitten, 10: 121.

12. Zhevakov, 1: 280–82.

13. Paléologue, 1: 98.

14. The first two chapters of Massie provide a beautifully written account of the last tsar's childhood.

15. Buxhoeveden, *Life and Tragedy*, 23.

16. Nicholas, *Journal intime*, 52; Nicholas, *Secret Letters*, 65.

17. Nicholas, *Journal intime*, 111.

18. Radziwell, *Memories*, 324–27.

19. Mouchanow, 162, is a reliable source of information on Alexandra's superstitions; the author was lady-in-waiting to the empress and knew her for 33 years. Dehn, 62–64, and Vyrubova, 150–51, argue the degree of Alexandra's superstition is often exaggerated by unfriendly writers.

20. Cohn, 94–96; Iliodor, 170–71; Smitten, 10: 129; Warth, 325–27.

21. Paléologue, 1: 203–5.

22. Paléologue, 1: 204.

23. Paléologue, 1: 206.

24. Spiridovich, *Dernières années*, 1: 100, 101; Yusupov, *Lost Splendor*, 62; Warth, 329.

25. Paléologue, 1: 207; Vyrubova, 151–52; AF to N, 98 (June 16, 1915). I find no clear evidence that Nicholas and Alexandra tried to communicate with the dead, and I doubt the charges are true.

26. Mouchanow, 159–61.

27. Radziwill, *Nicholas II*, 181; Buxhoeveden, *Life and Tragedy*, 125.

28. Tisdall, 243.

29. Alexander, 182–83.

Chapter 3, "A Man of God from Tobolsk"

1. de Jonge, 80.

2. Spiridovich, *Raspoutine*, 52.

3. For Feofan's role, see *Padenie*, 1: 397; 3: 236; 4: 147–48; also, Shavel'skii, 1: 50. According to Simanovich the two sisters met Rasputin by chance at a monastery in Kiev in 1903 (12–14); Pares (*Fall*, 135), Salisbury (207), and Spiridovich (*Raspoutine*, 37–38, 48–52) agree with him. I conclude that Feofan introduced Rasputin to the Montenegrins in St. Petersburg, possibly in 1903, probably in 1905.

4. Nicholas, *Dnevnik*, 229.

5. The Russian language has two forms of "you." *Ty*, the familiar form, is used with family members, friends, children, pets, oneself, and God. *Vy* is used with important people and in situations where the relationship is impersonal or professional. Rasputin

disregarded these distinctions and employed *ty* where *vy* would be expected. Some upper-class people were amused over this disdain for rank; they attributed it to peasant ignorance, boorish manners, a religious conviction that all people are equal—whatever. Others were offended. But from the beginning this easy manner charmed Nicholas and Alexandra.

6. This overlooked account comes from Alexander Damer, who for 19 years registered visitors to the palace and noted the purpose, time, and duration of each reception, and so on. "It fell to me to meet Rasputin at the court from his first appearance to his last visit" (1). See also Spiridovich, *Raspoutine*, 50–53.

7. Simanovich, 18; M. Rasputin, *Real Rasputin*, 36; Maevskii, 74. Concerning the second recorded visit, see Vyrubova, 152. The quotes are from Vinogradoff, 115–16.

8. The icon was just under 12 inches (30 centimeters) high, and was painted on wood. Concerning this visit, see Spiridovich, *Raspoutine*, 57–58, and "Nachalo Rasputina," 5; also Vyrubova, 152; Vinogradoff, 115–16; Simanovich, 18.

9. Smitten, 1: 99. Spiridovich, *Raspoutine*, 93. Medved was former confessor to Grand Duchess Militsa.

10. Compare M. Rasputin, *My Father*, 35–36, with Spiridovich, "Nachalo Rasputina," 1, and *Raspoutine*, 71–72. Spiridovich thought that Rasputin first healed Alexis in 1907. The garrulous Teliakovskii's friends included the minister of the court, and Spiridovich concludes his account "certainly contains a part of the truth."

11. This is from the discussion of hemophilia contained in the article "Pathology" in the *Encyclopaedia Britannica* (9th ed., 1885), 18: 375.

12. Lukhomskii, 28; Mosolov, 148; Shakhovskoi, 119; Fabritskii, 134–35; Vorres, 142.

13. Iliodor, 181–82, knew Alexis was "sick," but he was obviously ignorant of the boy's exact malady. For theories linking Badmaev to Rasputin, see Kerensky, *Road*, 70, and Anonymous, *Fall*, 48–49. M. Rasputin, *My Father*, 36, criticizes these theories. See further Buxhoeveden, *Life and Tragedy*, 142; Dehn, 99–100, 128; Gilliard, 62–70; Tisdall, 250; Alexander, 184.

14. Smitten, 12: 100; Mouchanow, 190; Semennikov, *Za kulisami tsarizma*, 17; Salisbury, 208, 658; Kurlov, 187–88.

15. Katkov, 203; Massie, 190–91; Trewin, 22.

16. Markov, 20; M. Rasputin, *My Father*, 34.

17. *Padenie*, 4: 502.

18. *Padenie*, 1: 28, 35; Yuspov, *Rasputin*, 102–3.

19. Massie, 190.

20. Poliakoff, 274–75. Buxhoeveden, *Before the Storm*, 116–19. L.M. de Basily, 78.

21. *Padenie*, 4: 354; Lukhomskii, 28; Simanovich, 18.

22. Dorr, 112–13.

Chapter 4, "The Secrets of Father Grigory"

1. M. Rasputin, *Real Rasputin*, 52–53; M. Rasputin, *My Father*, 59; Simanovich, 27, 29–30.

2. This account of Rasputin's family is based upon Maria Rasputin's memoirs and the reminiscences of Aron Simanovich. Iliodor offers a less charitable account. He claims Praskovaya was a "good-looking, but sickly woman" who knew about her husband's misdeeds but shielded him due to "mercenary considerations." Iliodor found Varvara to be a pleasant nine year-old girl "whose mouth was always open. . . . " Iliodor writes that

Dmitry went to Saratov (rather than Samara) to study. But the boy proved to be "very corrupt" and ignored the education that cost his father 25 rubles per month "and got two servant girls dismissed for their loose conduct with him. He returned to Pokrovskoe to do manual labor" (Iliodor, 115). M. Rasputin, *Real Rasputin*, 26–27, 37–38; M. Rasputin, *My Father*, 56–57; Rasputin and Barham, *Rasputin*, 160–61; Simanovich, 30.

3. Simanovich, 9–10, 21–22; M. Rasputin, *My Father*, 60; Betskii, 155.

4. Smitten, 10: 123; N. de Basily, 27; Evlogii, 215; Fülöp-Miller, 271; Dzhanumovaia, 101, 103, 108.

5. Smitten, 10: 122–23. See Evlogii, 217–18, for Uexkull.

6. *Padenie*, 4: 241; Smitten, 10: 123; Spiridovich, *Raspoutine*, 78–90.

7. *Padenie*, 3: 434; 4: 500; Smitten, 10: 122; Simanovich, 101; Paléologue, 1: 142–43; Iliodor, 187; Spiridovich, *Dernières années*, 1: 290.

8. Harsh judgments of Anna Vyrubova include Botkin, 47; Cantacuzène, 24–25; Gilliard, 83; Paléologue, 1: 229–30, and 2: 50–51; Simanovich, 162; and Protopopov (*Padenie*, 4: 8, and 2: 215). Favorable judgments are in Rudnev, 393, 394, and Gippius, 169.

9. Smitten, 12: 90; *Padenie*, 3: 233–334, 235; Vyrubova, 30–31.

10. Smitten, 12: 91; Vyrubova, 29–32, 153–54; Rasputin and Barham, *Rasputin*, 132–33.

11. *Padenie*, 3: 234–35; Vyrubova, 31–21; Paléologue, 1: 229; Spiridovich, *Dernièrs années*, 2: 207–8; Botkin, 51; Smitten, 12: 90.

12. *Padenie*, 3: 235; Smitten, 12: 94; Spiridovich, *Raspoutine*, 56–57; Massie, 150.

13. Paléologue, 1: 229–30; Bogdanovich, 304–5; Vyrubova, 258–59; Rudnev, 395–96.

14. Gilliard, 194; Spiridovich, *Dernières années*, 1: 294; *Padenie*, 3: 237, 250.

15. Zhevakov, 1: 275–80.

Chapter 5, "The Teachings of Father Grigory"

1. M. Rasputin, *Rasputin*, 15–16.

2. *Padenie*, 4: 506; Kilcoyne, 26–27; G. Rasputin, "My Thoughts," 134–35; M. Rasputin, *Real Rasputin*, 43; Radziwell, *Rasputin*, 95.

3. M. Rasputin, *Real Rasputin*, 49.

4. Zhevakov, 1: 275–80.

5. Paléologue, 1: 149.

6. Kilcoyne, 29–30.

7. Mosolov, 149–50.

8. Spiridovich, "Nachalo Rasputina," 2; Graham, 180.

9. Paléologue thinks Rasputin's teachings were similar to "a Phrygian sect" and the heretic Montanus (1: 150); Kilcoyne connects him with "the folk sects and Satanic cults of the Middle Ages" (30). These assertions do not seem accurate to me.

10. See George E. Munro, "Khlysty," *Modern Encyclopedia of Russian and Soviet History*, 16: 150–54.

11. Iliodor, 215.

12. M. Rasputin, *My Father*, 48; Smitten, 10: 121.

13. M. Rasputin, *Real Rasputin*, 21–22, 62–63; M. Rasputin, *My Father*, 90.

14. Judas, 36–40.

Chapter 6, "First Crisis"

1. Tisdall, 250; Rodzianko, 24; Kokovtsov, 2: 38; Voeikov, 69; Bonch-Bruevich, 94.

2. N. de Basily, 77–78.

3. *Padenie,* 3: 11–12; Rodzianko, 2; Kurlov, 178; Spiridovich, "Nachalo Rasputina," 4–5.

4. Kurlov, 178–80; Spiridovich, *Dernières années,* 1: 297–99, and "Nachalo Rasputina," 9; *Padenie,* 3: 11–12.

5. Spiridovich, *Dernières années,* 1: 208–9; *Padenie,* 3: 12; Spiridovich, *Raspoutine,* 91–92.

6. Vorres, 135.

7. Spiridovich, "Nachalo Rasputina," 9; Tisdall, 243; Zhevakov, 1: 270.

8. Spiridovich, *Raspoutine,* 73–74, and *Dernières années,* 1: 295.

9. Spiridovich, *Raspoutine,* 96–104; Vyrubova, 162–63.

10. Vorres, 132; Shavel'skii, 1: 67; Aronson, 74. The countess was the widow of the Duke of Meklenburg-Strelitskii; the book was entitled *Iurodovye sviatye russkoi tserkvi.*

11. Gilliard, 178; Buxhoeveden, *Life and Tragedy,* 142; Voeikov, 174. "It was extremely difficult to respond to this argument," Voiekov continued, "because both the emperor and the empress grew convinced, and with good reason, that every person who gained their confidence for that reason would fall victim to envious people and liars."

12. Rodzianko, 11; Oldenburg, 3: 83.

13. Gurko, *Tsar i tsaritsa,* 90.

Chapter 7, "Iliodor: Radical on the Right"

1. See Chapters 1–4 of Iliodor.

2. Iliodor, 30, 87–93.

3. Iliodor, 30–48.

4. Iliodor, 49–50.

5. Stremoukhov, 24

6. Iliodor, 50–56.

7. Iliodor, 95–97; Kilcoyne, 123–28.

8. Iliodor, 97–98.

9. Iliodor, 57, 97, 103.

10. Iliodor, 59.

11. *Padenie,* 7: 324; Oldenburg, 3: 199. For the citation from Hermogen's article, see Curtiss, *Church and State,* 254, 336. Hermogen was born in 1858 into a wealthy merchant family in the area of Kherson on the Black Sea. His lay name was Georgy Dalganev. At first the young man studied law. The call he felt to the priesthood was unusual at a time when the vast majority of Russian priests were the sons of priests. Georgy graduated from the St. Petersburg Seminary and became a monk under the name of Hermogen in 1892. Hermogen was made bishop in 1901 and two years later was assigned to Saratov.

12. Iliodor, 106. Hermogen's "critic" was Stremoukhov, 13, 21–22. Spiridovich, *Raspoutine,* 106; Evlogii, 198.

13. Kilcoyne, 131; Spiridovich, *Raspoutine,* 105–17; de Jonge, 182.

14. Semennikov, *Za kulisami,* 138; Iliodor, 116–21; Kilcoyne, 129.

15. Bulgakov, 84.

16. Nekliudov, 68–69. Bogdanovich, 277.

17. Spiridovich, "Nachalo Rasputina," 8, and *Raspoutine,* 128.

18. Iliodor, 186–87; Evlogii, 220; Spiridovich, *Raspoutine,* 104, 124–25; Kilcoyne, 133–34.

19. Iliodor, 216–20; Spiridovich, *Raspoutine,* 69.

20. Spiridovich, *Raspoutine,* 125–26; Iliodor, 216–20; Gurko, *Tsar i tsaritsa,* 43, 44, 70; Oldenburg, 3: 81. The Russian names of these three newspapers were *Moskovskie vedomosti, Rech',* and *Novoe vremia.*

21. Shavel'skii, 1:49; Kilcoyne, 134.

22. Smitten, 10, 132; Mosolov, 163–64; Dehn, 76; Vyrubova, 62, 64; de Jonge, 189; Bogdanovich, 300, 317–18.

23. Shavel'skii, 1: 62.

24. Rodzianko, 27; Smitten, 10, 132. Anna Vyrubova denies that Rasputin visited the royal children in their private quarters. She maintains that Tyutcheva never even saw Rasputin, and that Nicholas in their final interview suggested she meet the starets. Tyutcheva refused to do this, according to Vyrubova (62–64).

25. Iliodor, 202. Feofan suffered continuing signs of royal displeasure. When Nicholas and his family planned a visit to the Crimea in the fall of 1912, they realized protocol entailed a welcome from the bishop of the diocese. To prevent a disagreeable encounter, Nicholas sent Feofan to serve as bishop of Astrakhan, a still more remote place with even greater dangers to his health. Feofan returned to the central region of the empire as bishop of Poltava and Pereiaslavl' in 1913; he survived the revolution and civil war.

26. Iliodor, 135.

27. Rodzianko, 27–28; Pol'skii, 14.

28. Mandrika received a telegram from his cousin in the capital on February 11 that told him "You're in a fix now!" When the mother superior saw her cousin on February 14 she defended Rasputin, hoping to persuade Mandrika to qualify some of the information he had presented to the tsar. "Rasputin is a good man," Maria insisted. "He must be saved." Seeing that Mandrika would not relent, she predicted that he had destroyed his career. This proved untrue. Mandrika dined with the royal family again on February 16, 1911. If Alexandra was cool, Nicholas received Mandrika cordially and was "visibly quite satisfied with his envoy's journey and report" (Spiridovich, *Raspoutine,* 135). Mandrika's career moved forward at a reasonable pace. He dined a third time with the royal family in 1914 just before departing to become vice-governor of Nizhnyi-Novgorod. Mandrika was made governor at Tbilisi in 1916. Concerning the Mandrika episode, see Spiridovich, *Raspoutine,* 106–8, 132–36, and *Dernières années,* 2: 52–55; also, Gurko, *Tsar i tsaritsa,* 95–98, who offers this tantalizing information: "I drew these facts from the memoirs of A. N. Mandrika, which have not been published as of now."

29. Lukhomskii, 27.

30. According to Maria Rasputin (Rasputin and Barham, *Rasputin,* 162–68), the conspirators learned of his habits from Iliodor. They recruited the Finnish ballet instructor Lisa Tansin to ensnare Grigory. The night the trap was sprung he had already partied at his favorite restaurant, the Villa Rode. Tansin enticed Grigory to a party in progress at her house. She challenged Rasputin to toast her with vodka, knowing that he was more familiar with wine. Grigory was soon drunk, and at the mercy of his foes.

Chapter 8, "Jerusalem"

1. Graham, 99–100.
2. Spiridovich thinks Rasputin's book—entitled *Moi mysli i razmyshleniia*—was based upon a "series of interesting letters addressed to his admirers." (*Raspoutine*, 139–40, and *Dernières années*, 2: 55–59). The manuscript was published in 1915 in a deluxe edition with two portraits. Alexandra sponsored the effort in the hope it would help refute charges that Rasputin was a cynic, charlatan, agent of the Germans, and so on. *My Thoughts and Meditations* were not sold. Dzhanumovaia tells us that Rasputin gave complementary signed copies to his friends, often with notes of appreciation (106). It was reprinted by Semennikov, *Za kulasami*, 142–60, and translated into English in M. Rasputin, *My Father*, 121–57. My citations are from Semennikov.
3. G. Rasputin, "Moi mysli."
4. Graham, 8–9, 40, 99.
5. G. Rasputin, "Moi mysli."
6. Graham, 84–85, 88; G. Rasputin, "Moi mysli."
7. G. Rasputin, "Moi mysli."
8. G. Rasputin, "Moi mysli."
9. G. Rasputin, "Moi mysli."
10. In Rasputin's time Russia still used the Julian calendar; other European states had shifted to the Gregorian calendar. Russian dates are 13 days behind those of Western Europe during the twentieth century. The Bolsheviks ended the discrepancy by adopting Pope Gregory's calendar. The Orthodox Church retained the Julian calendar for religious purposes, and it still celebrates Easter later than non-Orthodox Christians.

Chapter 9, "Again a Brilliant Star"

1. Gurko, *Tsar i tsaritsa*, 97.
2. Iliodor, 140–53.
3. *Padenie*, 7: 432; 4: 368; Bulgakov, 83; Bogdanovich, 481; Miliukov, 334.
4. Miliukov, 334.
5. Bogdanovich, 481; the quote is from Kilcoyne, 214–15.
6. Witte, 3: 567–68.
7. *Padenie*, 1:3–5.
8. Witte, 3: 567.
9. Salisbury, 658–59; Simanovich, 81–83.
10. Shulgin, 260–63.
11. Spiridovich, *Dernières années*, 2: 188.
12. Kokovtsov, 2: 265, 493.
13. *Padenie*, 1: 3–5.
14. The Russian Church was headed by a patriarch from 1589 to 1700. Peter the Great replaced the patriarchate with the "Most Holy Synod," a governing board patterned after the Swedish Lutheran Church. Four of the 13 Russian church leaders sat *ex officio:* the metropolitans of St. Petersburg, Moscow, and Kiev; and the exarch of Georgia. The other nine bishops and church dignitaries rotated and were appointed for short terms. The Russian Synod was headed by an "Ober-Procurator" and his assistant; I translate this

German-Swedish term "director general." The tsar appointed these two officials, and they answered to him.

15. Oldenburg, 3: 89–90, 201–2.

16. Conroy, 31; Iliodor, 196–97.

17. *Padenie,* 7: 413; Byrnes, 175, 200, 228, 360–65; Nikon, 10: 137.

18. Rodzianko, 72–73; Semennikov, *Za kulasami,* 138; Curtiss, *Church and State,* 375. Pares, *Fall,* 143, characterizes Sabler as "a Rasputin man [who] was often reproached with having actually made an obeisance to him; Beletsky treats this charge as generally accepted and Kokovtsov repeats it." On this see Kokovtsov, 2: 32; Matthew Spinka, *The Church and the Russian Revolution* (New York, 1927), pp. 56–57.

19. Witte, 3: 552–53.

20. Harcave, 398; Spinka, 57–58.

21. Evlogii was critical of Sabler for permitting the appearance that Rasputin dominated him and the Holy Synod, but he praises Sabler at length in his memoirs (196). Stremoukhov, 15, 29, 39, 45, and Shavel'skii, 1: 282–88, also insist upon Sabler's high character and ability, but Witte included Sabler among the "dilettantes" who followed Pobedonostsev as Synod director general (3: 552). The American historian quoted is Harcave, 398.

22. Smitten, 12: 99; Maevskii, 115; Shavel'skii, 1: 369.

23. Maevskii, 115–16.

24. Shavel'skii, 1: 369–70; Maevskii, 115; *Padenie,* 4: 153.

25. Smitten, 12, 100; *Padenie,* 1: 385; Shavel'skii, 1: 87; Iliodor, 206–7 (quotation slightly revised in terms of the Russian original).

26. "V tserkovnykh krugakh," 204–11.

27. "V tserkovnykh krugakh," 211–212; Smitten, 2: 104; Maevskii, 117–19; Nikon, 4: 55–56. This last meeting occurred on August 8, 1911.

28. Maevskii, 116–17. Bishop Anthony of Tobolsk conveyed this information to M. A. Novoselov, editor of the *Religious–Philosophical Library,* and by now one of Rasputin's deadliest critics.

29. For Varnava's diet, compare Iliodor, 205–6, and *Padenie,* 4: 254. For Varnava and Rasputin, *Padenie,* 1: 385.

30. Smitten, 2: 105.

31. The quote is from Andronnikov in *Padenie,* 1: 385. See also *Padenie,* 4: 153, and Smitten, 12: 100.

32. Maevskii, 119–20.

33. Smitten, 12: 100.

Chapter 10, "Disgrace"

1. Hermogen actually saw an example of Rasputin's bad behavior. They once stayed in the same guest room of the Balashevskaia Convent. Hermogen pretended to be asleep to see if anything might happen to confirm the rumors about Grigory's sex life. At 1 A.M. Rasputin slipped away with Hermogen in quiet pursuit. Grigory tried to seduce the wife of a priest who was absent on a trip. A noisy altercation made Grigory leave. (Spiridovich, *Raspoutine,* 107, 130, 154).

2. Cunningham, 197; Curtiss, *Church and State,* 370–71; Oldenburg, 3: 109. Kulikowski, 77. See Almedingen, *An Unbroken Unity,* for a brief survey of Elizabeth's life.

3. Spiridovich, *Raspoutine,* 156.

4. Spiridovich, *Raspoutine,* 157–58; Iliodor, 106, 130, 158–59, 167, 215, 227–28; M. Rasputin, *Real Rasputin,* 63, and *My Father,* 20, 66–67.

5. Spiridovich, *Raspoutine,* 158–60; Iliodor, 229–36; Evlogii, 198; Pares, *Fall,* 145–46; Kulikowski, 77. Two accounts based upon Rodionov are Rodzianko, 15–17, and Vonliarliarskii, 202–5. Tikhomirov, 174–75, is useful in reconstructing the sequence of events in this bizarre "trial." Shavel'skii says an attempt was made to castrate Rasputin, but Grigory saved himself by flight. De Jonge gives a good account of this episode. He notes this was the first recorded attempt to harm Rasputin, and it occurred on December 16, the anniversary of his meeting Iliodor and the day he died in 1916 (202–3).

6. Gurko, *Features,* 259–60; Vonliarliarskii, 203–4, 272; Evlogii, 198.

7. Vonliarliarskii, 204; Iliodor, 237–38.

8. Curtiss, *Church and State,* 371–372; Kokovtsov, 293.

9. Iliodor, 244–45, 249–50.

10. Iliodor, 256, 259–60, 270; Oldenburg, 3: 206.

11. The title of Tikhomirov's newspaper was *Moskovskiia vedomosti;* the quotes are from entries in his diary under January 28 and 29, 1912 (see Tikhomirov, 174–75).

12. Kokovtsov, 293. The title of Novoselov's thick journal was the *Religious–Philosophical Library.*

13. Shulgin, 219; N. de Basily, 62–63; Oldenburg, 3: 80–81, 291.

14. Nekliudov, 67; see also Katkov, 337.

15. Rodzianko, 31–34; Kulikowski, 80; Shulgin, 230–31. Pares, *Fall,* 146–47. Guchkov's paper was *Golos Moskvy.* Another paper, *Vechernee vremia* (*Evening Times*), published excerpts from Novoselov's pamphlet on January 24, 1912.

16. Mosolov, 177; Nekliudov, 67–68. Concerning the editorial in *Russkiia vedomosti* (January 21, 1912) and news items in *Birzheviia vedomosti* (January 17, 1912), see Curtiss, *Church and State,* 372.

17. Kokovtsov, 290–91; Curtiss, *Church and State,* 374–75; Rodzianko, 31.

18. An "interpellation" could be voted by the Duma or the upper house, the State Council. It began with 30 or more members moving a debate on a particular issue; the motion could be approved by a simple majority vote. An interpellation was addressed to a specific minister who had a month to study the issue, express an opinion, take remedial action—whatever. The chamber that passed the interpellation could then debate the issue. Ministers were not required to answer questions or attend the debates, but the solemn procedure and newspaper coverage made a response of some sort desirable.

19. Rodzianko, 31–32; Eddy, 41; Thomson, 75.

20. Rodzianko, 33.

21. Rodzianko, 35–48; Pares, *Fall,* 147–48.

22. Concerning the cabal see Kilcoyne, 159–63; Kokovtsov, 294ff., and especially Spiridovich, *Dernières années,* 196–200. Its members included Guards General Drenteln; Alexander Mosolov, head of the court chancellery; Benckendorf; Alexandra Naryshkina, so close to the royal family that she was called "tante Sasha"; Prince Orlov, affectionately known as "Fat" Orlov, assistant-director of the tsar's personal military secretariat; Admiral Nilov; General Spiridovich, head of palace security.

23. Spiridovich, *Dernières années,* 2: 199–200.

24. Rodzianko, 49–50; Iliodor, 197; *Padenie,* 7: 332.

25. Compare Rodzianko, 51–52, and his testimony in *Padenie,* 7: 160–63.

26. *Padenie,* 7: 160; Kokovtsov, 294–95.

27. Oldenburg, 3: 111; Evlogii, 196–98; Kokovtsov, 317.

28. Iliodor passed the letters to Rodzianko through Rodionov. It is less clear who released them to the public by hectograph. Nicholas believed that Guchkov was the culprit, which is also what the "purveyors" of the letters claimed. Oldenburg (3: 112) thought this was not proven—a powerful statement considering his low opinion of Guchkov. Kokovtsov (291–300) and Miliukov (234) thought Guchkov was responsible.

29. Smitten, 10: 131–32; Kokovtsov, 293.

30. Makarov feared that the government's enemies might produce photographic copies of these letters, and this would create a greater scandal than the hectographed versions. Kokovtsov and Makarov decided to buy the letters; if this failed they were ready to use "other means." A few days later, Makarov phoned to tell the prime minister that it had not proved difficult to get the letters because the man who had them at that point was a "decent fellow" who also feared his possession of the letters might anger Rasputin and his friends (Kokovtsov, 300).

31. Compare the English translation of Kokovtsov's memoirs about this episode (300) with the Russian original (2: 44). See also Iliodor, 31, and *Padenie*, 4: 149.

32. Kokovtsov, 294; Iliodor, 254–55.

33. Rodzianko, 60–61.

34. Voeikov, 68–69, and Nekliudov, 226–28.

35. *Padenie*, 3: 384, 391–92, and 4: 150; Bonch-Bruevich, 93; Bogdanovich, *Dnevnik*, 496. The retired General Bogdanovich apparently organized a serious conspiracy against Rasputin. Beletskii later admitted that he provided the "Bogdanovich circle" with police information about Grigory. Interior Minister Makarov knew Beletskii was doing this and did not stop him. (*Padenie*, 4: 149).

36. Nekliudov, 226–28.

Chapter 11, "The Little One Will Not Die"

1. Nicholas, *Secret Letters*, 270–71.

2. Nicholas, *Secret Letters*, 271–76; Spiridovich, *Dernières années*, 2: 272–85; Gilliard, 28; Vyrubova, 90.

3. Vyrubova, 90–92.

4. Spiridovich, *Dernières années*, 2: 289; Nicholas, *Secret Letters*, 276; Vyrubova, 92; Buxhoeveden, *Life and Tragedy*, 131.

5. Buxhoeveden, *Life and Tragedy*, 131–32; Vyrubova, 92–93; Nicholas, *Secret Letters*, 276.

6. Gilliard, 28–30.

7. Buxhoeveden, *Life and Tragedy*, 132–33; Nicholas, *Secret Letters*, 276–77; Vyrubova, 93–94; Massie, 171–79; Paléologue, 1: 27.

8. Vyrubova, 94; Rasputin and Barham, *Rasputin*, 177–78; M. Rasputin, *My Father*, 72. The quote is from Kilcoyne, 110–11.

9. Paléologue, 1: 148. It is apparently impossible to determine the exact text of the telegram and one sees it cited in a variety of ways. Anna Vyrubova recalled that it read: "The little one will not die. Do not allow the doctors to bother him too much" (94). Spiridovich tells us Rasputin sent two telegrams to Spala. "The illness is not serious," the first asserted. "The doctors should not tire him." In the second telegram, Rasputin supposedly assured Alexandra that he had prayed, God heard those prayers and permitted Alexis to live (Spiridovich, *Dernières années*, 2: 290). The text that I cite here is from

Charles Sydney Gibbes, tutor to the royal children (Trewin, 24). Gibbes was not an eyewitness, but he was sufficiently close to the court to fill in gaps in his knowledge if he cared to do so. Rasputin's message parallels the text of Isaiah 38: 5: "Go and say to Hezekiah. Thus says the Lord, the God of David your father: I have heard your prayer, I have seen your tears; behold, I will add fifteen years to your life."

10. Mosolov, 150–51; Vyrubova, 95; Nicholas, *Secret Letters,* 277–78; Trewin, 24–25; Paléologue, 1: 148–49; Gilliard, 70; Darmer, 7.

11. Mosolov, 150–51; Vorres, 143.

12. Gilliard suggests that the doctors were not "bothering" Alexis. They applied remedies, probably topical drugs, to reduce the swelling and pain. Gilliard also notes that the tsarevich's "terrible sufferings" made a thorough examination impossible until the afternoon of the day that his recovery began (30). "I must admit it is always depressing to see so many doctors gathered together," Nicholas confessed to his mother, "but they were all so kind and sympathetic and considerate with Alexis that I shall always think of them with gratitude" (Nicholas, *Secret Letters,* 276). The team of doctors at Spala was made up of Eugene Botkin (general practitioner to the royal family), Professor Sergei Fedorov (court surgeon and a specialist on hemophilia), Rauchfuss (court pediatrician), and Ostrogorskii (characterized by Nicholas as "our usual doctor for the children"). A new physician called in at this time, Fedorov's assistant Vladimir Derevenko, continued to serve Alexis in later years (Nicholas, *Secret Letters,* 276; Mosolov, 149–50.)

Chapter 12, "As Long as I Live, I Will Not Permit War"

1. Oldenburg, 3: 126.

2. Rodzianko, 75–77.

3. Buchanan, 35–36; Vyrubova, 98–101; Spiridovich, *Dernières années,* 2: 315–16.

4. Oldenburg, 3; 127; Kokovtsov, 360–61.

5. Kokovtsov, 361; Oldenburg, 3: 127; Shavel'skii, 1: 61; *Padenie,* 4: 189.

6. Oldenburg, 3: 127; Narishkin-Kurakin, 205–6.

7. Voeikov, 30.

8. M. Rasputin, *My Father,* 79–82; Iliodor, 195; Salisbury, 249; Bertram D. Wolfe, *Three Who Made a Revolution* (New York: Dell, 1964), 607–8.

9. Semennikov, *Politika,* 227.

10. Semennikov, *Politika,* 227–28. The first newspaper was *Sankpeterburgskaia gazetta;* the second interviewer was A. Stolypin for *Novoe vremia.* A game of wits was probably in progress during these interviews. Stolypin seemed to want comments that could be twisted into damaging statements: Rasputin doesn't appreciate the importance of the outside world, he doesn't understand Russia's honorable tradition of defending the Balkan Slavs, and so on. Rasputin hints that Stolypin and his type traffic in lies, which Grigory saw through because he had travelled through the Balkans. An interesting performance, and one that leaves us wondering if Rasputin exerted too much influence in state affairs or not enough.

11. Nicholas, *Secret Letters,* 278–79; Simanovich, 153–54; *Padenie,* 6: 370.

12. Rodzianko, 97–98, 101–2; Curtiss, *Church and State,* 375–76. The Russian newspapers were *Kolokol* and *Vechernie vremia.*

13. Oldenburg, 3: 132–34, 139.

Chapter 13, "Nearly Assassinated—War"

1. M. Rasputin, *Real Rasputin,* 78–82; Rasputin and Barham, *Rasputin,* 193.
2. M. Rasputin, *Real Rasputin,* 82; *Padenie,* 7: 331; Spiridovich, *Raspoutine,* 201.
3. Rasputin and Barham, *Rasputin,* 194–95; M. Rasputin, *Real Rasputin,* 82–86, and *My Father,* 77; Massie, 244–45; Davidsohn sold articles on this story to several St. Petersburg newspapers. He might have learned of Guseva's plot from her or her friends; more likely he got a tip from the tangled world of police informants, agents, and double-agents. This would suggest that the police had some notion of what was about to happen, and were satisfied to let events take their course. See *Padenie,* 4: 449, and Amalrik, 179.
4. M. Rasputin, *Real Rasputin,* 87; Rasputin and Barham, *Rasputin,* 196–97; Spiridovich, *Raspoutine,* 202.
5. Spiridovich, *Raspoutine,* 202, and *Dernières années,* 2: 468–69.
6. Spiridovich, *Dernières années,* 2: 470; Spiridovich, *Raspoutine,* 203; Amalrik, 184.
7. Semennikov, *Monarkhiia,* 92; *Padenie,* 5: 101–2; Rodzianko, 105; Kulikowski, 95. There were signs that pogroms might break out in connection with the attempt against Rasputin. "Are the newspapers correct in reporting massive departures of Jewish artisans from Kiev?" Nicholas asked Makarov. "Give me a report about this."
8. Radziwell, *Rasputin,* 123; *Padenie,* 3: 233, 245; 6: 225–226; and 7: 331.
9. Kerensky, *Road,* 52; Mel'gunov, 383; Amalrik, 181–82, 183.
10. Kerensky, *Road,* 52. The original letter is in Yale's Beinecke Rare Book Library, and is cited in English translation by Massie, 268. Maria Rasputin published a similar document in all three memoirs of her father: *Real Rasputin,* 88–89; *My Father,* 77–78; and *Rasputin,* 198. I offer my own translation. See also *Red Archives,* 34, and Amalrik, 183.
11. Semennikov, *Dnevnik,* 15–16.
12. Vyrubova, 105.
13. Rodzianko, 108–9. Paléologue, 1: 50–52.
14. Paléologue, 1: 72–73; Bible.

Chapter 14, "Rasputin Returns"

1. Kokovtsov was a thorn in Rasputin's hide, and his downfall was widely attributed to Grigory. Rasputin supposedly pressured Alexandra to persuade her husband to fire Kokovtsov. I doubt that Nicholas was yet making major decisions in this way. Kokovstov thought that he might have offended Nicholas by upstaging him. Kokovtsov told Paléologue when Nicholas appointed him chairman in 1911 that the tsar warned him not "to treat me as your predecessor, Peter Arkadievich [Stolypin] did." Kokovstov replied, "Peter Arkadievich died for Your Majesty, Sire!" "He died in my service, true," the emperor conceded. "But he was always anxious to keep me in the background. Do you suppose I liked always reading in the papers that *the President of the Council has done this . . . the President of the Council has done that?* Don't I count? Am I nobody?" (1: 298).
2. An interesting view of Goremykin's relationship with Rasputin is contained in the memoirs of Prince V. N. Shakhovskoi, minister of trade and industry throughout the war. Rasputin did not know Shakhovskoi, and at one point (the prince claimed) Grigory asked

for an appointment. Shakhovskoi was not certain that he cared to enter into relations with the infamous starets, and he turned to Goremykin—ever a wise, fatherly figure—for advice. "Do you ever receive scoundrels in the course of your work?" the worldly chairman asked. Of course, that was among the costs of holding high office. "Then it would also be wise to receive Rasputin," Goremykin concluded. Whatever the truth of this episode, Vsevolod Shakhovskol became known as a member of the "Rasputin circle," appointed with Grigory's blessing and responsive to his will.

3. Hoare, 344; N. de Basily, 53, 68; Oldenburg, 4: 137; Paléologue, 2: 13–14.

4. M. Rasputin, *My Father*, 82; *Padenie*, 2: 54; Paléologue, 1: 137.

5. Some thought the royal family had a fortune in West European banks. Some of the "Anastasias" may have been part of conspiracies to collect this money. The son of the Cossack General Grabbe recalled, "the tsar told [my father] early in the war that he had liquidated his holdings abroad and contributed them to the war effort" (118). Sir Edward Peacock, director of the Bank of England during 1920–24 and 1929–46, was "pretty sure there never was any money of the imperial family of Russia in the Bank of England nor any other bank in England. Of course it is difficult to say 'never' but I am positive at least there never was any money after World War I and during my long years as director of the bank" (Vorres, 245).

6. Vyrubova, 5, 83, 143; Narishkin-Kurakin, 211; Radziwill, *Intimate Life*, 199; Spiridovich, *Raspoutine*, 207; Paléologue, 1: 133, 137–38; Gilliard, 82, 105, 127; M. Rasputin, *My Father*, 70.

7. Vyrubova, 346–47; Gippius, 1: 127; Spiridovich, *Raspoutine*, 89–90.

8. Kulikowski, 104; *Padenie*, 3: 248.

9. M. Rasputin, *My Father*, 88; Rasputin and Barham, *Rasputin*, 203–11; Dehn, 97.

10. *Red Archives*, 43, 49; *Padenie*, 3: 174, and 4: 199; Smitten, 10: 123.

11. Rasputin lived at the hostelry of the Alexander Nevskii Monastery in 1903 and during 1905–8. During 1909–12 he lived in succession with Olga Lokhtina, G. P. Sazonov, and Peter Damanskii. From 1912 to early 1914, he lived at 70 Nicholaevskii Avenue, next at 35 Baseinaia Street, then at 13 English Avenue. Smitten, 10: 123; Amalrik, 199; Kulikowski, 97–99.

12. Fülöp-Miller, 181; Spiridovich, *Raspoutine*, 197; Yusupov, *Rasputin*, 89–91; M. Rasputin, *My Father*, 58; Rasputin and Barham, *Rasputin*, 135; Dzhanumovaia, 107; Pascal, 10; Kulikowski, 98.

13. Spiridovich, *Raspoutine*, 197; Yusupov, *Rasputin*, 89; Dzhanumovaia, 116; *Padenie*, 1: 7, 23, 259; 2: 72; 3: 173.

14. *Red Archives*, 43–45.

15. For the stages of Rasputin's drunkenness in the order listed, see *Red Archives*, 43, 30, 45, 30, 43, 44, 41, 46, 48.

16. Lockhart, 128–29; Salisbury, 263–64; Paléologue, 1: 331–332; Kulikowski, 132–33, 140; *Padenie*, 5: 101–6; 4: 150–51. Dzhanumovaia, 101.

17. *Padenie* 5: 101–6; Pares, *Fall*, 225; *Padenie*, 4: 150–51; AF to N, 105 (June 22, 1915). Rasputin was in Pokrovskoe from July to September 1915, when Dzhunkovskii was dismissed. Grigory surprised his detective guards by telling them that their boss had just been forced to resign; Rasputin predicted that he would be blamed. Rasputin "disclaimed all knowledge of [Dzhunkovskii], however, and professed to have nothing to do with his dismissal." Rasputin admitted his sins at the Yar to a later police director, A. T. Vasil'ev, but still "denied emphatically that he had taken any part whatever in the dismissal of Dzhunkovskii" (Vasil'ev, 152).

The Russian public assumed that Rasputin and Alexandra pressured Nicholas to dismiss Dzhunkovskii because he had clashed with Grigory. It was also thought that the former assistant-minister of the interior was in disfavor with the tsar. The empress often expressed hostility toward Dzhunkovskii to her husband, and she wanted him discharged. But Nicholas's motives in dismissing him were probably more complex than the gossips realized. The tsar seems to have been displeased not so much by Dzhunkovskii's investigation and report—both of which came through royal command—as he was by Dzhunkovskii leaking his report to Rasputin's enemies. This information was used in a series of articles attacking Rasputin in *The Stock Exchange News* from August 14 to 18, 1915. Dzhunkovskii was dismissed on August 19. He blamed Alexandra. But the empress disavowed this in a letter to her husband on September 15, 1915: "[I am quite] disgusted with town & so pained by everything & that my name is always mentioned, as tho' I had cleared *Orlov & Dzhunkovsky* away because of our Fr[iend, Rasputin] etc." (AF to N, 166). It was not necessary for Alexandra to lie in this context! She was probably referring to a point she and Nicholas both knew was true: The decision to dismiss Dzhunkovskii was his, not hers. Kilcoyne notes Nicholas assigned Dzhunkovskii to a military post. This might had been to help the young man; many thought desk officers would not enjoy the better careers once the war ended (258). In short, Alexandra and Rasputin may have played no role in Dzhunkovskii's dismissal, and the dismissal might not indicate the general was in total disfavor with Nicholas II.

18. Dzhanumovaia, 108–10.
19. Korovin, 1–2.
20. Mosolov, 153; Anonymous, *Fall,* 51–52. Sliuzberg, 3: 348; Simanovich, 28.
21. Kulikowski saw several petitions mailed to Rasputin. A typical letter sought Grigory's help in averting a prison term; its author remarked he had written Rasputin several times without a reply (102, 114). Concerning the would-be opera singer, see Mosolov, 153. Vyrubova insists that Rasputin often told his petitioners he was powerless over affairs which concerned them; he admitted that his efforts to help might even hurt their cause. But he did not have the strength to refuse point-blank to help (164). See also *Red Archives,* 42–43.
22. *Red Archives,* 25–28; *Padenie,* 7: 151–52; Dzhanumovaia, 101.
23. *Red Archives,* 31; Lemke, 262; *Padenie,* 4: 31; Protopopov, "Dopros," 139; Semennikov, *Za kulisami,* 31–32. As of June 24, 1915 Rasputin received only 5,000 rubles from these Baptists. We know of some transactions involving Rasputin, but not the amount he received. For example a woman visited him on March 10, 1915 to get his help in securing a two million-ruble army underwear contract (*Red Archives,* 27).

V. P. Semennikov argues that Rasputin had links at every level from European trusts to local speculators operating on the "black market." These connections supposedly influenced policies he urged upon Nicholas. Semennikov offers no evidence of Rasputin's ties with bankers (*Politika,* 103–62). Ordinarily an absence of proof for a proposition demands its rejection. In Rasputin's case the problem is more complicated. Papers concerning Rasputin may have been destroyed in the early days of the revolution. Written evidence probably never existed in great quantities in the first place. Rasputin operated on the "black stock exchange," an "inner world where deals were sealed with words or glances or notes jotted down on slips of paper" (see the "Introduction" to Dzhanumovaia, 97–98).
24. *Padenie,* 4: 323–24, 356–57; Vasil'ev, 133.
25. Spiridovich, *Dernières années,* 2: 419–21; Katkov, 68–69; *Red Archives,* 51–52.

See Aronson, 82, concerning Rubinstein's rivalry with Manus. Alexandra wrote Nicholas on September 10, 1915 concerning Rubinstein's request for the rank of *Deistvitel'nyi statskii sovetnik,* the fifth highest of the 14 bureaucratic ranks that existed at this time (AF to N, 154–55).

26. In fact, Rubinstein did have ties with Germans throughout the war. Alexandra (no less) used him to forward money to needy relatives in Germany during the conflict. Although Rubinstein was widely regarded as pro-German, there is no evidence that he was disloyal to Russia. But his relations with Rasputin made each still more unpopular with his countrymen. Katkov, 68; Pares, *Fall,* 387; *Padenie,* 5: 239; Spiridovich, *Dernières années,* 2: 419–21.

27. Concerning Rasputin as "lampadary," compare Rodzianko, 7, and *Red Archives,* 48–49, with Buxhoeveden, *Life and Tragedy,* 147. Alexandra noted "people are so nasty" about Rasputin: "Now they pretend he has received a nomination at the *F[edorovskii] Cathedral* which obliges him also to light all the *lamps* in the palace in all the rooms! One knows what that means—but that is so idiotic that any sensible person can but laugh at it;—as do I—" (AF to N, January 7, 1916, 256; revised in terms of *Perepiska*). Spiridovich writes Anna Vyrubova's father paid Rasputin's rent from "Her Majesty's purse" (*Raspoutine,* 197), a point confirmed by Rudnev, 386. For Rasputin's complaints about Alexandra's supposedly miserly ways, see Dehn, 103, and Smitten, 10: 130. Vasil'ev told Protopopov that the bureau that paid for Rasputin's auto trips to Tsarskoe Selo also rented the car he used to sport about the capital (*Padenie,* 4: 30). Klimovich testified he paid Rasputin amounts up to 100 rubles in connection with his trips to the palace (*Padenie,* 1: 65–66) Concerning Rasputin's salary, see Protopopov, "Dopros," 139; also, *Padenie,* 4: 31, 63, and 2: 72. A. T. Vasil'ev headed the police after September 13, 1916. On one occasion Protopopov ordered him to pay Rasputin 1,000 rubles. "Larger sums than this he never received from the Ministry of the Interior" (142).

28. *Padenie,* 7: 374–75.

29. *Padenie,* 7: 374–76; Paléologue, 2: 167–68; Bonch-Bruevich, 89–91; *Padenie,* 1: 23–24, 272; 3: 173.

30. *Padenie,* 7: 375–76; Betskii and Pavlov, *passim;* Katkov, 67. Anonymous, *Fall,* 154–55, cites a telegram from Alexandra to Nicholas dated December 14, 1916: "I beg you to stop immediately, by wire, the trial of Manuilov. It commences at 11 o'clock in the morning and will be pitiless. I wrote to you and to General Batyushin [Chairman of the Commission for the Investigation of Activities Endangering the Home Front] concerning this circumstance, and asked you point-blank to stop this affair. This is absolutely necessary to your happiness." Supposedly the tsar did as he was asked, and on the following day Alexandra thanked him "from the depths of my heart for your dear letter. . . . I am so thankful that my telegram of yesterday influenced your noble order." These communications are not found in the published Nicholas–Alexandra letters, though we do find the empress writing: "Thanks so much (& fr. A[nna Vyrubova]. too) for *Manuilov, . . .* " (December 15, 1916, 457).

31. Vyrubova, 118–21; *Padenie,* 4: 501–2; 3: 65; Mosolov, 162.

32. Gurko, *Tsar,* 80. Vyrubova, 118–21, does not treat her recovery as a "miracle," but Voeikov makes it clear that she thought so at the time; see *Padenie,* 3: 65. Concerning the restoration of the old friendship between Alexandra and Anna, see Smitten, 12: 91, and Shavel'skii, 1: 193–94.

33. *Red Archives,* 40–41. This police account says that Rasputin was visiting his

brother Nicholas when the fight with his father occurred on September 9, 1915. See Chapter 1, note 13.

34. *Padenie,* 4: 324–25.

Chapter 15, "A New Saint, a National Scandal"

1. Shavel'skii, 1: 371–72. The quote is from de Jonge, 273.

2. Gilliard, 148–49; Marie, *Education,* 194–95.

3. Shavel'skii stresses that Grand Duke Nicholas and Prince Orlov inclined the tsar towards Samarin (1: 288–94). In the letter quoted here, Nicholas tells Alexandra, "Old Gorem[ykin], and Krivoshein and Shcherbatov have all told me the same thing [that it is necessary to replace Sabler], and believe that Samarin would be the best man for this post" (N to AF, 60; June 15, 1915; revised in terms of *Perepiska*).

4. AF to N, 95–97 (letters of June 15 and 16, 1915); revised in terms of *Perepiska.*

5. *Padenie,* 7: 415; D'iakin, 80; Riha, 237–38; Cunningham, 128–29; Gurko, *Features,* 357, 554, 569, 575, 661; Lockhart, *Memoirs,* 129.

6. Curtiss, *Church and State,* 387–89.

7. Paléologue, 2: 61. For the episode concerning *Sibirskaia torgovaia gazeta,* see Kulikowski, 56, 134, 141; Rasputin's telegram was published on July 29, 1915.

8. N to AF, 60 (June 15, 1915); Paléologue, 2: 35; Buchanan, 1: 247.

9. D'iakin, 112–13; *Krasnyi arkhiv* (1923), 277, and (1924), 278.

10. The ministers' secret meetings began on July 16, 1915 and ended on September 2, 1915. Shcherbatov later testified that Samarin acted against Rasputin on behalf of the entire council (*Padenie,* 7: 222) Concerning the ministerial crisis, see Pares, *Fall,* 264–78; Krivoshein, 251–252, 259; Katkov, 136–52.

11. N to AF, 241 (August 21, 1916), revised in terms of *Perepiska.* K. A. Krivoshein believes Nicholas's decision to take command "was made, as in most cases, by the emperor on his own, in agreement with 'the dictates of his conscience,' even if this decision coincided in the main with the empress's suggestions." Krivoshein minimizes Rasputin's role in such events: Father Grigory " 'influenced' the tsar only to the extent that he said and did what the tsar wished" (258–59).

12. Hoare, 344–45.

13. Smitten, 2: 106–7; Shavel'skii, 1: 370; Amalrik, 180; Spiridovich, *Raspoutine,* 200-207.

14. Curtiss, 389–390. Shavel'skii, 1: 370.

15. Smitten, 2: 114; Curtiss, *Church and State,* 390. The quote is from Paléologue, 2: 147.

16. Smitten, 2: 107. Archbishop Tikhon was a member of the Holy Synod. He was sent to Tobolsk to investigate the claims made for John Maximovich and found the affair to be quite "uncomplex": there was no reason to regard John Maximovich as a saint (Swan, 12).

17. Smitten, 2: 107; Zhevakov, 1: 86; AF to N, 128 (August 29, 1915).

18. Smitten, 2: 107; Maevskii, 122. Nicholas's telegram read: "Propet' velichanie mozhno, proslavit' nel'zia." Shavel'skii was at Stavka when Nicholas sent this telegram; he did not know if the tsar consulted anyone before acting. The chief chaplain criticized Nicholas's arrogance in this episode, and noted the instructions contained an "internal contradiction": if glorification was impossible, what made laudation possible? (1: 371–72).

19. Smitten, 2: 108.

20. AF to N, 146, 150, (September 7 and 9, 1915).

21. Shavel'skii, 1: 372; AF to N, 150 (September 9, 1915); Smitten, 2: 109; *Padenie,* 4: 168.

22. AF to N, 150–54 (September 9 and 10, 1915).

23. Smitten, 2: 108; Shavel'skii, 1: 373; *Padenie,* 4: 154; AF to N, 146–148 (September 7 and 8, 1915).

24. Krivoshein, 184; Gurko, *Features,* 555.

25. *Padenie,* 4: 168.

26. Gurko, *Features,* 555, offers interesting criticisms of Shcherbatov's policies as minister of the interior.

27. Naumov, 2: 306–7, 339.

28. Pares, *Fall,* 265, 288; Rodzianko, 158. Shavel'skii called this the "first swallow of the revolution: the Moscow nobility expressed grief over an action of the Sovereign!" (1: 373n).

29. Lockhart, 25.

30. Spiridovich, *Velikaia voina,* 1: 247; D'iakin in Anan'ich, 615, and *Russkaia burzhuaziia,* 625.

31. This quote is from Shulgin, 281. He was speaking of Rasputin and Protopopov in late–1916, but his observations seem equally applicable to Nicholas, Alexandra, and Rasputin in August–September 1915. For the "breakdown of authority" and so on, see Ulam, 276.

32. Semennikov, *Dnevnik,* 97, entry for September 29, 1915. The grand duke is actually quoting—with obvious agreement—a conversation with V. M. Volkonskii, a former assistant-procurator of the State Duma and then assistant-minister of the interior.

Chapter 16, "Rasputin and the Homosexual Prince"

1. Andronnikov's early life is shadowy. The information here is from *Padenie,* 7: 301–2; 4: 152. Simanovich, 93–94; Mel'gunov, *Legenda,* 407, 416–17.

2. Smitten, 12: 98; Mel'gunov, *Legenda,* 407–9; *Padenie,* 4: 152, 241.

3. Mosolov, 165; *Padenie,* 2: 9–23; Mel'gunov, *Legenda,* 408.

4. Smitten, 12: 98; *Padenie,* 1: 24; 4: 152; Semennikov, *Politika,* 104–5. Naumov, 2: 381.

5. Smitten, 12: 96.

6. *Padenie* 1: 370.

7. Smitten, 12: 98; Mel'gunov, *Legenda,* 407; *Padenie,* 2: 12–14.

8. Amalrik, 234–35; *Padenie,* 1: 21–22, 375–77; 4: 152.

9. *Padenie,* 1: 392; 7: 307; Amalrik, 234–35.

10. *Padenie,* 1: 375, 392–93; Salisbury, 299; Naumov, 2: 329.

11. *Padenie,* 1: 392–95; 4: 154.

12. Semennikov, *Politika,* 107–11; Chernov, 32.

13. AF to N, 127 (August 28, 1915), 129 (August 29, 1915).

14. AF to N, 157 (September 11, 1915), 170 (September 17, 1915). Khvostov's recollections of his first meeting with the empress are in Smitten, 1: 101. For the telegrams and the letter that followed, AF to N, 174–75 (September 17 and 18, 1915); N to AF, 92 (September 18, 1915). For concerns about Rasputin's security see Amalrik, 234, and

Padenie, 6: 74. Concerning Goremykin, *Padenie,* 1: 382; and 3: 309. Kilcoyne, 230–32, offers an interesting discussion of Khvostov's overtures to Nicholas and Alexandra.

15. A *troika* is a wagon or sleigh drawn by three horses. Russians use the word to indicate leadership by three people, in this case Khvostov, Beletsky, and Andronnikov.

16. Semennikov, *Dnevnik,* 97–99; *Padenie,* 7: 318.

17. *Red Archives,* 39, 41; AF to N, 169 (September 16, 1915).

18. *Padenie,* 4: 157–61. See also S. P. Beletskii, "Grigory Rasputin: iz vospominanii," *Byloe,* 20 (1922); 218–20.

19. *Padenie,* 4: 156–57.

20. *Padenie,* 4: 164–67; Curtiss, *Church and State,* 356–57.

21. *Padenie,* 4: 164; 7: 318.

22. *Padenie,* 164–65. "Well, Dear, here are a list of names, very little indeed, who might replace *Samarin.* Ania got them through *Andronnikov* who had been talking with the *Metropolitan* [Pitirim] as he was in despair that Samarin got that nomination, saying that he understood nothing about the Church affairs." AF to N, 146 (September 7, 1915); also 146–76 (September 7–17, 1915).

23. AF to N, 193 (October 8, 1915); *Padenie,* 4: 165, 168.

Chapter 17, "Rasputin and the Homosexual Bishop"

1. *Padenie,* 7: 396; Zhevakov, 1: 115–25; "Aleksandro-Nevskaia lavra," 200–201; Smitten, 2: 105.

2. Smitten, 2: 105–6, 114; *Padenie,* 4: 194; 7: 396. Zhevakov, 1: 125; Shavel'skii, 1: 376. Pitirim was an extreme conservative and played a counter-revolutionary role in 1905; see Cunningham, 206–8.

3. The governor was Alexander Naumov; he had the postmaster send the telegram to Rasputin (see *Padenie,* April 17, 1917). Smitten, 2: 109.

4. *Padenie,* 1: 367; Vyrubova, 192–93.

5. AF to N, 210 (November 6, 1915); *Padenie,* 4: 195–96; Polskii, 14–15, 24; Smitten, 2: 109; Zhevakov, 1: 106–7, 130–31.

6. See *Padenie,* 7: Naumov's interrogation of April 17, 1917. Rodzianko, 172–73.

7. Zhevakov, 1: 192–195; Protopopov, "Dopros," 147–48; *Padenie,* 4: 197; Cunningham, 144–45, 167–68, 198–99.

8. Shavel'skii, 1: 375–76, 383; 2: 85; Zhevakov, 1: 125.

9. *Padenie,* 4: 192, 197, 453; 7: 392.

10. *Padenie,* 1: 366.

11. *Padenie,* 3: 168–69; 6: 84; Rudnev, 391.

12. Radziwell, *Rasputin,* 81–82; Shavel'skii, 1: 385–86.

13. Brother Gerasim later testified "in general [the mistress] was involved in all the monastery's affairs." A special rug reserved her favorite spot in church; when she appeared the monks cried out "little Miss Filaret has arrived!" "I hold her in contempt for the shadow her relations with Filaret cast on the entire monastery," Gerasim concluded ("Aleksandro-Nevskaia lavra," 201–11).

14. "Aleksandro-Nevskaia lavra," 201, 204–5.

15. "Aleksandro-Nevskaia lavra," 202; Shavel'skii, 1: 384–85; *Padenie,* 6: 83; AF to N, 228 (November 27, 1915), 236 (December 13, 1915), 256 (January 7, 1916) 261 (January 10, 1916).

Chapter 18, "Rasputin—Master of the Russian Orthodox Church"

1. Naumov, 2: 207.

2. *Padenie*, 4: 191–92; Shave'lskii, 1: 373, 378–83; 2: 87. Smitten, 2: 108; Lemke, 822; Dehn, 108–12; Buxhoeveden, *Life and Tragedy*, 145.

3. *Padenie*, 1: 25, 26; 4: 166, 222–26, 355; 7: 341, 383; Smitten, 2: 104; "Aleksandro-Nevskaia lavra," 201.

Rasputin wanted Mudroliubov appointed secretary of the Mogilev consistory, but Sturmer (minister of internal affairs as well as prime minister) rejected the promotion. Rasputin and Pitirim then worked successfully to have Mudroliubov made head of the important department of foreign faiths within the ministry of internal affairs. Mudroliubov returned to the Holy Synod on November 1, 1916 to direct its chancellery until the collapse of the Old Regime four months later. He was born in 1864 and died in 1922. Mudroliubov and Solov'ev frequented the wild parties that Rasputin and Pitirim threw at the Alexander Nevskii Monastery.

4. *Padenie*, 4: 169; 7: 418.

5. Smitten, 2: 104.

6. *Padenie*, 4: 199; 7: 348–49; Smitten, 2: 110; AF to N, 421.

The disgraced Bishop Alexis (Molchanov) of Pskov became exarch of Georgia through Rasputin's influence. Shavel'skii credits Grigory with three other appointments: Alexis Dorodnitsyn (Vladimir), Seraphim Chichikov (Tver), and Palladii (Saratov). An additional bishop, Vasilii, was "ambitious and sought Rasputin's favor though he was actually handsome and talented" (Shavel'skii, 2: 59–60, 149). Makarii became metropolitan of Moscow upon Grigory's urging in 1912; Rasputin also made certain Makarii was replaced at Tomsk by Meletii, bishop of Barnaul. Meletii had encouraged Rasputin in his early years, giving him the title of "penitent" and commanding him to wander and "perform saintly exploits" (Iliodor, 209).

Pitirim brought an old friend from the Caucasus to Petrograd to serve as vicar bishop there. This was Antonii, who was "still relatively young with an expressive and beautiful exterior." Beletskii is perhaps hinting that Antonii, like Pitirim, was a homosexual. Rasputin introduced Antonii to Beletskii and Anna Vyrubova, claiming Antonii was devoted to himself and Pitirim. Grigory later explained that he did not know Antonii personally or well, but that "Antonii loved Pitirim" (*Padenie*, 4: 199). Alexandra praised the same man: "Bishop *Antony Guriysky*—charming impression, cosy *Georgian* intonation in his voice—knows our friend longer than we do—was rector years ago at Kazan." We can identify two other bishops from Alexandra's correspondence who were friendly to Rasputin and Pitirim. She speaks of Melchizedek, a young Georgian priest whom Pitirim brought to the capital to serve as bishop of Kronstadt: "our Friend says he will be a marvellous metropolitan in the future." "Churches full were [sic] he serves—very high—. . . talked so well & calmly—such a peaceful, harmonious *atmosphere*." (AF to N, 406, September 21, 1916; 418, September 28, 1916; 421, October 1, 1916). The empress also enjoyed the company of the bishop of Viatka. (She does not give his name.) Apparently Pitirim had brought this prelate before the Synod to clear the bishop of a charge of being overly familiar with women. I do not find all of Alexandra's remarks about Pitirim's friend intelligible, but she characterizes him "an old man, a friend of his & 'very high' therefore persecuted. . . . He is much higher than the Metropolitan & with *Gregory* one continues what the other begins, & still the Bishop looks up to Gregory" (409; September 22, 1916).

In short, sources indicate that 13 of the 70 or more Russian bishops had ties to Rasputin, ties ranging from a close alliance to benevolent neutrality: Metropolitans Pitirim (Petrograd) and Makarii (Moscow), Exarch of Georgia Alexis, Archbishop Varnava of Tobolsk and his vicar bishop Isidor, Alexis of Vladimir, Seraphim of Tver, Paladii of Saratov, Vasilii (his diocese or assignment is not specified), Meletii, bishop first of Tomsk, then Barnaul, Antonii, vicar bishop of Petrograd, Bishop Melchizedek of Kronstadt, and the unnamed bishop of Viatka.

7. *Padenie*, 4: 190; Curtiss, *Church and State* 397–98.

8. Curtiss, *Church and State*, 394; *Padenie*, 4: 310.

9. *Padenie*, 7: 39–50; Curtiss, *Church and State*, 397.

10. Curtiss, *Church and State*, 401–2.

11. Curtiss, *Church and State*, 403.

12. Paléologue, 2: 222–23.

13. Paléologue, 2: 173–74.

14. *Padenie*, 4: 308–10.

15. *Padenie*, 4: 289–91, 296; 7: 319; Curtiss, *Church and State*, 394–95; Woytinsky, 200–202, 237–38.

16. *Padenie*, 4: 289; 7: 319; AF to N, 188 (October 3, 1915); Curtiss, *Church and State*, 395.

17. Curtiss, *Church and State*, 395–96. *Padenie*, 4: 289. For Rasputin's opinion of parishes electing their priests, see AF to N, 340 (May 26, 1916): "Says the peasants cannot choose a suitable priest, that one cannot allow."

18. Zhevakov, 1: 191, 392.

19. Rodzianko, 158; Paléologue, 2: 148.

20. Shavel'skii, 1: 386–87, 391; Zhevakov, 1: 105, 139–41, 164–65; AF to N, 215 (November 10, 1915); 364 (June 25, 1916).

21. Shavel'skii, 2: 70–71; Zhevakov, 1: 88–95; AF to N, 152 (September 9, 1915); 194 (October 9, 1915); 196 (October 10, 1915). Concerning the icon, see de Jonge, 145.

22. *Padenie*, 4: 222–24; Zhevakov, 1: 103–5; AF to N, 210 (November 6, 1915).

23. Compare *Padenie*, 4: 222–25; Beletskii, with Zhevakov, 1: 103–5, 134–38.

24. *Padenie*, 2: 66; 4: 323. Pitirim nominated Shvedov, Zhevakov, Raev, and Kryzhanovskii (Semennikov, *Monarkhiia*, 141, 148). Rasputin did not know Raev, but he found him satisfactory, probably on the strength of Pitirim's approval. Kulchitskii became the last tsarist minister of education four months later when Rasputin was dead. Raev's "harsh critic" was Shavel'skii (2: 66).

25. AF to N, 365 (June 27, 1916); 386 (August 14); Zhevakov, 1: 163–64; Curtiss, *Church and State*, 404; *Padenie*, 4: 222–25.

26. *Padenie*, 7: 402; Shavel'skii, 2: 67–69; AF to N, 364 (June 25, 1916); Simanovich, 115.

27. AF to N, 391 (September 6, 1916); 395 (September 9); 406 (September 26).

28. Zhevakov, 1: 162–63, 190–91.

29. Shavel'skii, 2: 69–70. Alexandra wrote her husband concerning this episode: "The *Synod* gave me a lovely old Image & *Pitirim* read a nice *paper*—I mumbled an answer. Was rejoiced to see dear *Shavelsky*" (AF to N, 415 September 26, 1916).

Chapter 19, "The Troika Shatters"

1. Beletskii gave Rasputin 3,000 rubles early in their relationship. A bit later he gave Rasputin 8,000 rubles to cover a tour of north Russian monasteries that the troika hoped

Grigory would make before the Duma resumed its work on November 1, 1915. Beletskii gave Rasputin 3,000 rubles to cover the Christmas–New Year's day season plus an additional 5,500 rubles in January 1916 (*Padenie*, 4: 174, 437–39, 448).

2. *Padenie*, 3: 139–41; 4: 338–48; 7: 356–57; Hingley, 93; Vasil'ev, 85.

3. *Padenie*, 4: 349, 354; de Jonge, 270–72.

4. *Padenie*, 1: 251; 2: 70–71; de Jonge, 271–72.

5. *Padenie*, 1: 382; 4: 171, 335–36. Beletskii angered his lower-ranking Okhrana colleagues by insisting they avoid Rasputin. They would have used Grigory to advance their careers, but the chief personally handled all police dealings with Rasputin. Sitting in prison at the Peter and Paul Fortress in 1917, Beletskii felt his policy had been justified. "I think they [my former subordinates] have probably forgiven me now for my desire— which had no evil in it—to see their good names were preserved" (*Padenie*, 4: 328)

6. *Padenie*, 3: 169; 4: 241–42.

7. *Padenie*, 1: 39; 6: 80.

8. *Padenie*, 4: 229, 260, 360–61.

9. *Padenie*, 1: 43; 2: 47; 4: 386, 398; 6: 83; Spiridovich, *Velikaia voina*, 2: 39; Smitten, 2: 105.

10. Smitten, 2: 105; *Padenie*, 4: 174–76; 6: 80.

11. *Padenie*, 1: 43; 3: 170–71; 4: 367–68; Smitten, 2:106.

12. *Padenie*, 1: 43–44, 368, 378; 4: 363–64, 371–74; Simanovich, 93.

13. *Padenie*, 2: 40–42; 4: 136, 400–406; 5: 258; Iliodor, 296–311; Lemke, 609–15. Or—vskii, "Iz zapisok."

14. Harcave, 441; *Padenie*, 2: 42; 4: 417–26.

15. *Padenie*, 4: 421–22; AF to N, 283 (March 2, 1916).

Chapter 20, "Rasputin—Master of the Russian State"

1. *Padenie*, 2: 17.

2. Simanovich, 137–38.

3. N to AF, 87 (September 11, 1915); 91 (September 17); AF to N, 219 (November 13, 1915); 225 (November 15); Rodzianko, 162–63.

4. *Padenie*, 4: 282; Vasil'ev, 97, 134, 135, 147.

5. Vasil'ev, 135, 136, 273, 282–85, 309, 448; AF to N, 225 (November 15, 1915).

6. Rasputin suggested that Goremykin be retired and "promoted" to "chancellor" (*kantsler*), the highest of the tsarist government's 14 bureaucratic ranks. One of Maria Rasputin's women friends stole the letter. Beletskii retrieved it at a cost of 1,500 rubles. He and A. N. Khvostov showed a photographic copy to Goremykin! (*Padenie*, 4: 318– 21, 453; Betskii, 136–39).

One example of Alexandra's own difficulties with Goremykin involved her effort to recruit Alexander Naumov, a talented provincial governor—and a staunch, well-known anti-Rasputinite—as minister of agriculture. "It seems the old Man [Goremykin] did not propose the ministry in a nice way to *Naumov*," she complained to her husband, "so that he found himself obliged to refuse. [*A. N.*] *Khvostov* has seen *Naumov* since, & is sure that he would accept, or be happy if you simply named him. He is a very right man, we both like him. I fancy *Beletzky* worked with him before. Being very rich, (his wife is the daughter of Foros *Ushkov*) so not a man to take bribes—& the one, whom *Goremykin* proposes, is not worth much—have forgotten his name." "*Gregory* has asked to see me tomorrow in the little house [of Anna Vyrubova] to speak about the old man, whom I have not yet seen" AF to N, 206, 207 (November 3, 1915); 210 (November 7), and 214 (November 10).

7. AF to N, 214 (November 10, 1915); 216 (November 11); 219 (November 13).

8. Oldenburg, 4: 55–56. The Duma was in recess from its last meeting on September 2, 1915 to its next meeting on February 9, 1916.

9. N to AF, 131 (January 7, 1916).

10. Thomson, 60–95; *Padenie,* 7: 150, 438.

11. Thomson, Chapter 2; *Padenie,* 1: 233.

12. Shavel'skii, 2: 208; Thomson, 110; Francis, 104.

13. *Padenie,* 1: 273–75; 4: 388–89; M. Rasputin, *My Father,* 106; Anan'ich, 582.

14. N to AF, 136 (January 12, 1916).

15. AF to N, 251, 256, 260 (January 4, 7, 9, 1916).

16. N to AF, 133 (January 9, 1916).

17. Liebman, 79; *Padenie,* 1: 44; 5: 338–39; Gurko, *Features,* 188; Paléologue, 2: 166.

18. *Padenie,* 1: 67; 2: 46–47, 78; 4: 396; 5: 162–63; Korostovetz, 253; Paléologue, 3: 24–25.

19. *Padenie,* 2: 49–51; Kilcoyne, 48.

20. Kilcoyne, 48–49.

21. "Aleksandro-Nevskaia lavra," 208.

22. *Padenie,* 1: 34. Manasevich-Manuilov testified that he also broached this question with Rasputin. "You have influence. Fix it up so papasha will visit the Duma." Rasputin supposedly paced around the room, then suddenly declared, "Well, okay, papasha will visit the Duma. Tell the old man [Sturmer] papasha will be at the Duma." A few days later Nicholas appeared at the Duma's opening session. (*Padenie,* 1: 55)

23. Paléologue, 2: 186–88; Rodzianko, 176–77.

24. Thomson, 126–27; *Padenie,* 6: 329.

25. AF to N, 277 (February 10, 1916).

26. Beletskii published an interview in *The Stock Exchange News* followed by a letter in *The New Times* on the day he left office, February 12, 1916. Khvostov responded to Beletskii in an interview the same month charging "Grishka [Rasputin] is connected with world espionage"—whatever that might mean (*Arkhiv russkoi revoliutsii,* 12 [1923]: 76–82). See Thomson, 154, and Semennikov, *Za kulisami,* 23. Avrekh, 255, discusses the aura that attached to royal ministers before Khvostov's exposure.

27. Avrekh, 255; D'iakin, 180. The quote is from Ulam, 258–59.

28. Katkov, 188–89, discusses the Khvostov episode as a possible turning point in Nicholas's internal policies, though he assumes Alexandra was more contrite and Rasputin more discredited than was (unfortunately) the case. For the royal letters, see AF to N, 283 (March 2, 1916) and N to AF, 152 (March 5, 1916).

29. *Padenie,* 2: 50; *Krasnyi arkiv,* 77, 4 (1936), 207.

Chapter 21, "Our Friend's Opinions of People Are Sometimes Very Strange"

1. Semennikov, *Za kulisami,* iv; *Padenie,* 7: 304. Zhamsaran's godfather was the tsarevich, the future Alexander III. The Buriats became Russian subjects in the seventeenth century; their Russian-educated leaders were subsequently agents of Russian expansion

in Asia. Badmaev went farther than the others in converting to the Russian Orthodox Church and enjoying close relations with the tsar's family.

2. Semennikov, *Za kulisami,* iv, ix-x, xxxiii-xxxiv; Mel'gunov, *Legenda,* 229; Smitten, 1: 108; *Padenie,* 1: 115.

3. Semennikov, *Za kulisami,* iv, 3–14, 137–41. In a letter of October 8, 1916, Badmaev tells Rasputin of an unnamed entrepreneur who would pay Badmaev and his business partner Paul Kurlov 50,000 rubles for facilitating a certain transaction. "We refused to take money for this affair," Badmaev wrote, "but told him that we could ask you to direct this affair along the right channel since this affair is absolutely fair and needed as the ministers know and the tsar's eye will detect. Therefore, I and General Kurlov warmly ask you, dear Grigory Efimovich, to send this most humble request *in ways familiar to you* believing that our dear tsar, once he becomes familiar with its essence, will present it to the council of ministers for action" (Semennikov, *Za kulisami,* xiii-xiv, 31–32; emphasis added). I suspect this letter was carefully worded in case it fell into the wrong hands, but Badmaev and Kurlov were offering Rasputin 50,000 rubles if he could get their "affair" approved and funded. The passage in italics hints at earlier collaborations.

4. Zaslavskii, 19–23.

5. V. I. Gurko was hostile to Rasputin, but he thought the starets was sincerely trying to find office-holders who would strengthen Nicholas's government. Grigory often refused to support people who sought his help. "How can I make her husband a minister when he's a fool," Rasputin said of one request from an ambitious wife. "He's not suited to this work."

6. *Padenie,* 1: 115–16; 4: 12–13; Mel'gunov, *Legenda,* 229–30; Gurko, *Tsar,* 119–20; Dzhanumovaia, 106.

7. Buchan, 3: 383; Nabokov, 53–54.

8. N to AF, 233 (July 20, 1916); Massie, 336.

9. Mel'gunov, *Legenda,* 230; N to AF, 256 (September 9, 1916); *Padenie,* 2: 65; 4: 60.

10. Florinsky, 64, 86–90.

11. Pares, *Fall,* 337–48; *Padenie,* 2: 51–52.

12. AF to N, 393–96 (September 7, 9, and 10, 1916); *Padenie,* 1: 65–71; 4: 14. Klimovich was "promoted" to the Senate after Kurlov replaced him at the ministry of internal affairs.

13. N to AF, 256, 258 (September 9, 10, 1916); AF to N, 395 (September 9, 1916).

14. Pares, *Fall,* 381; Miliukov, 368.

15. *Padenie,* 2:65; AF to N, 398 (September 14, 1916); N to AF, 269 (September 23, 1916), 282 (October 17).

16. Zaslavskii, 5, 30; Cantacuzène, 83–84; Pares, *Wandering Student,* 209; Kerensky, *Russia,* 170–71.

17. Salisbury, 279–80; Pares, *Fall,* 331–32.

18. *Padenie,* 4: 62–63.

19. *Padenie,* 14: 77–78; 2: 67, 439.

20. Zaslavskii, 38, 49–54. Protopopov's newspaper was *Russkaia Volia, Russian Liberty.*

21. Zaslavskii, 37, 56–57; *Padenie,* 4: 6, 56–57, 75; 7: 364.

22. N to AF, 285 (October 28, 1916); Vorres, 150; Gilliard, 178; Salisbury, 285; Poliakoff, 301.

23. N to AF, 295 (November 8, 1916). Rasputin suggested that Sturmer remain prime minister and pacify his critics by relinquishing the foreign affairs ministry (AF to N, 437, November 9, 1916). But Nicholas made a decision—that Sturmer must leave—and he stood by it.

24. Ulam, 272; Florinsky, 111.

25. N to AF, 297–98 (November 10, 1916); Pares, *Fall*, 393–94.

26. AF to N, 439–41 (November 11, 12, 1916); N to AF, 299 (December 4, 1916); *Padenie*, 4: 30–31; Mel'gunov, *Legenda*, 383; Protopopov, "Dopros," 138, 143; D'iakin, 261–62; Massie, 344. Trepov actually persuaded Protopopov to go to Nicholas with an offer to resign, but the tsarina's campaign saved her favorite (D'iakin, 262).

27. AF to N, 442–50 (December 4–16, 1916).

28. Liebman, 78; Vonliarliarskii, 201.

29. Paléologue, 3: 107–8; Mosolov, 168–73; *Padenie*, 4: 15–16, 30.

30. *Sovetskaia istoricheskaia entsiklopediia*, 4: 486–89; *Padenie*, 2: 251–52; Ulam, 273.

Chapter 22, "The Rivers Will Flow with Blood"

1. N to AF, 86 (September 9, 1915).

2. Novomeysky, 187; *Marina Tsvetaeva, A Captive Spirit*, edited and translated by J. Marin King (Ann Arbor, MI: Ardis, 1980), 174; Zhevakov, 2: 165; Marie, *Education*, 248; Teffi, 274.

3. Preston, 105; Paustovsky, 408–9; Purishkevich, *Dnevnik*, 67.

4. Lemke, 561, 675–76, 683, 823; N. de Basily, 106–7; Lomonosov, 7–8.

5. Ossendowski, 98; Novomeysky, 197–98.

6. Dzhanumovaia, 115–16; Lemke, 561; Voeikov, 181.

7. *Red Archives*, 41; Paléologue, 1: 260; Ossendowski, 100; Dzhanumovaia, 116.

8. Teffi, 290; Pereverzev, 8; Simanovich, 35–37, 122–23. Beletskii insisted Grigory maintained his zest for life until the day he died, and continued to scoff at pleas "to be careful in making trips to unfamiliar houses" (*Padenie*, 4: 504).

9. *Padenie*, 4: 448; Vasil'ev, 141–42; M. Rasputin, "Moi otets," 7; Simanovich, 122.

10. Vyrubova, 174.

11. Buchanan, 138; Smitten, 10: 133; Paléologue, 2: 238–40; Novomeysky, 200.

12. Paléologue, 2: 265; D'iakin, 246.

13. Paléologue, 2: 240, quotation slightly revised; Dehn, 108; Blok, 6; Bonch-Bruevich, 88; "Aleksandro-nevskaia lavra," 208–9.

14. M. Rasputin, *My Father*, 32–33 and *Real Rasputin*, 152–53; Rasputin and Barham, *Rasputin*, 242. According to Maria Rasputin, her mother gave her this letter and she (Maria) kept it as a "supreme relic" testifying to her father's prophetic gifts.

15. Simanovich published this letter in *Rasputin*, 256. Pares cities it in *Fall*, 399, with information on the history of the document. I offer here my translation of the letter.

16. *Padenie*, 4: 503–4.

Chapter 23, "Conspiracy"

1. De Jonge, 308; Yusupov, *Lost Splendor*, 183–85; *Red Archives*, 101, 104–13. Concerning the charge that Yusupov made homosexual advances to Grigory, see Rasputin and Barham, *Rasputin*, 213–18.

2. Yusupov, *Lost Splendor,* 56–68; N to AF, 78 (August 31, 1915), 154 (March 9, 1916), and 203 (June 7).

3. Pares, *Fall,* 349–75.

4. AF to N, 377, 382, 411, 413 (July 25, 1916; August 8, 1916; September 23, 1916; September 25, 1916); N to AF, 267 (September 21, 1916). Simanovich, 153.

5. Yusupov, *Lost Splendor,* 60–68.

6. Yusupov, *Lost Splendor,* 60–66.

7. Yusupov, *Rasputin,* 75–76.

8. Yusupov, *Rasputin,* 80.

9. Yusupov, *Rasputin,* 79. "In a moment of indiscretion Rasputin told Yusupov that some of Badmaev's herbs and roots could 'cause mental paralysis and either stop or aggravate hemorrhage.' What more suggestive example could there be of the effect of Badmaev's treatment than the tsar with his wandering eyes and helpless smile? About this time the tsarina repeatedly reminded the tsar in her letters to take 'the drops prescribed by Badmaev' " (Kerensky, *Russia,* 161). See also Lloyd George, 5: 2534, and Kerensky, *Road,* 66–70.

10. Yusupov, *Lost Splendor,* 211–12, 288; Kerensky, *Road,* 68–70.

11. Purishkevich, *Murder,*"Introduction." *Padenie,* 7: 401.

12. Kalpashchnikoff, 179–84.

13. Eddy, 161–63; Paléologue, 3: 153.

14. Yusupov,*Rasputin,* 118–21; Purishkevich, *Dnevnik,* 11–13; Mel'gunov, *Legenda,* 369; Spiridovich, *Raspoutine,* 200.

15. Yusupov, *Rasputin,* 118; *Lost Splendor,* 214–15.

Yusupov may have been engaged in a more far-flung search for accomplices than we know. The English governess Rosamond Dawe was in Kislovodsk with her employers, the Miklashevskii family, when Felix visited them in late September 1916. "I heard him [Yusupov] ask if I spoke Russian," Dawe recalled, "and as I did, nothing but general topics were mentioned in my hearing. I realized later that Madame and her sisters were involved with the prince in a coup to destroy Rasputin, but, at the time, I was unaware of this plot" (Dawe, 17; Pitcher, 135).

16. Mel'gunov, *Legenda,* 369.

17. Yusupov, *Rasputin,* 121–23; Purishkevich, *Dnevnik,* 17–23.

18. Yusupov, *Rasputin,* 121, 122; Mel'gunov, *Legenda,* 367.

Chapter 24, "Murder"

1. AF to N, 458 (December 16, 1916);*Padenie,* 4: 504; de Jonge, 319–20; Vyrubova, 179–80; Simanovich, 161.

2. *Padenie,* 4: 31, 504.

3. Rasputin and Barham, *Rasputin,* 12–13.

4. Yusupov, *Rasputin,* 131–35, 137; Solov'ev, 214; Purishkevich, *Dnevnik,* 22.

5. Yusupov, *Rasputin,* and Purishkevich, *Dnevnik,* are our main sources about Rasputin's assassination. An interesting and overlooked account of the murder is in N. M. Romanov, "Zapiski." Yusupov's uncle by marriage recorded in his diary an account of the assassination provided by Felix on December 19, 1916, two days after the deed. A comparison of this and later accounts by Yusupov indicates that the subsequent versions were not retouched with time.

6. de Jonge, 323.

7. One of the fascinating aspects of Rasputin's murder was the apparent failure of the poison to work. But it seems Grigory now was beginning to feel the effects of the potassium cyanide. The poison probably lost enough potency to not deliver immediate results. The amateurish assassins jumped to the conclusion it would not work at all. This judgment was probably incorrect. If Rasputin had returned home he might have died later without fixing the blame so clearly upon his murderers.

8. Yusupov, *Rasputin*, 156.

9. Yusupov, *Rasputin*, 143–57; Purishkevich, *Dnevnik*, 69–79, 95; Yusupov, *Rasputin*, 158–60.

10. Purishkevich, *Dnevnik*, 79–83; Yusupov, *Rasputin*, 157–59.

11. Yusupov, *Rasputin*, 159–63; Purishkevich, *Dnevnik*, 84–92; M. N. Romanov, 99–101.

Chapter 25, "The Reckoning"

1. M. Rasputin, *My Father*, 13; Vyrubova, 179–80. "Ubiistvo Rasputina," contains police reports of this investigation.

2. "Ubiistvo Rasputina," 66–68.

3. Vyrubova, 180.

4. Vyrubova, 180–81; Purishkevich, *Dnevnik*, 93, 94, 96; Paley, *Memories*, 31; "K istorii ubiistva Grigoriia Rasputina," *Krasnyi arkhiv*, 4 (1923): 424–26; A. V. Romanov, 185–Z10; "Ubiistvo Rasputina," 68–81; de Jonge, 331.

5. Katkov, 426; Hoare, 138; Pollock, 120.

6. Pollock, 120–22; Paley, 30; Alekseev, 341; Avrekh, 250; Voeikov, 181; Marie, *Education*, 250; Hanbury-Williams, 145–46; Mel'gunov, *Legenda*, 372.

7. Shulgin, 79, 269; Alekseev, 67, 142; Bulgakov, 87–88; Cantacuzène, 101. Wolkonsky, 2: 159; Woytinsky, 238.

8. Mel'gunov *Legenda*, 374; Paléologue, 3: 188–89; Miliukov, 380–81; Oldenburg, 4: 116; M. Rasputin, *My Father*, 115; Markov, 147–48.

9. Chebyshev, 7; Shklovsky, 8–9, 150; "Ubiistvo Rasputina," 82–83.

10. N to AF, 312 (December 18, 1916); Gurko, *Memories*, 221–22, 225; Lukomskii, 49–50; *Padenie*, 4: 483; Paley, 35–36; Marie, *Education*, 257; Voeikov, 178; Gilliard, 183.

11. Vol'kenshtein, 1; *Padenie*, 4: 106; M. Rasputin, *My Father*, 16.

12. Dehn, 121; M. Rasputin, *My Father*, 16; *Padenie*, 4: 107; Anonymous, *Russian Diary*, 136–37; Vol'kenshtein, 1. "I read the secret report of the post-mortem examination," Robert Wilton claimed in *Russia's Agony*, 42. "It described the body as that of a man over forty-five years of age normally constituted." De Jonge thinks "there is no evidence to support the legend that [Rasputin] had twisted one hand free of his bonds and died making the sign of the cross" (332).

13. *Padenie*, 4: 106, 198–99, 480, 502–3, 505; Dorr, 116; Simanovich, 169; A. V. Romanov, 189.

14. Dehn, 121–24; M. Rasputin, *My Father*, 17; *Real Rasputin*, 149; *Padenie*, 4: 107, 480; 3: 62; Voeikov, 178–82; Vyrubova, 182–83; Nicholas, *Journal intime*, 73.

15. Dehn, 124; *Padenie*, 4: 480; A. V. Romanov, 188; Shavel'skii, 2: 251; Nicholas, *Journal intime*, 73.

16. Damer, 8; Dehn, 121; *Padenie*, 4: 6; A. V. Romanov, 190–91; The naval officer was Sablin.

17. Paléologue, 3: 191; Simanovich, 171–72; Dehn, 137.

18. Lloyd George, 3: 1585; Kerensky, *Crucifixion*, 244; *Russia*, 147; *Padenie*, 4: 483; Vyrubova, 141.

19. Chebyshev, "Navozhdenie;" Pereverzev, 6–11; Mel'gunov, *Legenda*, 372–73; Marie, *Education*, 258, 260–61, 270.

20. Marie, *Education*, 279; *Padenie*, 4: 108; Katkov, 210.

21. Vyrubova, 183. Nicholas felt he could rely only upon two sons of his cousin Alexander Michaelovich ("Sano"), Michael and Paul.

22. Marie, *Education*, 260, 267, 282; *Padenie*, 4: 232; Heald, 36; Houghteling, 12.

23. Simanovich, 174; Rasputin and Barham, *Rasputin*, 225; *Padenie*, 4: 353–54; Sokolov, 78.

24. M. Rasputin, "Moi otets," 10; *Real Rasputin*, 150–51; and *My Father*, 114. Alexandra Fedorovna asked Protopopov to provide 100,000 rubles for the Rasputin girls from the "special funds" at the disposal of the interior minister. The government's financial situation was so troubled that Protopopov could not carry out this order; nor could the once-wealthy capitalist find this sum among his own resources, though he was personally kind and attentive (*Padenie*, 4: 10, 483–84).

25. M. Rasputin, *Real Rasputin*, 157–62.

26. Paléologue, 3: 266–67; Anonymous, *Russian Diary*, 137; Shulgin, 269; M. Rasputin, *My Father*, 115–16. The "measurements" tale is from Shklovsky, 225; if this information is accurate it would refute the silly notion that Rasputin's penis was cut off during his assassination. But Shklovsky's tale may be a rumor. It is all too typical of sources pertaining to Rasputin's life that even a conscientious biographer is tempted to use one rumor to refute another! See also Kobylinsky, 171–72.

27. Long, 31.

28. Paley, 36.

Chapter 26, "The Fate of the Others"

1. The new Communist government adopted the Gregorian calendar used in the West; from this point on, my dates are "new styles," according to the Gregorian calendar. Massie, 416ff.

2. Gilliard, 263; Pares, *Fall*, 490; Bykov, 68–69; Kobylinskii, 209; Bulygin, 212. See the entry in Nicholas's diary for April 14/27, *Krasnyi arkhiv*, 27: 125.

3. Pares, *Fall*, 491; Massie, 484–85.

4. Massie, 485, 489–92.

5. Korostovets, 259.

6. Williams, 156.

7. Pares, *Fall*, 314; Pol'skii, 84–85.

8. *Padenie*, 1: 140, 161–62; 2: 299–300; 4: 482; Protopopov, "Iz dnevnika," 175–83; Shulgin, 281–83; Katkov, 211–14.

9. Sliuzberg, 2: 187.

10. Vonliarliarskii, 208.

11. Houghteling, 225; Pospielovsky, 1: 25.

12. Katkov, 386; Naumov, 2: 337–38; Kokovtsov, 295, 386–87; Cunningham, 318.

13. Kokovtsov, 579; Aleksandr Solzhenitsyn, *The Gulag Archipelago, 1918–1956*, vols. 1 and 2 (New York: Harper & Row, 1973), pp. 322–27. Nikon, 10: 142–44, reprints

an obituary of A. D. Samarin by Antonii Krapovitskii, metropolitan of Kiev under the old regime.

14. Naumov, 2: 375–76; Pospielovsky, 1: 113–42. I do not know the fate of Nicholas Raev; his biographical sketch in *Padenie,* 7: 402, tells us he was born in 1856, but it does not list a death date.

15. Cunningham, 348; Nikon, 7: 41; Shavel'skii, 2: 72. Zhevakov, 2: 150–61, says nothing about cheating Fedka, robbing Pitirim, and so on. Zhevakov describes Pitirim's death as if he witnessed it.

16. Evlogii, 198–99; Curtiss, *Russian Church,* 87. I do not know Varnava's fate.

17. Bykov, 47–51, 58–59. On Hermogen's fate compare Evlogii, 199, and the eye-witness account cited in Pol'skii, 30.

18. Massie, 502; Maevskii, 50. The quote is from Stremoukhov, 47–48. John J. Stephan, *The Russian Fascists, Tragedy and Farce in Exile, 1925–1945* (New York: Harper & Row, 1978), pp. 7–8.

19. Betskii, 239. I do not know Prince Andronnikov's fate. *Padenie,* 7: 301, lists his death date as 1919, but gives no details; he was born in 1875.

20. Massie, 502.

21. Massie, 502.

22. Kalpaschnikoff, 181–84; *Padenie,* 7: 401; Simanovich, 184–98.

23. Werner Gruehn, trans. and ed. *Der Zar, der Zauberer und die Juden* (Berlin and Leipzig: Nibelungen-Verlag, 1942).

24. Obolensky, 264.

25. *Krasnyi arkhiv,* 30 (1928): 200–209; 49 (1931): 92–111; Marie, *A Princess,* 103; and *Education,* 265–66, 282; Shulgin, 256. Yusupov's obituary is in *The New York Times,* September 28, 1967.

26. M. Rasputin, *Real Rasputin,* 182–223; Massie, 464–67; Simanovich, 201–4. Maria Rasputin did not doubt her husband's loyalties. Her obituary is in *Newsweek,* October 10, 1977.

27. Simanovich, *Rasputin,* 205; M. Rasputin, *My Father,* 117–18; and "Moi otets," 8.

28. de Jonge, 29.

Selected Bibliography

AF to N: Alexandra Fedorovna to Tsar Nicholas II. *Letters of the Tsaritsa to the Tsar, 1914–1916*. London: Duckworth, 1923. All quotations from this work are compared with the more accurate texts in *Perepiska* and revised when necessary.

"Aleksandro-nevskaia lavra nakanune sverzhdennia samoderzhaviia," *Krasnyi arkhiv* 77 (1936): 200–211.

Alekseev, S. A. *Fevral'skaia revoliutsiia i grazhdanskaia voina v opisaniiakh belogvardeitsev*. Moscow and Leningrad, 1925.

Alexander (Grand Duke Alexander Mikhailovich Romanov). *Once a Grand Duke*. Garden City, N.Y.: Garden City, 1932.

Allshouse, Robert H. *Photographs for the Tsar*. New York: Dial, 1980.

Almazov, Boris. *Rasputin i Rossiia*. Prague, 1922.

Almedingen, E. M. *The Empress Alexandra*. London: Hutchinson, 1961.

————. *An Unbroken Unity: A Memoir of Grand-Duchess Serge of Russia, 1864–1918*. London: The Bodley Head, 1964.

Amalrik, Andrei. *Raspoutine*. Translated and annotated by Basil Karlinsky. Paris: Seuil, 1982.

Anan'ich, B. V., et al. *Krizis samoderzhaviia v rossii, 1895–1917 gg*. Leningrad, 1984.

Anonymous. *The Fall of the Romanoffs: How the Ex-Empress and Rasputine caused the Russian Revolution*. New York: Dutton, 1917.

Anonymous. *The Russian Diary of an Englishman: Petrograd, 1915–1917*. London: Heinemann, n.d., probably 1919.

Aronson, Georgii. *Rossiia nakanune revoliutsii, istoricheskie etiudy: monarkhisty, liberaly, masony, sotsialisti*. New York: 1962.

Avrekh, A. I. *Tsarizm i IV Duma 1912–1914 gg*. Moscow, 1981.

Bariatinskii, V. V. "Oshibka istorii, delo ob ubiistve Rasputina." *Illustrirovanniia Rossiia* 16 (April 16, 1932): 4–6.

258   SELECTED BIBLIOGRAPHY

Beletskii, S. P. "Vospominaniia." *Arkhiv russkoi revoliutsii* 12 (1923): 5–75; reprint of "Grigory Rasputin: iz vospominanii." *Byloe* 20 (1922): 194–222, and 21 (1921): 237–69.

Bely, Andrei. *Mezhdu dvukh revoliutsii.* Leningrad, 1934.

Berry, Thomas. "Seances for the Tsar: Part VI: The Reign of Nicholas II: Section 1." *The Journal of Religion and Psychical Research* 8, 4 (October 1985): 231–42.

Betskii, K., and P. Pavlov. *Russkii Rokambol' (prikliucheniia I. F. Manasevicha-Manuilova).* Leningrad, 1925.

Blok, Aleksandr. "Poslednie dni st. rezhima." *Arkhiv russkoi revoliutsii* 4 (1922): 5–54.

Bogdanovich, (Madame) A. V. *Journal de la générala A. V. Bogdanovich.* Translated by M. Lefebvre. Paris: Payot, 1926; translation of *Tri poslednikh samoderzhtsa, dnevnik A. V. Bogdanovicha.* Moscow and Leningrad: L. D. Frenkel, 1924.

Bonch-Bruevich, Mikhail Dmitrievich. *From Tsarist General to Red Army Commander.* Translated by Vladimir Vezey. Moscow, 1966.

"Boris Nikolskii i Grigorii Rasputin." *Krasnyi arkhiv* 68 (1935): 157–61.

Botkin, Gleb. *The Real Romanovs.* New York: Revell, 1931.

Buchan, John. *History of the Great War* (4 vols.). Boston and New York: Houghton Mifflin, 1923.

Buchanan, Sir George. *My Mission to Russia, and Other Diplomatic Memories.* Boston: Little, Brown, 1923.

Bulgakov, Sergei. *Avtobiograficheskiia zametki.* Paris: YMCA Press, 1946.

Bulygin, Paul. *See* Alexander Kerensky.

Burtsev, V. L. "Rasputin v 1916 godu (iz moikh vospominanii)." *Illiustrirovanniia Rossiia* 17 (April 23, 1932): 4–8.

Buxhoeveden, Sophie. *Before the Storm.* London: Macmillan, 1938.

———. *The Life and Tragedy of Alexandra Feodorovna, Empress of Russia.* London: Longmans, Green, 1928.

Bykov, P. M. *The Last Days of Tsardom.* Translated with an Historical Preface by Andrew Rothstein. London: Lawrence, 1934.

Byrnes, Robert F. *Pobedonostsev, His Life and Thought.* Bloomington: Indiana University Press, 1969.

Cantacuzène, Princess. *Revolutionary Days, Recollections of Romanoffs and Bolsheviki, 1914–1917.* New York: Scribner's, 1926.

Case, Norman. "The Name 'Rasputin': A Study in Semantic Complexity." *Names* 17 (1969): 245–49. Disappointing.

Chebyshev, N. N. "Navozhdenie." *Illiustrirovanniia Rossiia* 20 (May 14, 1932): 6–8, 16.

Cherniavsky, Micheal, trans. and ed. *Prologue to Revolution: Notes of A. N. Iakhontov on the Secret Meetings of the Council of Ministers, 1915.* Englewood Cliffs, N.J.: Prentice-Hall, 1967.

Chernov, Victor. *The Great Russian Revolution.* Translated and abridged by Philip E. Mosley. New Haven: Yale, 1936.

Cohn, Norman. *Warrant for Genocide: The Myth of the Jewish World-Conspiracy and the Protocols of the Elders of Zion.* New York: Harper & Row, 1966.

Conroy, Mary Schaeffer. *Peter Arkad'evich Stolypin: Practical Politics in Late Tsarist Russia.* Boulder, Colo.: Westview, 1976.

Cunningham, James W. *A Vanquished Hope: The Movement for Church Renewal in Russia, 1905–1906.* Crestwood, N.Y.: St. Vladimir's Seminary Press, 1981.

Curtiss, John Shelton. *Church and State in Russia, The Last Years of the Empire, 1900–1917.* New York: Columbia, 1940.

———. *The Russian Church and the Soviet State, 1917–1950.* Gloucester, Mass.: Smith, 1965.

Damer, Aleksandr. "Rasputin vo dvorets, vospominaniia pridvornago skorokhoda." *Illiustrirovanniia Rossiia* 16 (April 16, 1932): 7–8. For nineteen years the author maintained the daily register of everyone Nicholas and Alexandra received in Russia or abroad. "It fell to me to meet Rasputin from his first appearance at the court to his last visit."

Dawe, Rosamond E. "Looking Back: A Memoir of an English Governess in Russia, 1914–1917," ed. John Fines (pamphlet issued by Bishop Otter College, 1973).

Deacon, Richard. *A History of the Russian Secret Service.* London: Frederick Muller, Ltd., 1972.

de Basily, Lascelle Meserve. *Memoirs of a Lost World.* Stanford: Stanford University Press, 1975.

de Basily, Nicholas. *Memoirs.* Stanford: Stanford University Press, 1973.

Dehn, Lili. *The Real Tsarista.* Boston: Little, Brown, 1932.

de Jonge, Alex. *The Life and Times of Grigorii Rasputin.* New York: Coward, McCann and Geoghegan, 1982.

Delevskii, I. "Rasputin kak psikhologicheskaia zagadka." *Illiustrirovanniia Rossiia* 13 (March 26, 1932): 6–8.

Denisov, L. I. *Pravoslavnye monastyri rossiiskoi imperii.* Moscow, 1908.

de Robien, Louis. *The Diary of a Diplomat in Russia, 1917–1918.* Translated by Camilla Sykes. New York: Praeger, 1969.

D'iakin, V. S. *Russkaia burzhuaziia i tsarizm v gody pervoi mirovoi voiny (1914–1917).* Leningrad, 1967.

Dorr, Rheta Childe. *Inside the Russian Revolution.* New York: Macmillan, 1917.

Dzhanumovaia, Elena F. "Moi vstrechi s Grigoriem Rasputinym." *Russkoe proshloe* 4 (1923): 97–116.

Eddy, Eleanor Madeleine. "The Last President of the Duma: A Political Biography of M. V. Rodzianko." Unpublished Ph.D. dissertation, Kansas State, 1975.

Evlogii Georgievskii. *Put' moei zhizni, vospominaniia mitropolita Evlogiia.* Paris: YMCA Press, 1947.

Fabritskii, S. S. *Iz proshlago vospominaniia fligel'-ad'iutanta gosudaria imperatora Nikolaia II-go.* Berlin, 1926.

Ferro, Marc. *The Russian Revolution of February 1917.* Translated by J. L. Richards. London: Routledge & Kegan Paul, 1972.

Florinsky, Michael T. *End of the Russian Empire.* New Haven: Yale, 1931.

Francis, David R. *Russia from the American Embassy.* New York: Scribner's Sons, 1921.

Fülöp-Miller, René. *Rasputin, The Holy Devil.* Translated by F. S. Flint and D. F. Tait. Garden City, N.Y.: Garden City Publishing Co., 1928.

Gessen, I. V. "Beseda s A. N. Khvostovym." *Arkhiv russkoi revoliutsii.* 12 (1923): 76–82.

Gibbes, Charles Sidney. *See* Trewin, J. C.

Gilliard, Pierre. *Thirteen Years at the Russian Court.* Translated by F. Appleby Holt. New York: Doran, 1921.

Gippius, Zinaida. *Zhivyia litsa, Blok, Briusov, Vyrubova, Rozanov, Sologub, o mnogikh.* In two volumes. Prague, 1925.

Glagolin, Boris Sergeevich. "Slovo za Rasputina." Mimeographed by Mary O'Dweyer, Hollywood, Calif., 1945. On file at Yale University.

Grabbe, Paul. *Windows on the Neva: A Memoir.* New York: Pomerica, 1977.

Graevenitz, Baron P. *From Autocracy to Bolshevism.* London: Allen & Unwin, 1918.

Graham, Stephen. *With the Russian Pilgrims to Jerusalem.* London: Macmillan, 1914.

Gurko, V. I. *Features and Figures of the Past; Government and Opinion in the Reign of Nicholas II.* Translated by Laura Matveev. Stanford: Stanford University Press, 1939; reprinted 1970.

———. *Memories and Impressions of War and Revolution in Russia, 1914–1917.* London: Lane, 1918.

———. *Tsar i tsaritsa,* Paris: Vozrozhdenie, n.d.

Hanbury-Williams, Sir John. *The Emperor Nicholas II as I Knew Him.* London: Humphreys, 1922.

Harcave, Sidney. *Years of the Golden Cockerel: The Last Romanov Tsars, 1814–1917.* New York: Macmillan, 1968.

Heald, Edward T. *Witness to Revolution: Letters from Russia, 1916–1919.* Edited by James B. Gidney. Kent, Ohio: Kent State University, 1972.

Hingley, Ronald. *The Russian Secret Police.* New York: Simon and Schuster, 1970.

Hoare, Sir Samuel. *The Fourth Seal: The End of A Russian Chapter.* London: Heineman, 1930.

Houghteling, James L., Jr. *A Diary of the Russian Revolution.* New York: Dodd, Mead, 1918.

Iliodor (Sergei Mikhailovich Trufanov). *The Mad Monk of Russia.* New York: Century, 1918.

Judas, Elizabeth. *Rasputin: Neither Devil nor Saint.* Los Angeles: Wetzel Publishing Co., 1942.

Kalpaschikoff, Andrew. *Prisoner of Trotsky's.* Garden City, N.Y.: Doubleday, Page, 1920.

Katkov, George. *Russia 1917: The February Revolution.* New York: Harper & Row, 1967.

Kazarinov, M. G. "Rasputinskii schet." *Illiustrirovanniia Rossiia* 22 (May 28, 1932): 1–6, and 24 (June 11, 1932): 6–11.

Kerensky, Alexander. *Crucifixion of Liberty.* London: Barker, 1934.

———. *Road to the Tragedy.* Republished in the same volume with Captain Paul Bulygin, *The Murder of the Romanovs: The Authentic Account.* Translated by Gleb Kerensky. New York: McBride, 1935.

———. *Russia and History's Turning Point.* New York: Duell, Sloan and Pearce, 1965.

Khatisov, A. I. "Pochetnaia ssylka iz istorii smeshch. velikago kniazia Nik. Nik. s posta verkhovnago glavnokomanduiushchago. . . . ," *Illiustrirovanniia Rossiia* 14 (April 2, 1932), 4–6, 14–15.

Kilcoyne, Martin. "The Political Influence of Rasputin." Unpublished Ph.D. dissertation, University of Washington, April, 1961.

Kleinmichel (Countess). *Memories of a Shipwrecked World.* Translated by Vivian le Grand. London: Brentano's, 1923.

Klibanov, A. I. *History of Religious Sectarianism in Russia.* New York: Pergamon, 1982.

Knox, Sir Alfred. *With the Russian Army, 1914–1917.* 2 vols. London: Hutchinson, 1921.

Kobylinskii, Colonel E. S. "Depositions" given to White Government at Omsk concerning the royal family's fate; in Robert Wilton, *Last Days of the Romanovs,* pp. 167–223. London: Thorton, Butterworth, 1920.

Kokovtsov, Count Vladimir Nikolaevich. *Out of My Past: The Memoirs of Count Kokovtsov.* Edited by H. H. Fisher. Translated by Laura Matveev. (Stanford, 1935). A useful abridgement of his two-volume Russian *Iz moego proshlago* (Paris, 1933). Each is cited in the text; citations with volume numbers refer to the two-volume Russian original.

Korelin, Avenir. *Collapse of the Russian Empire.* Moscow, 1980.

Korostovetz, Vladimir. *Seed and Harvest.* Translated by Dorothy Lumby. London: Faber and Faber, 1931.

Korovin, Konstantin. "Sviataia Rus', vospominaniia." *Illiustrirovanniia Rossiia* 14 (April 2, 1932).

Krivoshein, K. A. *A. V. Krivoshein (1857–1921 gg.)*. . . . Paris, 1973.

Kulikowski, Mark. "Rasputin and the Fall of the Romanovs." Unpublished Ph.D. dissertation, State University of New York at Binghamton, 1982.

Kurlov, P. G. *Konets russkogo tsarizma.* Moscow and Petrograd, 1923.

Lemke, Mikhail. *250 dnei v tsarskoi stavke (25 sent.–2 iulia 1916).* Petrograd, 1920.

Liebman, Marcel. *Russian Revolution: Origins, Phases and Meaning of the Bolshevik Victory.* Translated by Arnold J. Pomerans. London: Cape, 1970.

Lincoln, W. Bruce. *Passage through Armageddon: The Russians in War and Revolution, 1914–1918.* New York: Simon and Schuster, 1986.

———. *The Romanovs: Autocrats of All the Russias.* New York: Dial, 1981.

———. *In War's Dark Shadow.* New York: Dial, 1983.

Lloyd George, David. *War Memoirs: 1916–1917.* Boston: Little, Brown, 1934.

Lockhart, Robert Bruce. *The Diaries of Sir Robert Bruce Lockhart, Volume I: 1915–1938.* Edited by Kenneth Young. London: Macmillan, 1973.

———. *Memoirs of a British Agent.* London: Macmillan, 1932.

Lomonosov, George V. *Memoirs of the Russian Revolution.* Translated by D. H. Dubrowsky and Robert T. Williams. New York: The Rand School of Social Science, 1919.

Long, Robert C. *Russian Revolution Aspects.* New York: Dutton, 1919.

Lukomskii, A. S., "Iz vospominanii," *Arkhiv russkoi revoliutsii* 2 (1921): 14–44; 3 (1921): 247–70; 5 (1922): 101–90; 6 (1922): 81–160; appeared in English as *Memoirs of the Russian Revolution.* Translated by Mrs. Vitali. London: Unwin, 1922.

Maevskii, V. I. *Na grani dvukh epokh (tragediia imperatorskoi rossii).* Madrid; privately printed, 1963.

Margulis, M. S. "Rasputinshchina." *Illiustrirovanniia Rossiia* 19 (May 7, 1932); 6–7.

Marie, Grand Duchess of Russia (Marie Pavlovna Romanova). *Education of a Princess; A Memoir.* Translated under the editorial supervision of Russell Lord. New York: Viking, 1931.

———. *A Princess in Exile.* New York: Viking, 1932.

Markov, Sergei Vladimirovich. *Pokinutaia tsarskaia sem'ia, 1917–1918.* Vienna: Amalthea-Verlag, 1928.

Marsden, Kate. *On Sledge and Horseback to the Outcast Siberian Lepers.* New York: Cassell, 1892.

Marye, George Thomas. *Nearing the End in Imperial Russia.* Philadelphia: Dorrance, 1929.

Massie, Robert K. *Nicholas and Alexandra*. New York: Atheneum, 1960.

Mel'gunov, S. "Kak my priobretali zapiski Iliodora." *Na chuzoi storene* 2 (1923): 47–56.

———. *Legenda o separatnom mire (kanun revoliutsii)*. Paris: La Renaissance, 1957.

———. *Na putiakh k dvortsovomu perevorotu: zagovory pered revoliutsiei 1917 goda*. Paris; Libraire "La Source," 1931.

Miliukov, Paul. *Political Memoirs, 1905–1917*. Edited by Arthur P. Mendel. Translated by Carl Goldberg. (Ann Arbor: University of Michigan Press, 1967).

Mosolov (Mossolov), A. A. *At the Court of the Last Tsar*. Edited by A. A. Pilenco. Translated by E. W. Dickes. London: Methuen, 1935.

Mouchanow, Madame Marfa. *My Empress*. New York and London: Lane, 1918.

Nabokov, Konstantin. *Ordeal of a Diplomat*. London: Duckworth, 1921.

Narishkin-Kurakin, Elizabeth. *Under Three Tsars*. Edited by René Fülöp-Miller. Translated by Julia E. Loesser. New York: Dutton, 1931.

Naumov, A. N. *Iz utselevshikh vospominanii, 1868–1917*, 2 vols. (New York, 1954, 1955).

Nekliudov (Nekludoff), Anatoly Vasilievich. *Diplomatic Reminiscences before and during the World War, 1911–1917*. Translated by Alexandra Paget. London; Murray, 1920.

Nicholas (Romanov). *Dnevnik imperatora Nikolaia vtorago*. Berlin: "Slovo," 1923.

———. *Journal intime de Nicholas II*. Translated by A. Pierre. Paris: Payot, 1925.

———. *The Secret Letters of the Last Tsar, Being the Confidential Correspondence between Nicholas II and His Mother, Dowager Empress Maria Fedorovna*. Edited by Edward J. Bing. New York: Longmans, Green, 1938.

(Bishop) Nikon (Rklitskii). *Zhizneopisanie blazheineishago Antoniia, mitropolita Kievskago i Galitskago*, 10 vol. New York, 1956–1963. A biography of Antonii Krapovitskii, one of Rasputin's fiercest enemies in the church. This massive work contains valuable information about Rasputin, but only a portion of it is entered in the index.

Novomeysky, M. A. *My Siberian Life*. London: Parrish, 1956.

N to AF: Tsar Nicholas II to Alexandra Fedorovna. *The Letters of the Tsar to the Tsaritsa, 1914–1917*, Translated by A. L. Hynes, London: The Bodley Head, 1929. All quotations from this work are compared with the original texts in *Perepiska* and revised when necessary.

Obninskii, V. P. *Poslednii samoderzhets. Ocherk zhizni i tsarstvovaniia imperatora Rossii Nikolaia II-go*, Berlin, n.d.

Obolensky, Serge. *One Man in His Time*. New York: McDowell, 1958.

Oldenburg, S. S. *Last Tsar, Nicholas II: His Reign and His Russia*. Translated by Leonid I. Mihalap and Patrick J. Rollins. Gulf Breeze, Fla.: Academic International Press, 1975–1978.

Or—vsii. "Iz zapisok politseiskago ofitsera: 1. podgotovka k ubiistvu G. Rasputin," *Na chuzoi storone*, 9 (1925): 143–52.

Ossendowski, Ferdinand. *The Shadow of the Gloomy East*, Translated by F. B. Czarnomski. New York: Dutton, 1925.

Padenie. See P. E. Shchegolev

Paléologue, Maurice. *An Ambassador's Memoirs*, 3d ed. 3 vols. Translated by F. A. Holt. New York: Hippocrene Books, 1925.

Paley, Princess (Mme. Zinaida Morhange). *Memories of Russia, 1916–1919*. London: Jenkins, 1924.

Pares, Sir Bernard. *Fall of the Russian Monarchy*. New York: Knopf, 1939.

———. *My Russian Memoirs*. New York: AMS, 1969 (originally published London, 1931).

———. "Rasputin and the Empress: Authors of the Russian Collapse." *Foreign Affairs* 6 (1927): 140–54.

———. *A Wandering Student: The Story of a Purpose*. New York: Syracuse University, 1948.

Pascal, Pierre. *Mon Journal de Russie a la Mission Militaire Française, 1916–1918*. Lausanne, Switzerland: Editions L'Age d'Homme, 1975.

Paustovsky, Konstantin. *The Story of a Life*. Translated by Joseph Barnes. New York: Pantheon, 1964.

Pearlstein, Edward W., ed. *Revolution in Russia! As Reported by the New York* Tribune *and the New York* Herald, *1894–1921*. New York: Viking, 1967.

Perepiska Nikolaia i Aleksandry Romanovykh. Vols. 3, 4, 5, covering 1914–1917. Moscow, Petrograd, and Leningrad, 1923, 1926, 1927.

Pereverzev, P. N. "Ubiistvo Rasputina." *Illiustrirovanniia Rossiia* 21 (May 21, 1932): 6–11.

Pethybridge, Roger. *Witnesses to the Russian Revolution*. London: Allen & Unwin, 1964.

Pitcher, Harvey. *When Miss Emmie was in Russia: English Governesses before, during and after the October Revolution*. London: Murray, 1977.

Poliakoff, Vladimir. *The Empress Marie of Russia and her Times*. London: Thornton, 1926.

Pollock, John. *War and Revolution in Russia: Sketches and Studies*. London: Constable & Co., 1918.

Pol'skii, Mikhail, *Novye mucheniki rossiiskie, pervoe sobranie materielov*. Jordainville, N.Y., 1949. Abridged in English, *The New Martyrs of Russia*. Monteal: Brotherhood of St. Job of Pozhav, 1972.

Pospielovsky, Dimitry. *The Russian Church under the Soviet Regime, 1917–1982*, 2 vols. Crestwood, N.Y.: St. Vladimir's, 1984.

Preston, Thomas. *Before the Curtain*. London: Murray, 1950.

Price, M. P. *Siberia*. London: Methuen, 1912(?).

Protopopov, A. D. "Dopros." *Krasnyi arkhiv* 9 (1925): 133–55.

———. "Iz dnevnika." *Krasnyi arkhiv* 10 (1925): 175–83.

Prugavin, A. S. *"Starets" Grigory Rasputin i ego poklonnitsy*, part 1. 2nd ed. Moscow, 1917.

Purishkevich, V. M. *Dnevik*. Riga, n.d.

———. *The Murder of Rasputin*. Edited by Michael E. Shaw. Translated by Bella Costello. Ann Arbor: Ardis, 1985.

Radziwill, Princess Catherine. *The Intimate Life of the Last Tsarina*. London: Cassell, 1929.

———. *Memories of Forty Years*. London: Cassell & Co., 1914.

———. *Nicholas II: The Last of the Tsars*. London: Cassell, 1931.

———. *Rasputin and the Russian Revolution*. New York: Lane, 1918.

Rasputin, Grigory. "Life of an Experienced Pilgrim." In Iliodor, *The Mad Monk of Russia*, pp. 154–64. New York: Century, 1918.

———. "Moi mysli i razmyshleniia. Kratkoe opisanie puteshestviia po sviatym mestam i vyzvannye im razmyshleniia po religioznym voprosam." First published in V. P. Semennikov, ed., *Za kulasami tsarizma*, 142–160. Published in Maria Rasputin,

My Father, as "My thoughts and Meditations," but cited here from the Russian in Semennikov.

————. "Velikie dni torzhestva v Kieve! Poseshchenie vysochaishei sem'i! Angel'skii privet!" Reprinted as Appendix XIV to V. P. Obninskii, *Poslednii samoderzhets. Ocherk zhizni i tsarstvovaniia imperatora Rossii Nikolaia II-go.* Berlin, n.d.

Rasputin, Maria, "Moi otets, Grigorii Rasputin." *Illiustrirovanniia Rossiia* 13 (March 26, 1932): 8–10.

————. *My Father.* London: Cassell, 1934.

————. *The Real Rasputin.* Translated by Arthur Chambers. London: Long, 1929.

Rasputin, Maria, and Pattie Barham. *Rasputin: The Man behind the Myth.* Englewood Cliffs, NJ.: Prentice-Hall, 1977.

Red Archives. See C. E. Vulliamy.

Riha, Thomas. *A Russian European: Paul Miliukov in Russian Politics.* Notre Dame: Notre Dame University, 1969.

Rodzianko, M. V. *The Reign of Rasputin: An Empire's Collapse.* Translated by Catherine Zvegintoff. London: Philpot, 1927.

Romanov, A. V. "Iz dnevnika." *Krasnyi arkhiv* 26 (1928): 185–210, 306–10.

Romanov, N. M. "Zapiski," *Krasnyi arkhiv* 49 (1931): 92–111.

Rudnev, V. M. "The Truth concerning the Russian Imperial Family: Statement by Vladimir Michailovitch Roudneff, appointed by Minister of Justice Kerensky." In Anna Vyrubova, *Memories of the Russian Court*, pp. 383–99. New York: Macmillan, 1923.

Salisbury, Harrison E. *Black Night, White Snow: Russia's Revolutions, 1905–1917.* Garden City, NY.: Doubleday, 1978.

Sazonov, Serge. *Fateful Years, 1909–1916.* London: Cape, 1928.

Schlossberg, Heinrich. *See* Sliuzberg, G. B.

Semennikov, V. P., ed. *Dnevnik b. velokogo kniazia Andreia Vladimirovich, 1915 g.* Leningrad and Moscow, 1925.

————. *Monarkhiia pered krusheniem 1914–1917 gg., bumagi Nikolaia II i drugie dokumenty.* Moscow and Leningrad, 1927.

————. *Politika Romanovykh nakanune revoliutsii (ot Antanty k Germanii) po novym dokumentam.* Moscow and Leningrad, 1926.

————. *Za kulisami tsarizma; arkhiv tibetskogo vracha Badmaeva.* Leningrad, 1925.

Shakhovskoi, Prince Vsevolod. *"Sic Transit Gloria Mundi" (Tak prokhodit mirskaia slava"), 1893–1917.* Paris, 1952.

Shavel'skii, Georgii. *Vospominaniia poslednego protopresvitera russkoi armii i flota.* New York: Chekhov, 1954.

Shchegolev, P. E., ed. *Padenie tsarskogo rezhima; Stenografisheskie otchety doprosov i pokazanii, dannikh v 1917 g. v Chrezvychainoi Sledstvennoi Komissii Vremennogo Pravitel'stva*, 7 vols. Moscow and Leningrad, 1924–1927.

Shklovsky, Viktor. *Sentimental Journey: Memoirs, 1917–1922.* Translated by Richard Sheldon. Ithaca, NY: Cornell, 1970.

Shulgin, V. V. *The Years; Memoirs of a Member of the Russian Duma, 1906–1917.* Translated by Tanya Davis. New York: Hippocrene Books, 1984.

Simanovich, Aron. *Rasputin i evrei; vospominaniia lichnago sekretaria Grigoriia Rasputina.* Riga, n.d., probably 1928.

Sliuzberg, Genrikh Borisovich. *Dela minuvshikh dnei, zapiski russkago evreiia,* 3 vols.; vol. 3. Paris: privately printed, 1934.

Smitten, B. N. "Poslednyi vremenshchik poslednego tsaria. (Materialy Chrezvychainoi Sledstvennoi Komissii Vremennogo Pravitelstva o Rasputine i razlozhenii samoderzhaviia.)" Edited by A. L. Sidorov and published in four parts in *Voprosy istorii* 10 (1964): 117–35: 12 (1964): 90–103: 1 (1965): 98–110: 2 (1965): 103–21.

Sokolov, N. A. *Ubiistvo tsarskoi sem'i*. Buenos Aires: Rossiiskii Imperskii Soiuz-Orden, 1969.

Solov'ev, M. E. "Kak i kem byl ubit Rasputin?" *Voprosy istorii* 3 (1965): 211–17.

Sovetskaia istoricheskaia entsiklopediia, 16 vols. Edited by E. M. Zhukov. Moscow: Gosudarstvennoe nauchnoe izdatel'stvo, "Sovetskaia Entsiklopediia." 1961–1976.

Speranskii, V. N. "Istoricheskie svideteli o Rasputine, iz besed s vel. kn. Nikolaem Mikhailovichem." *Illiustrirovanniia Rossiia* 19 (May 7, 1932): 8–11.

Spiridovich, Alexander. *Les dernièrs années de la cour de Tzarskoie-Selo*, 2 vols. Translated by M. Jeanson. Paris: Payot, 1928, 1929.

———. "Nachalo Rasputina," *Illiustrirovanniia Rossiia* 15 (April 9, 1932): 1–9. Adds valuable information to his books.

———. *Rasputine, d'après les documents russes et les archives privees de l'auteur*. Translated by M. Benouville. Paris: Payot, 1935.

———. *Velikaia voina i feveral'skaia revoliutsiia 1914–1917 g.g.*, 3 vols. New York: Vseslavianskoe izdatel'stvo, 1960.

Stosova, E. D. *Vospominaniia*. Moscow, 1969.

Stremoukhov, P. P. "Moia bor'ba s episkopom Germogenom i Iliodorom." *Arkhiv russkoi revoliutsii* 16 (1925): 5–48.

Swan, Jane. *A Biography of Patriarch Tikhon*. Jordainville, NY.: Holy Trinity Monastery, 1964.

Teffi, N. A. (pseudonym of Nadezhda Aleksandrovna Buchinskaia) (Lokhvitskaia). *Vospominaniia*. Paris: Vozrozhdenie, 1931.

Thomson, Thomas John. "Boris Sturmer and the Imperial Russian Government, February 2–November 22, 1916," Unpublished Ph.D. dissertation, Duke, 1972.

Tikhomirov, Lev. "Iz dnevnika," *Krasnyi arkhiv* 74 (1936): 162–91.

Tisdall, E. E. P. *The Dowager Empress*. London: Paul, 1957.

Trewin, J. C. *House of Special Purpose: An Intimate Portrait of the Last Days of the Russian Imperial Family* [compiled from the papers of their English tutor, Charles Sydney Gibbes]. New York: Stein & Day, 1975.

"Ubiistvo Rasputina: ofitsial'noe dozanie." *Byloe*, 1 n.s. (1917): 64–83. Seventeen police reports from the murder investigation.

Ulam, Adam. *Russia's Failed Revolutions*. New York: Basic Books, 1981.

Vasil'ev (Vassilyev), A. T. *The Ochrana [sic]: The Russian Secret Police*. Edited by Renè Fülöp-Miller. Philadelphia and London: Lippincott, 1930.

Vinogradoff, Igor. "The Emperor Nicholas II, Stolypin, and Rasputin: A Letter of 16 October 1906," *Oxford Slavonic Papers* 12 (1965): 112–16.

Voeikov, V. N. *S tsarem i bez tsaria, vospominaniia posledniago dvortsovago komendanta gosudaria imperatora Nikolaia II*. Helsingfors, 1936.

Vol'kenshtein, L. F. "Kak eto bylo," *Illiustrirovanniia Rossiia* 9 (February 27, 1932): 1–7; and 10 (March 6, 1932): 1–7.

von Bock, Maria Petrovna. *Reminiscences of My Father, Peter A. Stolypin*. Edited and Translated by Margaret Patoski. Metuchen, NJ.: Scarecrow, 1970.

Vonliarliarskii, V. *Moi vospominaniia, 1852–1939* g.g. Berlin, n.d.

Vorres, Ian. *The Last Grand Duchess: Her Imperial Highness Grand Duchess Olga Alexandrovna*. New York: Scribner's, 1964.

"V tserkovnykh krugakh pered revoliutsii: iz pisem arkhiepiskopa Antoniia volynskogo k mitropolitu kievskomu Flavianu," *Krasnyi arkhiv* 31 (1928): 202–13.

Vulliamy, C. E. ed. *Red Archives: Russian State Papers and Other Documents relating to the Years 1915–1918*. Translated by A. L. Hynes, London: Geoffrey Bles, 1929. Contains "Letters [of the Yusupov family] relating to the Last Days of the Tsarist Regime," 98–130, and "Rasputin as Known to the Secret Police (Okhrana)," 21–56.

Vyrubova (Viroubova), Anna. *Memories of the Russian Court*. New York: Macmillan, 1923.

Warth, Robert D. "Before Rasputin: Piety and the Occult at the Court of Nicholas II." *The Historian*, 67 (1985): 323–37.

Williams, Albert Rhys. *Journey into Revolution: Petrograd, 1917–1918*, Edited by Lucita Williams. Chicago: Quadrangle, 1969.

Wilson, Colin. *Rasputin and the Fall of the Romanovs*. New York: Farrar, Straus & Co., 1964.

Wilton, Robert. *Last Days of the Romanovs*. London: Thornton, Butterworth, 1920.

———. *Russia's Agony*. New York: Dutton, 1919.

Witte, S. Iu. *Vospominaniia*. 3 vols. Moscow, 1960.

Wolkonsky, Serge. *My Reminiscenses*, 2 vols. Translated by A. E. Chamot. London: Hutchinson, n.d.

Woytinsky, W. S. *Stormy Passage*. New York: Vanguard, 1961.

Yusupov, Price Felix. *Lost Splendour*, Translated by Ann Green and Nicholas Katkoff. London: Cape, 1953.

———. *Rasputin*. New York: Dial, 1927.

Zaslavskii, D. *Poslednyi vremenshchik Protopopov*. Leningrad, n.d. Based upon the same author's "A. D. Protopopov," *Byloe*, n.s. 23 (1924): 208–42.

Zavadskii, S. V. "Na velikom izlome: otchet grazhdanina o perazhitom 1916–17 godakh," *Arkhiv russkoi revoliutsii* 8 (1923): 5–42.

Zavarzin, Pavel Pavlovich. *Zhandarmy i revoliutsionery, vospominaniia*. Paris, 1930.

Zernov, Nicholas. *The Russian Religious Renaissance of the Twentieth Century*. London: Darton, Longman & Todd, 1963.

Zhevakov, Prince N. D. *Vospominaniia*, 2 vols. Munich, 1923.

Index

Agafangel (bishop of Yaroslavl), 136

Alexander Nevsky Monastery, 12–13, 14, 150–52, 158, 173

Alexander Palace, 18, 24–26, 101–2, 161, 193

Alexander III (tsar, 1881–1894), 13, 17, 18, 20, 100, 249 n.1

Alexandra Fedorovna, before the war: early life, 17–18; appearance, 17; despair over son's hemophilia, 21–22, 27–31, 53; determination that Alexis must rule, 53–54, 95, 132; spiritual interests, 18–22, 24; love for peasantry, 54, 100–101; character, 24, 30–31, 34, 147, 160–61, 185; early friendship with Rasputin, 24–30, 35; understood Rasputin's faults, 51–53; Rasputin's fall from favor, 64–65; Rasputin restored, 71; letters controversy and Rasputin's second fall, 87, 89, 90–91, 222; Spala episode, Rasputin forgiven, 94–98

Alexandra Fedorovna, during the war: desire for peace in 1914, 108–9; wartime activities, 116, 124, 132–39; military influence, 197–98; and Vyrubova, 116–17, 126; and Rasputin, 116–20, 124, 126, 130–38, 164–67, 170–76, 185, 191–95, 242 n.27; public anger against, 138–39, 191–95; 209; reacts to Rasputin's murder, 207–15, 254 n.24; imprisoned and executed, 216–17, 223, 225

Alexandra Fedorovna, relations with other people: Iliodor, 58, 82; Stolypin, 73, 74; Sabler, 76; Kokovtsov, 239 n.1; Samarin, 130–32; Volzhin, 146–47, 158–59, 245 n.22; Pitirim and his circle, 152, 155, 159–61, 246–47 n.3; A. N. Khvostov, 164–67; Sturmer, 165, 172–75; Goremykin, 169–71, 248–49 n.6; Protopopov, 178–87

Alexis (bishop of Tobolsk, exarch of Georgia), 79, 155, 246 n.3

Alexis (bishop of Vladimir), 246 n.3

Alexis (the tsarevich), 87, 129, 183–84; hemophilia, 20–21, 25–31, 107–8; near death at Spala, 94–97; wartime health, 116; imprisoned and executed, 216–17

Anastasia (Montenegrin sister): introduces

About the Author

JOSEPH T. FUHRMANN has been intrigued with Russian civilization since the time, as a teenager, he encountered Mussorgsky's *Boris Godunov*. His B.A. is from Emory; his graduate degrees are from Indiana University. Fuhrmann was a graduate exchange student at Moscow University during 1965–66, working on a dissertation that was the core of his first book, *The Origins of Capitalism in Russia: Industry and Progress during the Sixteenth and Seventeenth Centuries*. His other books include *Tsar Alexis, His Reign and His Russia* and *The Life and Times of Tusculum College*, where he taught from 1970 to 1978. Dr. Fuhrmann is now a professor of history at Murray State University in Murray, Kentucky. Recent publications include "Lenin and Privilege" in *The Historian*, May 1989. Dr. Fuhrmann is currently editing the wartime letters of Nicholas II and Alexandra Fedorovna. He and his wife Mary are the parents of two children, Maria and Christopher.